"With a masterly command of details crafted into unfolding narratives, *Reformed and Evangelical across Four Centuries* provides a sweeping overview of the precedents and pressures that have shaped evangelical Presbyterianism. It is comprehensive and meticulous in research. This is not mere denominational history. The authors introduce us to an astonishing array of people, some familiar and others fetched out of obscurity. They depict events and ideas with marvelous texture set upon the broad canvas of their political, social, and intellectual context. Theological controversies are explained with subtlety; social forces, such as immigration and civil rights, are freshly considered; the impact of intellectual movements in fomenting change is clarified. This rigorous work will serve as an indispensable guide to all who wish to understand evangelical Presbyterianism."

— WALTER KIM
PCA pastor and president of the National Association of Evangelicals

"*Reformed and Evangelical across Four Centuries* is a useful introductory survey of Presbyterian history with an eye to the mainline Presbyterian Church's legacy. The team of scholars represent various Presbyterian traditions who document the unity and diversity of many of the denominational, doctrinal, ethical, and ethnic challenges and developments that Presbyterians have encountered through the centuries. This book will serve as a helpful aid for a first study of the Presbyterian tradition and a ready reference for review and to gain perspective."

— PETER A. LILLBACK
president of Westminster Theological Seminary, Philadelphia

"A much-needed updated history of the Presbyterian and evangelical movement since the Reformation that reflects twenty-first-century scholarship. However, the unique contribution of the book is that it addresses the key divisions that have occurred since 1971—the formation of the PCA, EPC, and ECO. Writing from their denominational perspectives, Rosell (PCUSA), Stewart (PCA), Fortson (EPC), and Feldmeth (ECO) offer a careful and scholarly assessment of the impact of these three ruptures. By incorporating these separate streams into the 'broader Presbyterian story,' they challenge the reader to consider commonalities in addition to the readily acknowledged differences between each of these streams."

— JEFFREY J. JEREMIAH
Stated Clerk of the Evangelical ⌐ ˙

T0272617

Reformed and Evangelical across Four Centuries

The Presbyterian Story in America

Nathan P. Feldmeth, S. Donald Fortson III,
Garth M. Rosell, and Kenneth J. Stewart

William B. Eerdmans Publishing Company

Grand Rapids, Michigan

Wm. B. Eerdmans Publishing Co.
4035 Park East Court SE, Grand Rapids, Michigan 49546
www.eerdmans.com

© 2022 Nathan P. Feldmeth, S. Donald Fortson III, Garth M. Rosell,
and Kenneth J. Stewart
All rights reserved
Published 2022
Printed in the United States of America

28 27 26 25 24 23 22   1 2 3 4 5 6 7

ISBN 978-0-8028-7340-8

Library of Congress Cataloging-in-Publication Data

Names: Feldmeth, Nathan P., 1945– author. | Fortson, S. Donald (Samuel Don-
    ald), 1956– author. | Rosell, Garth, author. | Stewart, Kenneth J., author.
Title: Reformed and Evangelical across four centuries : the Presbyterian story in
    America / Nathan P. Feldmeth, S. Donald Fortson, III, Garth M. Rosell, and
    Kenneth J. Stewart.
Description: Grand Rapids: Wm. B. Eerdmans Publishing Co., 2022. | Includes
    bibliographical references and index. | Summary: "A definitive history of the
    Presbyterian church in the United States, from its British foundations to its
    present-day expression in multiple American Presbyterian denominations,
    with special attention to Presbyterianism's evangelical influences"—Provided
    by publisher.
Identifiers: LCCN 2021029599 | ISBN 9780802873408 (paperback)
Subjects: LCSH: Presbyterian Church—United States—History. | United
    States—Church history.
Classification: LCC BX8935 .F45 2022 | DDC 285/.173—dc23
LC record available at https://lccn.loc.gov/2021029599

To the teachers who shaped us

Feldmeth: Geoffrey Bromiley, David F. Wright
Fortson: Will Barker, David Calhoun, Clair Davis
Rosell: Arthur Holmes, Lefferts Loetscher, Timothy Smith
Stewart: Ian S. Rennie, W. Stanford Reid

Contents

Foreword

Reformed and Evangelical across Four Centuries has a number of distinctive strengths. First, it offers a detailed and reliable new history of American Presbyterianism. Second, it is unusual among such histories in the thoroughness with which it recounts the British background. Third, it explicitly emphasizes "the symbiotic relationship that has frequently existed between American Presbyterianism and American evangelicalism." Finally, the emphasis on such relationships orients the recent history toward the realignments among the more evangelical Presbyterians.

The interactions between American Presbyterianism and the larger evangelical movement in America have been a source of some strengths and also of some challenges for American Presbyterians. Since those interactions are so close to the center of this history, it may be helpful to reflect on some of the major similarities and differences between the two traditions.

One difference that comes out clearly in the early history of Presbyterianism in England and Scotland is that Presbyterianism was originally designed to provide a model for the state churches of Christendom. That goes back to the fact that the mainstream Protestant Reformation, including its Calvinist branch, was not designed to dismantle Christendom but rather to reestablish it on a new, more consistent basis. Early Reformed Christians, like Lutherans and Roman Catholics, typically assumed that princes or magistrates should support one true church and not permit counterfeits that might dishonor God and deceive the populace. In England and Scotland, Presbyterian efforts to establish such state churches were sharply contested. Many Presbyterians accordingly developed outlooks as dissenters even as aspirations to shape a state-supported establishment remained an important part of the heritage. Even after Scotland gained a secure Presbyterian establishment, various Presbyterians seceded from that to found what they saw as purer church institutions.

What became known as evangelicalism emerged as a major force within Protestantism by about the mid-1700s. As among the pietists in Germany or the Methodists in England, it was a collection of loosely related movements marked by efforts to revitalize established churches that had lost spiritual vitality. Rather than depending on church authority and formal privilege, evangelicals shifted the locus of concern toward individuals, emphasizing conversion, deep commitment, and practices of personal piety. Many evangelicals were or became Baptists who explicitly opposed state establishments.

Some Presbyterians in America wholeheartedly embraced the evangelical awakenings. Others did not. In either case, Presbyterians typically remained ambivalent about state establishments. In New England, where Congregationalists often were referred to as "Presbyterian," state support survived until after the American Revolution. Throughout the colonies Presbyterians strongly supported the Revolution and aspired to help shape the American national project. Even while not aspiring to be state churches, they still exercised their cultural privilege, especially as leaders in education. Throughout the first half of the nineteenth century, for instance, most of the nation's leading colleges or universities, including state schools, were led by Presbyterians or their New England Congregationalist allies.

Many of these same Presbyterians and Congregationalists actively supported the ongoing awakenings of the early nineteenth century and so were part of the larger evangelical movement. That also led again to some conflict. Such tensions helped lead to the split in 1837 between the more conservative "Old School" Presbyterians, who opposed some of the doctrinal and practical innovations of the awakenings, and their "New School" counterparts, who supported such innovations.

These differences among various kinds of Presbyterians pointed to larger differences between the Presbyterian heritage and the characteristic emphases of the more popular sorts of evangelicalism of the American awakenings. The most significant of these differences is that Presbyterians emphasized theology grounded in tradition and an accompanying emphasis on education. The Presbyterian heritage going back to the Reformation included the idea that its teachings should be based on the best theological and biblical interpretations in the longer Augustinian tradition. A corollary has been that the clergy should be highly educated. Furthermore, educational levels among Presbyterian laypeople typically have been higher than among most of their other evangelical counterparts.

Meanwhile, the otherwise valuable evangelical emphases on personal conversion and growth in holiness had a tendency to undermine the importance of theological tradition as guided by learned clergy. Some of the clearest examples of that can be seen in how the American evangelical tradition often interpreted the meaning of "the Bible alone." The major Reformers, such as Luther and Calvin, meant by that the Biblicist ideal that church traditions had to be tested and refined according to how they comported to the higher authority of Scripture. In American evangelicalism, by contrast, "the Bible alone" often became associated with what have come to be called "primitivist" outlooks. Rather than emphasizing that church teachings should be grounded in the best theological and biblical scholarship of the ages, evangelical primitivists have seen "the Bible alone" as meaning that they should go back to the primitive practices of the New Testament church, skipping over the history that has intervened since then. One major American example of such teachings was in the Disciples of Christ movement and related Christian Churches, or Churches of Christ, founded by ex-Presbyterians such as Alexander Campbell in the early nineteenth century. Around the same time in Ireland, John Nelson Darby offered a more radical version of such primitivism that developed into the Plymouth Brethren movement and then into dispensational teachings associated with *The Scofield Reference Bible* (1909). Dispensational premillennialism had immense influence in shaping twentieth-century American fundamentalism, which in turn had many interactions with conservative Presbyterianism. Dispensationalism tended to jettison church history and to encourage the New Testament sensibility that Jesus would return in the very near future. A still larger and eventually more influential version of primitivism is found in the Pentecostal movements that emerged after 1900 and typically included teachings that modern Christians could replicate New Testament practices of tongues, other spiritual gifts, and miracles.

One way of characterizing such primitivist tendencies has been what historian Nathan O. Hatch described as *The Democratization of American Christianity* (1989). These characteristics, which first became widespread in the era after the American Revolution, might also be described as the "populist" tendencies among American evangelicals. They are democratic in that they appeal to the spiritual experiences of ordinary individuals. At the same time, they are populist in the sense that they often involve strong authoritarian leaders who can sway popular opinion. Such tendencies have led to some of the greatest strengths in American evangelicalism. They have fostered the emergence of exceptionally talented evangelists who have had immensely successful ministries, often reaching well beyond denominational bounds. Furthermore, by appealing to the spiritual experiences of ordinary people, populist revivalist movements have cultivated deep grass roots among American Christians. The benefits of such roots can readily be seen in contrast to British and European counterparts, where major churches have been much more dependent on state support. While in recent generations such Old World churches have experienced dramatic membership declines, in the United States evangelicalism has thrived. Even in the twenty-first century, when there has been some attrition, American evangelicalism has remained remarkably resilient.

At the same time, there are some evident downsides and dangers involved in dependence on such democratic or populist tendencies. Lack of grounding in historical theology invites superficial theological innovations. Strong popular leadership invites authoritarian empires in which there is little check on abuses of power. Populist based evangelicalism may have even stronger tendencies than do churches generally to reinforce the preexisting prejudices of their constituents, rather than prophetically challenging them.

It is inevitable that evangelical Presbyterians today will be constantly interacting with the larger and more populist evangelical movements and that those interactions will have both benefits and drawbacks. Evangelicals of all sorts of denominations today are closely interrelated and often learn from each other. One has only to look at the wide commonalities of popular music and worship practices to recognize such interdependence. Since churches are voluntary organizations, they are shaped in part by the market. Fortunately, among the countless varieties of evangelical churches, some of the teachings that have had the widest perennial appeal involve the core gospel message of salvation from sin based on the atoning work of Christ on the cross and the necessity of a life of holiness and service.

In considering the possible interrelationships of Presbyterians with the many varieties of evangelicals, there is a good case for emphasizing the positive. Richard Lovelace, in his classic *Dynamics of Spiritual Life* (1979, republished 2020 with a foreword by Tim Keller), offers a helpful approach. While recognizing that often there are heresies and unacceptable practices to be avoided, Lovelace suggests that we should also recognize that most errors in various church teachings involve taking some truth too far. So instead of just dismissing another tradition because we can identify its errors, we should also be asking: "What can we learn from them?" The Body of Christ is made up of many members with differing gifts, and they need each other. Often some of the strongest members and leaders of Presbyterian or Reformed churches are those who were initially converted through the ministry of a more intensely evangelical ministry. It is frequently the case that such Christians have come to appreciate the more deeply grounded Reformed theology, yet without their evangelical background they may never have become Christians at all.

Historical study is one of the best ways of gaining perspective on a tradition. When we Christians study our own traditions, our approaches should be distinguished from those of most other insider histories in that we will not just be celebrating our virtues and successes. Rather, as sinful, fallible humans dependent on God's grace, we should also be alert to identifying faults in our heritage and to be learning from those as well. The present volume offers an excellent resource for such edifying study and critical reflection.

George M. Marsden

Abbreviations

Presbyterian bodies listed appear on the genealogical table in appendix 2.

ABCFM	American Board of Commissioners for Foreign Missions
ACLU	American Civil Liberties Union
APA	American Psychiatric Association
ARP	Associate Reformed Presbyterian Church
BPC	Bible Presbyterian Church
CEF	Child Evangelism Fellowship
CFP	Covenant Fellowship of Presbyterians
COCU	Consultation on Church Union
CP	Concerned Presbyterians
CPC	Cumberland Presbyterian Church
CPCA	Cumberland Presbyterian Church in America
C-67	UPCUSA Confession of 1967
DOMA	Defense of Marriage Act
ECO	Covenant Order of Evangelical Presbyterians
EPC	Evangelical Presbyterian Church
ETS	Evangelical Theological Society
JCOU	Joint Committee on Union (preliminary to north-south union in 1983)
LAM	Latin American Mission
NAE	National Association of Evangelicals
NAPARC	North American Presbyterian and Reformed Council
NCC	National Council of Churches
OPC	Orthodox Presbyterian Church
PCA	Presbyterian Church in America
PCCSA	Presbyterian Church in the Confederate States of America

PCUS	Presbyterian Church in the United States
PCUSA	Presbyterian Church in the United States of America (to 1958)
PC(USA)	Presbyterian Church in the United States of America (since 1983)
PEF	Presbyterian Evangelistic Fellowship
PJC	Permanent Judicial Commission
PLC	Presbyterian Lay Committee
PUBC	Presbyterians United for a Biblical Confession
RPCES	Reformed Presbyterian Church, Evangelical Synod
RPCNA	Reformed Presbyterian Church of North America
RPCNA, GS	Reformed Presbyterian Church in North America, General Synod
RUF	Reformed University Fellowship
SIM	Sudan Interior Mission
SPCK	Society for the Promotion of Christian Knowledge
SPG	Society for the Propagation of the Gospel in Foreign Parts
SSPCK	Society in Scotland for the Propagation of Christian Knowledge
TEAM	The Evangelical Alliance Mission
UCC	United Church of Christ (combined Congregational and Evangelical Reformed bodies)
UPCNA	United Presbyterian Church of North America
UPCUSA	United Presbyterian Church in the United States of America (post-1958)
WCC	World Council of Churches
WCRC	World Communion of Reformed Churches

Preface

The idea for this book began during a conversation between two of its authors over lunch. With a shared interest in Presbyterian history and a mutual love for the church, Ken Stewart and Don Fortson soon found themselves discussing the need for a single volume that they could recommend to help students and Christian leaders grasp the thread of Presbyterian history. A number of fine studies of Presbyterian history already existed, to be sure, but none seemed to provide exactly the right themes and emphases. Existing literature seemed to suffer from one or more limitations.

First, there was the challenge of age. Highly commendable treatments produced in the middle of the twentieth century by writers such as Leonard Trinterud, Lefferts Loetscher, and Ernest Trice Thompson are, in addition to being dated, now only found in libraries or through scouring the used-book market.[1]

Second was the challenge of changed context. Trinterud, Loetscher, and Thompson, writing at midcentury, aimed to explain how what was a still largely cohesive Presbyterian family (admittedly existing in northern and southern expressions) had come to be. But as is evident to many, the period since 1970 has been characterized, on the one hand, by a reunion of Presbyterians north and south (realized in 1983) and, on the other, by the recurring fragmentation of the former "Presbyterian mainline." That fragmentation—in three distinct movements, in 1973, 1981, and 2012—reflected deep dissatisfaction with the biblical, theological, and ethical teaching of what had until then been the main-

---

1. Leonard Trinterud, *The Forming of an American Tradition: A Re-examination of Colonial Presbyterianism* (Philadelphia: Westminster, 1949); Lefferts Loetscher, *The Broadening Church* (Philadelphia: University of Pennsylvania Press, 1957); Ernest Trice Thompson, *Presbyterians in the South*, 3 vols. (Atlanta: John Knox, 1963–1972).

stream. These three movements, now aggregately numbering about 655,000,[2] had all concluded that their freedom to continue as robustly Presbyterian and evangelical had vanished. After extended efforts to sustain their position within the then-mainline, they concluded that alternative ways of continuing as Presbyterian and evangelical needed to be found. Yet the hidden "price tag," which came into view following these decisions to depart, was the evaporation of any sense of a common Presbyterian heritage or shared story.

The writing of Presbyterian history did not, of course, come to a halt as a result of these denominational divisions. With this fragmentation under way, writers such as Bradley Longfield produced commendable modern materials from within the former mainline; but these could not attempt to address either the causes of the fragmentation or its sizable consequences.[3] On the other hand, historians within the groups that had withdrawn since 1971 (for example, Frank J. Smith, Sean Lucas, Don Fortson), along with historians who detailed an earlier fragmentation in 1936 (D. G. Hart and John Muether), focused mostly on recounting the circumstances that warranted their own communion's separate existence.[4] No such effort, from any quarter, amounted to a comprehensive history of the whole. Over that initial meal discussion, then, we determined that a new, comprehensive approach was required.

Third was the concern that American Presbyterianism has largely lost a sense of connectedness to Presbyterian origins in the sixteenth and seventeenth centuries. Differences of conviction and approach already in existence in Tudor and Stuart times have continued to exert their influence since the

2. The figure of 655,000 reflects the aggregate membership of the Presbyterian Church in America (PCA), Evangelical Presbyterian Church (EPC), and Covenant Order of Evangelical Presbyterians (ECO), all gathered since 1971. Adding two Korean American bodies, two Cumberland churches, Associate Reformed Presbyterians, Orthodox Presbyterians, and Reformed Presbyterians to the equation raises this cumulative figure to 953,000 members. The Presbyterian Church in the United States of America (PC[USA]), while claiming 3.2 million members at the north-south reunion of 1983, now reports only 1.25 million.

3. Bradley J. Longfield, *The Presbyterian Controversy: Fundamentalists, Modernists, and Moderates* (New York: Oxford University Press, 1991); Bradley J. Longfield, *Presbyterians and American Culture: A History* (Louisville: Westminster John Knox, 2013).

4. Frank J. Smith, *The History of the Presbyterian Church in America*, 2nd ed. (Lawrenceville, GA: Presbyterian Scholars Press, 1999); Sean Lucas, *For a Continuing Church: The Roots of the Presbyterian Church in America* (Phillipsburg, NJ: P&R, 2015); Don Fortson, *Liberty in Non-Essentials: The Story of the Evangelical Presbyterian Church* (Livonia, MI: Evangelical Presbyterian Church, 2016). D. G. Hart and John Muether have prepared a substantial denominational history of their denomination, begun in 1936, entitled *Fighting the Good Fight: A Brief History of the Orthodox Presbyterian Church* (Philadelphia: Committee for the Historian of the OPC, 1995). They also collaborated to write *Seeking a Better Country: 300 Years of American Presbyterianism* (Phillipsburg, NJ: P&R, 2007).

era when immigrants first crossed the Atlantic. Ongoing issues as diverse as attitudes toward the state, terms of confessional subscription, and communion practice can only be properly understood with reference to that earlier period. And yet the standard literature available to American Presbyterians has more and more ignored these roots.

Fourth was the challenge of ethnic diversity. If at mid-twentieth century Presbyterian historians Trinterud, Loetscher, and Thompson could still write from the standpoint of a majority-white culture with fleeting reference to racial minorities, current history of the church can no longer be written this way. American Presbyterians (black and white) are now joined by Korean American, Brazilian American, Cuban American, and sub-Saharan African American congregations, *in numbers.* In sum, today's Presbyterian history must reflect this expanding coalition.

As we discussed the possibility of producing a volume that might address these four challenges, we rapidly concluded that a team approach was needed. With the Presbyterian Church in America (PCA) and Evangelical Presbyterian Church (EPC) constituencies already represented by Ken and Don, respectively, we wanted to be sure that other Prebyterian voices were also included in the preparation of the book. Consequently, Garth Rosell, a longtime member of the PC(USA), the Presbyterian Church in the United States of America, and a good friend of Don's and a professor of church history at Gordon-Conwell Theological Seminary, was invited to join the project. Nate Feldmeth, a member of the Covenant Order of Evangelical Presbyterians (ECO) and a member of the faculty of Fuller Theological Seminary, was subsequently invited to participate. Each contributor has brought historical expertise as well as his life experience as a Presbyterian evangelical to the task. In addition, Dale Johnson, a church historian in the Associate Reformed Presbyterian Church's (ARP) Erskine Seminary, assisted the project in a consultative capacity. The fine genealogical table of the American Presbyterian family that appears as an appendix to this volume is the work of Vic King of Baltimore. His original may be viewed at http://king.page.link/presbyterian.

Our book is a team effort that we offer to you as a faithful account of what it has meant in the past and what it means today to be Presbyterian and evangelical in America.

Kenneth J. Stewart and S. Donald Fortson III, editors

CHAPTER 1

Increasing Divergence after Common Origins in the British Reformations

A common notion among Presbyterians is that our branch of the Christian family is chiefly descended from John Calvin (1509-1564) and emanates from Geneva, the city where he labored. While this notion contains elements of truth, a too-rapid emphasis on Genevan influence becomes an obstacle to a fuller understanding. We should instead accept the principle that the heritage of the Reformation came to us by diverse means; some of these were native to the regions from which our forebears came; others crossed national boundaries.

Initially, we will focus chiefly upon the nations of England and Scotland and how the Protestant movement took hold there. Welsh and Irish Protestants would eventually make their own impact in the New World; yet, because of the vastly greater numbers of Protestant immigrants to America from England and Scotland,[1] these latter nations will occupy center stage.

England and Scotland were influenced—in tandem—by the European events set in motion by Luther's 1517 protest at Wittenberg. His writings were soon available in both countries. Into each, Baltic traders illegally imported Lutheran literature.[2] At the universities of Cambridge and St. Andrews there were students ready to read and espouse the Lutheran teachings about the supreme authority of the Bible and salvation in Christ received by faith alone.

---

1. In treating Scottish immigration to the New World, we will eventually employ the term "Scots-Irish" to describe immigrants of Scottish heritage who came to America from Ulster.

2. A. G. Dickens, *The English Reformation*, 2nd ed. (London: Batsford, 1989), 91–92; W. Ian P. Hazlett, *The Reformation in Britain and Ireland* (Edinburgh: T&T Clark, 2003), 135; G. R. Potter, "The Initial Impact of the Swiss Reformers in England," in *Discordia Concors* II (1968), 396; Jenny Wormald, *Court, Kirk, and Community: Scotland, 1470–1625* (London: Edward Arnold, 1981), 91, 104.

Arrests and executions followed in both countries.[3] We must also acknowledge that in both nations Luther's tracts found a reception in regions where there had been an earlier popular religious movement known as Lollardy.

Lollardy: A Force in England and Scotland

Originating through the teaching of the Oxford theologian John Wycliffe (1320–1384), the Lollard movement consisted of roving preachers and their followers. Lollard preaching oriented people to the supreme authority of the Bible; the preachers stressed that only scriptural teaching could provide the standard by which the life of the church and the individual could be judged. The Lollards also critiqued the medieval church's wealth (accumulated in land and money) and the readiness of its bishops and archbishops to function as ministers of state (to the neglect of their churchly duties). They also contested the requirement of celibacy for the clergy, of the confessing of one's sins to a priest, and of offering prayers for the dead; such practices lacked adequate biblical foundation. Most notoriously, they opposed the medieval Christian teaching that in the Holy Communion there is a physical transformation of the bread and wine into Christ's body and blood.[4]

Late in the lifetime of Wycliffe, Lollards translated the Latin Bible into the English of that day. At least five persons collaborated in the initial production of this word-for-word rendering of the Scriptures. It was an arduous and extended process, but the translation yielded from it was stilted and awkward. Later, Wycliffe's associate John Purvey (c. 1351–c..1414) improved the initial effort by utilizing what is today called an idiomatic translation strategy, which he termed "translation according to the sentence."[5] This superior method had first entailed the establishing (by comparison) of the best text of the Vulgate

3. Dickens, *The English Reformation*, 98–99; W. James K. Cameron, "Aspects of the Lutheran Contribution to the Scottish Reformation," *Records of the Scottish Church History Society* 22 (1984): 1–12.

4. See the "Twelve Lollard Conclusions," reprinted in Henry Gee and W. J. Hardy, *Documents Illustrative of English Church History* (London: Macmillan, 1898), 126–32. Errors with which the Scottish Lollards were charged are listed in Gordon Donaldson, ed., *Scottish Historical Documents* (Glasgow: Scottish Academic Press, 1974), 90.

5. Margaret Deanesly, *The Lollard Bible* (1920; reprint, Cambridge, Cambridge University Press, 1966), 262. Purvey supplied details explaining the translation process in a document attached to his revision of the Lollard Bible, circa 1388. A modern English rendering of Purvey's document is viewable here: http://www.bible-researcher.com/wyclif2.html, accessed March 11, 2021.

among numerous variants. Purvey also consulted patristic and medieval Bible commentaries to establish the meaning of passages difficult to translate.[6]

We can note both the pervasive extent of Lollardy's spread and the persistence of its influence. Whole regions of England's south, east, and midlands were influenced by this teaching; so also was the southwest of Scotland in the regions of Ayrshire and Lanarkshire.[7] In both countries, those found holding Lollard opinions or possessing Lollard Scriptures were arrested and executed. That some 250 copies of this hand-copied Lollard Bible survive (some consisting of individual books of Scripture, others of complete Bibles) tells us something of this movement's spread.[8] The movement also had staying power: in spite of the persecution that raged against it, it persisted in families and in local communities.

In the south of England, the later Bible translator William Tyndale (c. 1494–1536) came from a Gloucestershire family with Lollard associations.[9] After completing his studies at Oxford, he would be influenced by the teachings of Luther and of Zwingli, but one modern researcher claims to have found earlier Lollard themes expounded in his writings as well.[10] In Ayrshire, Scotland, a Lollard disciple and contemporary of Tyndale, Murdoch Nisbet, had turned the New Testament portion of the improved second (Purvey) Lollard Bible into the Scots dialect by the early 1530s.[11] According to the preface to his translation, Nisbet had been reading Luther and had been exposed to the Tyndale New Testament, available in English in 1525.[12]

---

6. F. F. Bruce, *The English Bible* (London: Lutterworth, 1970), 16–17.

7. Margaret H. B. Sanderson, *Ayrshire and the Reformation* (East Linton, UK: Tuckwell, 1997), chap. 4. More recently, Richard Rex has contested the extent of the enduring influence of this movement. See his *The Lollards* (London: Palgrave Macmillan, 2002), 112–20.

8. "Wycliffe's Bible," Wikipedia, last edited January 1, 2021, https://en.wikipedia.org/wiki/Wycliffe%27s_Bible.

9. David Daniell, *William Tyndale* (New Haven: Yale University Press, 1994), 15, 16.

10. Dickens, *The English Reformation*, 93–98; Donald Dean Smeeton, *Lollard Themes in the Reformation Theology of William Tyndale* (Kirksville, MO: Sixteenth Century Journal, 1986).

11. Hazlett, *Reformation in Britain and Ireland*, 136. In a 2002 Edinburgh University dissertation, "The Emergence of Evangelical Theology in Scotland to 1550," Martin Dotterweich reports that Nisbet's Lollard New Testament is only one of two such Scottish Lollard Bibles to have been preserved. See p. 56.

12. The Nisbet New Testament was published in a three-volume edition prepared by T. G. Laws and published as *The New Testament in Scots* (Edinburgh: Blackwood, 1901). The significance of Nisbet's work is explored in T. M. Lindsay, "A Literary Relic of Scottish Lollardy," *Scottish Historical Review* 1 (1904): 260–90, and T. M. A. MacNabb, "The New Testament in Scots," *Records of the Scottish Church History Society* 11 (1951): 82–103.

Thus, there are ample indications that the preexisting Lollard movement had both survived into the age of the Reformation and, as it were, "passed the baton" to these later developments in both countries. To urge this is not to maintain the strict identity of Lollardy with later Protestantism, but only to observe that a definite overlap of concerns existed. In consequence, when Luther's pamphlets did reach English and Scottish seaports, there was a segment of the population predisposed to take them up and to devour them.

THE ERA OF LUTHERAN INFLUENCE WITHIN BOTH COUNTRIES

That there was a definite Lutheran "phase" in the progress of the Reformation in the two neighboring countries is also beyond controversy. The early illegal importation of Luther's writings meant that, in both countries, student populations were among the first to be affected. At the White Horse Inn at Cambridge and St. Leonard's College, St. Andrews, students—by now exposed to the Greek New Testament edited by Erasmus in 1516[13]—began also to read and debate Luther.[14] Other students came in contact with Luther's ideas while studying in Paris, Louvain, and Cologne. Some of those caught up in this new theology went subsequently to Wittenberg to sit at the feet of Luther and Melanchthon. Tyndale did so temporarily; he was followed by fellow Englishman Robert Barnes. The Lutheran center of Marburg was the temporary destination of another future English martyr, John Frith. Lutheran Wittenberg was also the destination of choice for the St. Andrews graduate Patrick Hamilton. One whom he influenced for the gospel while at St. Andrews, Alexander Alesius, eventually made Lutheran territory his permanent domain; he served as professor of theology initially at Frankfurt an der Oder and subsequently at Leipzig.[15]

The migration to Lutheran territory was usually a preliminary to attempting something for one's homeland. In Tyndale's case, while at Wittenberg he gained momentum in translating the New Testament from Greek into English; presses

---

13. The "Novum Instrumentum," a two-column Latin-Greek New Testament of 1516, was printed at Basel. It was released in improved editions in 1519, 1522, 1527, and 1536.

14. The role of Cambridge's White Horse Inn is described in E. G. Rupp, *The Making of the English Protestant Tradition* (Cambridge: Cambridge University Press, 1947), chap. 2, and Dickens, *The English Reformation*, 91. Lutheran interest at St. Andrews in the same era is described by Cameron, "Aspects of the Lutheran Contribution," 2–3.

15. On the career of Alesius, see John T. McNeill, "Alexander Alesius, Scottish Lutheran (1500–1565)," *Archiv für Reformationgeschicte* 55, no. 4 (1964): 161–91, and Gotthelf Wiedermann, "Alexander Alesius' Lectures on the Psalms at Cambridge, 1536," *Journal of Ecclesiastical History* 37, no. 1 (1986): 15–41.

in Antwerp printed his efforts, until he was arrested and executed there in 1534. For Patrick Hamilton, the Wittenberg sojourn was a prelude to his open-air preaching in St. Andrews, leading to his arrest and martyrdom in 1528.

Thereafter, the Lutheran connection developed very differently in the two neighboring nations. In Scotland, Luther's teaching continued to be opposed with arrests and prosecutions. Well into the 1540s, these policies of opposition ensured an ongoing migration of Scottish university graduates into Lutheran territories. They sometimes remained there until the theological climate changed at home.[16]

But England was about to pass through uncharted perils that followed King Henry VIII's obtaining a parliamentary divorce from his first wife, Catherine, in 1533. Faced with the prospect of a retaliatory invasion led by the Holy Roman emperor Charles V (nephew to Queen Catherine), Tudor England looked abroad for potential military allies. The Tudor regime found Lutheran Saxony open to such an alliance, but Saxon support was contingent on England's endorsing of the Augsburg Confession of 1530. On again, off again negotiations involving diplomats of both countries never quite succeeded in bringing the matter to resolution; King Henry VIII—while antipapal—was not in fact pro-Lutheran. As the threat of imperial invasion receded, so did Henry's interest in Saxon diplomacy. During the last decade of Henry's reign the Church of England followed a course that might be called "national Catholicism." The era of Lutheran influence in England had clearly crested.[17] By 1530, two things had become clear about the fledgling European Protestant movement.

The Limitations of Magisterial-Style Reformation

First, it was no longer realistic to expect that Protestantism would remain one movement extending across western Europe, since strong disagreements about the Lord's Supper had emerged between Luther and the Swiss pastor-theologians Zwingli and Oecolampadius. At the Marburg Colloquy (October

16. James Kirk, "John Gau," in *Scottish Dictionary of Church History and Theology*, ed. Nigel M. Cameron (Downers Grove, IL: InterVarsity Press, 1993), 352. Cameron, "Aspects of the Lutheran Contribution," 2. It is also notable that some Scottish university graduates of Lutheran sympathy migrated into England in the late 1520s and 1530s. John Spottiswoode and John McAlpine belong to this group. See entries for each in Cameron, *Scottish Dictionary of Church History and Theology*.

17. The era of Anglo-Lutheran negotiation is surveyed in Basil Hall, *Humanists and Protestants, 1500–1900* (Edinburgh: T&T Clark, 1990), chap. 7, "The Early Rise and Gradual Decline of Lutheran Influence in England."

1529) and after, Luther was unbending in insisting that his literal understanding of the words of Jesus, spoken in instituting Holy Communion (Matt. 26:26), was nonnegotiable. This position was not one that the Swiss could endorse.[18] Similarly, it had become clear—both at Wittenberg while Luther was hiding in Wartburg Castle (1521–1522) and at Zurich in 1522–1523—that there would be dissenters from the young reformation that began in 1517. At Wittenberg, spiritualists or prophets demanded revolutionary changes based on claimed promptings of the Spirit.[19] As well, at Zurich, a fledgling Anabaptist movement dissented against the role played by the cantonal government in determining the pace of religious reform; they also repudiated the universal baptism of infants practiced within the canton. It was clear that early Protestantism would not remain unified. But there was a second limiting factor.

The Lutheran movement had relied upon what was becoming the dominant method of advancing religious reformation: dependence on a regional ruler to authorize and defend church reform within his territories. This came to be known as the magisterial pattern of reform. Thus, in Saxony, for instance, the approval and support of Prince Frederick was absolutely fundamental to the advancing of reform; were it withdrawn, Luther and his colleagues would have faced all the hostility that the Roman Catholic Church and the Holy Roman Empire could muster. Accordingly, Frederick had protected Luther from arrest after the Diet of Worms in 1521 by having him kidnapped and hidden in Wartburg Castle. At Frederick's death in 1525, his brother, John, continued in this supportive role. The number of German princes who would act similarly and advance a reformation of religion in their territories increased in the period leading to the 1530 Diet of Augsburg. But, in England and Scotland, it had become clear by the 1540s that lack of similar royal support would not allow the cause of reform to advance in any orderly way.

The Tudor monarchy, while it had proved to be antipapal, was at the same time unprepared to support church reform as it had gone forward in Europe. Permission for clergy to marry was granted, only to be revoked. The freedom to own and read a Bible was granted, only to be restricted. As for the Stuart monarchy to the north, there is no evidence that it ever became antipapal

---

18. A report of the Luther-Zwingli contest at the 1529 Marburg conference is provided in D. Ziegler, *Great Debates of the Reformation* (New York: Random House, 1969), chap. 3. Reformed and Lutheran perspectives on the Marburg Colloquy are provided, respectively, by James I. McCord, *Marburg Revisited: An Examination of the Lutheran and Reformed Traditions* (Minneapolis: Augsburg, 1966), and Hermann Sasse, *This Is My Body: Luther's Contention for the Real Presence in the Sacrament of the Altar* (Minneapolis: Augsburg, 1959).

19. These were the Zwickau Prophets. See James M. Kittelson, *Luther the Reformer* (Minneapolis: Augsburg, 1986), 246–48.

enough to support efforts to uproot corruption. Thus, the question naturally arises whether church reform on the magisterial plan was within the realm of possibility. The answer to this question, prior to 1547, would have to be no. There could be no nationwide Reformation for England or Scotland without royal protectors, like the Saxons Frederick and John.

The death of Henry VIII in 1547 did open the way for a brief, energetic endorsement of further reformation under the sponsorship of the boy-king Edward VI. Ruling at first through two different "lord protectors" (regents) and, eventually, in his own right, Edward became the energetic promoter of further Protestant advance. Archbishop Thomas Cranmer (1489–1556) began to actively cultivate relationships with various European leaders of reform in Strasbourg, Zurich, and Geneva. In Edwardian England, Scottish Protestant refugees such as John Knox (1513–1572) and John Willock (1515–1585) found a liberty to preach that had been denied them in Scotland. Draft Protestant articles of faith were prepared for the Church of England, and a prepared service book, the Book of Common Prayer, rapidly went through two editions.[20] During this five-year window of time, it appeared that the magisterial model of advancing Reformation might yield results in England after all. But as is well known, Edward's death in 1553 opened the way for a religious reaction directed by his Roman Catholic half sister, Mary Tudor.

Because of Mary's half-decade reign of oppression, she is justifiably remembered as the great persecutor of Protestants. Thus, during her reign, no case could be made that the mere emergence of what was called the "godly prince" was bringing England into a "promised land" of Protestant stability. The lack of a stable Protestant royal succession seemed to render this model of reformation moot.

In Scotland, not only had members of the Stuart royal house supported the harsh treatment of Protestants in these years, but the death of King James V in 1542 (followed by the twelve-year regency of James Hamilton, second Earl of Arran) brought no more than a temporary respite from persecution. Arran's temporary flirtation with the Reformation (later derided as Arran's "godly fit") and more cordial relations with England soon ended.[21] If the elevation of the Catholic royal widow of James V, Mary of Guise, to the role of regent from 1554 to 1560 brought no intensification of persecution of Protestants, it also brought no support for them. In short, the model of advancing Reformation by

---

20. John Knox was forthright in dissenting from certain features of these prayer books, known as the First and Second Prayer Books of Edward's reign. Jane Dawson, *John Knox* (New Haven: Yale University Press, 2016), chap. 6.

21. This critical period is described in Wormald, *Court, Kirk, and Community*, 103–4.

the endorsement of a godly monarch seemed to be beyond the reach of these neighboring nations. In both countries, therefore, in 1558–1559, reformation went forward by stealth, in defiance of royal policy and by resort to exile. The principle learned in this period was that the Protestant Reformation could make only meager advances without magisterial support.

A distinguishable method of advancing reformation had already been displayed in certain imperial free cities of south Germany such as Strasbourg and in Swiss cantons such as Zurich. Reformation had been established in such places already in the early 1520s; reform efforts had secured the active support of the city fathers, who would endorse religious change while controlling the speed of its advance. To this extent, such cities and cantons might be said to be following the magisterial method. Yet in truth, these local reformations had been sparked by public agitation, by the hanging of posters highlighting the corruptions of church and clergy needing to be amended, by petitioning city fathers to appoint preachers of reform, and by what were considered acts of religious violence. The approval and endorsement of city fathers for reform came, on this plan, reactively.[22]

In response to this kind of agitation, city fathers would customarily agree to a public disputation with two sides represented; in the disputations, well-prepared advocates of reform would regularly carry the day. In the aftermath of such disputations, city fathers could—now with plausibility—pronounce in favor of reform.[23] This model of reform did not deny the magistrate a role in matters of religion, but it required efforts to persuade, even to cajole, political authorities into sanctioning reform efforts already favored.

It was this broad approach that came to be adopted in the troublesome 1550s in both England and Scotland. English Protestants relied on it because their fledgling reformation had been aborted by Edward's untimely death in 1553. Belligerent Protestants who remained in England during Mary's reign and who assembled clandestinely while maintaining some outward conformity to Roman Catholicism made this stance their own.[24] So also did the approximately eight hundred Protestants (many of them church leaders) who fled to various European cities such as Emden, Wesel, Frankfurt am Main, Zurich, Strasbourg, Basel, and Geneva and who, upon arrival, gained permission to meet as English refugee congregations.[25] Together, these groups asserted their right to worship as Protestants irrespective of the royal opposition at home. A subgroup of ref-

22. Lewis W. Spitz, *The Renaissance and Reformation Movements*, rev. ed., 2 vols. (St. Louis: Concordia, 1987), 2:369–70.

23. Such disputations were held in Strasbourg, in Zurich, and, later, in Berne. See Bruce Gordon, *The Swiss Reformation* (Manchester: Manchester University Press, 2002), 57–60.

24. Andrew Pettegree, *Marian Protestantism: Six Studies* (Aldershot, UK: Scolar, 1996).

25. The classic study is Christina H. Garrett, *The Marian Exiles* (Cambridge: Cambridge

ugees (particularly those assembled at Emden and Geneva) asserted their right to advance the Reformation of King Edward's time so as to bring it more fully into conformity with European Reformed practice. Their insistence on this principle was full of implications for what would follow after exile.[26]

Similarly, in the second half of the 1550s, Scottish Protestants assembled clandestinely under the sponsorship of lesser nobles in Ayrshire, Angus, Perth, and elsewhere.[27] Legal statutes prohibited them from doing so, and yet— borrowing a measure of legitimacy from the support of lesser nobles—they carried on. With the support of these lesser nobles, their gatherings could post sentries for protection. In preaching tours in mid and late decade, refugee Scottish preachers John Willock (from Emden) and John Knox (from Geneva) slipped into Scotland and moved from one clandestine gathering to another. Knox styled these gatherings "privy kirks."[28] Though they were unauthorized congregations, they appointed pastors and elders, established membership rolls based on professions of faith, and held worship services utilizing (among other things) the English Book of Common Prayer (1552).

LUTHERAN INFLUENCES SURPASSED BY SWISS

Something else became very clear during this period, beyond the limitations of the magisterial Reformation as practiced among the Lutherans. It was that Scots and English friends of the advance of reformation were looking more and more to Switzerland to find a way forward. Future Anglican bishop John Hooper (c. 1495–1555) went first to Strasbourg and then to Zurich when imperiled for his Protestant doctrine late in Henry VIII's reign. There he began a relationship with Zwingli's successor, Heinrich Bullinger (1504–1575), which was carried on by correspondence into the next decade.[29] In this same period, following the termination of a period of refuge in late Henrician England, the

---

University Press, 1938). More recent is Dan G. Danner's *Pilgrimage to Puritanism: The History and Theology of the Marian Exiles at Geneva, 1555–1560* (New York: Lang, 1999).

26. Dawson, *John Knox*, chap. 7.

27. One such sponsoring noble was John Erskine of Dun. See the entry in Cameron, *Scottish Dictionary of Church History and Theology*, and Frank Bardgett, "John Erskine of Dun: A Theological Reassessment," *Scottish Journal of Theology* 43 (1990): 59–85.

28. John Knox, *History of the Reformation in Scotland* (New York: Philosophical Library, 1950), 1:148, 2:277–78. The functioning of these secretive congregations is investigated in James Kirk, *Patterns of Reform: Continuity and Change in the Reformation Kirk* (Edinburgh: T&T Clark, 1989), chap. 1.

29. Andrew Pettegree endorses the opinion of C. H. Smyth that Hooper was "the leading disciple of the Swiss Reformation." *Foreign Protestant Communities in Sixteenth-Century London* (Oxford: Oxford University Press, 1986), 30.

Scottish preacher George Wishart (c. 1513–1546) went to Zurich and similarly became acquainted with Bullinger. When he returned to Scotland in 1543, he brought with him an important document, generated in Zurich in 1536: the First Helvetic Confession. Wishart's doing so is an indicator of a changed theological orientation. Supporters saw to it that this important confessional document was published in English soon after Wishart's execution in 1546.[30]

The reorientation toward Swiss and south German lands accelerated within England. By 1547 (the year of King Henry's death), Peter Martyr Vermigli (1499–1562) had come from Strasbourg to take up a post at Oxford; he was soon followed by his Strasbourg colleague Martin Bucer (1491–1551), who was invited to Cambridge University. This migration of scholars was part of a grand scheme developed by Archbishop Thomas Cranmer to accelerate the cause of the Reformation in young King Edward's time and to see England become an international bastion of Protestantism at the very time Emperor Charles V was making life increasingly difficult for Protestants in his German territories and the Low Countries. As part of this same grand scheme, Cranmer accommodated the settlement of foreign Protestant refugees from the Low Countries and France in London and granted them religious liberty. Cranmer placed these congregations (with their pastors and elders) under the jurisdiction of a foreign Protestant leader, Jan à Lasco (1499–1560), whom he named superintendent.[31]

The various foreign congregations, with their pastors, were not required to conduct their services according to the English Book of Common Prayer, still in its first edition of 1549.[32] This provision was more than a kind accommodation extended to foreign refugees. It was in fact a kind of laboratory experiment authorized by an archbishop who was ready to consider different methods by which the retarded process of English Reformation might be accelerated.[33]

Could the foreign Reformed pastors and congregations in London provide a way forward? The concept was controversial and disliked by bishops, who opposed the creation of congregations outside their jurisdiction, freed from the required liturgical uniformity. Their daily challenge was to maintain religious uniformity in the tumultuous period of young Edward's reign.

30. Martin Holt Dotterweich, ed., *George Wishart Quincentennial Conference Proceedings* (2014), 4.

31. Hall, *Humanists and Protestants,* chap. 6, shows that á Lasco was clearly in the theological orbit of Bullinger at Zurich.

32. Frederick A. Norwood, "The Strangers Model Churches in Late Edwardian London," in *Reformation Studies in Honor of Roland Bainton,* ed. Franklin Little (Richmond, VA: John Knox, 1962), 181–96.

33. Pettegree, *Foreign Protestant Communities,* 25, maintains that this development of 1550 "was part of a concerted effort to effect a substantial revision of the 1549 Prayer Book and to introduce into England a radical Reformed polity on the Swiss model." See also p. 35.

WHAT A CHANGE OF MONARCH WOULD BRING

The death of King Edward and his succession by his half sister, the fervently Roman Catholic Mary Tudor, in 1553 sent repercussions across the country. Many who had supported Protestantism under Edward confirmed Mary's expectation that they would support a church resembling what her father had left at his death in 1547. Others were openly resistant and either utterly refused to conform to the newly Romanized church (by worshiping clandestinely) or conformed in a minimalist fashion. Some three hundred suffered execution.[34] Yet, especially significant for our purpose here were the eight hundred who fled England to seek their fortunes in European cities spread between Emden and Venice. While a small proportion of these seem to have gone abroad primarily to further business ventures or to advance their education, the vast majority had an earnest Protestant motivation for being outside England. Yet, these Protestants were divided.

At Zurich, Strasbourg, Basel, Wesel, and (in time) Frankfurt am Main, the refugees were guided by loyalty toward the Church of England as it had existed in King Edward's time. This entailed conformity to the pattern of worship set out in the Book of Common Prayer (1552). Back in England, Christian leaders were still dying on account of their attachment to the Protestantism of the Edwardian era. Why would solidarity not be kept with them and their legacy?

But there was also a party that—having from the start been conscious of the imperfections of the prayer book—wished not to be bound by it. This outlook was most closely associated with the refugee congregations at Emden and Geneva. At Emden, under the pastoral leadership of Willock, and at Geneva, under Knox, with Christopher Goodman (1520–1603), the preference was for a Protestantism only in broad conformity with what had existed in Edward's time. There was no uncritical loyalty to the Book of Common Prayer.

As the Marian era ended in November 1558 and the hitherto-conforming Protestant Elizabeth Tudor succeeded her half sister, these differences—clearly displayed among the refugees abroad—would take on deeper significance. So far as the future of Elizabethan Protestantism was concerned, many of the exiles determined to preserve the Reformation in its Edwardian expression found their way into positions of influence in the Elizabethan church. Edmund Sandys, who divided his exile between Augsburg, Frankfurt, and Zurich, became bishop of Winchester in 1559 and, later, archbishop of York. John Jewell, who divided his exile between Frankfurt, Strasbourg, and Zurich, became the bishop of Salisbury in 1560. Edmund Grindal, who spent his exile years at Strasbourg, was chosen

---

34. Lacey Baldwin Smith, *This Realm of England: 1399–1688*, 8th ed. (Boston: Houghton Mifflin, 2001), 163.

archbishop of Canterbury in 1575. Such returning exiles are fairly described as Low Church Anglicans, supportive of the reformations at Strasbourg and Zurich and loyal to the formulas of Edward VI. They all supported the gradual advancing of reformation beyond the state of things left at Edward's passing while withholding their support from the restless sort of Protestant who carped at the limitations of the religious settlement that came in under Queen Elizabeth.

By contrast, not only the Scottish refugee preachers Knox and Willock, who labored in Geneva and Emden, respectively, but also their English refugee congregations were strongly oriented to a Protestantism that was less liturgical, less tied to forms, and more determined to appropriate ways of worshiping God already in use in the European Reformed churches. Among those admitted to the membership of each church were tradesmen, merchants, and Anglican clergy and scholars.[35] Both churches included clergy who had previously served the Edwardian Church of England. Though they returned to the Elizabethan Church of England, none were put in high office. William Whittingham and Miles Coverdale, who had both served the English church under Edward, collaborated in the production of the Geneva Bible while at Geneva. Though Coverdale had earlier been bishop of Exeter (1550–1553), he returned to England only to serve a parish. Whittingham, a scholar and linguist prior to the Marian era, returned to England as dean of Durham. The two pastors of the English congregation at Geneva, Christopher Goodman and John Knox—though they had both served the Edwardian Church of England—were not invited to resume ministry. Their authorship of treatises protesting the tyranny of Mary Tudor and of women rulers in general had deeply offended the rising queen Elizabeth, who forbade their reentry to the country.[36]

England's and Scotland's Reformations circa 1559–1560

When Elizabeth ascended to the throne in late 1558 (the restoration of Protestantism followed, through an Act of Uniformity adopted in 1559), the cause of the Reformation in Scotland was still laboring against the opposition of the queen regent, Mary of Guise. While the Reformation in England would now rely upon a fresh attempt at magisterial style (with the monarch both supporting and controlling the advance of Protestantism), Scotland seemed set for more years of

35. The list of refugees at Emden is reprinted as appendix 2 in Pettegree's *Marian Protestantism*, 170–71. Membership lists of the English congregation at Geneva are provided in A. F. Mitchell, ed., *Livre des Anglois: or Register of the English Church under the Pastoral Care of Goodman and Knox, 1555–1559* (Edinburgh: Constable, 1889), 1–5.
36. Dawson, *John Knox*, 169.

reformation by stealth. Yet this Reformation-from-below in Scotland had been yielding better and better results. After 1555, both Knox and Willock had slipped into the country to conduct wide-ranging preaching tours hosted in the homes of lower aristocracy—those to whom Knox would refer to in his history as "Lords of the Congregation."[37] These nobles had been mustering private armies that were sympathetic to Protestantism and engaging in conflict with forces loyal to the queen regent. In Angus and the Mearns, in Perth, and in Fife, these armies aimed at the forcible destruction of Roman Catholic places of worship.

They met with the most concentrated resistance as they approached the capital, Edinburgh. Out of concern that the outcome might be lost, the Lords of the Congregation negotiated with the new government of English Queen Elizabeth I to secure military help in bringing the conflict to an end. Queen Regent Mary, also sensing how high were the stakes in this conflict, had secured French military help in the form of troops and ships. At a crucial point in 1560, two things happened. First, combined English and Scottish Protestant forces defeated troops loyal to the queen regent in a crucial battle at Leith. By the resultant Treaty of Edinburgh, signed in July 1560, both England and France agreed to withdraw all forces from Scotland, and the new queen regent, Mary—daughter of Mary of Guise—agreed to abandon all claim to England's throne.[38]

But second, the death of the queen regent, at Edinburgh in June 1560—the month preceding the end of the fighting—left Scotland in a greater political vacuum than when her husband, James V, died in 1542. Her only successor was her daughter, Mary, now married to the young king of France. The marriage to Francis proved very short-lived; he passed away in December of that same crucial year, and young Mary, his widow, to be known as "Queen of Scots," had returned to Scotland by August 1561.

These factors, taken in combination, created a situation in which the rising Protestant sentiment promoted by Knox and Willock, the mushrooming influence of the unregistered congregations of Protestants, and the military leadership of the lesser nobles were able to press legislatively for a reformation unrestrained by any member of Scotland's still–Roman Catholic monarchy. Here was a parliamentary and magisterial reformation with monarchy left on the sidelines.

This Parliament, hopeful of the successful outcome of the fighting against the combined forces of those loyal to the queen regent and those sent by France, had met at Edinburgh in the spring of 1559 and authorized a committee

37. Knox, *History of the Reformation in Scotland*, 1:137.
38. Donaldson, *Scottish Historical Documents*, 120–24. Note especially p. 121. Mary Stuart's aspirations after the English throne were based upon her descent from Margaret Tudor (sister to England's late Henry VIII) and her first husband, Scottish king James IV. These aspirations were kept alive by James VI, son to Mary.

of six men to prepare a document (called the *Book of Reformation*) elaborating how the existing church could be restructured along Protestant lines.[39] A collaborative Protestant confessional document, the Scots Confession, was also produced later in the same year and was received as the standard of teaching of the church as reformed.[40]

PROTESTANTISM UNDER ELIZABETH AND UNDER MARY

At the outset of her reign, Elizabeth was cautioned by her councilors to proceed cautiously in matters touching religion in light of the wild oscillations introduced by her half siblings in the preceding decade. The policy was very congenial to Elizabeth; she seems never to have departed from it. While certainly a Protestant herself,[41] her policies seemed intent on securing an outward conformity to a centrist Protestantism capacious enough to enfold all her subjects. Extremists of all kinds she loathed. And she showed this loathing toward those who would not cooperate with her plans for religious comprehension. Beginning with the Acts of Supremacy and Uniformity in 1559, she made plain that she expected full support for her royal prerogative in matters of church and state and compliant use of the formularies in place in the last year of Edward's reign.[42] And it was not only the queen who was determined to achieve uniformity: by the promulgation of the "Advertisements" of 1566, her archbishop, Matthew Parker (1504–1575), made plain that he would tolerate no opposition to the required clerical dress and the prescribed use of ceremonies.[43] Elizabethan policies equally singled out those who supported expressions of clandestine Catholicism, for they—equally—did not wish to make peace with her broadly Protestant national church.[44]

By 1570, Thomas Cartwright (1534/35–1603) had used his position within Cambridge University to draw attention to the absence of biblical support for

39. This was later designated as the *First Book of Discipline*, to distinguish it from a fuller treatment, the *Second Book*, ratified in 1576.

40. The collaborative nature of these documents is highlighted by Kenneth J. Stewart in "Somewhere between Zurich and Geneva? The Scottish Reformation Stance in 1560," *Scottish Bulletin of Evangelical Theology* 35, no. 2 (2017): 156–71.

41. Susan Doran, "Elizabeth I's Religion: The Evidence of Her Letters," *Journal of Ecclesiastical History* 31, no. 4 (2000): 699–720.

42. Printed in Gee and Hardy, *Documents Illustrative*, 442, 438.

43. Gee and Hardy, *Documents Illustrative*, 467. The Scottish Church, freed from regulations such as the Advertisements, took note of the multiple clergy who were suspended because of the application of the Advertisements. The Scots General Assembly of 1566 appealed for their restoration. See Knox, *History of the Reformation in Scotland*, 2:199–201.

44. "The Act against Recusants," in Gee and Hardy, *Documents Illustrative*, 498.

England's continued hierarchy of bishops. For his efforts, Cartwright forfeited his post as Lady Margaret Professor of Divinity.[45] Dissent came not only from ministers who were reluctant to toe the line on matters of costume and liturgy, but also from members of Parliament who wanted to see the Church of England move further and faster in a robustly Protestant direction. Various petitions were submitted to Parliament purporting to show popular demand for greater conformity between the Church of England and what were called "the best Reformed churches."[46] A particular shortcoming in the English church (in the eyes of such critics) was its failure to address the need for the pastoral admonition and discipline of wayward members at the local level.

But such appeals not only made no difference; they provoked sterner measures. Queen Elizabeth did not wish her Parliament to meddle in the nation's religious affairs. Further, in 1577 she instructed her second archbishop of Canterbury, Edmund Grindal, himself a returned exile of the Marian period, to forbid the periodic ministerial gatherings known as "prophesyings."[47] She suspected that these regional gatherings for theological and sermonic discussion were seditious. When Grindal (who was sympathetic toward these gatherings) declined to act, Elizabeth ordered his sequestration; this (a kind of house arrest) prevented his functioning as archbishop until his death. The last decade of Elizabeth's reign further aggravated those wishing for greater uniformity of practice with the family of Reformed churches with the Act against Puritans.[48] In sum, the Elizabethan period had largely tended to frustrate the aspirations of not only the nonconforming Anglicans who had refused to accept the Book of Common Prayer as the last word but also many who used it willingly. Hopes would be pinned on Elizabeth's eventual successor.

More than two years elapsed between Elizabeth's succession of her half sister (in November 1558) and the time when Mary (now) Queen of Scots returned to her homeland after her bereavement in France. In the intervening period, not only had a Scottish army (assisted by English forces) driven French troops out of Scotland, but also the Scottish Parliament had legislated the Roman

45. Patrick Collinson, "Thomas Cartwright," in *Oxford Dictionary of National Biography* (Oxford: Oxford University Press, 2004), 10:409-13.

46. W. H. Frere and C. E. Douglas, eds., *Puritan Manifestoes: A Study of the Origin of the Puritan Revolt* (London: SPCK, 1907). Two printings of John Knox's Genevan Service book, adopted by the Church of Scotland in 1564 as the *Book of Common Order*, were prepared in England in these years. See Horton Davies, *Worship and Theology in England from Cranmer to Baxter and Foxe* (Grand Rapids: Eerdmans, 1996), 255, 276.

47. The "prophesyings" of Elizabethan England were a regional manifestation of a practice employed throughout regions of Reformed Europe. At Zurich, the gatherings were named the "prophezei"; at Geneva the "congregation"; in the Netherlands the "coetus"; and in Scotland the "exercise."

48. "The Act against Puritans," in Gee and Hardy, *Documents Illustrative*, 492.

Catholic Church in Scotland out of existence and endorsed that new expression of Christianity, the Reformed Church of Scotland. The Parliament, acting in the absence of a monarch, had ratified a confession of faith and received (with general approval) the plan for the reorganization of the church that we today call the *First Book of Discipline*. Though the core of six ministers who stood at the center of the reform of the Scottish church did not occupy entirely the same ground (some having only just embraced Protestantism), their achievements were sizable.[49] In the space of a year, there had come into existence a national church that—though vastly understaffed due to a shortage of Protestant clergymen—had defined geographic districts supervised by superintendents, ranks of examined readers and exhorters to supplement its ministers, and local church elders to assist with community discipline. It was thus functioning as a Presbyterian body, with a structure determined by itself. In 1564, it endorsed a liturgical manual, *The Book of Common Order*, to provide a template for the various services of the church. The book was an adaptation of a preexisting service manual brought home by John Knox and Christopher Goodman from the refugee congregation they had served at Geneva during the reign of Mary Tudor. Its guidance was advisory; ministers enjoyed reasonable liberty in adapting it to their local situations. By 1578, the Church of Scotland had advanced sufficiently from its early struggle for existence that it endorsed a revised book of polity, the *Second Book of Discipline*. Now, in addition to regional synods (which roughly corresponded to pre-Reformation dioceses), there would be geographical groupings of congregations called presbyteries. Within twenty years of its official sanction by the Scottish Parliament, persons in the southern kingdom, disgruntled with the lack of real change in the Church of England, would ask, "Is discipline good for Scotland and not for England?"[50]

This Reformed Church of Scotland assumed governance over the nation's young universities, and in the space of a few years, St. Andrews, Aberdeen, and Glasgow were transformed into institutions capable of producing Protestant ministers as well as community leaders. A fourth, at Edinburgh, was added in 1583. The Church of Scotland, from the beginning, enjoyed full and free relationships with the various Reformed churches of the Continent.

49. The six were: John Knox, John Willock, John Spottiswoode, John Winram, John Douglas, and John Erskine.
50. "First Admonition to Parliament" (1572), in Frere and Douglas, *Puritan Manifestoes*, 19.

CHAPTER 2

Stuart Pressures against Presbyterians and Puritans

We have seen that the employment of the magisterial framework for support of a reformation of the Church of England in Elizabethan times had left a portion of English Protestants with a sense of growing frustration.

By contrast, the Reformed Church of Scotland had begun its formal existence in August 1560 with the authorization of the nation's Parliament but *not* the consent of the monarch. When Mary of Guise, the royal widow and regent of the land, had departed this life in June 1560, the Scottish Parliament proceeded without the concurrence of any monarch. It ended the jurisdiction of the pope and of Roman Catholicism within the nation and gave legal standing instead to the new Reformed church. Yet this arrangement, because of its irregularity, ensured that the Reformed church would need to come to terms with the eventual monarch, Mary, Queen of Scots, upon her return from France to reign in August 1561. Here lay the seeds of future trouble.

Mary, Queen of Scots, while never directly challenging the right of the Reformed church to exist, steadfastly refused to give her royal assent (by signature) to the legislation of 1560 that had brought the Protestant church into statutory existence.[1] As a result, a kind of awkward coexistence unfolded: Mary kept a Roman Catholic chaplain at her palace while the now-Protestant Church of Scotland simultaneously worked to extend the Reformation outward from the major towns to the countryside. This awkward arrangement merely postponed eventual troubles.

Instability within the royal household provoked much trouble. Queen Mary generated national turmoil by her unwise marriages, and this turmoil in turn threatened the stability and unity of the young Reformed church. Having returned from France as a young widow, Mary married a Catholic relative,

---

1. This royal assent would only be secured in the reign of Mary's son, James VI.

Henry Stuart, Lord Darnley, in July 1565. As Mary had not adequately gauged the character of this future husband, the marriage soon proved to be an unhappy match. Then, Darnley—who had proved to be abusive—died under mysterious circumstances in February 1567. After an explosion in a room below his bedchamber, he was found outside, dead by strangulation. As if this situation was not confused enough, by May of that same year, Queen Mary had remarried (again). Her third husband, James Hepburn, the fourth Earl of Boswell (a nominal Protestant), was suspected of involvement in Darnley's murder. Though an inquiry subsequently cleared Boswell, his marriage to Mary—following immediately his divorce of his second wife—provoked a national tumult.

The nation was now divided, not (as one might expect) along Catholic-Protestant lines, but between those supporting the queen's decision to remarry while under a cloud of suspicion and those demanding greater rectitude in their head of state. After an armed struggle between supporters (the Queen's Party) and opponents (the King's Party),[2] Queen Mary was captured and imprisoned. Before her eventual escape, powerful nobles obliged her to abdicate from the throne in favor of her infant son, James.[3] James (now James VI) would not reign in his own name until 1579, and only exercised his full powers commencing in 1583.

King James in His Minority

It became clearer with the passage of time that the government of the infant king James VI of Scotland stood somewhat in reaction to developments in Scotland since 1560, the year Parliament endorsed the reformation of the national church. His government, led from 1571 by a regent, James Douglas, fourth Earl of Morton,[4] was supportive of magisterial reformation, yet on the plan displayed in the southern kingdom. There was within Morton's government a growing expectation that James would eventually function like Elizabeth, his southern kinswoman, as guide and protector of the Protestant church. Morton (and young James after him) could see that the role of the

2. So named because the alternative to Mary was her infant son, the future James VI.

3. The escape of Queen Mary from this imprisonment, across the border to England in 1568, opened the way to her being confined in England as a security threat until her eventual execution in 1587.

4. Morton was the fourth and longest-serving regent during the minority of King James VI. See George R. Hewitt, *Scotland under Morton, 1572–80* (Edinburgh: John Donald, 1982).

monarch in Scottish religious affairs had been diminished by the estrangement from Protestantism that had existed during Mary's reign in the 1561–1567 period. Since 1560, under these conditions of estrangement, the conception of the respective influence of church and Crown that developed in Scotland was that they represented not *one* jurisdiction with a monarch supreme over all but two parallel jurisdictions. In the state, the monarch was undoubtedly supreme; in the church, the king (as a professed Christian) stood on level ground with other Christians. Even in his youth, King James sought to undermine this somewhat republican conception of the roles of monarchy and state.[5]

One of the earliest indicators that the government of Regent Morton intended to modify the self-governing structure of the Reformed church was shown by its determination in 1571–1572 to reinstate bishops into the national church. The Reformed church had made no provision for the continuation of bishops in 1560; instead, it had created the office of superintendent.[6] Inasmuch as no Roman Catholic monk, priest, or bishop had been required to resign his office in 1560, a majority of these continued (though inactive) with their honorific titles intact. While they lived, they continued to receive whatever revenues and stipends had earlier been promised them. The ecclesiastical title of bishop was therefore not available to be bestowed on any range of new persons.[7]

Regent Morton, acting in the interests of the young king, had two reasons for wishing to see bishops restored.[8] First, there was a constitutional reason. Traditionally, bishops had been given a place in Parliament in order to represent the interests and concerns of the church; they had similarly been eligible to serve on the council of state (i.e., the cabinet) and in the college of justice. This constitutional role had withered since 1560, as former bishops

5. Biographer Roger Lockyer indicates that James stood in particular reaction against the republican sentiments of his boyhood tutor, humanist scholar George Buchanan. *James VI and I* (London: Longman, 1998), 37–38.

6. The office of superintendent as originally conceived of in 1560 is described in *The First Book of Discipline*, ed. James K. Cameron (Edinburgh: St. Andrew Press, 1972), 115–28. The significance of this office is explored by James Kirk in *Patterns of Reform: Continuity and Change in the Reformation Kirk* (Edinburgh: T&T Clark, 1989), chap. 5, "The Superintendent: Myth and Reality."

7. In an isolated instance, former Queen Mary had—though Roman Catholic—made the Protestant superintendent of Argyll, John Carswell, the titular bishop of the Western Isles in 1565. D. E. Meek, "John Carswell," in *Scottish Dictionary of Church History and Theology*, ed. Nigel M. Cameron (Downers Grove, IL: InterVarsity Press, 1993), 140–41.

8. D. G. Mullan, *Episcopacy in Scotland: 1560–1638* (Edinburgh: John Donald, 1986), 34–35, enumerates five factors that made the reintroduction of episcopacy an attractive proposition from the vantage point of the governing powers.

who were still resolute Catholics kept their titles but forfeited their former spheres of influence. Thus, there remained a kind of constitutional basis for the continuation of bishops at least until the constitutional framework was officially altered.

But there was also a second reason. Morton and his government also sought to gain greater access to the considerable land-derived revenues that these bishops had customarily received. Earlier, in pre-Reformation Scotland, the Scottish Crown and nobility had regularly turned to the Scottish church for financial grants; Morton sought to extend this arrangement into the Protestant era. The civil war that had so recently divided Scotland into pro- and anti-Mary factions had driven the government into a precarious financial situation. After 1572, as the titular (but nonactive) Catholic bishops began to pass away (thus leaving their titles vacant), Morton nominated Protestant ministers as their successors.[9] Each person accepting such a nomination from Morton's government would have understood that any revenues associated with that episcopal see would now be diminished in order to address two emerging needs. Beyond guaranteeing a suitable annual sum to the new bishop, these revenues would henceforth benefit both a national government that was struggling to stay solvent and a Reformed church that a dozen years after 1560 had made little progress in possessing the land-based revenues long promised to it.

It should be clear that the Reformed church did not initiate this state of affairs inasmuch as the church *itself* had no intrinsic interest in the restoration of episcopacy. It had seen to it that the pastoral oversight associated with bishops would be provided through its superintendents. It also considered the representation of the church in Parliament by bishops (though long-accepted practice) to be nonnecessary, as ample pious nonclerical Christians were already present in those assemblies. Yet, having been given Morton's assurance that with Protestant ministers installed in these episcopal roles one-third of the revenues of their sees could now be diverted to the common funds of the church to provide stipends for the new ministers, the Reformed church could not reject this proposal out of hand. Under duress, the Reformed church agreed to this proposal, all the while seeking to draw attention to the unsavory aspect of an arrangement that diverted still-additional church revenues to the state. It described these arrangements as "tulchan."[10] The Reformed church accepted the arrangement with the provision that any such bishops, nominated by the government, needed to be church ministers in good standing,

9. See note 7 above, for an earlier instance in 1565.

10. The term referred to a straw-filled calfskin matched with a milk-giving cow in order to induce the yielding of milk.

would be reckoned to be members of presbyteries, and would be answerable for the conduct of their office to the General Assembly. This agreement, when formalized, was called the Concordat of Leith.[11]

Yet, within five years it became abundantly clear that this arrangement, under which General Assembly–appointed superintendents and government-nominated bishops existed (and sometimes labored) side by-side, was a failure in two respects. First, the bishops nominated by government initiative did not effectively provide pastoral oversight during the existing shortage of ministers. Their readiness to carry out that supervisory task had never been the primary consideration of those who nominated them.[12] Second, these bishops—having a sense of obligation toward the public officials who had nominated them—proceeded to enrich these patrons by diverting church revenues and lands to them in a manner almost identical to what had characterized the church in its pre-Reformation days.[13] Deep dissatisfaction with the 1572 arrangement led to calls for the settling of matters on a less-improvised basis. The Reformed church was determined to be self-governing and to recover lands and revenues critical to its operation and expansion. This new, more coherent conception was realized in 1578 as the *Second Book of Discipline*.

This was the work of a committee of thirty, the majority of which were veteran ministers who had been serving since the *First Book of Discipline* had been introduced in 1560. They knew firsthand the limitations of the existing arrangement, agreed to at Leith in 1572. At this time, a participating layman, Lord Glamis, entered into correspondence with Theodore Beza (1519–1605), Genevan successor to John Calvin, regarding certain contested questions. He wished to know whether in Reformation times there ought to be ecclesiastics representing the church in a legislature, and whether the maintenance of ranks within the Christian ministry (a thing required by episcopacy) was a valid practice. One particular rising star of the younger generation and the by-then principal of Glasgow University, Andrew Melville (1545–1622), played a signif-

11. It is interesting to note that John Knox, no supporter of bishops, eventually gave his support to this scheme. Yet he refused to take any part in the admission to office of the new archbishop of St. Andrews, John Douglas, in 1572. Knox maintained that the already-aged Douglas was unable to function energetically in the episcopal role. Mullan, *Episcopacy in Scotland*, 39. The account as given by James Kirk, ed., *The Second Book of Discipline* (Edinburgh: St. Andrew Press, 1989), 37–42, more fully details the strong opposition of John Knox to this scheme. See the terms of the 1572 agreement in Gordon Donaldson, ed., *Scottish Historical Documents* (Glasgow: Scottish Academic Press, 1974), 137–38.

12. Two bishops nominated by the government in this period (the bishops of Dunblane and of Moray) had not even been ministers of the church. Kirk, *Second Book of Discipline*, 53.

13. Kirk, *Second Book of Discipline*, 37–42.

icant, though not dominant, role in this work of reassessment.[14] Authorized subcommittees met in five Scottish cities; their reports were widely discussed in the General Assembly of 1578; that Assembly approved the document.

Under its provisions, there were to be no further episcopal appointments made from among the church's ranks of ministers, nor any further encroachments by government or nobility upon its property and revenues. Also, a clear line of demarcation was to be drawn between the national Parliament and the jurisdiction of the church. Strong opposition was articulated to ideas of royal or kingly authority extending into matters of religion. Yet, significantly, this document (like its predecessor, the *First Book of Discipline*), while operative in the church, was never ratified by the nation's Parliament. The church's forthright claim to the entirety of its lands and revenues called into question many preexisting bargains struck by the nobility with the bishops of earlier times.

King James in His Majority

From the year 1579, young King James began to involve himself more directly in the rule of the kingdom. Sweeping aside his regent, Morton, in 1581, he attempted a more direct rule, now taking advice from the French-born cousin of his late father, Esmé Stuart, Seigneur d'Aubigny. James made him Earl of Lennox, and subsequently Duke of Lennox. This Francophone relative's guiding principle was to thwart the pro-English policies of Regent Morton and to turn Scotland once more toward France, its old ally.[15] Their opposition to Lennox led Scottish nobles to forcibly sequester the young king in what was called the "Ruthven Raid"; the named price of young James's liberation was his consenting to the forced return of Lennox to France.

In this period of political intrigue, the church's determination to govern itself without royal intervention (whether direct, or through bishops loyal to the crown) gained ground. Yet the young King James struck back in 1584 by introducing, through Parliament, the so-called Black Acts, which required the subordination of the church to a comprehensive royal supremacy, forbade any preaching that opposed this arrangement, and resumed the practice of governmental nomination of bishops from within the ranks of the Protestant

---

14. Hewitt, *Scotland under Morton, 1572–80*, 105–7, and Lockyer, *James VI and I*, 11, assert this Melvillian dominance. Kirk, *Second Book of Discipline*, 46–47, counters with evidence indicating Melville's more confined role. A recent returnee to Scotland from the Continent, Melville would successively be principal of the universities of Glasgow and St. Andrews.

15. Lockyer, *James VI and I*, 12.

ministry.[16] Such bishops would henceforth have the authority to select and appoint ministers, usurping the right of congregations to do so. Andrew Melville, outspoken in his opposition to this reassertion of royal supremacy in religion, fled to England to avoid arrest.[17] Yet, within two years of the passage of the Black Acts, the political balance of power shifted once more and James consented to modifications to this arrangement that blunted his efforts to suppress the Presbyterian self-government of the church. His nominated bishops were now required to secure the collaboration of presbyteries in their work; they were also subject to potential censure by the General Assembly. In the light of threats both of a Spanish invasion and of hostile Highland Catholic nobility who had never reconciled themselves to Protestantism, James opted for religious policies aimed at securing the support and solidarity of his Protestant subjects.[18] Consistent with this desire for consolidation, in 1592 James granted to the Church of Scotland legislation restoring to it the liberties sought after in the two books of discipline of 1560 and 1578. This Act Authorizing Presbyterian Government granted the Reformed Church of Scotland the long-sought liberty to order its own affairs. It did not, however, resolve the still-lingering need to secure for the church the lands and revenues that had been at the disposal of the pre-Reformation church.[19]

King James VI *and* I

As death approached in March 1603, aged Queen Elizabeth I included among her last spoken instructions an indication that her kinsman, James VI of Scotland, was her intended successor. Though this was her first public utterance on the subject of the succession, there had in fact been governmental correspondence and negotiations with James about this, extending back years. For an even longer period, James had contemplated this outcome—conscious both that Elizabeth's father, Henry VIII, had been brother to his great-grandmother, Margaret Tudor, and that the never-married Elizabeth was leaving no heirs. James was thirty-seven years of age as he assumed the reign of the neighboring nation.

A certain reputation preceded James as he relocated to the south in the

---

16. Donaldson, *Scottish Historical Documents*, 153–56.
17. Lockyer, *James VI and I*, 16–17.
18. Lockyer, *James VI and I*, 18.
19. "Act Authorizing Presbyterian Government," in Donaldson, *Scottish Historical Documents*, 160–61, and Lockyer, *James VI and I*, 23.

spring of 1603. Citizens of the southern kingdom may have wondered about the fitness of James—monarch of the more provincial and less densely populated realm to the north—to ascend to the throne of their richer and more powerful nation. It was duly noted that in his youth, James had struggled to exert his authority over Scottish nobility. Yet, at the same time, Christian leaders in the southern kingdom—if of the type that had hankered after a more thorough reformation than what Queen Elizabeth would authorize—entertained hopes that under James the Church of England might now see significant changes. Among them there existed the long-standing perception that Scotland's Reformation had advanced more thoroughly than England's. As early as 1566, leading ministers of the Reformed Church in Scotland had written to the bishops of the Church of England appealing for latitude in matters of liturgy and clerical dress, knowing that English ministers of their own persuasion were being suspended from service.[20] These advocates of further reform in the Church of England reckoned the Church of Scotland to rank among the "best Reformed churches."[21] Had not James, after a prolonged contest, come to some kind of an amicable understanding with the Church of Scotland?

Yet, what would become clear over time is that James's policies were aimed at securing a religious convergence between the neighboring nations that would compel Scotland to conform increasingly to English patterns. His expectation was that the Church of Scotland would increasingly resemble its southern counterpart by recognizing royal supremacy in religious matters, one part of which was accepting the government of the church by bishops.

Hampton Court

As James journeyed southward to take up English residence, signatures were being gathered across England on a petition. The petition, delivered to the king as he traveled, sought a conference with James and major leaders of the Church of England regarding long-standing grievances about liturgy and the exercise of discipline.[22] The approximately one thousand who signed what came to be

20. This letter, "The Superintendents with other Ministers and Commissioners of the Church of God in the Kingdom of Scotland to their Brethren, the Bishops . . . ," dated December 27, 1566, is reprinted in W. C. Dickinson, ed., *John Knox's History of the Reformation in Scotland* (New York: Philosophical Library, 1950), 2:199–201.

21. This was the language used by "First Admonition to Parliament" of 1572. See Walter H. Frere and C. E. Douglas, eds., *Puritan Manifestoes* (London: SPCK, 1906), 6, 28, 113, 150.

22. See the discussion in Christopher Durston, *James I* (London: Routledge, 1993), 56–57, and Lockyer, *James VI and I*, 102–9.

called the Millenary Petition had reason to believe that the Scot ascending to the throne of England would look favorably upon their request. Signatories were of the moderate Puritan outlook that sought not the overthrow of the Church of England's episcopal system but the improvement of it.[23] The conference took place at Hampton Court palace in January 1604.

It is regularly recalled that the king—who suspected that their calls for increased discipline at the congregational level implied a determination to overthrow episcopacy in favor of a Presbyterian order—denounced the Presbyterian system as "agreeing as well with monarchy as God with the Devil."[24] But this was hardly the whole story.

Serious back-and-forth took place among the Puritan representatives, the bishops (led by the archbishop of Canterbury, Richard Bancroft), and the king. James gradually came to accept that calls for enhanced congregational discipline were not, in fact, a mere front for the elimination of episcopacy. It is often supposed that the only thing of value granted to the Puritan faction was authorization for the production of a new Bible translation.[25] But on closer examination, there is strong reason to believe that King James came to some kind of a meeting of minds with his petitioners.

The preserved list of modifications of practice agreed to by the conferees is highly impressive. Private baptism by laymen and nurses was to be discontinued. Excommunication—to this point purely within the prerogative of bishops—would henceforth require the concurrence of local ministers. Readings from the apocryphal (intertestamental) writings were to be discontinued in church services. The practice of confirming children was to be renamed "Confirmation or Further Examination" of the children's faith.[26] Regrettably, James, having entrusted the summarization of these discussions to his bishops (led by Bancroft), also left the implementation of these resolutions to the same bishops. Implementing these changes was clearly no priority of the attending bishops, who had never endorsed the sentiments of those who had signed the petition.[27]

23. See the text of the Millenary Petition in Henry Gee and W. J. Hardy, *Documents Illustrative of English Church History* (London: Macmillan, 1898), 508–11.

24. J. R. Tanner, *Constitutional Documents of the Reign of James I* (Cambridge: Cambridge University Press, 1930), 67, as quoted in Lockyer, *James VI and I*, 107.

25. This was the Authorized Version, issued in 1611.

26. See the report of the Hampton Court Conference in G. W. Prothero, *Statutes and Select Constitutional Documents Illustrative of the Reigns of Elizabeth I and James I* (Oxford: Oxford University Press, 1914), 416–17.

27. There has been considerable debate as to the outcome of the Hampton Court Conference. The revisionist essay of Mark H. Curtis, "Hampton Court Conference and Its Af-

Archbishop George Abbot

In naming George Abbot (1562–1633) to succeed Richard Bancroft as archbishop of Canterbury in 1611, King James put forward a man known for his moderate Puritan sympathies. Abbot had been a university administrator at Oxford before coming to the king's attention in 1606 as one ready to defend the rightness of hereditary monarchy. King James then used Abbot, a donnish individual, as his emissary to Scotland in 1608, where he persuasively made a case for the previously unpopular episcopal government within the Church of Scotland. Episcopacy had faded in Scotland since the king had introduced a guarantee of Presbyterianism's continuance in 1592; yet in 1600 the king had resumed agitation for episcopacy by naming three bishops for Scotland. Now in 1608, James was using a moderate Puritan to urge on the Scots what they would surely have rejected if presented by a theological opponent; James was pleased to see Abbot prevail. A Scottish General Assembly at Linlithgow in 1608 gave its assent to Abbot's arguments.[28]

By the time of Archbishop Bancroft's passing, Abbot had left university life and had served in rapid succession as bishop of Lichfield and of London.[29] It seems that his fruitful working relationship with the king to that point made him a natural choice for royal nomination—even though his university career meant he had bypassed all pastoral ministry. In the initial years of being named archbishop of Canterbury in 1611, Abbot's relationship with the king yielded some productive results. We may speak of an overlap of concern between James and Abbot, for James himself (like Abbot) had had a somewhat austere and puritanical upbringing. James also, like his archbishop, had little enthusiasm for the rising ritualist party in the Church of England, centering around William Laud (1573–1645). Laud was well known to Abbot on account of their overlapping years of service as heads of colleges in Oxford University.

---

termath," *History* 46 (1961): 1–16, emphasized concessions gained by the Puritan petitioners. More cautious assessments followed from Patrick Collinson, "The Jacobean Religious Settlement: The Hampton Court Conference," in *Before the English Civil War: Essays on Early Stuart Politics and Government*, ed. Howard Tomlinson (London: Macmillan, 1981), 27–51, and Frederick Shriver, "Hampton Court Revisited: James I and the Puritans," *Journal of Ecclesiastical History* 33, no. 1 (1982): 48–71. Collinson and Shriver emphasized the hollowness of concessions gained but never implemented by bishops entrusted with the task.

28. Paul A. Welsby, *George Abbot: The Unwanted Archbishop* (London: SPCK, 1962), 30–31.

29. "George Abbot," in *Oxford Dictionary of the Christian Church*, ed. F. L. Cross (Oxford: Oxford University Press, 1957), 2–3.

The Synod of Dordt

Early in his English reign, James found himself as the most powerful Protestant monarch in western Europe. Through extensive diplomacy, he early on sought to summon a general council of European Protestants and Catholics to seek a resolution of religious differences.[30] In such a council, James would not have ensured any weighty role for the bishop of Rome. Consistent with this rising role in Europe, his daughter Elizabeth had married the Elector of the Palatinate in 1613. Exercising this enhanced role, and because of shared theological concern between Archbishop Abbot and himself, it was natural for James to accept the invitation to send English delegates to the international Synod of Dordt (1618–1619). This synod was called to address the destabilizing effects of the teaching of the Dutch Remonstrants, the disciples of the late Jacob Arminius (1560–1609).[31] King James himself had a pronounced interest in such theological questions. Once he had reached school age, he had been entrusted to the tutelage of the Scottish humanist and supporter of the Reformation, George Buchanan (1506–1582). This education imparted to him a definite theological acumen. Though he stood in reaction against Buchanan, by creed James remained consciously Calvinist.[32] It was James who took primary responsibility in the selection of those who represented England at Dordt. The English delegates were treated with honor in this international synod and exercised a moderating influence while there.

Of the delegates to Dordt, only one possessed a Scottish connection: Walter Balcanquall. Of Scottish birth and education, Balcanquall was of Episcopalian sympathies and spent his entire ecclesiastical career in England. Consistent with his desire to bring the Scottish church to acknowledge his supremacy in religious matters, in the same period, James had his agents in Scotland secure passage of the Five Articles of Perth in the 1618 General Assembly, meeting in that city.[33] The articles established quasi-Anglican features in Scottish church life such as permitting private ceremonies of baptism and Holy Communion and requiring

30. W. B. Patterson, *King James VI and I and the Reunion of Christendom* (Cambridge: Cambridge University Press, 1997), chap. 2.

31. M. W. Dewar, "The British Delegation to the Synod of Dort 1618–1619," *Evangelical Quarterly* 46, no. 2 (1974): 103–16; Anthony Milton, ed., *The British Delegation and the Synod of Dort (1618–1619)* (Woodbridge, UK: Boydell, 2005); Patterson, *King James VI and I*, chap. 8.

32. John Coffey, "Church and State 1550–1750: The Emergence of Dissent," in *T&T Clark Companion to Nonconformity*, ed. Robert Pope (London: Bloomsbury T&T Clark, 2013), 53.

33. The articles received the approval of the Scottish Parliament in 1621. See the articles in Donaldson, *Scottish Historical Documents*, 184–85. The king's strategy of using the Perth Articles to secure religious conformity between the two kingdoms is explored in Ian B. Cowan, "The Five Articles of Perth," in *Reformation and Revolution*, ed. Duncan Shaw (Edinburgh: St. Andrew Press, 1967), 160–77.

both that Communion be received kneeling and that children be confirmed by a bishop. Christmas, Easter, Ascension, and Pentecost were now to be observed in the Scottish churches, which had not been the case since 1560.[34]

James had proved to be a difficult "godly prince"; yet he represented difficulty in different ways for each nation. Though at a distance from Scotland (to which he returned only once after his accession to the English throne), James never left off working to advance his royal supremacy in religion. Yet, in England, with the religious supremacy issue having been settled under his predecessor, the king proved to be (1) a spendthrift whose expenditures regularly exceeded his revenues, (2) partial to a fault in lavishing his bounty on courtiers who migrated with him from the north, and (3) autocratic—in that he summoned Parliament as seldom as he could. He was also regularly given over to debaucheries of several kinds and shocked the populace in ways his predecessor never had.[35] Archbishop Abbot, who earlier had proved so useful to him, was gradually marginalized because of his determined opposition to a proposed marriage between the heir to the throne, Charles, and a Spanish Catholic princess, and because of his resistance to an unethical divorce and remarriage endorsed by James.[36] A marginalized Abbot survived James, only to be marginalized further by his son and successor, Charles.

The Ascension and Reign of Charles I

Charles was not the intended heir to his father's throne. An older brother, Henry Frederick, had died unexpectedly of typhoid in 1612. Ascending to the throne at his father's death in March 1625, Charles was in many ways like and in as many ways unlike his father. Neither liked to negotiate with Parliament if this could be avoided; and to avoid it, each sought alternative sources of royal income that did not require parliamentary accountability. Charles was, if anything, more of an autocrat than his father. His marriage to the French princess Henrietta Maria in 1625 brought him into contact with French ideas of royal absolutism that were more advanced than those embraced by his father. He spoke of this autocracy as "self-rule" or "personal rule."

Yet Charles was fastidious in dress and manner, whereas his father had

---

34. Laura A. M. Stewart, "The Political Repercussions of the Five Articles of Perth: A Reassessment of James VI and I's Religious Policies in Scotland," *Sixteenth Century Journal* 38, no. 4 (2007): 1013–36.

35. Durston, *James I*, 17.

36. Welsby, *George Abbot*, 60–61, 107.

often seemed other-than-refined. These tendencies showed themselves also in his preferences in church matters. Charles prized order, ceremony, and decorum. Whereas moderate Puritans had quietly flourished in the reign of James, once Charles named William Laud archbishop of Canterbury in 1633, pressures against the Puritans increased to a remarkable degree.[37] Transatlantic colonization, already under way at such sites as the James River (1607) and Plymouth Colony (after 1620), received an additional impetus during the reign of Charles. About one thousand Puritan folk took part in the initial migration to the Massachusetts Bay colony 1630. In the decade leading to 1640, some forty thousand English citizens in all departed for the American colonies and the Caribbean; they constituted what has come to be called "the Great Migration."[38]

The Appointment of Laud

William Laud's promotion to the archbishopric of Canterbury in 1633 (he was previously bishop of London) was hardly a surprise. In George Abbot's final years as archbishop, Charles had regularly preferred the company and counsel of Laud. It is true that Abbot was in failing health and often confined to his house, but King Charles had found a kindred spirit in Laud. Laud, like Charles, was fastidious, a lover of order, and committed to the united use of power by church and monarchy,

In the early years of his reign, Charles had distanced himself from the broadly Calvinist stance of his father, who sent an English delegation to the Synod of Dordt. By a royal declaration of 1628, the king had insisted that the Anglican Articles of Religion would go on being used plain and simple, without any reference to the now-published canons of the Dutch synod.[39] Laud came to be termed "Arminian." This was not because he was a vocal supporter of the Dutch Remonstrants who had continued the teachings of Jacob Arminius, but because he stood in decided reaction to what he considered the gloomy theology of Calvinistic Puritans within the national church. He disliked the Puritan conception of fallen human nature as depraved. Under Laud, the designation "Arminian" was as much about anti-Puritanism and

---

37. Coffey, "Church and State 1550–1750," 54, speaks of an "open assault on Puritanism" in the Laud era.

38. Lacey Baldwin Smith, *This Realm of England: 1399–1688*, 8th ed. (Boston: Houghton Mifflin, 2001), 262. See Roscoe Lewis Ashley, *American History* (New York: Macmillan, 1908).

39. Gerald Bray, ed., *Documents of the English Reformation* (Minneapolis: Fortress, 1994), 481, notes that this declaration of 1628 was aimed at dampening appeals to the documents of Dordt within the ministry of the English church.

High Church liturgical tendencies as it was about soteriology. His was a theological perspective that emphasized the efficacy of sacramental grace rather than the efficacy of the preached Word.[40]

King Charles, in tandem with Laud—who served not only as archbishop but also as an important member of his Privy Council—pursued policies that maximized the directing of the two nations and the nations' churches from "above," that is, with as little consultation with houses of Parliament and Convocation as necessary. The adjective used to describe this approach was apt: "thorough."[41]

The Prayer Book Controversy of 1637 and Bishops' Wars

Though William Laud had no actual jurisdiction over Scotland as archbishop of Canterbury, he overreached himself by preparing a prayer book (a comprehensive liturgical guide for church services of all kinds) for the Protestant church of the north. The introduction of this book into Scotland by royal authority in 1637 perturbed two kinds of Scots. Some rejected outright the idea that Scottish Christians should be instructed by royal authority in how to worship God. Scotland had an existing manual of aids to guide corporate and private devotion: the *Book of Common Order*, which had been approved by the General Assembly in 1564. There were also those who, though open to a more extensively liturgical approach to worship and a greater exercise of royal authority in matters of religion, knew from the start that the introduction of Laud's book was a terrible mistake. It was an English book foisted on a Scottish church.[42]

The royal pronouncement that the book be utilized across Scotland without delay provoked opposition from both kinds. There were public outcries, most notably at Edinburgh. Under the leadership of a prominent lawyer, Archibald Johnston of Wariston, and the Fife pastor Alexander Henderson, there was

---

40. It remains true that there were outspoken soteriological Arminians within England and Scotland at this time. See John Coffey, *John Goodwin and the Puritan Revolution* (Woodbridge, UK: Boydell, 2006), and Nicholas Tyacke, *Anti-Calvinists: The Rise of English Arminianism, c. 1590–1640* (Oxford: Oxford University Press, 1987). For an overview of Scottish developments during these same decades, see David Mullan, "Arminianism in the Lord's Assembly: Glasgow, 1638," *Records of the Scottish History Society* 26 (1996): 1–30.

41. Smith, *This Realm of England*, 286–91.

42. Gordon Donaldson maintained that preliminary work toward the book of 1637 had been carried out by Scottish bishops sympathetic to Laud and to Charles's intention to secure religious uniformity between the two kingdoms. See Donaldson's *The Making of the Scottish Prayer Book of 1637* (Edinburgh: Edinburgh University Press, 1954), chap. 3.

drawn up in February 1638 the important National Covenant.[43] Signatures were solicited for the document in all corners of the land. The introduction of the prayer book of 1637 provoked the 1638 General Assembly of the Church of Scotland to take aim at what it believed to be the underpinnings of this latest royal intrusion into the free exercise of religion: accordingly, the Assembly moved to abolish the office of bishop (itself a practice reintroduced into the Scottish church at the insistence of King James).

But even before the Assembly could meet, King Charles had determined to take military action punishing the Scots for their agitation in support of the National Covenant. His agent at the Glasgow Assembly, James, third Marquess of Hamilton, was fully aware of this royal intention, even as he attempted to impede the determined action of the Assembly commissioners.[44] Charles, acting without the authorization or funding of the English Parliament, launched the first Bishops' War in September 1638; this ended in a debacle for commanders and forces loyal to Charles just south of the Scottish border. The Scots showed far greater military preparedness than the king had anticipated.

Obliged to grant to the Scots the concessions they demanded regarding their church (an end to episcopacy and the withdrawal of the prayer book of 1637), King Charles returned home determined to reverse this humiliation. Summoning the English Parliament for the first time in eleven years, he now unsuccessfully sought funding for renewed military hostilities against Scotland. But the Parliament, after being ignored for so long, saw no urgency in funding war on the king's northern subjects, with whom many members stood in sympathy. The king then dissolved this "Short Parliament." In late summer 1640, Charles—still without parliamentary funding—made war on the Scots a second time. In this skirmish the king suffered the further indignity of seeing two northern English counties (Northumberland and Durham) fall into Scottish hands.[45] The Scots occupied these territories until Charles could pay them war indemnities. To secure funding for those indemnities, Charles was obliged to call back Parliament.

---

43. On Henderson's role, see the recent biography of L. Charles Jackson, *Riots, Revolutions, and the Scottish Covenanters: The Work of Alexander Henderson* (Grand Rapids: Reformation Heritage, 2015), chap. 2. The now-standard work on this period is Mark Charles Fissel, *The Bishops' Wars: Charles I's Campaigns against Scotland* (New York: Cambridge University Press, 1994).

44. C. V. Wedgwood, *The King's Peace: 1637–1641* (New York: Macmillan, 1956), 236, 237.

45. Rosalind Mitchison credits the efficiency of the Scots armies in this second of the "Bishops Wars" to the return to Scotland in the interim between the first and second hostilities of a class of professional Scots soldiers who had returned home from European wars. See her *Lordship to Patronage: Scotland, 1603–1745* (London: Edward Arnold, 1983), 46.

This "Long Parliament" (called this because it technically remained in session until 1653) then presented its own accumulated grievances to the king preliminary to the question of indemnity funding. This list of grievances, given the name the Grand Remonstrance, recorded the growing sense of opposition to the steady drift away from the rule of law and the expansion of Stuart "personal rule." It represented an "alliance" of the concerns of two groups: (1) those agitated over an erosion of the rule of law and of fiscal accountability in which private property was no longer secure in the face of a monarch who forced nobles to grant him "loans," and (2) those of moderate Puritan sympathy who saw affairs in state as well as church steadily oriented in a Rome-ward direction.[46]

The Remonstrance also highlighted both the sale of honorific titles and offices and the awarding of commercial monopolies as methods by which Stuart monarchs surreptitiously raised their needed revenues. It faulted the king for favoring in both state and church those who sought to advance a Roman Catholic agenda, and protested against the steady expansion of the powers of the bishops of the Church of England. Supporters of the Grand Remonstrance also recorded their sympathies with their neighbors, the Scots, who had so recently been ready to fight in defense of their religious liberties.[47]

Further, one can detect in the Grand Remonstrance a particular anxiety common to Puritan ministers of the English church. Since 1640 they had been under obligation to take the "Et Cetera Oath," which required them to pledge both to do nothing to advance the influence of the Roman religion and to never seek any alteration of the present government of the English church by bishops.[48] The latter spurred many to think less well of the existence and operation of the episcopal system of church government. It was one thing to consent to work under the episcopal system as tolerable and workable, but quite another to pledge that it ought never to be modified or replaced.

Of course, the Remonstrance was looked on by the king as provocative. It was intended to checkmate his penchant for autocratic rule. After two military

46. Robert S. Paul, *The Assembly of the Lord* (Edinburgh: T&T Clark, 1985), 54, offers a helpful discussion of the emergence of this alliance of concern. John Morrill, "The Religious Context of the English Civil War," *Transactions of the Royal Historical Society* 34 (1984): 157, while allowing that this alliance of concerns was critical, maintained that "it was the force of religion that drove minorities to fight and forced majorities to make reluctant choices."

47. Excerpts from the Grand Remonstrance are printed in Gee and Hardy, *Documents Illustrative*, 553–62. English concern for the harm done by royal actions toward Scotland had been recorded in Parliament as early as the "Root and Branch Petition" in December 1640. See Gee and Hardy, 545.

48. See Gee and Hardy, *Documents Illustrative*, 536.

attempts to force religious conformity with England upon Scotland, Charles had been forced, on one hand, to relent and confirm the Scots in their religious preferences and, on the other, to give attention to an English Parliament that had reached a state of exasperation with him. Within a year, the Parliament had passed legislation requiring that no more than three years could elapse without its being called into session.[49] Two major associates of the king, one being Archbishop Laud, had been brought down.[50]

To make a tense situation even worse, October 1641 brought a large-scale rebellion of Irish Catholic peasants against the Protestant citizens of that country. It was suspected that Charles was at least cognizant that this uprising would happen, as he earlier planned to use Irish troops loyal to himself to assist him in his campaigns against the Scots.[51] In 1642, determined to prohibit further unauthorized royal military campaigns, Parliament ratified the Militia Bill as an ordinance since the king, understandably, would not sign into law a bill that ensured that, in the future, military forces and the navy would be answerable to Parliament rather than himself.[52]

49. This was the Triennial Act.

50. One, the king's favorite advisor, Thomas Wentworth, Lord Strafford, had been executed for treason in May 1641. The other, Archbishop William Laud, while accused of treason, was eventually convicted by Parliament under a bill of attainder and executed in May 1645. There was not again an archbishop of Canterbury until William Juxon was named such in 1660.

51. Smith, *This Realm of England*, 288.

52. Smith, *This Realm of England*, 290.

CHAPTER 3

Two Attempts at Protestant Religious Uniformity

Parliament's stripping away of what Charles considered his royal prerogative moved the king to conclude that a line had been crossed. When he gave no ground in light of the Grand Remonstrance of 1641, the House of Commons responded in June 1642 with its "Nineteen Propositions"; these encapsulated the main concerns from the previous, larger document. To these, Charles responded with an "Answer" in which he claimed that he had never sought to be other than benevolent in his exercise of kingly power. He refused to agree to demands that he believed altered the separation of powers between monarch and Parliament. "We do not wish the laws of England to be changed," he maintained.[1]

CIVIL WAR NECESSITATES MILITARY ALLIANCE

Already in April of 1642, Charles had sought to prepare for conflict by attempting to seize a military arsenal at Hull. But in keeping with the Militia Ordinance, which Parliament had just proclaimed as law (without his assent), this attempt was repulsed. By August, the king was at Nottingham gathering a military force. And so began a first year of war in which the initiative and early success fell mostly to the king's forces. With London in parliamentary hands, the king and his forces soon made Oxford their capital.

The English Parliament, which had yet to provide its own military force with professional soldier-commanders,[2] had good reason to be discouraged

1. Both the "Nineteen Propositions" and the King's "Answer" are printed in Lacey Baldwin Smith, *The Past Speaks: Sources and Problems in English History* (Boston: D. C. Heath, 1993), 346–49.
2. The parliamentary army was originally comprised of troops under the command of various notable and wealthy members of Parliament.

with that first year of war. Parliamentary troops lacked clarity as to their war aims. They meant to oppose the king's attempts to persist in "personal rule" by the use of force, but what did they contemplate—beyond resistance to that style of rule? It seemed that a negotiated settlement with the king would have satisfied those in command.[3] It was in this context that an idea, earlier mooted, received fresh attention: a military alliance with Scotland. What would it take to secure the involvement of the Scots, given that the Scots had only just secured their own peace with Charles under the Treaty of London (1641)?

We have noted that the English House of Commons had shown concern for the Scots in their struggles against the policies of Charles.[4] That solicitude was strengthened by the activity in London of Scottish representatives sent there to conclude the Treaty of London, which secured for Scotland the payment of the £850 per day earlier promised in the interim Treaty of Ripon (1640). That interim treaty had secured the cessation of the king's hostilities against the Scots, who had taken control of the whole of the English counties of Northumberland and Durham, as guarantee.

In this same period, the newly invigorated House of Commons had been calling for a parliamentary investigation of unresolved religious tensions exacerbated by recent royal policies.[5] What had in January 1640 been one of five new parliamentary committees, a Grand Committee on Religion, by December 1641 gave way to something further. The Grand Remonstrance had enunciated that there be "a general synod of the most grave, judicious and learned divines of this island assisted with some from foreign parts . . . who may consider of all things necessary for the peace and good government of the church."[6] This appeal was reiterated once more in the "Nineteen Propositions" submitted to King Charles in June 1642.[7] Charles was no more inclined to grant this request a year later in 1643 when—after a year of civil war—an off-ramp from further hostilities was offered to him in a draft document styled the "Treaty of Oxford." But this appeal, like others emanating from Parliament, went unheeded by a monarch who was determined to maintain control over the life of the nation and the national church.[8]

---

3. Rosalind Mitchison, *Lordship to Patronage: Scotland, 1603–1745* (Edinburgh: Edinburgh University Press, 1983), 54.

4. Chap. 2 above.

5. Robert S. Paul, *The Assembly of the Lord* (Edinburgh: T&T Clark, 1985), 58, 59.

6. "Grand Remonstrance" item 284, in S. R. Gardiner, ed., *Constitutional Documents of the Puritan Revolution: 1625–1660* (Oxford: Oxford University Press, 1951), 229.

7. See the helpful narrative in Paul, *Assembly of the Lord*, 61, 62.

8. Paul, *Assembly of the Lord*, 63.

With the civil war a year old, the two houses of Parliament acted together on June 12, 1643, to authorize the calling of just such an assembly.[9] At this point, the stated intention of this joint "ordinance" (as before, a pronouncement reckoned to have the force of law, though lacking the monarch's signature) was only to advance "a more perfect reformation" in the English church.[10] But as events unfolded, it became clear that a wider purpose was in view.

In England, matters were proceeding toward the opening of this Assembly on July 1, 1643. The Assembly's opening weeks were spent in an investigation (never completed) into the adequacy of the Thirty-Nine Articles of Religion, the existing doctrinal articles of the Church of England. As before, the civil war still offered little encouragement to the parliamentary side, yet now, by joint action of this Assembly and the English House of Commons, English representatives were sent both to the Scottish Parliament and the Church of Scotland General Assembly, to seek their collaboration. Ministers Stephen Marshall and Philip Nye—both members of the English Assembly—advised the Scots of the Assembly's determination to deliberate concerning the "liturgy, discipline, and government of the church" and invited them to send a delegation.[11] The Scottish authorities agreed to pursue consultations further.

It is safe to say that the primary motivation of the English Parliament in consulting with the Scots was military, that is, to secure the help of Scottish troops in their struggle against King Charles's forces. The Scots, having already engaged twice in combat with King Charles's armies, were not currently engaged in any such military action. Thus, their primary motivation in the summer of 1643 was to obtain guarantees of security for a common Protestantism in both nations. The Scots foresaw that any defeat of the English parliamentary army would likely open the way for the king to renew his conflict with their nation.[12] It was thus in their own security interest to assist the English parliamentary forces. The Scots were also ready to believe that

9. B. B. Warfield, *The Westminster Assembly and Its Work* (1931; reprint, Grand Rapids: Baker Books, 1981), 10, 11, notes that the House of Commons had framed and passed enabling legislation for such an assembly as early as November 1641; but by the king's refusal to sign this legislation, it lapsed.

10. The ordinance of the joint houses of Parliament is reprinted in standard editions of the Westminster Confession of Faith and Catechisms. See, for example, *The Confession of Faith and the Larger and Shorter Catechisms* (Glasgow: Free Presbyterian Publications, 1973), 11.

11. Charles A. Briggs, "A Documentary History of the Westminster Assembly," *Presbyterian Review* 1, no. 1 (1880): 139.

12. Edward Furgol, "The Civil Wars in Scotland," in *The Civil Wars: A Military History of England, Scotland, and Ireland, 1638–1660*, ed. John Kenyon and Jane Ohlmeyer (New York: Oxford University Press, 1998), 49. David Stevenson, *The Covenanters: The National*

the Assembly of Divines at Westminster was ready to seriously consider the Scottish presbyterian system of church government as a remedy for their own recurring ecclesiastical difficulties.

Accordingly, the Scots devised the Solemn League and Covenant, which predicated their armies joining with the English parliamentary forces upon there being support for a cross-border pledge to seek a uniform Protestantism. The language of the Solemn League seems to have sought to assure the subscribing nations that their somewhat distinguishable objectives could be achieved together: "the preservation of the reformed religion in the Church of Scotland, in doctrine, worship, discipline and government, against our common enemies; the reformation of religion in the kingdoms of England and Ireland, in doctrine, worship, discipline and government according to the Word of God."[13]

Ratified by both the Scottish Parliament and the General Assembly on August 17, 1643, it was approved by both houses of the English Parliament on September 25.[14] In Edinburgh, then at Westminster, there were public signing ceremonies at which all members of government were expected to demonstrate their support. And with that, the way was opened for Scottish commissioners to enter the ranks of the Westminster Assembly.[15] The first Scottish commissioners to the Assembly were already present on the day the English signed.

And with the covenant formally signed, the way opened for Scottish troops to enter the military conflict on the parliamentary side.[16] By early 1644, these Scots would be fighting in northeast England, besieging Newcastle—a royal

---

Covenant and Scotland (Edinburgh: Saltire Society, 1988), 52, maintained that "The Scots concluded that they had to intervene in England to protect their own revolution."

13. "Solemn League and Covenant" first head, in Henry Gee and W. J. Hardy, *Documents Illustrative of English Church History* (London: Macmillan, 1898), 569; William Ferguson, *Scotland's Relations with England: A Survey to 1707* (Edinburgh: Saltire Society, 1994), 125, insists that "the Covenanters erred in believing that Presbyterians were a major force in English politics."

14. "Solemn League and Covenant," in *Oxford Dictionary of the Christian Church*, ed. F. L. Cross (Oxford: Oxford University Press, 1957), 1268. The full text is provided in Gee and Hardy, *Documents Illustrative*, 569–74. The Solemn League was an adaptation of the preexisting National Covenant, circulated and supported in Scotland in the aftermath of the royal imposition of the prayer book in 1637.

15. It appears that at least three Scottish commissioners, Alexander Henderson, George Gillespie, and Archibald Johnson, were on hand as early as September 15, with others (Robert Baillie and Samuel Rutherford) not arriving until November. Briggs, "Documentary History," 139. Paul, *Assembly of the Lord*, 135. Sketches of the members of the Assembly (Scots included) are provided in William Barker, *Puritan Profiles: 54 Puritan Personalities Drawn Together by the Westminster Assembly* (Fearn, UK: Christian Focus, 1996).

16. The Scots appointed to be present in the Assembly were there only in an advisory

stronghold. By summer of that same year, Scottish troops assisted in a major military victory for the parliamentary forces at Marston Moor, Yorkshire.[17] Though the war had begun poorly for the parliamentary forces, the hitherto ineffective armies of Parliament soon experienced a reversal. The parliamentary armies took on a new character under the direction of commanders such as Thomas Fairfax (1612–1671) and Oliver Cromwell (1599–1658).

There were also setbacks, including some in Scotland that the advocates of the Solemn League failed to anticipate. By 1644, Irish and Scottish Highland royalist troops combined under the command of James Graham, Earl of Montrose, began to raise havoc in Scottish locales (such as Aberdeen) that had supported the current Scottish intervention into the English Civil War.[18] These royalist military actions at home were intended to divert Scottish forces away from the conflict in the southern nation. Nevertheless, the tide of war had turned in favor of the forces loyal to the Parliaments.

By May 1646, Charles had surrendered himself into the hands of a Scottish army at Southwell, Nottinghamshire. After six months of futile negotiation with Charles in the hopes of securing his support for the Solemn League and Covenant, and with their owed wages finally paid by the Parliament, the Scottish forces transferred the king into parliamentary jurisdiction and crossed over into Scotland. Their English business was done, as the king's ability to make war in any of his kingdoms was now past. By February 1647 he was under house arrest in Northamptonshire, guarded by parliamentary agents.

Yet Parliament, having exhausted its financial resources in paying the wages owed to the Scots, had left its similar obligation toward its own "New Model Army" unmet. This army now chafed against the Parliament both for that reason and because, increasingly, the army favored a free religious toleration (with no national church) that the Presbyterian-leaning Parliament could never countenance under the Solemn League with Scotland. Representatives of the army then seized control over the king in June 1647 and brought him to London, where separate negotiations with both Parliament and army leaders were intensified.[19] At this point, it was still within the realm of possibility that

---

role. As citizens of the neighboring kingdom, they were not accountable to the English Parliament but to their own.

17. Furgol, "The Civil Wars in Scotland," 54.

18. See note 14 above. Furgol, "The Civil Wars in Scotland," 52, 55. Montrose is an example of a Scottish aristocrat who, while supportive of Scotland's interest in the recent Bishops' Wars, and who had signed the National Covenant in 1638, desired no part in Scottish antiroyal invasions of England. The standard work is that of C. V. Wedgwood, *Montrose* (1966; reprint, London: Palgrave Macmillan, 1996).

19. Robert Ashton, *The English Civil War: Conservatism and Revolution; 1603–1649* (London: Weidenfeld & Nicolson, 1978), 312, 313.

Charles would remain king under terms insisted upon by either one party or the other. Then the king fled—hoping to escape to France—and was detained and reimprisoned on the Isle of Wight, off England's south coast.

Meanwhile, the ecclesiastical deliberations of the Westminster Assembly were still taking place at Westminster under the terms of the existing Solemn League. These deliberations continued even as the political situation began to stalemate because of the standoff between the New Model Army and the Parliament.

THE WESTMINSTER ASSEMBLY AT WORK

Up to 121 representatives from the various counties, the two English universities, three Channel Islands, and New England were joined by 20 members of Parliament.[20] First in the King Henry VII chapel and subsequently in the Jerusalem Chamber of the House of Parliament, they had already been examining the adequacy of the existing Anglican Articles of Religion. The concluding of the Solemn League in September 1643 and the arrival of the Scottish commissioners provided the occasion for fresh parliamentary instructions to the Assembly; the subject of deliberation was changed from the question of the adequacy of the English Articles of Religion[21] to the discipline and governance of the church.[22] Such a discussion could raise very ultimate questions.

Directories for Church Government and Worship

The Church of Scotland, acting in its General Assembly of 1638, had terminated the office and function of bishops within its own jurisdiction.[23] There was a similar growth of sentiment against episcopacy (at least of the hierarchical type, under which bishops were considered officers of the Crown) amongst many Church of England divines present in the Assembly. This growing suspicion of hierarchical episcopacy had already moved the Parliament in January 1641 to suspend English bishops from their traditional duties in the House of Lords; this had left them with purely ecclesiastical functions to per-

20. Briggs, "Documentary History," 135, 136.

21. Paul, *Assembly of the Lord*, 99.

22. Paul, *Assembly of the Lord*, 135, makes quite clear that the change of mandate reflected the importance assigned to the governance of the church by the Scottish signatories of the Solemn League.

23. We have observed in the preceding chapter the ongoing tension between the Church of Scotland and the late King James VI over this question.

form.[24] But what, if anything, might replace the traditional practice of episcopal oversight in the church was a very open question among the English at the Assembly. There seems to have been an English hopefulness that episcopacy could survive as a pastoral office, shorn of past accretions; this hope would only die slowly. With the exception of London ministers, there was initially only modest English support for the Presbyterian system of government in the Assembly.[25] This support would grow, over time, as it became clearer that support was lacking within the Assembly for episcopacy's continuance. But Parliament would not formally abolish the office of bishop in England until October 1646.[26]

Discussion and debate over the form of government and disciplinary procedure of the church continued from October 1643 until July 22, 1644. This eventually yielded a brief document, "The Form of Presbyterial Church Government."[27] Yet, as the deliberation advanced, opposition toward the Presbyterian scheme had emerged within the Assembly from five advocates of Congregational Independency. Their tract, *An Apologetical Narration*, was submitted not to the Assembly itself but to the House of Commons—to which the Assembly was subject.[28] As if this unforeseen development were not distraction enough, the Assembly had without prior consultation also been tasked

24. This was the Clerical Disabilities Act. It is printed in Gardiner, *Constitutional Documents of the Puritan Revolution*, 241, 242.

25. Paul, *Assembly of the Lord*, 111; E. W. Kirby, "English Presbyterians in the Westminster Assembly," *Church History* 33 (1964): 418–28. So also C. G. Bolam and Jeremy Goring, "Presbyterians in the Parish Church," in C. G. Bolam et al., *The English Presbyterians from Elizabethan Puritanism to Modern Unitarianism* (London: Allen & Unwin, 1968), 38. Warfield, *The Westminster Assembly and Its Work*, 18n28, notes that English divines sympathetic to Presbyterian order had only a "purely theoretical" understanding of it. Robert Letham, *The Westminster Assembly: Reading Its Theology in Historical Context* (Phillipsburg, NJ: P&R, 2009), 24, views the English attachment to Presbyterianism as being more extensive. The difference of interpretation is rooted in the fact that English divines present in the Assembly identifying as Presbyterian were primarily concerned about the right ordering of congregations and local exercise of church discipline rather than the hierarchy of courts associated with Presbyterianism as established in Scotland.

26. Peter King, "The Episcopate during the Civil Wars, 1642–1649," *English Historical Review* 83, no. 328 (July 1968): 523. During the first phase of war, the bishops were sequestered and hindered from exercising their functions. The abolition of the episcopate followed the surrender of the king.

27. This was received and endorsed by the General Assembly of the Church of Scotland in February 1645. The English Parliament adopted an ordinance providing for its implementation in March 1646. Bolam, *The English Presbyterians*, 43n1.

28. The text of the *Apologetical Narration* may be read at http://quintapress.webmate.me /PDF_Books/Apologetical_Narration.pdf.

by the House of Commons with the additional responsibility of investigating complaints of idleness or corrupt living made against existing clergymen and examining ministerial candidates who aspired to fill the pastoral vacancies that the removal of the first would create. Such tasks had devolved to the House of Commons because it had marginalized the corps of bishops who, however imperfectly, had earlier addressed these needs.[29]

About the time work on that first directory was completed, efforts were begun to produce a companion manual: the Directory for Public Worship.[30] Given long-accumulated Puritan dissatisfaction with obligatory use of the Church of England's Book of Common Prayer, and given that the attempted introduction of an equivalent volume in Scotland in 1637 had provoked a revolt, this was an initiative fraught with difficulty. While it preserved the principle that divine worship should be deliberate and ordered, the Directory also allowed for adaptation and discretion.[31] In this respect, it continued a stance exhibited in the earlier Scottish *Book of Common Order*.[32] This project was completed by December 27, 1644, and ratified by the House of Commons on January 3 of the year following.[33] The Scottish Parliament and General Assembly did the same in February of the same year.

Writing a Confession of Faith

In August 1644, the House of Commons instructed the Westminster Assembly to compose a new doctrinal confession, but, because of multiple tasks laid on the Assembly, the work did not commence until April 1645.[34] Earlier attempts had been made at this task. In July-August 1643 the Assembly had

---

29. This work, once assigned to the Assembly by Parliament, would continue on in the years immediately following the conclusion of the formal sessions of the Assembly in 1646. This work has recently been described by Chad Van Dixhoorn in *God's Ambassadors: The Westminster Assembly and the Reformation of the English Pulpit, 1643–1653* (Grand Rapids: Reformation Heritage, 2017), chaps. 4 and 6.

30. The commencing of this project is described in Van Dixhoorn, *God's Ambassadors*, chap. 7. Briggs, "Documentary History," 150, indicates May 24, 1644, as the beginning of consideration.

31. This historical background and rationale are provided in the preface to the Directory. See this in the Directory as printed in *The Confession of Faith and Larger and Shorter Catechisms*, 373, 374.

32. Discussed above in chap. 2.

33. Briggs, "Documentary History," 50.

34. Briggs, "Documentary History," 151, provides the date of August 20, 1644, as the time when Parliament issued its directive to the Assembly. See also John H. Leith, *Assembly at Westminster: Reformed Theology in the Making* (Atlanta: John Knox, 1973), 60.

been occupied scrutinizing the existing Articles of Religion of the English church, progressing to article 15 of the thirty-nine articles before the fresh directive came from Parliament. The Assembly had also been comparing the Anglican articles with one preexisting effort to improve them, the Irish Articles of Religion (1615).[35] The Assembly most likely discontinued this effort at improving existing articles because, with the endorsing of the Solemn League and Covenant in late summer 1643, the new objective was to seek all possible conformity in the Protestantism practiced in the two nations.[36] Neither of the confessional documents in existence, the Anglican articles or the Scots Confession of 1560, could serve this purpose.

The use of such earlier models as the Irish Articles was important for several reasons. The Assembly worked under pressure of time (it had, after all, been assigned several concurrent tasks). It was also comprised of men who, though competent and thorough, were not academic theologians.[37] One of the two universities of England, Oxford, had become the headquarters of the king and the royalist forces. Thus, not only existing Oxford University theologians but also any bishops (assembled at Oxford) of advanced theological ability could not be expected to involve themselves in the Assembly effort. Theologians in Cambridge, the other university, if they served by royal appointment, were likewise obliged to shun involvement.[38] Thus, with the Assembly supported by the Parliament yet opposed by the king and those loyal to him, participants would by necessity be competent pastor-teachers. Only a few had published theological works beforehand.[39]

35. The Irish Articles of Religion are reprinted in Gerald Bray, ed., *Documents of the English Reformation* (Minneapolis: Fortress, 1994), 437–52. Editor Bray terms them a "bridge" between the earlier Anglican articles and the work of the Assembly. The influence of Irish archbishop James Ussher (1581–1656) in the composing of the Irish Articles and the subsequent utilization of them within the Westminster Assembly have recently been investigated. See Harrison Perkins, "The Westminster Assembly's Probable Appropriation of James Ussher," *Scottish Bulletin of Evangelical Theology* 37, no. 1 (2019): 45–63.

36. This was, in effect, the attempt to provide for a united Protestantism that was distinct from that which King Charles had intended for both countries.

37. Formal invitations had been given to theologians in both English universities, but these were declined.

38. Both universities, then, as now, had Regius and Lady Margaret Professorships of Divinity. There was consultation between members of Parliament and Irish archbishop James Ussher on questions of church government. It is said that he "moved easily" between Parliament and the royal court at Oxford. Alan Ford, "James Ussher," in *The Oxford Dictionary of National Biography*, vol. 57 (Oxford: Oxford University Press, 2004), 11.

39. Leith, *Assembly at Westminster*, 46, draws particular attention to the abilities of Anthony Tuckney. After his work at the Westminster Assembly, he left pastoral work for an academic career at Cambridge.

Theological Posture of the Westminster Assembly

"*Calvinistic* in emphasis, *Federal* in its basic structure, and *Evangelical* in its view of the relationship between God and man" is how one late twentieth-century evangelical theologian described the product of the Assembly's deliberations.[40] There was also a strong concern to counter a recent surge of antinomianism in England.[41] A range of opinions was held on contested subjects such as church government and the order of the divine decrees.[42] The confession of faith and catechisms "provide the most formal legacy of Puritan engagement with Reformed theology."[43] But it is at the same time clear that the consensus expressed in these documents did not encompass the perspectives of either theological voices allied with the king or leading non-Puritan thinkers still in English university posts.[44]

The Assembly finished the confession in early December 1646 and submitted it to the House of Commons for ratification. The Commons returned the document asking that Scripture proofs be added to it; this was completed by late April 1647.[45] What happened next must surely have disappointed the members of the Assembly.

Adoption in Scotland, Yet Not England

Political developments in the opening months of 1647 had altered the landscape. In March, the New Model Army, under the effective command of Sir Thomas Fairfax and Oliver Cromwell, took the last of the fortified strongholds loyal to the king (himself in custody since May 1646). As we have seen, in that spring of 1647, this army was growing estranged from the English Parliament

---

40. Sinclair B. Ferguson, "The Teaching of the Confession," in *The Westminster Confession in the Church Today*, ed. Alasdair I. C. Heron (Edinburgh: St. Andrew Press, 1982), 29. See also Chad B. Van Dixhoorn, "Unity and Diversity at the Westminster Assembly (1643–1649)," *Journal of Presbyterian History* 79, no. 2 (2001): 103–17.

41. Whitney Gamble, "Theology of the Westminster Confession," in *Oxford History of Scottish Theology*, vol. 1, ed. David Fergusson and Mark W. Elliott (New York: Oxford University Press, 2019), 265–78.

42. Robert Letham, *The Westminster Assembly: Reading Its Theology in Historical Context* (Phillipsburg, NJ: P&R, 2009), 283.

43. Susan Hardman Moore, "Reformed Theology and Puritanism," in *The Cambridge Companion to Reformed Theology*, ed. Paul T. Nimmo and David A. S. Fergusson (New York: Cambridge University Press, 2016), 211.

44. The best example of non-Puritan theological contemporaries is the individuals designated "Cambridge Platonists." See chap. 5 below.

45. Leith, *Assembly at Westminster*, 30.

(to whom it ostensibly answered). Fairfax, Cromwell, and many troops in this army favored the system of church government known as Congregational Independency; they had no sympathy with the parliamentary aim of achieving uniformity in religion, entailing Presbyterian polity, as allowed for in the Solemn League and Covenant. As Independents, they wanted no state supervision of the churches, whatsoever. And now, relations between Parliament and the army were deteriorating.

Representatives of this army seized the king from his quarters at Holdenby, Northamptonshire, from agents loyal to Parliament. A year after the king's initial surrender to the Scots, Parliament had still not secured concessions from their defeated but still willful king. The sudden seizure of the king now openly pitted the New Model Army against the priorities of the Parliament; Charles now became a kind of bargaining chip in army hands. The army produced a document entitled *The Solemn Engagement*, which assured the House of Commons that while it remained answerable to the Parliament, it would not disband (as Parliament requested) until the soldiers were paid their accumulated wages.[46]

It became clear through military representation in conferences known as the Putney Debates that a large segment of the army was seeking radical changes in the constitution of England as part of any settlement with the king. They now demanded universal male suffrage as well as an elevation of the House of Commons above both the monarchy and the House of Lords.[47] The House of Commons, by now increasingly nervous about the loyalty of the New Model Army, lacked confidence to implement the provisions of the Westminster Assembly in these unsettled circumstances. The captive king would not ratify this style of uniformity in religion while large segments of the army were determined not to live under it.[48]

---

46. For *The Solemn Engagement*, see https://quod.lib.umich.edu/e/eebo/A60729.0001.001 ?view=toc, accessed March 13, 2021. Writing in 1998, Ian Gentles estimated the arrears to be £2.8 million. See his "The Civil Wars in England," in *The Civil Wars: A Military History of England, Scotland, and Ireland, 1638–1660*, ed. John Kenyon and Jane Ohlmeyer (New York: Oxford University Press, 1998), 147.

47. Gentles, "The Civil Wars in England," 149–50.

48. Stevenson, *The Covenanters*, 54, speaks of the Confession becoming a "dead letter" to the English Parliament from this point on. The Parliament's earlier conception of the needed reform of the church no longer corresponded to popular aspirations. See John Coffey, "Church and State 1550–1750: The Emergence of Dissent," in *T&T Clark Companion to Nonconformity*, ed. Robert Pope (London: Bloomsbury T&T Clark, 2013), 58.

Fissure Opens between Scotland and England

With the English House of Commons hindered in enacting into law the documents produced by the Westminster Assembly, the question of their official future in England was beginning to become moot.[49] The opposite was true, however, north of the border, where by August of 1647 the General Assembly of the Church of Scotland had ratified the Confession and begun to employ it as the new standard of orthodox teaching.[50] This English parliamentary limbo notwithstanding, the Westminster Assembly completed the Larger and Shorter Catechisms in autumn 1647.[51] As with the Confession, ratification of the catechisms by the Scottish General Assembly followed in short order; no corresponding English implementation was forthcoming.[52] The authority of the English Long Parliament, which oversaw the Assembly, had deteriorated steadily in the aftermath of the capture of the king by elements of the New Model Army.

A Scottish Faction Makes War on England

Observing this stalemate and the prospects of the promised transnational religious uniformity ebbing away, a faction of Scottish nobles—who were subject neither to the Scottish Parliament nor to the Church of Scotland General Assembly—entered into private negotiations with the captive King Charles. Conferring at his lodgings on the Isle of Wight, these Scottish nobles, all of

---

49. This is not to say, however, that the Westminster documents found no uses in England. Their use among Puritan clergy is testified to by the production of popular commentaries on the Shorter Catechism, such as those by Thomas Vincent, *An Explanation of the Assembly's Shorter Catechism* (1675; reprint, Edinburgh: Banner of Truth, 1980), and John Flavel, *An Explication of the Assembly's Shorter Catechism* (1692), reprinted in vol. 6 of *The Works of John Flavel* (London: Banner of Truth, 1968).

50. The good will with which the documents produced by the Westminster Assembly were taken up in Scotland is illustrated by the fact that David Dickson, professor of divinity first at Glasgow and then (from 1650) at Edinburgh, gave lectures on the Confession of Faith from the 1650s onward. These were published posthumously in 1684 as *Truth's Victory over Error*. The lectures are available in a modern edition of the same name produced by the Banner of Truth (Edinburgh, 2007).

51. Leith, *Assembly at Westminster*, 30.

52. The Church of Scotland General Assembly ratified the Larger Catechism on July 2 and the Shorter Catechism on July 28, 1648. *Confession of Faith and Larger and Shorter Catechisms*, 128, 286.

whom had earlier endorsed the Solemn League and Covenant, agreed—along with English royalists—to throw fresh support behind King Charles. This support would enable the king to resist concessions demanded by the Parliament and hold out the hope of reversing his earlier military defeat. The support was offered on the basis of conditions (all of which Charles pledged to fulfill). Among these were the following:

- The Solemn League and Covenant would remain in force, though neither the king nor his closest supporters would be obliged to sign it.
- The Presbyterian form of government would continue uninterrupted in Scotland and would commence a three-year trial in England, after which its utility could be evaluated. Congregational Independency would be opposed.
- The king would nominate twenty representatives of his own preference to confer with the Westminster Assembly of Divines.[53]

But these undertakings, though ostensibly intended to advance the cause of religious uniformity between the kingdoms, splintered Scottish opinion. The Scottish faction supporting these policies (which came to be known as the "Engagers") was opposed by a faction that objected to the king not being required to support the Covenant.[54] Shortly, the faction promoting this "Engagement" led troops into England in an attempt to liberate King Charles and restore him to the throne. Not only were these Scottish forces defeated by English troops led by Oliver Cromwell, but the king came to be recognized as dangerous, even when held captive. By his collusion, Charles had strengthened the case for his own end and also an end to the Stuart monarchy.[55] His supporters, needing yet again to be put down by the army, strengthened the latter's hold on national life at the expense of Parliament. Cromwell, returning to London, expelled from Parliament elected members (many of them Presbyterian sympathizers) who were understood to have favored the restoration of the king through negotiation; he left in Parliament only those sympathetic to

---

53. Gardiner, *Constitutional Documents of the Puritan Revolution*, 347–48.

54. The negotiations involving Charles and royalist supporters drawn from Ireland, England, and Scotland are helpfully explained in Furgol, "The Civil Wars in Scotland," 63.

55. Charles would now be tried for treason, found guilty, and executed on January 30, 1649. Gentles, "The Civil Wars in England," 152, notes that from this "Second Civil War" onward, King Charles is often referred to as a "man of blood" in that he actively collaborated in a resumption of a civil war that had been considered closed.

army concerns.[56] Thus ended the "Second Civil War."[57] Charles I was shortly tried and executed for treason.

CHARLES II PROCLAIMED KING: CONSEQUENCES

While Scots had disagreed strongly among themselves about the rightness of supporting military efforts to restore King Charles to his throne, they remained strongly attached to the Stuart monarchy; they recalled that this same dynasty had ruled Scotland before being transplanted to the southern kingdom. They also believed the Stuart monarchy could still prove viable if it supported their preferred principles regarding the government and worship of the church.[58] Consistent with these commitments, the Scottish Parliament proclaimed the surviving son of their late monarch as king.[59] At the time of this proclamation at Edinburgh in February 1649, the new king's father had only been dead a week. The Scottish Parliament made clear, however, that Charles II could be crowned only if and when he pledged to uphold the Solemn League and Covenant.[60] There followed extensive negotiations with Charles II, who was then residing at Breda, the Netherlands, with his mother and siblings. In May 1650, Charles II gave the assurances required by the Scots. In the Treaty of Breda, signed at his landing in Scotland the next month, he pledged allegiance to the Solemn League and Covenant. Yet, his being officially crowned at Scone in January 1651 ensured that there would be military conflict with England; Scotland's action had, in effect, countered the English abolition of monarchy achieved by the execution of the new king's father. His being crowned in Scotland was, in effect, a reassertion of his claim to be monarch over three kingdoms.

56. The portion of Parliament remaining in session came to be known as the "Rump" Parliament. The expulsion of parliamentarians who favored further negotiations with the king has come to be called "Pride's Purge."

57. Mitchison, *Lordship to Patronage*, 59, 60. Bolam, *The English Presbyterians*, 45, indicates that 140 members of Parliament characterized by Presbyterian and royalist sympathies were expelled at this time.

58. It was, after all, these dual concerns that had moved the Scots to military resistance to Charles I in the two "Bishops Wars" that preceded the Civil War itself.

59. Stevenson, *The Covenanters*, 57.

60. Mitchison, *Lordship to Patronage*, 60. The proclamation of Charles II as king followed one month later in Ulster. In the same month (March 1649) the Rump Parliament, meeting at London, voted to abolish the monarchy altogether. See "Act Abolishing the Office of the King," in Gardiner, *Constitutional Documents of the Puritan Revolution*, 384–87.

CROMWELL INVADES SCOTLAND

A military debacle now followed. Oliver Cromwell, the leader of the parliamentary army of England, moved north and, after skirmishes in the north of England (into which Scottish forces loyal to Charles had penetrated), entered Scotland to quell this reassertion of Stuart right to reign. Young Charles II conveniently slipped out of Scotland and made his way to France. But Cromwell and his armies, having entered Scotland, declined to leave; they remained as an occupying army under the command of Cromwell's associate, George Monck. Scotland, having pledged fresh allegiance to the Stuart monarchy, and having been prepared to invade England in support of Charles II, was now reckoned a threat to English security.[61] There followed a temporary political union of Scotland with England; henceforth Scottish representatives would sit in England's Parliament. This English military occupation of Scotland continued until the death of Cromwell in September 1658.[62]

PROSPECT OF RELIGIOUS UNIFORMITY GIVES WAY
TO PLURIFORMITY

Looking back on the two preceding decades from the vantage point of 1658 (when the English military occupation of Scotland ended), we clearly see that neither Scotland nor England had obtained quite what they had aimed at fifteen years earlier. Each nation had chafed under the autocratic excesses of Charles I; he had driven a large proportion of his subjects in each nation to distraction with his style of autocratic rule. Both nations had come to resent and suspect his direction of their respective national churches in liturgical forms and hierarchical structure. The parliaments of each country had been willing to believe that, after military defeat, he might be brought to concede the sought-after changes. But in the event, not only did Charles not concede (forfeiting his life for his relentless determination to restore his autocratic rule by renewed conflict), but the two nations subsequently lost any prospect of Protestant religious uniformity. The Cromwell era, both in England and in Scotland, came to be characterized by the official toleration of a variety of forms of Protestantism never earlier sanctioned.

In England, one could now find congregations worshiping in the conventional Anglican style, as well as self-consciously Presbyterian congregations.

61. Mitchison, *Lordship to Patronage*, 63.
62. Mitchison, *Lordship to Patronage*, 68.

The latter utilized the literary productions of the Westminster Assembly.[63] Meanwhile, Baptist, Quaker, and Congregational Independent congregations came out into the open and flourished.[64] North of the border, the preexisting Church of Scotland lost its earlier monopoly on Protestant worship; it shortly had to contend with the same forms of alternative Protestantism now visible in the south. Cromwell's toleration policies under the political union decreed the same religious liberty in the north as in the south.[65]

The Church of Scotland, represented by delegates to the Westminster Assembly, had been ready enough to adopt the confession of faith and the catechisms, the Directory for Public Worship, and the Form of Presbyterial Church Government if offered a reciprocal gesture by the English church. This Scottish readiness for ecclesiastical collaboration had coaxed them beyond reliance on their earlier doctrinal confession (of 1560) and service book (of 1564), when no domestic fault had been found with either.[66] In retrospect, the Solemn League and Covenant had produced nothing but frustration.

63. Particular regions of England, notably Greater London, Lancashire, and Cheshire, saw serious attempts to implement Presbyterian discipline by elders (joined with a minister) not only in the local congregation but also in widespread associations linking congregations together. See Elliot Vernon, "A Ministry of the Gospel: The Presbyterians during the English Revolution," in *Religion in Revolutionary England*, ed. Christopher Durston and Judith Maltby (Manchester: Manchester University Press, 2006), 118–19. On the other hand, furtive Anglican prayer book services continued to be held; see Bolam, *The English Presbyterians*, 45.

64. John Coffey, "The Toleration Controversy," in Durston and Maltby, *Religion in Revolutionary England*, chap. 2.

65. R. Scott Spurlock, *Cromwell and Scotland* (Edinburgh: John Donald, 2007), chap. 5.

66. Gordon Donaldson, "Covenant to Revolution," in *Studies in the History of Worship in Scotland*, ed. Duncan Forrester and Douglas Murray (Edinburgh: T&T Clark, 1984), chap. 4.

CHAPTER 4

What Restored Monarchy Meant
for England and Scotland

The English Civil Wars had thrown Scotland and England into a state of uncertainty, both political and religious. Change was coming, and this change, in retrospect, seemed inevitable.

In England, the death of Lord Protector Oliver Cromwell in the opening days of September 1658, by malarial fever and septicemia, came almost without warning. As he had only reached his fifty-ninth year, the death caught the country unprepared.[1] There followed a hasty transition under which his son, Richard—the designated successor—was elevated to his position.[2] The changeover piled uncertainty upon uncertainty. Unlike his father, Richard had not been a military man; he thus had no particular influence with the army. He had only briefly been a member of Parliament during the 1650s, and so had no great influence there. On account of the government's crisis of finance, Richard Cromwell (1626–1712) acted on advice and recalled the Rump Parliament.[3]

The recalling of this Parliament, which represented a mind-set reflecting values that prevailed in the early 1650s, provoked radical elements in the army to offer resistance. Having more recently relied on a still smaller and more pliable "Protectorate Parliament" to support them, the army was justifiably concerned that the recent parliamentary deference paid to their views would

1. H. F. McMains, *The Death of Oliver Cromwell* (Lexington: University Press of Kentucky, 2015), 75.

2. Evidently, no written indication of the senior Cromwell's plan of succession could be located at the time of his death; this, in spite of his government's urging that forethought be given to the issue. Richard Cromwell was named lord protector after his dying father issued oral instructions to that effect. See Peter Gaunt, "Richard Cromwell," in *The Oxford Dictionary of National Biography* (Oxford: Oxford University Press, 2004), 14:359, 360.

3. The "rump" was the portion of the Parliament left in place after the purge of Presbyterian and royalist MPs by members of the army in late 1648.

now end; elements in the army now demanded that the younger Cromwell dissolve this Parliament. In time, he complied; his resignation as lord protector followed in short order.[4]

There now emerged the alarming prospect that—without a head of state to lead the nation—unbridled military rule would follow. Yet, this growing prospect was countered by the southward march of a second English army, which had been occupying Scotland since 1653. George Monck, who had served the late king and then served as Cromwell's governor in Scotland, led this army. At his initiative, the Long Parliament was recalled. It contained many members of Presbyterian and promonarchy sympathies; these now agreed to negotiations for the possible return of the Stuart monarchy. This recalled assembly was, in effect, the last parliamentary opportunity for those of Presbyterian sympathies to influence the future conditions under which they would live and worship.

Monck played a prominent role in the negotiations with Charles II. Initial indications of the terms put forward by Charles II were highly encouraging; toleration, forbearance, and peace were subjects much discussed.[5] No one could know in detail what the proposed restoration of monarchy would bring, inasmuch as not Charles II but a soon-to-be-elected new Parliament would determine the details. Even so, English supporters of the Presbyterian way remained hopeful.[6] At the king's arrival in England, several Presbyterian sympathizers (one being Richard Baxter [1615–1691]) were named honorary chaplains to the king.[7] A series of conferences followed in which such Presbyterian representatives (the term now referred to those who would have been prepared for an incorporation of Presbyterian features within a restored episcopal government) laid out the concerns of their constituency. In this period, Baxter was invited to preach before the House of Commons. Initially, there

4. Gaunt, "Richard Cromwell," 363.

5. In the Declaration of Breda of April 1660, Charles II had assured his subjects that in matters of religion he sought "a liberty to tender consciences and that no man shall be disquieted or called in question for differences of opinion in the matter of religion." S. R. Gardiner, ed., *Constitutional Documents of the Puritan Revolution: 1625–1660* (Oxford: Oxford University Press, 1951), 466.

6. John Coffey, "Church and State 1550–1750: The Emergence of Dissent," in *T&T Clark Companion to Nonconformity*, ed. Robert Pope (London: Bloomsbury T&T Clark, 2013), 60, writes, "Presbyterians hoped to continue where they belonged within the parishes of the national church. In their own eyes they were establishment men utterly distinct from the wild sectaries who had supported the regicide and disrupted the unity of the parish."

7. C. G. Bolam et al., *The English Presbyterians from Elizabethan Puritanism to Modern Unitarianism* (London: Allen & Unwin, 1968), 74, mentions Edmund Calamy, Richard Baxter, and Edward Reynolds.

was reason for quiet hopefulness; Presbyterians demonstrated this hope by presenting the king, newly arrived in London, with a gold-clasped Bible.[8]

Surely the incoming king was aware that English Presbyterian sympathizers clearly favored the continuation of monarchy at the end of the Civil War when Cromwell and the New Model Army had pushed in the opposite direction. Surely it was common knowledge that they had been expelled from Parliament on account of their opposition to the trial and execution of the late king; that sixty English Presbyterian ministers had petitioned Cromwell to save the life of captive King Charles;[9] and that a prominent London Presbyterian minister, Christopher Love, had been executed for treason for passing communications to and from the late king on behalf of his English parliamentary sympathizers.[10] But now, in 1660, new parliamentary elections were called for and the political landscape was about to be altered. In the event, the newly elected house was markedly less sympathetic to those who had been seeking substantive changes within the national church.

If the situation in London lacked clarity, the state of things in Scotland was even less transparent. With no Scottish representation in the negotiations with Charles carried on by the English Parliament, no one in Scotland knew what to expect. Scots who had supported the 1649 invasion of England in support of the king's late father, the imprisoned King Charles I (known as the Engagers), wanted to believe that this costly Scottish gesture had not been forgotten.[11] Also, in accepting their crown in 1651, this same Charles II had assured the Scots that he would support the Presbyterian government of the Kirk (as re-

---

8. Representatives of the Presbyterians met with English bishops at Worcester House in October 1660 and subsequently in the Savoy Conference in April 1661. The first conference focused upon questions of church order, the second upon the questions of modification to the prayer book. Bolam, *The English Presbyerians*, 70, 72, 77–78. David J. Appleby, "From Ejectment to Toleration in England," in *The Great Ejectment of 1662*, ed. Alan F. Sell (Eugene, OR: Wipf & Stock, 2012), 70, 71, stresses how intimately acquainted with the Presbyterians was Charles's chief advisor, Edward Hyde (Lord Clarendon). "He and the King recognized that the overwhelming majority of Presbyterians were respectable, socially conservative members of society who believed implicitly in the institution of monarchy."

9. William Barker, "Thomas Watson's 'A Body of Divinity,'" in *The Devoted Life: An Invitation to the Puritan Classics*, ed. Kelly Kapic and Randall Gleason (Downers Grove, IL: InterVarsity Press, 2004), 201.

10. E. C. Vernon, "Christopher Love," in *Oxford Dictionary of National Biography* (Oxford: Oxford University Press, 2004), 34:493–96; William Ferguson, *Scotland's Relations with England: A Survey to 1707* (Edinburgh: Saltire Society, 1977), 144: "none knew better than Charles himself that it was the Presbyterians, English as well as Scottish, who had made the Restoration possible."

11. We have noted (see pp. 46–47 above) that this Scottish military action on behalf of the late king was predicated on religious guarantees granted to the Scots.

stored in 1638) and uphold the Solemn League and Covenant of 1643. In 1660, the Scots wanted to believe that those assurances of 1651 still stood. But, ominously for the Scots, in 1660, *all* negotiations were in the hands of English emissaries.[12] The newly elected English Parliament would have the most to say.

RECKONING WITH THE LEGACY OF THE INTERREGNUM

The interregnum period had obliged Presbyterian sympathizers in both nations to accept religious pluralism as part of the stalemate that had followed the era of civil wars. Yet England and Scotland found themselves in this limbo for quite different reasons.

Scotland

Cromwell's policy for England as well as Scotland was to oppose religious monopolies and, with that, religious uniformity (the express intention of the Solemn League and Covenant of 1643). As we have noted above,[13] Cromwell had purposed to end the dominant position of the Church of Scotland and its vocal General Assembly. That church was already polarized at the time of Cromwell's 1651 military invasion. One faction, the Engagers (or "Resolutioners"),[14] was led by nobles and members of Parliament who had entered into the military engagement meant to secure the liberty and restoration of the late King Charles I. The other, variously known as the "Protesters" or "Kirk party," was led by church leaders who had both opposed that ill-conceived military invasion of England and adopted a healthy wariness about the Stuart dynasty's actual intentions regarding the church. The two factions, both Presbyterian, and both supportive of the National Covenant of 1638 and the Solemn League of 1643, were now totally estranged.

While Cromwell's 1651 invasion came in response to the military activity of the first group, once in control, the Protector pursued policies that prevented either party from gaining a clear ascendancy. He forbade the annual General

12. On this point, see Ferguson, *Scotland's Relations with England*, 142. Rosalind Mitchison puts it pithily: "The central fact of this period is that both restoration and revolution were made in England." See her "Restoration and Revolution," in *The Scottish Nation*, ed. Gordon Menzies (London: BBC, 1972), 133.

13. See p. 48 above.

14. Those known as "Resolutioners" in 1660 had earlier been known as "Engagers." See "Resolutioner," in *Dictionaries of the Scots Language*, accessed March 15, 2021, https://www.dsl.ac.uk/entry/snd/resolutioner.

Assembly to meet, since the two rival groups were proposing to meet separately. This prohibition denied each party the opportunity to debate openly its stance relative to changed circumstances. Because the Scottish Parliament was dominated by Resolutioners, he forbade that body to meet; instead, he governed Scotland by a council (chiefly comprised of non-Scots) appointed by himself. To exacerbate matters further, occupying English soldiers serving in Scotland brought with them their strong religious preferences from the south, so that Scotland now witnessed layman-advocates representing Baptist, Quaker, and Congregationalist viewpoints.[15] This latter viewpoint was further agitated in Scotland by Cromwell's own military chaplains, including the renowned John Owen (1616–1683). These openly urged the advantages of Congregational Independency.[16] The late monarch had pressured the Scots to make peace with episcopal oversight and to embrace liturgical uniformity with England; now, under Cromwell, this had been replaced by pressure of a completely different tendency.

England

In the 1650s, Presbyterianism established itself (as provided for in the earlier legislation of the House of Commons) only in certain regions of England. Greater London, Cheshire, and Lancaster parishes were notable in embracing not only the governance of congregations by a minister and elders but also a style of worship in accord with the Directory for Worship, the product of the recent Assembly of Divines.[17] In such locales regional presbyteries or classes functioned and candidates for the ministry were examined and ordained. But elsewhere in England, many supporters of the prewar Church of England worshiped with the now-forbidden Book of Common Prayer. In addition, there were gathered congregations of Baptists, Independents, and Quakers meeting without hindrance under the same tolerationist principles. Only Roman Catholic and anti-Trinitarian assemblies were banned. Supporters of the Pres-

15. See Ivan Hoy, "The Entry of Sects into Scotland," in *Reformation and Revolution: Essays Presented to Hugh Watt*, ed. Duncan Shaw (Edinburgh: St. Andrew Press, 1967), 178–211.

16. D. W. Bebbington, *The Baptists in Scotland* (Glasgow: Baptist Union of Scotland, 1988), 10, 11; Harry Escott, *A History of Scottish Congregationalism* (Glasgow: Congregational Union of Scotland, 1960), 9, 10; R. Scott Spurlock, *Cromwell and Scotland* (Edinburgh: John Donald, 2007), 45.

17. Elliot Vernon, "A Ministry of the Gospel: English Presbyterians during the Interregnum," in *Religion in Revolutionary England*, ed. Christopher Durston and Judith Maltby (Manchester: Manchester University Press, 2006), 118; Charles Augustus Briggs, "The Provincial Assembly of London: 1647–1660," *Presbyterian Review* 2, no. 1 (1881): 54–78.

byterian way in England found themselves in a conflicted position they had never anticipated: as supporters of the national church ideal, they *opposed* the toleration of competing forms of Christianity, which tended to skim earnest believers out of parish churches into gathered congregations.[18] But at the same time, by their inability to pervade the whole of the Church of England with their Presbyterian polity, they were gradually consenting to function in a way very like that of the Baptists, Independents, and Quakers.

Reconnoitering with Royalty

In the wake of the English Civil War, religious controversy in both England and Scotland was settled in the same general way: religion in both nations was restored to its prewar state. We take up the events in the southern kingdom first.

England

English Presbyterians had been represented in the parliamentary negotiations with Charles II, both before and after he took the throne.[19] Yet these latter negotiations during 1660–1661 were undermined because the newly elected parliamentary body was overwhelmingly made up of "cavaliers," that is, royalists deeply opposed to the Parliament's earlier military action leading to the defeat and ultimate execution of King Charles I.

The election of this cavalier parliament accelerated a period of reaction, already under way prior to the passing of the major legislation, that would give the reaction a permanent form. Some examples will help to elucidate this. The possibility that the former episcopal government might yet be modified in the direction many Presbyterians had urged was precluded when vacant bishoprics began to be filled with persons loyal to the pre–Civil War (and Laudian) state of the church.[20] A number of Presbyterians were offered such episcopal appointments, and some accepted.[21] Already, the restored bishops were threat-

18. The ally of Richard Baxter, Adam Martindale of Lancashire opined that Congregational Independents would "spoil many (parish) churches for the new making of one." *Life of Adam Martindale* (Chetham Society, 1845), 66, as quoted in Bolam, *The English Presbyterians*, 55.

19. Bolam, *The English Presbyterians*, 73.

20. Anne Whiteman, "The Church of England Restored," in *From Uniformity to Unity, 1662–1962*, ed. Geoffrey Nuttall and Owen Chadwick (London: SPCK, 1962), 63.

21. Bolam, *The English Presbyterians*, 76. "Richard Baxter was offered the see of Hereford,

ening ministers who neglected to use the Book of Common Prayer. Already, the Church of England ministers found guilty by parliamentary "triers" (examiners) and removed from their pastoral charges were insisting on returning to their former posts (to the great disadvantage of those appointed to replace them).[22] The English church was beginning to change in ways that portended trouble when the cavalier-dominated Parliament actually began to legislate.

When new legislation was first tabled beginning in November 1661, not only Presbyterians (who had persisted in wishing to find a way to conscientiously align themselves with the national church) but also Congregational Independents and Baptists (who wanted the legal right to exist outside any restored national church) found themselves in the crosshairs. The new Parliament was determined to "put the clock back to 1642."[23] Hard-hitting parliamentary action came in short order. It began with the public burning of the Solemn League and Covenant, which all parliamentarians and ministers had been obliged to sign in the summer of 1643. Members of Parliament were required to partake in Holy Communion, administered according to the Book of Common Prayer.[24] Soon, the same expectation was laid on civic leaders (mayors and aldermen). Attempts were made to officially reinstate the version of that book current in 1604 (the first year of the English reign of the Stuarts).[25]

Yet these items, which irritated those who had been free from such regulations for a decade, paled in comparison with the legislation that followed. An Act of Uniformity, advocated from November 1661 onward, was passed into law in May 1662. It stipulated suspension from parish ministry effective August 24 for those who:

1. lacked ordination from a Church of England bishop (or would not submit to reordination by such an official),
2. would not "assent and consent" to everything in the prayer book, and
3. would not renounce the Solemn League and Covenant of 1643.[26]

Edmund Calamy that of Lichfield and Coventry, and Edward Reynolds that of Norwich, while (Thomas) Manton and (William) Bates were offered deaneries. All except Reynolds declined." Whiteman, "The Church of England Restored," 66.

22. Bolam, *The English Presbyterians*, 74.

23. The apt phrase is that of Bolam, *The English Presbyterians*, 79.

24. George R. Abernathy, *The English Presbyterians and the Stuart Restoration: 1648–1663* (Philadelphia: American Philosophical Society, 1965), 81.

25. Bolam, *The English Presbyterians*, 80. G. N. Clark, *The Later Stuarts: 1660–1714* (Oxford: Oxford University Press, 1949), 20.

26. Bolam, *The English Presbyterians*, 80, 81. Abernathy, *The English Presbyterians*, 81, makes plain that with the adoption of the Act of Uniformity in May 1662, King Charles II

This legislation represented a calculated gamble that the Church of England could be forced back into its pre–Civil War shape with minimal dislocation; yet, the likelihood of total success can never have been great.[27] The king and his chief minister, Edward Hyde (Lord Clarendon), were still at work behind the scenes, attempting to mitigate the severity of this bill; they were attempting to honor assurances given to the Presbyterians involved in the original negotiations leading to the king's return from the Netherlands. Yet they failed in these attempts.[28]

With the prospect of mitigation having evaporated, the act was set to take effect in August. Richard Baxter and others resigned their pastorates on the spot once the legislation was passed in May. They perceived that the purpose of the time lapse between the bill's passage and its enforcement was to erode the readiness of ministers to resist; the lapse played on the fear of the loss of their livelihoods. By their prompt resignations, individuals like Baxter were determined to both forewarn the Parliament of the dire consequence of the new policy and to steel the resolve of other ministers now in jeopardy.[29]

When August 24 came, the readiness of ministers to surrender their pulpits, on principle, over these oppressive requirements, surpassed all expectation. That the wave of resignations was so sizable was also an ominous development. There is good reason to believe that very many who waited until August had been just as deliberate in preparing for the day as Baxter had been in his drastic resignation months before. In England and Wales, approximately two thousand ministers resigned their positions, salaries, and housing.[30] Ordained ministers holding posts within the two universities faced the same stark choices; many of these also resigned. Soon there appeared in print individual "farewell sermons," and

---

had in effect been thwarted in his genuine attempts to provide an accommodation for ministers uneasy with the return to pre–Civil War policies of the Church of England.

27. Clark, *The Later Stuarts*, 17.

28. Abernathy, *The English Presbyterians*, 83. Gardiner, *Constitutional Documents of the Puritan Revolution*, 465.

29. Bolam, *The English Presbyterians*, 80. Geoffrey Nuttal, "The First Nonconformists," in Nuttal and Chadwick, *From Uniformity to Unity, 1662–1962*, 182.

30. Bolam, *The English Presbyterians*, 83, 84, speaks of a total for England and Wales of 2,000, which constituted one-fifth of all clergy in the national church of the Restoration era. This figure of one-fifth has more recently been endorsed by John Coffey, in his 2013 essay, "Church and State 1550–1750," 69. John Gwynfor Jones, "The Growth of Puritanism, c. 1559–1662," in Sell, *The Great Ejectment of 1662*, 61, gives the figure of 1,909 ministers for England and 139 for Wales. Notable examples of those ejected from their ministries would include Philip Henry (1631–1696) (father to the commentator Matthew), John Owen, and Edmund Calamy. Bolam (85) notes that Devonshire was the county with the highest number of ejected ministers.

soon after that, compendiums of such sermons; all were printed illegally, as the government had no intention of licensing the circulation of this kind of printed resistance.[31] Such publishing efforts suggest a coordinated strategy of protest. In due course, a late Puritan chronicler, Edmund Calamy the younger, composed a four-volume work memorializing many who had been ejected in 1662.[32]

The two thousand who vacated their positions, however, did *not* represent the totality of English Christian leaders of Puritan sympathy. Many of this conviction remained at their posts in the restored Church of England. One of the better known was the Puritan William Gurnall, minister of Lavenham, Suffolk.[33] Edward Reynolds,[34] who accepted the bishopric of Norfolk, was not the only person of Presbyterian sympathies to come to terms with the Uniformity Act and find advancement; John Tillotson eventually served as dean and then archbishop of Canterbury (1691–1694). Tillotson would use his influence to seek ways of softening the harsh treatment meted out to Nonconformists.[35]

Yet such cases were the exception, not the norm. Because the government quickly concluded that this level of noncompliance by ministers presaged large-scale resistance by churchgoers, further pieces of legislation were introduced to quell potential grassroots resistance. By the Five Mile Act of 1665, ejected ministers were obliged to separate themselves by at least five miles from their former congregations. By the Conventicle Act of 1670, nonconforming preaching services—whether out of doors or in private dwellings—were strictly forbidden; fines and prison awaited those who transgressed.[36] And yet, so sizable was the constituency represented by the approximately two thousand ejected ministers,

31. Collections of these sermons are still available to us today. See, for instance, *Sermons of the Great Ejection* (Edinburgh: Banner of Truth, 1962). Historian David Appleby found that by late 1663 there had been ten or twelve printings of three large collections of these farewell sermons, totaling approximately thirty thousand copies. "From Ejection to Toleration in England," in Sell, *The Great Ejectment of 1662*, 88.

32. Calamy's work, originally entitled *Account of the Ministers and Others Ejected and Silenced, 1660–2*, is available to modern readers in a revised edition, that is, A. G. Matthews, ed., *Calamy Revised* (Oxford: Clarendon, 1934).

33. Gurnall has caught the attention of readers in the last half century through the republication of his treatise on Ephesians 6:11ff., *The Christian in Complete Armour* (1662; reprint, London: Banner of Truth, 1964).

34. See the reference in n. 7 above.

35. "Tillotson, John" in *New International Dictionary of the Christian Church*, ed. J. D. Douglas (Grand Rapids: Zondervan, 1974), 975.

36. The Baptist preacher John Bunyan was imprisoned on and off between 1660 and 1672 for such offenses. See "John Bunyan," in Douglas, *New International Dictionary of the Christian Church*, 166. Appleby, "From Ejectment to Toleration in England," 88, speaks of "thousands imprisoned." Philip Henry noted in his diary on August 24, 1663 (his birthday), "This year thirty two years ago, I was born; this day twelve-month I died." J. B. Williams, *Lives of Philip and Matthew Henry* (1828; reprint, London: Banner of Truth, 1984), 1:103.

that this community (now collectively termed "Nonconformist" because they declined to endorse the 1662 Act of Uniformity) showed surprising resilience. At the expiration of an Act of Indulgence (1672) in 1675, 1,339 Nonconformist ministers had been granted licenses to preach. Of these, 923 were Presbyterians.[37]

These draconian measures sometimes brought militant responses from harassed Nonconformists. By October 1663, there were armed uprisings in Yorkshire, Westmoreland, and County Durham; while bad weather did much to frustrate them, these were at least potentially "large-scale insurrections."[38] Twenty-six men were condemned to death for their roles in these rebellions. It is safe to say that such disorders only served to confirm the Cavalier Parliament in the opinion that Nonconformity represented a danger to society.

King James II (reigned 1685–1688) attempted to extend relief to Nonconformist Protestants (Presbyterians among them). But as the king's proposed Declarations of Indulgence (1687 and 1688) were motivated as much by his desire to enlarge the liberties of his fellow Roman Catholics as they were to enlarge those of Nonconforming Protestants, English Presbyterians were cool toward them and did not (unlike Congregational Independents, Baptists, and Quakers) take advantage of their provisions, lest they ally themselves with the advance of Roman Catholicism.[39]

It was not until the passage of the Toleration Act (1689) under the subsequent monarch, William III (reigned 1689–1702), that English Presbyterians— along with Congregational Independents, Baptists, and Quakers—secured the right to open their own places of worship and to employ their own settled ministers. These ministers, while freed from the obligation to use only the Book of Common Prayer and to be ordained by a bishop of the national church (the terms set out in 1662), were still required to give assent to the greater part of the Church of England's Thirty-Nine Articles of Religion.[40] Under King William, English and Welsh Nonconformists together built 1,000 places of worship. In the reign of George I (1715 onward), the number of existing Nonconformist places of worship in England and Wales rose to 1,150.[41]

---

37. Bolam, *The English Presbyterians*, 90. Regions most prominently represented in the granting of these licenses were Devonshire and London.

38. These "Northern Rebellions" were partly driven by antimonarchical sentiment and partly by religious anxiety that the policies being pursued by Charles II were tending to open the way for a Roman Catholic resurgence. See Appleby, "From Ejectment to Toleration in England," 87.

39. "Declarations of Indulgence," in Douglas, *New International Dictionary of the Christian Church*, 274–75.

40. "Toleration Act," in Douglas, *New International Dictionary of the Christian Church*, 978–79.

41. Clark, *The Later Stuarts*, 26. Coffey, "Church and State 1550–1750," 65, indicates that in 1715, the number of Nonconformists in England and Wales was at least four hundred

In retrospect, it seems evident that the likelihood of a form of Presbyterianism ever displacing the episcopal order of the Church of England was never higher than in late 1648, when the deliberative work of the Westminster Assembly was complete. To that point, the House of Commons had been commending the use of the Directory of Worship and the Presbyterian Form of Government (both products of the Assembly) across England and Wales. But the intervention of Oliver Cromwell and the New Model Army in December 1648, both to halt further parliamentary negotiations with King Charles I and to banish from Parliament the sizable Presbyterian representation that favored the salvaging of Charles's kingship, meant that the moment of opportunity had passed.[42] The actions of the Scottish Engagers, who, by secret negotiations with King Charles I in December 1647, agreed to invade England on his behalf in 1648, can only have discredited the Presbyterian cause; now the threat to England's stability came from *Presbyterian* Scotland. Thereafter, Presbyterian efforts would survive only in select regions of England. The general tendency of the interregnum period, both through Cromwell and the diminished Parliament, was to advance the interests of Congregational Independency.

It is important to note that the Great Ejection of 1662 and its uprooting of Puritan ministers and university staff from their posts did not mean any immediate utter uprooting of Reformed theology from the Church of England and its two universities. The failure of the Westminster Assembly to establish itself nationally could be attributed, in considerable part, to the fact that its aspiration that the Church of England stand in greater conformity with other Reformed churches in western Europe was not widely enough held. But this did not mean that all who sought that conformity necessarily departed in 1662. Modern research has shown the stubborn persistence of Reformed theology within the Church of England and its universities into the reign of George I (commenced 1715). And yet, to affirm this is only to acknowledge that Reformed theology continued in the Church of England as but one voice among others that were actually in the ascendant.[43] Within Nonconformity, the affinity with Reformed theology was deliberately preserved.

---

thousand, representing 7 percent of the population. The collective experience of the range of Nonconformity, under the disabilities imposed from 1662 onward, is well described in Raymond Brown, *Spirituality in Adversity: English Nonconformity in a Period of Repression* (Milton Keynes, UK: Paternoster, 2012).

42. Abernathy, *The English Presbyterians*, 91.

43. See Dewey D. Wallace, *Shapers of English Calvinism: 1660–1714* (New York: Oxford University Press, 2011). Wallace's seventh chapter, on John Edwards (1637–1716), a Cambridge fellow and prolific author, demonstrates the virility of Anglican Reformed theology half a century after the Ejection. Stephen Hampton, *Anti-Arminians: The Anglican Reformed*

Scotland

We have acknowledged that there was no Scottish negotiation with Charles II preliminary to his return to Britain in 1660.[44] In general terms, the settlement of religious affairs in the northern kingdom followed the same broad contours we have observed in England: religion was restored to its prewar state. Yet as applied to Scotland, such a policy did not entirely overthrow the maintenance of a Presbyterian form of church government (restored by General Assembly action in 1638); neither did it reimpose the discredited prayer book of 1637. As in the southern kingdom, Charles pursued religious policies that met with the approval of the landed classes (the Resolutioners/Engagers), who had belatedly come to his late father's aid in 1647–1648 with their invasion of England.[45] This party had, after all, signed the National Covenant.

Charles's way forward represented a reversal of the policy and priority of the protectorate under Cromwell. As we have seen, Cromwell's government had preferred to work with the "Protester" or "Kirk" party in the northern kingdom; the Engagers/Resolutioners had been his enemy. At his accession to the throne, Charles—working with a council drawn from this latter party—determined that all religious legislation since 1633 would be overturned by an Act Rescissory (1661).[46] This legislation was intended to dissolve obligations undertaken in 1638 to abolish the Scottish episcopate, to call into question the Solemn League and Covenant of 1643, and to undermine the legitimacy of the calling of the Westminster Assembly and any subsequent parliamentary ratifications of the documents produced there. There followed a parliamentary Act concerning the League and Covenant, which declared that the Solemn League document was no longer applicable and ought not to be agitated for.[47]

Bishops (outlawed since 1638) were restored to their offices; they were now described as exercising "presidencies" and as holding the powers of ordination and

---

Tradition from Charles II through George I (Oxford: Oxford University Press, 2008), while acknowledging the importance of Edwards, also points out the role played by the Oxford Lady Margaret Professor of Divinity William Delaune (1659–1728).

44. See p. 48 above.

45. Rosalind Mitchison, *Lordship to Patronage: Scotland, 1603–1745* (Edinburgh: Edinburgh University Press, 1983), 68–69, makes plain that at Charles II's arrival in England, Scottish nobles converged there for the purpose of securing advantageous terms. They obtained for their troubles "an aristocratic re-establishment."

46. The text is printed in Gordon Donaldson, ed., *Scottish Historical Documents* (Glasgow: Scottish Academic Press, 1974), 225–26.

47. See the description of the act in J. D. Douglas, *Light in the North: The Story of the Scottish Covenanters* (Grand Rapids: Eerdmans, 1964), 92.

discipline.[48] The existence and operation of presbyteries and kirk sessions were not directly threatened by this enactment, but their powers were reduced. What would prove most explosive, however, was a fourth piece of legislation, the Act concerning Benefices and Stipends.[49] This restored to local lords (or "heritors") the privilege, shorn in 1649, of holding the power to nominate parish clergy. The new act insisted that those who had entered their current pastoral posts apart from this protocol (the local lord nominating an individual to the local bishop, who, in turn, would make the appointment, if the candidate was deemed satisfactory) now needed to retroactively seek ratification by observing the protocol. This change directly threatened every minister who had taken up a post since 1649 because it pitted persons of rival allegiances against one another; it required ministers (who were more often aligned with the Protester faction) to seek the approbation of local lords (more likely of Engager/Resolutioner loyalties).

The results of this legislation were direct and dramatic: the rapid resignation of some 262 ministers concentrated chiefly (though not exclusively) in the southwest of Scotland.[50] They withdrew, not because of a refusal to abide by a liturgical standard or submit to a hierarchical polity (as in the southern kingdom), but because they would not acknowledge that they held their ministerial posts as the gift of a landed aristocrat. This resistance soon mushroomed to include both former Resolutioners and Protesters.

What followed was almost predictable. With so many preachers out of their pulpits, it was natural that they would preach and hold services outside the system whose jurisdiction they had found oppressive. In some cases, whole congregations followed their ministers away from the parish church. And so there followed more legislation: the Act against Covenants and Conventicles (1662), which forbade agitation against the current royal religious settlement and the holding of private religious gatherings, other than family devotional exercises.[51] But in truth, such legislation could not catch up with the recurrence of the practices it sought to prohibit. Some ministers were banished from Scotland at this time, lest they foment further resistance to the government's will. Fines were imposed for absenting oneself from the parish church.[52] But the conventicles, led by ministers who had resigned their charges, continued apace.

---

48. "Act Restoring Episcopal Government" (1662), in Donaldson, *Scottish Historical Documents*, 226–27.

49. Donaldson, *Scottish Historical Documents*, 228–29.

50. Mitchison, *Lordship to Patronage*, 73. The author points out that the 262 ministers constituted almost half the ministers in the Scottish lowlands. Douglas, *Light in the North*, 100, reports that about one-third of the entire body of 950 ministers were expelled at this time.

51. Donaldson, *Scottish Historical Documents*, 229–31.

52. Douglas, *Light in the North*, 100, 102.

In September 1663 the Scottish government sent troops to the southwest to collect fines imposed for nonattendance in parish churches, to disrupt illegal conventicles, and to intimidate the population into compliance with the law through the billeting of soldiers in community homes.[53] Such heavy-handed treatment provoked armed uprising; in November 1666, religious dissidents pushed back against military harassment and captured a commanding officer. The two thousand or so dissidents—who were by this time coming to be known as "Covenanters"[54]—began to march on Edinburgh to draw attention to their grievances. This "Pentland Rising" was intercepted south of Edinburgh, where marchers were overtaken by government troops and decimated. Prisoners were thrown into an Edinburgh dungeon, and ten of their leaders were hanged in that city, with other hangings following in the southwest.[55] Before these conflicts between covenanting Presbyterians and the government of King Charles II had run their course, eighteen thousand would perish or be banished to lands beyond Scotland. The period was justly known as "the killing times."

As this carnage unfolded, the rest of Presbyterian Scotland looked on and drew its own conclusions. The "presidential" bishops introduced at the Restoration were sometimes exemplary Christians and kind men: Robert Leighton, bishop of Dunblane and then archbishop of Glasgow, genuinely sought to be a reconciler and peacemaker. Yet such men were alternately exasperated by the tenacity of the antigovernment sentiment and scandalized by the legitimation of savage cruelty used by government forces against these dissidents. Leighton resigned his archbishopric in 1674.[56] Scotland came gradually to the conclusion that the restoration of royal supremacy in religion—something acceptable enough to the landed nobility—was contrary to the public interest and the exercise of liberty. Meanwhile, Charles II, who exercised this royal supremacy in religion, was a man notorious for his immoralities and thus peculiarly unsuited to exercise this prerogative.

In his capacity as Duke of York, James (who would succeed his brother Charles as king in 1685) had led military expeditions in Scotland against the covenanting Presbyterians in 1679. Those suspected of covenanting resistance against the government were at this time likely to be shot on sight if, when detained, they refused to renounce the Solemn League and Covenant. A steady

53. Douglas, *Light in the North*, 102.

54. Earlier, the term had applied to all who signed or were in sympathy with the Covenants of 1638 and 1643. Now, it pertained to those who maintained the perpetuity of those obligations along with an implied resistance against those who would threaten the continuation of Protestantism.

55. Douglas, *Light in the North*, 114.

56. Douglas, *Light in the North*, 134–35. Leighton contended for a modification of episcopacy very much along the lines of Irish archbishop James Ussher.

flow of citizens now chose to leave Scotland rather than remain under such intimidation and threat.[57] Once he became king in 1685, James II proposed religious toleration within Scotland (a toleration having in view primarily his fellow Roman Catholics).[58] By 1687, James II had used his royal prerogative to rescind all laws in Scotland restricting the practice of Roman Catholicism. The king wished to see the Roman Mass celebrated in a chapel within his palace of Holyrood, Edinburgh.[59] Yet, the logic of his own position forced the king to recognize that what he sought for his fellow Catholics (hitherto meeting secretly) could not be denied to the harassed covenanting Presbyterians. Thus, two Declarations of Indulgence, issued by him, ended all harassment.[60] There was plenty of relief and little regret within Scotland, as within England, when in 1688 James abdicated his throne by fleeing to France, thus opening the way for his son-in-law and daughter—William and Mary—to succeed him.

The Scottish legislative reaction to this abdication and succession came swiftly and decisively. The Scottish Parliament now ended the episcopal government of the Scottish church and reinstated the government of the church by presbyteries.[61] Such a sweeping change was, ironically, facilitated by the fact that Scotland's existing bishops would not swear that they accepted William as legitimate king.[62] Yet the carnage of the Restoration era for the Scottish church was so great that not only the covenanting Presbyterians of the southwest but also many others were unprepared to be reconciled with the national church. As in England, so in Scotland, the Stuart restoration had cemented the division of Protestant Christianity into conformist and nonconformist factions.

57. Douglas, *Light in the North*, 145.

58. Donaldson, *Scottish Historical Documents*, 248, 249.

59. Douglas, *Light in the North*, 177.

60. "Proclamations on Toleration i and ii" (February and June 1687), in Donaldson, *Scottish Historical Documents*, 251–52.

61. "Act Abolishing Prelacy" (1689) and "Act Establishing Presbyterian Government and Transferring Patronage" (1690), in Donaldson, *Scottish Historical Documents*, 258, 260. The difficulties faced in reintroducing a national Presbyterianism into Scotland from 1690 onward are described in A. Ian Dunlop, *William Carstares and the Kirk by Law Established* (Edinburgh: St. Andrew Press, 1964).

62. This same phenomenon, called "non-juring," occurred simultaneously in England; clergy believed that having earlier sworn allegiance to James II, they were bound to him as legitimate monarch so long as he lived.

CHAPTER 5

Developments in Evangelism, Mission, and Theology

In a century so dominated by conflict between the Stuart monarchs and their subjects, one might suppose that this was a period characterized by nothing but sterility in church life. With so much that now seems regrettable, what in this era could be judged memorable?

Yet, this same century displays impressive developments. In both Scotland and England, these Puritan Protestants,[1] navigating through a troubled period, exhibited many of the features associated with robust evangelical Christianity.[2] This is more significant because the idea has spread that "evangelical religion," characterized by the interplay of the four features of biblicism, conversionism, crucicentrism, and activism, only manifested itself clearly after 1730.[3]

---

1. The writer applies the term "Puritan" to Scots (as well as English) Protestants with care. "Puritan" has an obvious reference to the southern nation. David G. Mullan allowed a limited application of this term to early seventeenth-century Scots, given (1) that Scots of this outlook read English Puritan literature, in editions printed within Scotland; (2) that Scots writers of this outlook were read avidly by English Puritans in editions published in London; and (3) the theological convergence demonstrated in the Westminster Assembly, 1643–1647. See Mullan's *Scottish Puritanism: 1590–1638* (New York: Oxford University Press, 2000), 3–7. See also John Coffey, "The Problem of 'Scottish Puritanism,'" in *Enforcing Reformation in Ireland and Scotland*, ed. Elizabethanne Boran and Crawford Gribben (Farnham, UK: Ashgate, 2006), 66–90, and Margo Todd, "The Problem of Scotland's Puritanism," in *The Cambridge Companion to Puritanism*, ed. John Coffey and Paul C. H. Lim (New York: Cambridge University Press, 2008), 175–76.

2. Encouragement to think along such lines is furnished by John Coffey, "Puritanism, Evangelicalism and the Evangelical Tradition," in *The Emergence of Evangelicalism*, ed. Michael Haykin and Kenneth J. Stewart (Leicester: IVP, 2008), 252–77; Chad Van Dixhoorn, *The Westminster Assembly and the Reform of the English Pulpit: 1643–1653* (Grand Rapids: Reformed Heritage, 2018), 177; and Rick Kennedy, *Cotton Mather: America's First Evangelical* (Grand Rapids: Eerdmans, 2015), chap. 5.

3. The historian David Bebbington, in his *Evangelicalism in Modern Britain: A History*

The Early Evangelical Tradition in Operation

We here consider how clear was the commitment of pastors and people in England and Scotland to the combined emphases of biblicism, conversionism, crucicentrism, and activism in the previous century.

Biblicism as Displayed in Church and the Home

No Christians of this era were so Bible-centered as the Puritan-Nonconformist constituency of England and Scotland. It was because of a Puritan proposal made at the 1604 Hampton Court Conference[4] that the Authorized Version of the Bible was prepared and released in 1611. However, until approximately 1650, most Bible readers of Puritan sympathy continued to prefer the earlier Geneva Bible of 1560. While first released at Geneva, editions were subsequently printed in both England and Scotland. These retained their popularity because they came with explanatory marginal comments, which were lacking in other Bibles. Many Geneva Bibles also included Calvin's Geneva Catechism.[5] This version had been the work of English Protestant refugees, gathered at Geneva during the persecutions of Queen Mary Tudor (1553–1558).

The Puritan constituency went on to produce major aids to the study of the Bible; two were by notable English Presbyterians. Matthew Poole was deprived of his pulpit in the Great Ejection of 1662. Forbidden to exercise a public ministry of the Word, he devoted the balance of his life to compiling two major works that have put later generations in his debt. The first was the five-volume *Synopsis Criticorum*, a digest of the commentary of major Bible interpreters from rabbinic times forward.[6] The second, near completion at the time of his passing in 1679, was the still-in-print *Annotations upon the Holy Bible*; this work was brought into final form by friends who relied on resources available in Poole's earlier *Synopsis*.[7] Of the next generation, and still better known, is the commentator Matthew Henry (1662–1714), a Presbyterian minister first

---

from the 1730s to the 1980s (London: Unwin Hyman, 1989), chaps. 1 and 2, was the first to popularize this "quadrilateral." Bebbington allowed that several elements of the quadrilateral existed independently, prior to 1730—yet only in full combination after that time.

4. The importance of this event at the onset of James's rule has been explored in chapter 2 above.

5. Bruce Metzger, "The Geneva Bible of 1560," *Theology Today* 17, no. 3 (1960): 348, 351.

6. Completed in 1676, this multivolume work is in process of English translation.

7. Alexander Gordon, "Matthew Poole," in *Dictionary of National Biography* (London, 1885–1900), vol. 46. The contemporary edition of *Annotations* is termed *Matthew Poole's Commentary on the Bible*, 3 vols. (1685; reprint, Edinburgh: Banner of Truth, 1996).

at Chester and finally at Hackney (a London suburb). Henry's careful sermon preparation yielded addresses praised for their great clarity; behind them lay the careful research from which his commentary was eventually composed. As with Poole, Henry's *Exposition of the Old and New Testaments* was completed after his death by pastoral friends who drew on his extensive research.[8]

North of the border there labored a Scots contemporary of Poole, David Dickson; he was first a pastor and subsequently a professor in two Scottish universities (Glasgow and Edinburgh); Dickson authored biblical commentaries on the Psalms, the epistles of Paul and Peter, and the Epistle to the Hebrews.[9]

Conversionism as Displayed in Early Evangelical Awakenings

The value placed on "conversionism" (i.e., aggressive efforts at converting the unbelieving) was as much in evidence in the late Puritan era as in the era following 1730.[10] We see this in the wide circulation of evangelistic literature that urged conversion. Richard Baxter circulated such a work in 1658: his *Call to the Unconverted to Turn and Live*. Another Presbyterian, Joseph Alleine (1634–1668), like Baxter ejected in 1662, circulated *An Alarm to the Unconverted* (1672). This Puritan practiced what he preached; when he forfeited his pulpit, he became an itinerant preacher and evangelist and was subsequently imprisoned for preaching without a license.[11] There were also guides available to help in evangelizing; the Scottish Presbyterian Thomas Boston penned *The Art of Man-Fishing*.[12] Those who wrote this kind of material did not confine their preaching to the four walls of a church or meetinghouse; they were ready to itinerate and travel to where hearers were.[13]

---

8. J. B. Williams, *Lives of Philip and Matthew Henry* (1828; reprint, London: Banner of Truth, 1984). We today know this work as "Matthew Henry's Commentary."

9. Some have been reprinted by the Banner of Truth Trust. We have noted (p. 45 n. 50, above) Dickson's preparing of a commentary on the Westminster Confession of Faith.

10. It remains true, however, that movements *after* 1730 encouraged the idea that conversion was sudden. The treatment of this issue by Bebbington repays consideration; see his *Evangelicalism in Modern Britain*, 5–10, and subsequent article, "Evangelical Conversion, c. 1740–1850," *Scottish Bulletin of Evangelical Theology* 18, no. 2 (2000): 102–27.

11. See the treatment of Alleine in Dewey J. Wallace, *Shapers of English Calvinism, 1660–1714* (New York: Oxford University Press, 2011), chap. 4.

12. Published posthumously in 1773.

13. It is supposed that itinerant preaching commenced in the time of the awakening, circa 1730. Biographer Charles Chapman, *Matthew Henry: His Life and Times* (London: Arthur Hall, Virtue & Co., 1859), 62, names twelve communities in the vicinity of Chester where Henry preached either weekly or monthly after 1687.

Movements of spiritual awakening also occurred sporadically in seventeenth-century Britain. Once more, it is worth remarking how this feature of evangelical life, so generally associated with the era of Whitefield and Wesley in the century following, was on display earlier. Such movements were not confined to England, Ireland, and Scotland, however; they also occurred in circumstances of religious oppression generated by the Counter-Reformation efforts of Roman Catholicism.[14] This connection with oppression is borne out by a number of instances in our period.

The first was a remarkable development occurring in connection with the Church of Scotland General Assembly in 1596, a year when Spain—having seen its initial 1588 Armada come to nothing—was threatening new invasions of England and Scotland. In this time of national peril, ministers were rebuked in the General Assembly for their carelessness and distraction with worldly pursuits; this led to multiple tearful confessions of sin. Similar admonitions were carried to the parishes of the nation and to the royal palace; there young King James VI was reportedly moved to confess faults of his own.[15]

Only a few decades later, there was another manifestation. This came in connection with the ministry of David Dickson, the minister at Irvine who opposed the reintroduction of bishops at the insistence of King James. For five years under Dickson's ministry local folk were being converted to faith in Christ in such great numbers that this movement was derided as "the Stewarton sickness."[16] Churchgoers were known to swoon under conviction so that they needed to be carried from the church.

Similar events occurred among the Scots who had migrated across the Irish Sea to Ulster as part of King James's "Plantation of Ulster" after 1609.[17] Still reliant on the Church of Scotland, these migrants were served by Scots ministers who crossed the Irish Sea on a seasonal basis. At a location known as the Six-Mile Water, county Antrim, open-air preaching in 1628 met with amazing success: "the power of God did sensibly accompany the word with an unusual motion upon the hearers, and a very great catch as to the conversion of souls to Christ."[18]

---

14. Reginald H. Ward, *The Protestant Evangelical Awakening* (Cambridge: Cambridge University Press, 1992) and *European Evangelicalism: A Global Intellectual History; 1670–1789* (Cambridge: Cambridge University Press, 2006).

15. See Kenneth J. Stewart, *Ten Myths about Calvinism: Broadening the Reformed Tradition* (Downers Grove, IL: InterVarsity Press, 2011), 110–11.

16. Stewarton is a country town in the vicinity of Irvine, where Dickson served.

17. A scheme begun by King James in 1609, after rebellion by Irish Catholics, to boost the Protestant population in Ireland by immigration.

18. Robert Fleming, *Fulfilling of the Scriptures* (1743), 185, quoted in John Gillies, *Histor-*

There were similar happenings and similar consequences, once more in the west of Scotland, when at the Kirk of Shotts, Lanarkshire, in 1630, there was a "strange unusual motion on the hearers . . . of divers ranks; it was known that near five hundred had at that time a discernible change wrought on them, of whom most proved lively Christians afterwards."[19] The preacher that day, young John Livingston—just like Dickson—had experienced the opposition of Stuart-appointed bishops to his ministry. Neither minister had sought pastoral appointment under the bishops who claimed territorial jurisdiction. Such events of awakening also occurred in the Western Isles and Highlands of Scotland in 1675 and 1724.[20]

Because these examples come from the north of Ireland and Scotland, one might infer that the absence of similar reports from elsewhere in Britain suggests something about these manifestations that was unique to Scots-Irish Protestantism. Two things stand in the way of such a conclusion. First, the terminology of "revival" was current among contemporary English Puritans even if documentation of actual incidents has not come down to us. John Owen, the celebrated Congregational Independent, had written about spiritual revival in 1674.[21] New England preacher Jonathan Edwards (1703–1758) was fully aware of multiple previous seasons of "harvest" under the ministry of his grandfather, Solomon Stoddard (1643–1729).[22] For such reasons, the modern writer J. I. Packer has described the Puritan movement as "a movement of revival."[23] Second, the earliest phase of what is variously called "the Evangelical Revival" or "the Great Awakening" was *not* in Scotland but in Wales in 1735.[24] We can

ical Recollections Relating to Remarkable Periods of the Success of the Gospel (1754; reprint, Kelso: John Rutherford, 1845), 206.

19. Fleming, *Fulfilling of the Scriptures*, 185, quoted in Gillies, *Historical Collections*, 198–99.

20. John MacInnes, *The Evangelical Movement in the Highlands of Scotland* (Aberdeen, UK: Aberdeen University Press, 1951), 154–56.

21. Peter Toon, *The Correspondence of John Owen: 1616–1683* (London: James Clarke, 1970), 159.

22. Thomas Kidd, "Prayer for a Saving Issue: Evangelical Development in New England before the Great Awakening," in *The Advent of Evangelicalism: Exploring Historical Continuities*, ed. Michael Haykin and Kenneth J. Stewart (Nashville: B&H, 2008), 136, 137. The UK edition of this book was entitled *The Emergence of Evangelicalism* (Leicester: IVP, 2008).

23. In an article of this name in the *Evangelical Quarterly* 52 (1980): 2–16, reprinted in the same author's *A Quest for Godliness: The Puritan Vision of the Christian Life* (Wheaton, IL: Crossway, 1994). In the same era, New England Puritans such as Cotton Mather were referring to spiritual awakenings as "effusions of the Spirit" or "harvests." See the discussion of this in Stewart, *Ten Myths about Calvinism*, 112. See also Rick Kennedy, *The First American Evangelical: A Short Life of Cotton Mather* (Grand Rapids: Eerdmans, 2015).

24. Arthur Skevington Wood, *The Inextinguishable Blaze* (Grand Rapids: Eerdmans, 1960), chap. 3.

conclude, therefore, that such events were anticipated, prayed for, and savored across the English-speaking world. It is worth noting that many of these intense periods of spiritual awakening were associated with renewed attention to the Lord's Supper. Recognizing this brings us to a consideration of another element of the "quadrilateral" of evangelical characteristics: crucicentrism.

Crucicentrism Displayed in Attentiveness to the Lord's Supper

We most naturally think of these Puritans, north and south, as fervent preachers of the cross of Christ. That they were. It is equally important that we recognize that they were keen promoters of the regular use of the Lord's Supper, the symbol and reminder of Christ's sacrifice. Of the two rites Christ ordained, the Supper was the practice that struggled most to come into its own in the post-Reformation period. The reasons for this are less than obvious.

While pre-Reformation communion practice had entailed the administration of multiple masses—often simultaneously at side altars in cathedrals—since the Fourth Lateran Council of 1215, rank-and-file Christians had only been obliged to commune once per year; this customarily happened in the Easter season. At the Reformation, churches faced the challenge of drawing professed Christians into more frequent observance than had been expected earlier. This existing challenge was exacerbated for more than a generation by a shortage of Protestant clergy.[25]

Within the Church of England—which saw a higher proportion of pre-Reformation clergy carried over into Protestantism—the general expectation was that Holy Communion might be administered monthly. In the Church of Scotland, however, with great shortages of clergy after 1560 and a significant dependency on persons named as "readers" and "exhorters" (as substitutes for ministers), there was a recognition that a marked increase in frequency of observance would be highly difficult.[26] The 1564 *Book of Common Order* set out a differentiated expectation for town churches (more likely to have a settled minister) and country churches (less so): town churches would receive the

25. Some but by no means all who served previously as Roman Catholic priests and monks were adjudged fit to serve the churches of the Reformation. The shortfall of clergy was sometimes compensated for by the appointment of persons as "readers" and "exhorters"; such persons were permitted to read set liturgical forms or to expound a Scripture passage, but *not* to administer baptism or the Lord's Supper. See James Kirk, *Patterns of Reform: Continuity and Change in the Reformation Kirk* (Edinburgh: T&T Clark, 1989), chap. 4, "Recruitment for the Ministry in Reformation Scotland."

26. James K. Cameron, ed., *The First Book of Discipline* (Edinburgh: St. Andrew Press, 1972), 183.

Lord's Supper monthly; country churches, according to a less definite schedule. In actual practice, however, the in-between policy of four times annually was settled upon.[27]

Yet, even this low frequency of administration was met with considerable indifference by the churchgoing population of Scotland. Thus, in the early seventeenth century, Scottish ministers devised a scheme of combining a twice-yearly administration of the Lord's Supper with an outdoor preaching festival that brought together multiple preachers and large crowds drawn from diverse communities. Like pre-Reformation communion practice (focused chiefly on the Easter season), here the Lord's Supper was administered with an element of pageantry. Extensive evangelistic preaching would be followed by the personal interview or examination of those seeking to participate in the communion. Those whose preparedness was judged satisfactory were furnished with metal communion tokens ensuring them admittance to the closely guarded outdoor communion meal.[28]

English and Scottish Puritans in the Westminster Assembly discussed the administration of the Lord's Supper and related questions of church practice. That Assembly's deliberations about communion practice, set out in the Westminster Directory for Worship, were: "The communion, or supper of the Lord, is frequently to be celebrated; but how often may be considered and determined by the ministers and other church-governors of each congregation as they shall find most convenient for the comfort and edification of the people committed to their charge. And, when it shall be administered, we judge it convenient to be done after the morning sermon."[29]

This may have been a chastely stated policy, yet the pattern of Scottish communion practice that followed the era of the Westminster Assembly and its Di-

---

27. Church of Scotland, *The Liturgy of John Knox: Received by the Church of Scotland in 1564* (Glasgow: Thomas D. Morton, 1886), 138.

28. The development of these communion festivals is described in Leigh Eric Schmidt, *Holy Fairs: Scotland and the Making of American Revivalism* (Grand Rapids: Eerdmans, 2001). In the eighteenth century, a reaction set in over the negative consequences of the infrequency of these festivals. See Kenneth J. Stewart, "Accelerating the Rhythm: Eighteenth Century Evangelicals and the Frequency of the Lord's Supper," in *In Search of Ancient Roots: The Christian Past and the Evangelical Identity Crisis* (Downers Grove, IL: InterVarsity Press, 2017), chap. 8. Raymond Mentzer traces the introduction of communion tokens to Calvin and Beza and describes their extensive use across the Reformed churches of western Europe. See his "The Reformed Churches of France and the Visual Arts," In *Seeing beyond the Word: Visual Arts and the Calvinist Tradition*, ed. Paul Corby Finney (Grand Rapids: Eerdmans, 1999), 220–21.

29. See the text itself in *The Confession of Faith and Larger and Shorter Catechisms* (Glasgow: Free Presbyterian Publications, 1967), 384.

rectory can only properly be termed as random and other-than-focused. The determination of the Cromwell government to oppose religious monopolies in both kingdoms, followed by efforts of the restored monarchy to reintroduce common practices, led to a range of bewildering and uneven communion practices in Scotland. What ensued in the period of restored monarchy and the eventual restoration of Presbyterianism (in 1690) represented the opposite of uniformity.[30]

Activism as Displayed in Early Missionary Efforts

Evangelical Christians have often traced our earliest modern missionary efforts (an example of the "activisim" of the quadrilateral) to the pioneering mission to India of William Carey (1761–1834) in 1793.[31] Yet an examination of Carey's important survey of world mission, *An Inquiry into the Obligations of Christians to Use Means for the Conversion of the Heathens*,[32] discloses how much Carey had learned from earlier Protestant missionary efforts.[33] In writing this work, Carey had benefited by digesting the book of an earlier eighteenth-century chronicler of mission, the Scottish minister Robert Millar (1672–1752).[34] Here it is our purpose to draw attention to two of these earlier missionary efforts inasmuch as they testify to the existence of missionary zeal both in the Puritan age and in what immediately followed it.

The Society for the Propagation of the Gospel in New England

The Massachusetts Bay Colony, begun in 1628, had initially named the evangelization of native peoples as one of the reasons justifying the effort to plant a transatlantic society. It was known that Jesuit missionaries were already working among the native population to the north; thus, "It will be a service to the Church of great consequence to carry the Gospell into those parts of

30. Gordon Donaldson, "Covenant to Revolution," in *Studies in the History of Worship in Scotland*, ed. Duncan Forrester and Douglas Murray (Edinburgh: T&T Clark, 1984), 52–64. The standard work on Scottish practice is G. B. Burnet, *The Holy Communion in the Reformed Church of Scotland* (Edinburgh: Oliver & Boyd, 1960).

31. Chapter 10 (below) will highlight the launching of cross-cultural missionary efforts from within the young USA.

32. 1792; reprint, London: Carey Kingsgate Press, 1961.

33. Examples include the 1706 mission to Tranquebar, South India, of Lutheran Pietists Heinrich Plutschau and Bartolomaus Ziegenbalg, sent with the support of the king of Denmark, and the various missions of the Moravians to Greenland and the Caribbean.

34. Ronald E. Davies, "Robert Millar: An Eighteenth Century Scottish Latourette," *Evangelical Quarterly* 62, no. 2 (1990): 143–56.

the world, to helpe on the coming of the fulness of the Gentiles, & to raise a Bulwork against the kingdom of AntiChrist which the Jesuits labour to rear up in those parts."[35]

Yet, by 1642, no observable effort had been made in pursuit of this objective. An English visitor to Massachusetts Bay, Thomas Letchford, returned home and registered his concern in print: no colonist of Massachusetts had thus far done anything about Indian evangelization.[36] Letchford had successfully applied the spurs. One New England pastor, John Eliot (1604–1690), of First Church Roxbury, began to write about initial missionary efforts in a 1643 pamphlet, *New England's First Fruits*.[37] This tract was intended primarily for an English readership, a portion of which were Puritan members of England's Parliament and of the Westminster Assembly of Divines. Eliot's pamphlet led to the publication of others; these related his regular visits with the aboriginal people of his region, his gradual work of learning their language to the point where he could preach in it, and his eventual translation of Scriptures into their language.[38] Moreover, Eliot carried on extensive personal correspondence with one individual in particular (not a member of the Assembly): Richard Baxter.[39]

Sympathetic members of England's Parliament were ready to pass legislation in support of such work. There arose, in consequence of an Act of Parliament of 1649, the Society for the Propagation of the Gospel in New England;

35. R. C. Winthrop, *Life and Letters of John Winthrop*, 2 vols. (Boston: Little, Brown, 1869), 1:309, excerpted in Lacey Baldwin Smith, ed., *The Past Speaks*, 2 vols. (Boston: D. C. Heath, 1992), 411.

36. John Hinkson, "Missions among the Puritans and Pietists," in *The Great Commission: Evangelicals and the History of World Missions*, ed. Martin Klauber and Scott Manetsch (Nashville: B&H, 2008), 25.

37. See Richard Cogley, *John Eliot's Mission to the Indians before King Philip's War* (Cambridge, MA: Harvard University Press, 1999). Eliot's pamphlets (published for an English readership) were republished as *The Eliot Tracts: With Letters from John Eliot to Thomas Thorowgood and Richard Baxter* (London, 2003).

38. Hinkson, "Missions among the Puritans and Pietists," 25. The tracts were gathered together by Michael P. Clark as *The Eliot Tracts* (Westport, CT: Praeger, 2003). See the synopsis of the various tracts in Sidney H. Rooy, *The Theology of Missions in the Puritan Tradition* (1965; reprint, Laurel, MS: Audubon, 2006), chap. 3.

39. This correspondence was edited and published by the early twentieth-century historian F. J. Powicke in two extended essays. See F. J. Powicke, "Some Unpublished Correspondence of the Rev. Richard Baxter and the Rev. John Eliot, 'Apostle to the American Indians,' 1652–1686," *Bulletin of the John Rylands Library* 15, no. 1 (1931): 138–76, and 15, no. 2 (1931): 442–66. Baxter's role as an advocate of missionary effort is sketched in Rooy, *The Theology of Missions in the Puritan Tradition*, chap. 2. See also J. A. DeJong, *As the Waters Cover the Sea: Millennial Expectations in the Rise of Anglo-American Missions, 1640–1810* (Kampen, the Netherlands: J. H. Kok, 1970).

this was the first known instance of an English Protestant missionary society.[40] While its formal leadership was London based, a supervisory committee was located in Boston. Over a century, some £16,000 were contributed in England and Wales in support of these efforts.[41] Not only was the missionary labor and translation work of Eliot supported in this way, the Society—which continued after the Restoration period as a cause supported by both Nonconformists and Anglicans—supported many additional ministries to native people until the era of the Revolutionary War. The missionary work at Stockbridge, Massachusetts, continued by Jonathan Edwards after the conclusion of his Northampton pastorate, was directly supported by this society through its Boston committee.[42]

The Society in Scotland for the Propagation of Christian Knowledge

After the reestablishment of Presbyterianism in 1690, Scottish Presbyterians became increasingly aware that vast northern portions of their own country had not yet been evangelized. These regions were strongholds of Roman Catholicism (which had been legislated out of formal existence in 1560) and were also most susceptible to the efforts of the dethroned Stuart dynasty to stir up insurrection.[43] Thus, there was founded in Edinburgh in 1709, by royal charter, the Society in Scotland for the Propagation of Christian Knowledge (SSPCK). It was intended to be the Scottish counterpart of a similar society that had existed in England since 1698, the Society for the Promotion of Christian Knowledge.[44]

Among those associated with the founding of the Society in Scotland were the early mission historian Robert Millar, Church of Scotland minister

40. DeJong, *As the Waters Cover the Sea*, 43–48, maintains that it was the circulation of the Eliot tracts in England that stimulated the eventual act of Parliament establishing the mission society.

41. Hinkson, "Missions among the Puritans and Pietists," 28.

42. George Marsden, "Jonathan Edwards, the Missionary," *Journal of Presbyterian History* 81, no. 1 (Spring 2003): 7–9. Marsden appears not to recognize that the Boston committee represented the London Society, rather than being a separate organization.

43. James II of England had taken refuge in France at the time (1688) of the invasion of England by William III. James lived only until 1701; his son and grandson attempted to rally the Highlands to their support in 1715 and 1749.

44. On the founding of the SSPCK, see Donald E. Meek, "Scottish Highlanders, North American Indians and the SSPCK: Some Cultural Perspectives," *Scottish Church History Society Records* 23, pt. 3 (1989): 378–96. The dealings of the society within colonial America are described in Frederick V. Mills, "The Society in Scotland for Propagating Christian Knowledge in British North America, 1730–1775," *Church History* 63, no. 1 (1994): 15–30.

at Paisley,[45] and the English writer Daniel Defoe, who had lived in Scotland as the agent of the English government to advocate the political union of the neighboring countries.[46] Soon this young society had established seventy-eight schools across the Scottish Highlands; these provided literacy, numeracy, and Scripture knowledge.[47] But then came something unforeseen: the London Presbyterian minister Daniel Williams left a bequest to the society with the stipulation that it be used to send missionaries to "bring heathens to the knowledge of Christ." This funding eventually enabled young ministers to do American mission work in two particular fields: the colonies of Massachusetts and Georgia. The most renowned of these was David Brainerd (d. 1746), whose short but productive ministry among the Delaware Indians was memorialized in a work by Jonathan Edwards, *An Account of the Life of the Late Reverend David Brainerd* (1749). The work of the SSPCK in colonial America expanded southward to Virginia and Georgia; it remained strong until the Revolutionary War.[48] We are thus entitled to say that both in England and in Scotland in the decades following the Westminster Assembly, there was considerable concern that the gospel be carried to indigenous peoples in the New World; all this took place well before Carey.

CHANGES IN THE WORLD OF THEOLOGY

That the winds of theology had begun to blow against the theological consensus reflected in the work of the Westminster Assembly is illustrated by the virulence of the religious reaction accompanying the restoration of monarchy. Landed aristocrats and a majority of clergy in both England and Scotland were prepared to turn back the clock to a state of things in which royal supremacy over religion again prevailed and theological latitude was tolerated. We will concern ourselves exclusively with the latter.

In both nations, there had been a party in the national church that had continued to adhere to the theology of the Reformed churches while accepting

45. Mentioned on p. 72 above.

46. These Scottish involvements of Defoe (a Presbyterian) are described in Paula Backscheider, *Daniel Defoe: His Life* (Baltimore: Johns Hopkins University Press, 1989), 289.

47. Clare Loughlin, "Concepts of Mission in Scottish Presbyterianism: The SSPCK, the Highlands and Britain's American Colonies," *Studies in Church History: The Church and Empire* 54 (2018): 197.

48. Mills, "The Society in Scotland," 25–30, indicates that the well-being of the SSPCK both in Scotland and in colonial America was tied to its being seen as loyal to the House of Hanover; this relationship was disturbed by the Revolution.

a royally appointed episcopacy,[49] as well as a party with the same theological loyalty resistant to episcopacy.[50] But these had never been the only alternatives. Prior to the calling of the Westminster Assembly in 1643, the great vexation of English Puritans and their Scottish counterparts had been the advancement under King Charles I of a point of view associated with Archbishop William Laud. A modern writer has named this the "Durham House" perspective.[51] This position, while not at first openly hostile to Reformation theology, tended to subvert it by a reckoning that patristic learning and patristic theology were to be preferred to it. Puritan charges of "Arminianism" among the hierarchy were in many cases complaints against this viewpoint.[52]

This theological outlook, which was the cause of Puritan consternation prior to the Civil War, survived the period of the interregnum and flourished again in the Restoration period, being especially associated with individuals such as John Cosin, bishop of Durham, and George Bull, the eventual bishop of St. David's. In the eighteenth century, the outlook would come to be known as "High Church." In Scotland, those keen to perpetuate this stance did not enter the Church of Scotland as reestablished in 1690 but continued as the Scottish Episcopal Church.

Distinct from the foregoing was a viewpoint associated with but by no means confined to Cambridge University. Rising in its various colleges (including Emmanuel College, a stronghold of Puritanism) was a viewpoint that sought to find a middle way between the Puritan expression of Reformed orthodoxy and the patristic–High Church emphasis. This affirmed that each represented a form of excess. This moderating viewpoint, which since the nineteenth century has been termed "Cambridge Platonist," stressed that the heart of the Christian message had to do not with dogma or articles of faith (each of which had its place) but with right conduct. The heart of the Christian faith commended itself to reasonable men and did not require wrangling

49. Of the first category, in Scotland, Bishops Robert Leighton and Henry Scougall; in England, Bishops George Abbot and Edward Reynolds.

50. Of this second category, in Scotland, Alexander Henderson and Samuel Rutherford; in England, Richard Baxter and John Howe.

51. Bryan Spinks, *Sacraments, Ceremonies, and the Stuart Divines* (Aldershot, UK: Ashgate, 2002), 81–88, has named this point of view after its chief meeting place, the London residence of the bishop of Durham. He uses the term interchangeably with "Reformed Sacramentalism." We noted above in chapter 3 that negotiations with King Charles I, after his capture, might have led to the king choosing twenty divines to augment the conclusions of the Westminster Assembly. We should assume that this viewpoint, the "Reformed Patristic," would have been at the forefront of any group so nominated.

52. Spinks, *Sacraments, Ceremonies*, chap. 3; Owen Chadwick, *The Reformation* (Grand Rapids: Eerdmans, 1965), 218.

over.[53] The same House of Commons in London that regularly heard sermons from Puritan members of the Westminster Assembly also heard Cambridge philosopher-theologian Ralph Cudworth (reckoned a Cambridge Platonist) affirm: "Do we not nowadays open and lock up heaven with the private key of this and that opinion of our own, according to our several fancies as we please? And if anyone observes Christ's commandments never so sincerely, and serves God with faith and a pure confidence, that yet haply skills not of some contended-for opinions, some darling notions, he has not the right shibboleth, he has not the true watchword, he must not pass the guards into heaven."[54]

Devotees of the High Church approach made conformity with Christian antiquity their hallmark; those of the Reformed and Puritan way—while ready to draw on Christian antiquity—made Scripture and the Reformed confessions their standard. Yet this "third way" of Cambridge Platonism[55] grew up alongside both (sometimes in the same colleges) and sought a pacific way forward. It stressed the universal accessibility of grace, the rationality and sensibility of the heart of Christianity, and the supreme importance of ethical conduct. The need for divine revelation was not denied; yet this revelation was deemed universally accessible to all who would employ reason. On this approach, the number of distinctively Christian doctrines to be affirmed and defended was reduced and doctrinal controversy defused.

Yet the pupils of the Cambridge Platonists did not simply affirm what their tutors had said and written; as what were called "latitudinarians," they went further.[56] With them there was a continuation of the idea that controversy should be shunned and dogmatic speculation avoided. Such individuals as Daniel Whitby and Edward Stillingfleet "appealed to considerations which any intelligent person could appreciate and assess. This approach set a high value on the kind of religion that reason can discover for itself."[57] There was not yet a disparaging of the role of Scripture; this was still treated as possess-

53. Numbered among the Cambridge Platonists were Benjamin Whichcote, Henry More, Ralph Cudworth, John Smith, Peter Sterry, and Nathaniel Culverwell. A chapter-length treatment of Sterry is provided in Dewey D. Wallace Jr., *Shapers of English Calvinism: 1660–1714* (New York: Oxford University Press, 2011).

54. Ralph Cudworth, "A Sermon Preached before the House of Commons March 17, 1647," in *Cambridge Platonist Spirituality*, ed. Charles Taliaferro and Alison J. Teply (Mahwah, NJ: Paulist, 2004), 65.

55. Taliaferro and Teply show that at least two who are numbered among the Cambridge Platonists (Nathaniel Culverwell and Peter Sterry) remained Calvinist in their theology (p. 28); the second was appointed to the Assembly of Divines (p. 33).

56. On the link between Cambridge Platonists and latitudinarians, see Gerald L. Cragg, *The Church and the Age of Reason* (London: Hodder & Stoughton, 1962), 70.

57. Cragg, *The Church and the Age of Reason*, 71.

ing authority. But other authorities now needed to be recognized, with the new science particularly demanding recognition. The latitudinarian therefore was "in a position half-way between the unquestioning reliance on authority which was characteristic of the seventeenth century and the rationalism of the early eighteenth."[58]

And what was the Presbyterian reaction to these developments? In England, Scotland, and abroad, thoughtful Christian leaders could not be unaware of these unfolding changes; it was only a matter of time until they would respond.[59] While some of the adaptations already named had been stimulated initially by the writings of Thomas Hobbes (1588–1679) and René Descartes (1596–1650), as the century advanced the contributions of John Locke (1632–1704) also had to be considered. Of Presbyterian sympathies and working in Oxford at the time monarchy was restored (1660), the ejected Locke spent much of the rest of his life in Europe; from there he completed major works such as *An Essay on Human Understanding* (1690) and *The Reasonableness of Christianity* (1695). While Locke was self-admittedly a Christian believer who revered the New Testament, he was at the same time ready to maintain that the proportion of the Christian faith that was reliant on special revelation (as opposed to empirical observation) was modest.[60]

The cumulative effect of such intellectual developments upon Presbyterian thinking in the late seventeenth and early eighteenth centuries was to create a divergence in place of an earlier broad unity. This early broad unity we may designate "Reformed Orthodoxy" as represented in the Westminster Confession of Faith and Catechisms and the derivative documents produced by Congregational Independents and Baptists.[61] Now, in light of these emerging challenges, instead of a broadly united theological stream, we can observe several emerging late in the century among those who in 1662 endured the hardships of ejection.

58. Cragg, *The Church and the Age of Reason*, 72.

59. For evidence of the repercussions of these developments in the American colonies, see E. Brooks Holifield, *Theology in America* (New Haven: Yale University Press, 2005), chap. 3, "Rationalism Resisted."

60. Alan F. P. Sell, *John Locke and the Eighteenth Century Divines* (1997: reprint, Eugene, OR: Wipf & Stock, 2006), chap. 6.

61. That is, the Savoy Confession of Faith (1658) and London Baptist Confession of Faith (1689). The progress of Reformed theology through this period is addressed in three notable works: Carl Trueman and R. S. Clark, *Protestant Scholasticism: Essays in Reassessment* (Carlisle, UK: Paternoster, 1999); Willem J. Van Asselt and Eef Dekkert, eds., *Reformation and Scholasticism: An Ecumenical Enterprise* (Grand Rapids: Baker Academic, 2001); and Willem J. Van Asselt, ed., *Introduction to Reformed Scholasticism* (Grand Rapids: Reformed Heritage, 2011).

In Scotland, which in 1690 returned to a Presbyterian allegiance,[62] it soon became apparent that there was not just one stance vis-à-vis the Westminster Standards. To these, the Church of Scotland had officially returned. One writer has identified four points of view among Scottish Presbyterians as the eighteenth century dawned. These were the "scholastic Calvinist" (which upheld strict subscription to the Westminster Standards), the "Evangelical Calvinist" (concerned above all to maintain the free offer of the gospel), the "Liberal" (concerned to restate the Christian faith in light of the rationalistic spirit of the age), and the "Speculative" (tending to Arianism).[63]

In these decades, a similar range of stances could be found among the Nonconformists of England and the American colonies. Outside Scotland, even though strict confessional subscription was not yet maintained or required, at least as broad a range of views emerged.[64] Strict adherents of the doctrines championed in the Westminster Standards there were; these, like their Scottish counterparts, have been designated "scholastic Calvinists," in that they were committed to the perpetuation and defense of Reformed doctrine exactly as it had been received.[65] Within England, after the restoration of monarchy and the enforcement of the Act of Uniformity (1662), this emphasis was more likely to be perpetuated within Congregational Independency than among those committed to a Presbyterian polity.

Distinct from the first point of view, it is also possible to speak of the continued existence of an "evangelical Calvinism" as represented by figures such as Joseph Alleine or John Flavel.[66] The concern of this emphasis was not so much the perpetuation of the system of Reformed theology set out in the Westminster documents per se as the application of these doctrines to vital Christian experience. Most English Presbyterians of this era who are

62. The exceptions to this being the two groups: Cameronian Covenanters and Episcopalians who declined to enter the reestablished Church of Scotland.

63. Stewart Mechie, "The Theological Climate in Early Eighteenth Century Scotland," in *Reformation and Revolution: Essays in Honour of Hugh Watt*, ed. Duncan Shaw (Edinburgh: St. Andrew Press, 1967), 267–72. Mechie took the view that, over time, the first and most rigid of the positions (the Scholastic) tended to give way to the last (the Speculative).

64. The reason for this is that within Scotland, from 1690 onward, the Church of Scotland was the established church of the land; its doctrinal articles were enforced in a way analogous to that of the Articles of Religion of the Church of England. English Nonconformists can be observed, over time, making far more frequent references to the Larger and Shorter Westminster Catechisms than to the Confession.

65. Wallace, *Shapers of English Calvinism*, 14, 15. The use of the term "scholastic" is not intended to disparage; it implies an approach to theology dependent on earlier authors: reformation, medieval, and patristic.

66. Wallace, *Shapers of English Calvinism*, 121–22.

remembered today were of yet another affiliation, however. When the term "moderate Calvinist" is applied to the commentator Matthew Henry,[67] his near-contemporary John Howe,[68] or Daniel Williams—after whom a famous London library is named—what is being signified is that they were prepared to engage in careful restatement of Reformed theology in light of intellectual currents of the time. They did so with the apologetic interest of commending Reformed theology in the face of a changed intellectual atmosphere. There was, in addition, a grouping of Presbyterians who came to be called "Rational Dissenters"; these moved beyond both Scripture and Reformed confessions to establish unaided human reason as the arbiter of what was to be believed.[69] All points of view just described here as existing in England and Scotland had their counterparts in the American colonies.

67. At his ordination by other Dissenting ministers in 1687, Henry presented a doctrinal summary of his faith that, though consonant with the Westminster Standards, made no reference whatsoever to them. Williams, *Lives of Philip and Matthew Henry*, 2:48. The theological outlook of the younger Henry has recently been explored in a doctoral dissertation: David Murray, "Matthew Henry (1662–1714): The Reasonableness and Pleasantness of Christianity" (PhD diss., Free University of Amsterdam, 2019). Note especially chap. 2.

68. David P. Field, *Rigide Calvinisme in a Softer Dress: The Moderate Presbyterianism of John Howe, 1630–1705* (Edinburgh: Rutherford House, 2004). One sees the same effort at theological restatement in the Congregational Independent Isaac Watts (1674–1748). See Graham Beynon, *Isaac Watts: Reason, Passion, and the Revival of Religion* (London: T&T Clark, 2016).

69. Alasdair Raffe, "Presbyterians," in *Oxford History of Protestant Dissenting Traditions*, ed. Andrew Thompson (New York: Oxford University Press, 2017), 2:13; Wallace, *Shapers of English Calvinism*, 31–33.

CHAPTER 6

New World Immigration and the First Presbytery

The account of immigration to New England begins with a group of English Separatists who had left their homeland for the Netherlands in 1609. The Separatists were convinced that King James and the Anglican establishment had no right to impose forms of worship. Part of the group eventually sailed to North America in 1620 aboard the ship *Mayflower*, establishing Plymouth Plantation as the first permanent English colony in the New World. These so-called Pilgrim Fathers would become symbols of the American ethos in their determined pursuit of self-government and freedom of religion. Half of them would die during the first year in the New World. Their story was chronicled by William Bradford (1590–1657), who served as the governor of the colony for thirty years.[1] By 1626 the remaining Plymouth settlers had moved to Salem. They were soon joined by additional waves of immigrants, who reached the shores of New England after arduous journeys across the Atlantic. The Massachusetts Bay Colony was established near Boston in 1630 by English Congregationalists fleeing Anglican oppression under Charles I in the years leading up to the English Civil War. Massachusetts Bay Puritans were dissenters of the nonseparating variety who had never formally separated from the mother Church of England but were looking for the opportunity to experiment with congregational polity in the New World.

CONGREGATIONALISTS AND PRESBYTERIANISM

Cotton Mather of Boston (1663–1728), in his 1698 history of New England churches, claimed that over four thousand Presbyterians had come to New

---

1. See William Bradford, *History of Plymouth Plantation* (Boston: Massachusetts Historical Society, 1912).

England in the years up to 1640.[2] While ships full of Congregationalists arrived in the seventeenth century, a trickle of Presbyterians also made their way to the New World, many of them settling in Massachusetts and Connecticut. Congregationalists practiced leadership by elders and ministers in autonomous congregations, but Presbyterian sentiments were also found among the growing New England population. The influence of Presbyterian principles within New England Congregationalist practice was evident in the collaboration among the churches.[3] The Cambridge Platform of 1648 was a response to English requests for a definitive statement of New England practice and included biblical justification for congregational principles. The Cambridge Synod, which produced the document, consisted of clergy and lay representatives elected by the churches of New England. Churches shared "Church-communion," aiding, admonishing, and consulting on issues in congregations. The document also provided for representative synods "orderly assembled, & rightly proceeding according to the pattern, Acts. 15."[4] This plan was remarkably similar to Presbyterianism in its corporate understanding of New England church life—it has been called "Presbyterianized Congregationalism."[5]

Presbyterians and Congregationalists in parts of England had attempted union during the Commonwealth, entering into an agreement in 1656. Presbyterians had abandoned the dream of a modified established church and, in light of the Toleration Act of 1689, were more interested in collaboration with Congregationalists. In 1690, a joint General Fund was established to aid struggling congregations and educate candidates for the ministry. In 1691, Congregationalists and Presbyterians in London subscribed to a Heads of Agreement, which announced a formal union between the groups. Increase Mather (1639–1723) was in England at the time and participated in the negotiations that produced the agreement. The Heads of Agreement got significant attention among Congregationalists in the colonies through the writings of Increase's son, Cotton Mather of Boston. The document called for affirming the Scriptures as the "perfect and only Rule and Faith and Practice," and either the doctrinal parts of the Thirty-Nine Articles or the Westminster Confession and catechisms. The Heads of Agreement acknowledged differences in under-

2. Cotton Mather, *Magnalia Christi Americana*, vol. 1 (Carlisle, PA: Banner of Truth, 1979), 80.

3. See Edmund S. Morgan, *The Puritan Dilemma: The Story of John Winthrop* (Boston: Little, Brown, 1958), 124–29.

4. Williston Walker, *The Creeds and Platforms of Congregationalism* (New York: Charles Scribner's Sons, 1893), 229–34.

5. Leonard J. Trinterud, *The Forming of an American Tradition: A Re-examination of Colonial Presbyterianism* (Philadelphia: Westminster, 1949), 21.

standing the office of elder and asserted that no "particular Churches shall be subordinate to one another." However, in the selection and examination of ministers, congregations should "consult and advise with *Pastors* of Neighbouring Congregations." Likewise, ministers of several churches should "be consulted and advised" in difficult cases, and churches "ought to have reverential regard to their judgment so given, and not dissent therefrom, without *apparent* grounds from the word of God."[6]

In America, the Heads of Agreement was explicitly affirmed in the 1708 Saybrook Platform of Connecticut Congregationalists. The Saybrook Platform established local "consociations" of neighboring congregations and a general "council" with clergy and lay representatives, to render binding judgments in church discipline. Ministerial "associations" for clergy oversight and examination of ministerial candidates were also established. Not all colonial Congregationalists accepted these polity revisions; some rejected Saybrook as a de facto Presbyterianism that compromised their understanding of local church autonomy.[7]

SOUTHERN COLONIES

The story in the southern colonies begins in Jamestown (1607), the first English settlement in the New World. The Jamestown immigrants included Puritan clergy, some of whom were of Presbyterian persuasion. Alexander Whitaker and George Keith were two early Virginia clergy with Presbyterian convictions. Whitaker immigrated to Virginia in 1611, serving a parish along the James River below Richmond. He was from a Presbyterian Puritan family, his father, William, a divinity professor at Cambridge, a hotbed of Puritanism. One of Alexander Whitaker's cousins would later serve in the Westminster Assembly in the 1640s. George Keith was a Presbyterian Scot who entered the Virginia colony in 1617 and served several parishes. He did not use the prayer book and instituted Presbyterian structure. Keith wrote: "I have by the help of God, begun a Church government by ministers and elders. I made bold to choose four elders publickly by lifting up of hands and calling upon God."[8]

The early Presbyterian presence was short-lived, as the Virginia Assembly in 1629 declared that all ministers within the colony must conform to the Church of England. Tension in the colony continued as Puritan clergy from

---

6. Walker, *The Creeds and Platforms of Congregationalism*, 440–62.
7. Walker, *The Creeds and Platforms of Congregationalism*, 502–6.
8. John Gardiner Jr., "The Beginnings of the Presbyterian Church in the Southern Colonies," *Journal of the Presbyterian Historical Society* 34 (March 1956): 38, 39.

New England came south to serve parishes in Virginia. One group of Puritans removed themselves in 1649 to Maryland at the invitation of the governor of the colony. Presbyterians were suppressed in Virginia, and over time were assimilated by the Anglican establishment of the colony.[9]

Reformed and Presbyterian groups began arriving in the low country of South Carolina in the last quarter of the seventeenth century. Among the first were the Huguenots, who entered Charles Town and surrounding areas beginning in 1669. After the 1685 revocation of the Edict of Nantes by King Louis XIV, officially outlawing the Reformed faith in France, Huguenot immigration to the low country increased significantly. Eight separate Huguenot settlements have been identified in the region. One French immigrant was Benjamin Marion, grandfather of the famous general Francis Marion ("the Swamp Fox"), who would be instrumental in defeating the British in the southern colonies during the War of Independence. The Huguenot Presbyterian Church of Charleston traces its roots back to 1687 when the Reformed Church of Charleston was established. Most Huguenots were eventually absorbed into the established Anglican Church in South Carolina. Multiple reasons may account for this melding into Anglicanism—economic and political realities, difficulty in securing their own clergy, and similarity of the French Reformed liturgy to the prayer book.[10]

Scots also entered the Carolinas during the seventeenth century. Some of them, like Henry Erskine (Lord Cardross), were escaping persecution in Scotland at the hands of Charles II. Erskine planted a Scottish settlement at Port Royal, south of Charleston, but it was destroyed by the Spanish, who killed settlers and burned their homes. Some Scottish "Covenanters," who had taken a solemn oath to support only national Presbyterianism, were "banished" to Carolina for refusing to acknowledge the English king's supremacy. In Charleston, Scots joined with Scots-Irish brethren, English Puritans, and Huguenots to establish the Independent Church in 1690, which would come to be known by several different names, including the Presbyterian Church. One of the Independent Church's ministers, Archibald Stobo, planted several South Carolina Presbyterian congregations after he left the Charleston congregation in 1704. Stobo and three other Scottish ministers in the Charleston region established a presbytery in 1722. In 1731, twelve Scottish families withdrew from the Independent Church and formed what would become the First (Scots) Presbyterian Church

9. Ernest Trice Thompson, *Presbyterians in the South*, vol. 1, *1607–1861* (Richmond, VA: John Knox, 1963), 12–15.

10. See Arthur Hirsch, *The Huguenots of Colonial South Carolina* (Durham, NC: Duke University Press, 1928); George Howe, *History of the Presbyterian Church in South Carolina*, vol. 1 (Columbia, SC: Duffe & Chapman, 1870).

of Charleston. Scottish emigration from northern Ireland into the Carolinas began in 1732 with a group that settled near the Sante River and established a congregation with an Irish Presbyterian minister. This congregation and several others became members of the Charleston presbytery in the 1730s.[11]

MIDDLE COLONIES

As Puritans began moving into the middle colonies in the 1640s, those of Presbyterian persuasion organized themselves into particular Presbyterian congregations. There is evidence of an organized Presbyterian congregation established on Long Island by 1662 (Jamaica Church), and there were other Presbyterians throughout New York. The governor of New York in 1678 reported on the religious groups in the colony: "There are Religions of all sorts, one Church of England, severall Presbiterians and Independents, Quakers and Anabaptists, of severall sects, some Jews, but Presbiterians and Independents most numerous and substantiall."[12] By the 1690s, Huguenots fleeing the tyranny of Louis XIV had established four churches in the city of New York. Most Huguenots eventually conformed to Anglicanism, but the New Rochelle congregation would join the Presbyterians.

Families from Connecticut churches, along with clergy provided by New England, moved into eastern Long Island in the mid to late seventeenth century. Following New England patterns, town churches ("meetinghouses") and parsonages were constructed, and taxes provided for the support of ministers. Connecticut Congregationalism had a significant Presbyterian element, and most of these Long Island churches with Connecticut connections would eventually join the Presbyterian fold. Congregational town churches throughout New York faced a significant threat from those who wished to establish Anglicanism in the colony. The Society for the Propagation of the Gospel in Foreign Parts (SPG), established in London in 1701, supplied the Anglican clergy. Oppression of non-Anglican ministers was especially egregious under Lord Cornbury (1661–1723), who became governor in 1702.[13]

Scottish Covenanter refugees entered New Jersey in several waves in the 1680s and 1690s, most uniting with New England settlers in Congregational churches. A number of Scots were banished to America in exchange for re-

11. Thompson, *Presbyterians in the South*, 1:31–36.

12. *Ecclesiastical Records State of New York*, 1:709, quoted in Trinterud, *The Forming of an American Tradition*, 23.

13. Robert Hastings Nichols, *Presbyterianism in New York State: A History of the Synod and Its Predecessors* (Philadelphia: Westminster, 1963), 9–21.

lease from brutal prison conditions. Imprisoned for nonconformity—field preaching or attending conventicles in defiance of the king's suppression of Dissenter worship—they emigrated to the colonies for freedom of worship. One group of more than one hundred sailed for America in September 1685, arriving in New Jersey in December. Of the Scots on board, twenty-two died during the voyage; most of the survivors eventually settled in New England. Numerous other small bands of Scots made their way to the eastern seaboard and scattered throughout the colonies.[14]

The presence of Presbyterian churches in Delaware is identified with the Dutch Calvinist church in New Castle. The congregation's membership included Dutch, English, Scots, Scots-Irish, and Huguenots, and would become a Presbyterian church under John Wilson of Boston, who began his pastorate at New Castle in 1703. In Maryland, under Roman Catholic Lord Baltimore's policy of religious toleration, Presbyterians prospered, along with multiple other groups. In 1677 Baltimore wrote: "The greatest part of the inhabitants of that province (three of four at least) do consist of Praesbiterians, Independents, Anabaptists and Quakers, those of the church of England as well as those of the Romish being the fewest."[15] Presbyterian clergyman Samuel Davis of Ireland served congregations in Maryland (Snow Hill, 1691) and Delaware (Lewes, 1698). When Presbyterian immigrants arrived in Philadelphia, they joined with Baptists for worship. Eventually the two groups divided, and by 1701, Jedediah Andrews, a Harvard graduate, had become the ordained pastor of the Presbyterian group.

THE FIRST PRESBYTERY

Scots-Irish entered Virginia and Maryland in the 1680s and 1690s, and appeals went out for Presbyterian clergymen to be sent to the colonies. From the Irish Presbytery of Laggan, William Trill arrived in Maryland in 1682, and Francis Makemie (1658–1708) followed him the next year. Makemie would become an itinerant, preaching in Maryland, Virginia, and North Carolina in his early American years. He also spent three years in Barbados (1695–1698), returning

14. Richard Webster, *A History of the Presbyterian Church in America, from Its Origin until the Year 1760* (Philadelphia: Joseph M. Wilson, 1857), 68–73.

15. J. William McIlvain, *Early Presbyterianism in Maryland*, Note Supplementary to the Johns Hopkins University Studies in Historical and Political Science, no. 3 (Baltimore: Johns Hopkins University, 1890), 5.

to Accomack County, Virginia, in 1698; he helped organize five churches, including those in Snow Hill and Rehoboth in Maryland. Makemie financed his itinerant ministry through his five-hundred-acre farm in Accomack County, with the aid of a wealthy father-in-law.

Makemie was very concerned about strengthening the Presbyterian work in America. During a trip to London, he secured funds to support two young ministerial graduates from the University of Glasgow. John Hampton and George McNish traveled back with Makemie to Maryland in 1705. Soon afterward, Makemie was instrumental in getting Hampton and McNish, along with Samuel Davis, Nathaniel Taylor, Jedediah Andrews, and John Wilson, to join forces in establishing the first presbytery in the American colonies. Their backgrounds were diverse—three were New Englanders, three Scots-Irish, and one Scot.[16]

In 1706 Makemie was chosen as moderator of a "meeting of ministers" in Philadelphia. In a letter to a friend, he related that seven had been in attendance, "but expect a growing number." In the letter he described the purpose of the presbytery: "Our design is to meet yearly, and oftener, if necessary, to consult the most proper measures for advancing religion and propagating religion in our Various Stations, and to mentain Such a Correspondence as may conduce to the improvement of our Ministeriall ability by prescribing Texts to be preached on by two of our number at every meeting, which performance is Subjected to the censure of our Brethren."[17] The first two pages of the minute book are missing, and only a brief record from the conclusion of the first meeting is found—a Mr. John Boyd is being examined for ordination: he preached, defended his thesis, and "gave Satisfaction as to his Skill in the Languages & answered to extemporary questions: all which were approved of & sustained." At the second meeting in March 1707, several elders were also in attendance, but an absent minister, Samuel Davis, was sent a letter "requiring him to be present at our next meeting in this place." It appears that many elements of Presbyterian government were in place from the beginning—ministerial ordination trials before the presbytery, participation by both ministers and elders, and mandatory clergy attendance.[18]

16. Trinterud, *Forming of an American Tradition*, 31.

17. Makemie to Mr. Benjamin Colman, March 28, 1707, in Charles Augustus Briggs, *American Presbyterianism: Its Origin and Early History*, appendix X, "Letters of Makemie" (New York: Charles Scribner's Sons, 1885), l.

18. Guy S. Klett, ed., *Minutes of the Presbyterian Church in America, 1706–1788* (Philadelphia: Presbyterian Historical Society, 1976), 1–3. Subsequent citations of Synod minutes (including both the Synod of Philadelphia and the Synod of New York) will come from

One reason Presbyterians formed a presbytery was to strengthen religious toleration in the middle colonies. Dissenting worship had become difficult in the city of New York due to the installation of an Anglican priest, William Vesey (a former Dissenter), as rector of Trinity Church. The governor of New York, Lord Cornbury, was in full support of the Church of England in the colony, and Presbyterian ministers John Hubbard of Jamaica and Joseph Morgan of Westchester were forced to leave their church buildings.[19] In January of 1707, Makemie and John Hampton, on a trip to Boston, stopped in New York, where they were invited to preach by the Presbyterians. On the same day, Makemie preached in a private home on Pearl Street and Hampton preached at Newtown on Long Island. Soon afterward, Makemie and Hampton went together to preach again at Newtown, but this time they were arrested for preaching without Cornbury's permission. They were imprisoned for forty-six days.

Charges against Hampton were dropped, but Makemie was released on bail and ordered to stand trial in June. In a letter to a friend, Makemie expressed his concern for religious freedom in the colonies: "The penall laws are invading our American Sanctuary, without the least regard to the Toleration, which should justly alarm us all."[20] Under the rights of the 1689 Toleration Act of William and Mary, Makemie and other ministers had secured licenses as Dissenters. The act allowed Trinitarian Dissenters, with the exception of Roman Catholics, to secure such a license. Makemie's house had been designated an authorized preaching point in Anglican-established Virginia; he had obtained a Dissenters license from Barbados.

In June of 1707, Makemie appeared in court with three skilled lawyers, who argued that Cornbury's requirement for an additional license to preach in New York was illegal. He participated in his own defense during the trial, being rather well versed in colonial laws related to religious freedoms. Makemie would publish an account of his trial in *A Narrative of a New and Unusual Imprisonment of Two Presbyterian Ministers and Prosecution of Mr. Francis Makemie.*[21] Though acquitted at the trial, Makemie was forced by the governor to pay court costs for both the defense and the prosecution. Cornbury defended his actions in a letter to the Lords Commissioners of Trade and Plantation in London. He wrote that Makemie was a "Jack of all Trades he is

---

Klett's critical edition of the original manuscript minutes. Spelling, capitalization, and abbreviations from the original manuscripts are preserved.

19. Nichols, *Presbyterianism in New York State*, 17–22.

20. Makemie to Colman, March 28, 1707, xlix.

21. The full manuscript is printed in *The Life and Writings of Francis Makemie*, ed. Boyd S. Schlenther (Philadelphia: Presbyterian Historical Society, 1971), 189–244.

a Preacher, a Doctor Physick, a Merchant, an Attorney, or Counsellor at Law, and, which is worse of all, a Disturber of Governments."[22]

Responding to Cornbury's unjust treatment of Makemie, the New York Assembly charged Cornbury with violating the liberties of the people and removed him in 1709. Widespread knowledge of the trial gave Presbyterians an enhanced reputation as advocates of religious liberty in the colonies. The judge in the case observed that this was the first public trial over religious persecution in the colonies.[23] Boston minister Cotton Mather wrote to a friend: "That brave man, Mr. Makemie has after a famous Trial at N.York, bravely triumphed over the Act of Uniformity and the other Poenal Lawes for the Ch. of England. . . . The Non-Con[formist] Religion and Interest, is, thro' the Blessing of God on the Agency of that Excellent person, Likely to prevail mightily in the Southern Colonies."[24]

Makemie returned to his farm in Accomack, Virginia, where his health would deteriorate over the next year. He continued as pastor of the Rehoboth church in Maryland. In his will, written in April 1708, he left the land at Rehoboth, which had a new church building, "for ye ends and uses of a Presbyterian Congregation as if I were personally present and to theire successors forever and none else but to such of ye same persuasion in matters of Religion." The May presbytery minutes do not indicate that Makemie was present, although a letter written by him is mentioned. Makemie likely died in July on his farm in Virginia.[25]

PRESBYTERY PRACTICE

The presbytery gave specific directions on ministerial duties. A 1708 overture was agreed upon that stipulated the following: "First that evry minister in their respective congregations reade & comment upon a chapter of the bible every Lords day as discretion [and] ye circumstances of tyme, place &c. will admit. Second over: that it be recommended to evry minister of the Presbytery set on foot & encourage private christian societies. Third over: that every minister of the Presbytery supplie neighbouring desolate places where a minister is

---

22. *The Life and Writings of Francis Makemie*, 24. It was not uncommon during this era for clergy to practice medicine. One of Makemie's Presbyterian colleagues, Samuel Davis, also practiced medicine; see 276n77.

23. *The Life and Writings of Francis Makemie*, 24, 25.

24. *Diary of Cotton Mather*, 1:599, quoted in *The Life and Writings of Francis Makemie*, 25.

25. *The Life and Writings of Francis Makemie*, 28.

wanting & opportunity of doing good offers."[26] The member churches of the presbytery looked to the gathered ministers and elders to resolve disputes in the congregations (3, 4). That same year, the congregation at Woodbridge called Nathanial Wade as pastor; Wade had been ordained by ministers in Connecticut. Letters from the congregation to the presbytery reveal that a "Difference betwixt yt People and Mr Wade" had developed. Three ministers were directed to read over the letters and give a summary report to the 1708 presbytery meeting. The controversy was prolonged by many letters written by the presbytery to the congregation. Wade would eventually leave the congregation, and there were calls for peace (5–6).

In 1709 the presbytery sent a letter to the ministers in Boston pleading for ministers and financial support, which were so desperately needed in the middle colonies. They reference the evangelizing efforts of Makemie (now deceased) and state that they are ready to start eight congregations. The Presbyterians appealed for help "to carry on so necessary and glorious a work, otherwise many people will remain in a perishing Condition as to spiritual things" (73, 74 "Letter Book"). One of the primary tasks of the presbytery was to prepare and examine candidates for ministry. The 1710 minutes of the Philadelphia Presbytery mention a "great-Valley" congregation in Chester County, Pennsylvania, and its lay preacher David Evans. The presbytery censured Evans for acting "irregularly" and appointed three ministers to assist in "Learning & Study" so that Evans could be prepared for examination and licensed "publickly to teach or preach." While he was a "candidate," Evans was allowed to preach "under the Direction & Inspection" of these ministers; he was also chosen as the presbytery clerk (9–13). Finally, in 1714, having been satisfied with his "ministerial Qualifications," five ministers "by fasting, prayer and Imposition of hands solemnly set him apart to the work of the Ministry" (15–23).

The presbytery encouraged the important ministry of elders in the local churches. Presbytery minutes in 1714 recorded, "For the better establishing and settling Congregations, It is ordered and appointed, that in every Congregation there be a sufficient Number of Assistants [elders] chosen, to aid the Minister in the Management of Congregation Affairs, and that there be a Book of Records [Session minutes] for that Effect, and that the same be annually brought here to be revised by the Presbytery" (22). Congregations were represented in the presbytery by elders as well as ministers. A presbytery meeting on September 18, 1716, lists as those present eight ministers and four elders; those absent were nine ministers "and their Elders" (26).

---

26. Klett, *Minutes*, 3. Hereafter, page references from this work will be given in parentheses in the text.

The presbytery expanded rapidly, with additional churches joining her ranks over the next decade. Churches on Long Island (Southampton, Jamaica, Newtown, Setauket, Goshen) entered the presbytery, along with a New York City congregation of Presbyterians that had organized themselves in 1717. Presbyterians had difficulty flourishing in Maryland and Virginia due to the established Anglicanism of those colonies. Scots-Irish immigrants and Presbyterian clergy tended to avoid these colonies, but there were a few Presbyterians there. In the Jersey colonies, the congregations of Woodbridge, Newark, Elizabethtown, Shrewsbury, Pittsgrove, Fairton, and Cold Spring joined the presbytery. The colonial Jersey provinces, which had been purchased by Quakers in 1677 (West Jersey) and 1682 (East Jersey), allowed for freedom of worship.[27]

Pennsylvania became the home of thousands of Scots-Irish beginning in the early decades of the eighteenth century. Charles II in 1681 had granted the large Pennsylvania territory (present-day Pennsylvania and Delaware) to Quaker leader William Penn (1644–1718) to satisfy a debt owed to Penn's father. Penn instituted a "charter of liberties" for his "Holy Experiment" in the new province, which guaranteed freedom of religion. Pennsylvania would become a haven for Quakers, Mennonites, Lutherans, Catholics, Jews, and Presbyterians. Pennsylvania congregations of Scots-Irish heritage began trickling into the presbytery, and by 1715 included the Great-Valley and Welch-Tract congregations in Chester County. In the following decades, Presbyterians would proliferate in Pennsylvania.[28]

With the increasing number of congregations, and their geographic dispersion, it seemed prudent to consider expanding the Presbyterian organization in America. A plan to establish a synod, consisting of four distinct presbyteries, was put forward in 1716. One of the presbyteries never came into existence, but three new presbyteries began to function: Long Island, New Castle, and Philadelphia. The number of clergy in the synod had increased to twenty-five. The jurisdiction of the synod over the three presbyteries was not clear, and this would cause tension among the Presbyterians in the years to come. One means of review and control was the required submission of "Presbytery-Books" (minutes) at the meetings of the synod. The 1717 minutes of the synod noted that some presbyteries were "being defective in not bringing their Presbytery-books."[29] Increasing the number of presbyteries was timely, as more Presbyterian immigrants were arriving in the colonies.

27. Trinterud, *Forming of an American Tradition*, 33, 34.

28. See Guy S. Klett, *Presbyterians in Colonial Pennsylvania* (Philadelphia: University of Pennsylvania Press, 1937).

29. Klett, *Minutes*, 31.

IMMIGRATION FROM ULSTER

One of the largest migrations to the American colonies during the eighteenth century was that of the Scots-Irish. These immigrants were descended from lowland Scots who had settled in northern Ireland during the reign of James I. The "Ulster Plantation" had been an attempt to Anglicize Ireland, expand influence, and provide economic opportunity. There had been attempts at emigration in the previous century, and by the time of the Great Migration of 1717, there were a few Ulstermen in most of the colonies. The first major wave of immigration began in 1717, and afterward a steady stream of Ulster Scots arrived in the middle colonies, particularly the frontier in western Pennsylvania. Their number in America would approach half a million by the end of the century.[30]

The Ulster Plantation had been an economic success, but its success caused the English Parliament to begin restricting Irish exports, fearing competition with English goods. The restrictions imposed upon the wool industry were devastating to Scots-Irish prosperity, making immigration to America more inviting. Another contributing factor to the first mass Scots-Irish emigration of 1717 was the practice of "rack-renting" (raising land rental) in Ulster. One reason Scots had been drawn to northern Ireland in the late seventeenth century was the availability of land to lease at low cost and for a long term. Lease agreements were typically thirty-one years, which allowed farmers time to develop their land. In the first two decades of the eighteenth century, a large number of these leases were expiring, and the landlords, interested in increased profits, often doubled or tripled the rent when the leases expired. Numbers of dispossessed farmers returned to Scotland or decided to take their chances in America. The immediate economic catalyst leading up to the exodus of 1717 was a series of bad years for farmers. Successive years of drought in Ireland from 1714 to 1719 devastated the yield of crops, which included flax needed for thread by the linen industry. As a result, food costs soared in the towns. In addition, in 1716 the sheep were struck with disease. The economic factors—trade restrictions, rack rent, crop failures, etc.—were all incentives to risk the arduous Atlantic voyage.

The religious context also prodded departure from Ulster. In addition to economic oppression, Presbyterian Dissenters also faced religious discrimination. Religious toleration had taken a leap forward in William and Mary's

---

30. For an overview of statistics on Scots-Irish immigration to America, see James G. Leyburn, *The Scotch-Irish: A Social History* (Chapel Hill: University of North Carolina Press, 1962), 179–83.

Revolution of 1688–1689, which relieved some of the oppression Presbyterians had experienced under Charles II and James II. Anglican bishops in Ireland had been rather tolerant of the Presbyterians, but the accession of Queen Anne in 1702 put the High Church party in power, and the Irish bishops pressed for ecclesiastical uniformity. The 1703 Test Act requiring all officeholders in Ireland to take the sacrament according to the Anglican rubric was intended to suppress Roman Catholics, yet it was also used against the Presbyterians. Many Presbyterian ministers were forced to leave their pulpits, which meant weddings and funerals now required an Anglican priest. Presbyterians in government or the military faced a new religious test of their conscience.

The first wave of emigration in 1717–1718 commenced after four straight years of drought; for many, there were few reasons left to remain in Ulster. Over five thousand Scots-Irish set sail for America during the first year. Many of these Presbyterian pioneers entered the colony of Pennsylvania, where they found cheap land, fertile soil, and religious liberty. As word returned to Ulster about the good fortunes of their brethren in the New World, more were encouraged to consider immigration to the colonies. Jonathan Dickinson (1688–1747) wrote about the Scots-Irish immigration into Philadelphia in the summer of 1717: "we have had 12 or 13 sayle of ships from the North of Ireland with a swarm of people."[31]

Essential and Necessary Articles

When the first presbytery was organized in 1706, the Presbyterians did not immediately craft a constitution with doctrinal standards, a plan for church government, or directions for worship. Though personally committed to Reformed theology, they did not see the immediate necessity of adopting an official constitution. However, as time passed, increasingly more of them believed that a key ingredient for the future strength of the young ecclesiastical body would be official adoption of a public statement of faith. This issue became divisive as discussions unfolded in the 1720s. The debate and final compromise over confessional subscription would be a defining moment for American Presbyterians.[32] To comprehend why contemplating a confession

31. Leyburn, *The Scotch-Irish*, 170.

32. For an overview of the confessional subscription debates, see S. Donald Fortson III, *The Presbyterian Creed: A Confessional Tradition in America, 1729–1870* (Milton Keynes, UK: Paternoster, 2008), and *The Practice of Confessional Subscription*, ed. David W. Hall (Lanham, MD: University Press of America, 1995).

became an American controversy, one must understand how Presbyterians in the Old World had dealt with this question in recent decades. Arguably, the most important situation for the Americans was how this issue had unfolded in northern Ireland.

The Synod of Ulster in 1689 had declared that "young men licensed to preach be obliged to subscribe to our Confession of Faith in all the articles thereof, as the Confession of their faith."[33] Facing a threat of Arian theology in Dublin Presbytery, the General Synod tightened the subscription formula in 1705. In reaction, some Presbyterians formed the Belfast Society in opposition to strict subscription. To secure peace among the brethren, Robert Craighead of Dublin, the moderator of Synod in 1720, proposed a conciliatory plan. The 1720 Irish Pacific Act was a compromise intended to harmonize the stances of the disparate parties; it allowed for candidates and ministers to state exceptions: "if any person called upon to subscribe shall scruple any phrase or phrases in the Confession, he shall have leave to use his own expressions, which the Presbytery shall accept of, providing they judge such a person sound in the faith and that such expressions are consistent with the substance of the doctrine, and that such explications shall be inserted in the Presbytery books."[34]

Allowing persons to register "scruples" regarding confessional statements affirmed liberty of conscience, which was attractive to the Americans; they would likewise use the language of "scruple" in their own approach. Contributing to American reluctance to require subscription, however, was the fact that the Irish Pacific Act had not deterred schism. Irish ministers declining to subscribe were excluded and organized themselves into the Presbytery of Antrim in 1726. Conservatives in the Synod of Ulster announced that they were no longer able to maintain ministerial communion with the nonsubscribers and ejected them from the Synod in 1727.[35] The Irish rupture was fresh in the minds of American Presbyterians as they approached their own battle over subscription just two years after the Irish division. In many American minds, pushing confessional subscription meant potential schism.

In 1727 John Thomson (c. 1690–1753), of New Castle Presbytery, introduced an overture to Synod in favor of requiring confessional subscription. Thomson claimed it was not his intention to bring "any heat or contention"

33. Briggs, *American Presbyterianism*, 201.

34. Briggs, *American Presbyterianism*, 216–10; Trinterud, *The Forming of an American Tradition*, 49.

35. See George Ellswood Elis, "Nation, Creed and Unity: The Significance of the Subscription Controversy for the Development of Colonial Presbyterianism" (PhD diss., Temple University, 1983), 570.

to the Synod, but he was concerned for the "vindication and defense of the truths we profess, and for preventing the ingress and spreading of error." The infant Presbyterian church, which did not have its own seminary, was defenseless in an era "of so many pernicious and dangerous corruptions in doctrine."[36] Thomson recommended that Synod "publically and authoritatively adopt the Westminster Confession and Catechism, &c., for the public confession of our faith." Further, his overture asked Synod to "make an act to oblige every Presbytery within their bounds, to oblige every candidate for the ministry to subscribe or otherwise acknowledge, coram presbyterio, the said Confession of Faith, and to promise not to preach or teach contrary to it." In addition, it was proposed "that if any minister within our bounds shall take upon him to teach or preach anything contrary to any of the said articles, unless, first, he propose the said point to the Presbytery or Synod, to be by them discussed, he shall be censured so and so."[37] The overture, after initial resistance, was brought to Synod again by the New Castle Presbytery in 1728. It was deferred to the next year when all members of the Synod could be present to debate the question.

The Thomson/New Castle overture was opposed by a number of presbyters, the most influential being Jonathan Dickinson of Elizabethtown, New Jersey. The essence of Dickinson's objection was not disagreement with the Calvinistic theology of Westminster but resistance to imposing any creed in principle. Dickinson wrote to Thomson in April 1729, stating that he believed "a joint agreement in the same essential and necessary articles of Christianity, and the same methods of worship and discipline, are a sufficient bond of union . . . we have already all the external bond of union that the Scriptures require of us." The sole authority of Scripture would be undermined because "a subscription to any human composure as the test of our orthodoxy is to make it the standard of our faith, and thereby to give it the honour due only to the word of God."[38] Instead of imposing subscription, Dickinson suggested that candidates be carefully examined, that strict discipline against immoral ministers be enforced, and "that the ministers of the gospel be most diligent, faithful, and painful in the discharge of their awful trust."[39] While a number of Presbyterians sympathized with Dickinson's position, the climate of Synod was advantageous for moving ahead with Thomson's overture. Nevertheless,

36. Charles Hodge, *The Constitutional History of the Presbyterian Church in the United States of America*, pt. 1, 1705–1741 (Philadelphia: Presbyterian Board of Publication, 1851), 137–39.

37. Hodge, *The Constitutional History*, 140, 141.

38. Hodge, *The Constitutional History*, 144.

39. Briggs, *American Presbyterianism*, 213.

Dickinson's concerns would be incorporated into the final 1729 subscription principles that attempted to accommodate both sides.[40]

Twenty members were present for the September 1729 Synod meeting; seven were absent. The affair of the Confession was remitted to a committee of eight (including Dickinson and Thomson) to draft a recommendation for the Synod. The committee members represented the spectrum of opinion on the question; therefore a unanimous proposal would have to satisfy all parties if unity was to be preserved.[41] On the morning of September 19, the committee's overture was presented to the whole Synod. It was unanimously adopted "after long debating upon it." In the preamble, Synod declared, "we are undoubtedly obliged to take Care that the faith once delivered to the Saints be kept pure and uncorrupt among Us, and so handed down to our Posterity."[42]

After the preamble, the Synod pronounced its unanimous consent that all ministers "shall declare their agreement in and approbation of the Confession of Faith with the larger and shorter Catechisms of the assembly of Divines at Westminster, as being in all the essential and necessary Articles, good Forms of sound words and systems of Christian Doctrine; and do also adopt the said Confession and Catechisms as the Confession of our Faith." It was agreed that a candidate or minister must declare "his Agreement in opinion with all the Essential and Necessary Articles of said Confession, either by subscribing the said Confession of Faith and Catechisms, or by a verbal Declaration of their assent thereto, as such Minister or Candidate shall think best" (103, 104). The Synod also endorsed a method whereby ministers could exercise liberty of conscience by stating scruples publicly before the brethren. These scruples, however, must "be only about articles not essential and necessary." The Synod or presbytery was to make final judgment on these scruples and determine whether or not said scruples were "only about articles not Essential and necessary in Doctrine, Worship or Government" (104).

In the afternoon session, after the morning session minutes were read, which articulated the agreed-upon meaning of subscription, each member of the Synod was given the opportunity of "proposing all the Scruples yt any of them had to make against any Articles and Expressions in the Confession of Faith and larger and shorter Catechisms." After individual scruples were "unanimously agreed" to be acceptable, that is, not about "essential and necessary" doctrines, the whole Synod "unanimously declare[d]" exceptions to certain statements in

40. See Bryan F. Le Beau, *Jonathan Dickinson and the Formative Years of American Presbyterianism* (Lexington: University of Kentucky Press, 1997), 27–44.

41. Trinterud, *Forming of an American Tradition*, 49; Briggs, *American Presbyterianism*, 216.

42. Klett, *Minutes*, 103. Hereafter, page references from this work will be given in parentheses in the text.

chapters 20 and 23, which spoke of the civil magistrate's power over church affairs. Since these scruples were held in common by every member present, they were recorded in the minutes. These uniform exceptions having been noted, the Synod declared the "Confession and Catechisms to be the Confession of their faith" (104). The afternoon session thus completed the work that had begun in the morning. Having openly acknowledged every scruple before one another as the morning minutes had directed, the Synod had now completed their work of adopting the Westminster Standards. Anticipating that there would be differences of opinion, the Adopting Act concluded with these words: "And the Synod do solemnly agree, that none of us will traduce or use any opprobrious Terms of those yt differ from us in these extra-essential and not-necessary points of doctrine, but treat them with the same friendship, kindness and brotherly Love, as if they had not differed from us in such Sentiments" (104).

The first heresy trial in American Presbyterian history, the trial of the Reverend Samuel Hemphill of Philadelphia, would directly relate to the Adopting Act. Hemphill was received by the Synod in 1734 from the Presbytery of Straban in Ireland, where he had been ordained. Hemphill had subscribed to the Confession according to the formula used in Ireland, and he was recommended to the Synod with "satisfactory Certificates from the same Presbry of his Qualifications for and Ordination to the sacred Ministry." Synod minutes record simply that he was "admitted a member of this Synod." Hemphill served as an assistant to Jedidiah Andrews at the (First) Presbyterian Church in Philadelphia and quickly drew attention in the city as a fine preacher. It was soon discovered, however, that Hemphill had plagiarized a number of sermons, including a sermon from a Dr. Samuel Clarke (1675–1729), an English clergyman identified with Unitarian theology.[43] A commission of Synod, acting on behalf of the whole Synod, investigated the situation, and charges were brought against Hemphill for Arminianism and Socinianism (anti-Trinitarianism). The charges were sustained unanimously, and Hemphill was suspended from ministerial office in 1735.[44] The Hemphill trial became a public controversy; a twenty-nine-year-old Benjamin Franklin used his Philadelphia printing press to criticize the Presbyterians.[45]

---

43. Samuel Clarke's book, *Scripture-Doctrine of the Trinity* (1712), was condemned by many in England; he was labeled an "Arian" by his opponents.

44. Le Beau, *Jonathan Dickinson*, 45–63; William S. Barker, "The Heresy Trial of Samuel Hemphill (1735)," in *Colonial Presbyterianism: Old Faith in a New Land*, ed. S. Donald Fortson III (Eugene, OR: Pickwick, 2007), 87–111; Marilyn Westerkamp, *Triumph of the Laity: Scots-Irish Piety and the Great Awakening, 1625–1760* (New York: Oxford University Press, 1988), 158–61.

45. Melvin Buxbaum, *Benjamin Franklin and the Zealous Presbyterians* (University Park: Pennsylvania State University Press, 1975), 76–115; Merton A. Christensen, "Franklin on the

Jonathan Dickinson wrote a formal defense of the Synod's action in 1735, *A Vindication of the Reverend Commission of the Synod In Answer to Some Observations On their Proceedings against the Reverend Mr. Hemphill,* responding to Franklin's critique.[46] According to Dickinson, Hemphill had brought this trouble on himself. At his admission into the Synod, Hemphill assented to the Confession without exception, as he had done previously in Ireland. This was dishonest. Hemphill "should have particularly offered his objections, and submitted it to the judgment of the Synod, whether the articles objected against were essential and necessary or not." Dickinson adds, "Nor is it any excuse that the Synod have not defined how many fundamental articles there are in the Confession, since they have reserved to themselves the liberty to judge upon each occasion what are, and what are not, fundamental."[47] The basic principles of the Adopting Act were recounted by Dickinson as the pattern that should have been followed and would have prevented this embarrassment over Hemphill.

The controversy over Hemphill would be just the beginning of Presbyterian struggles with confessional subscription. The Adopting Act, while intended as a bond of union for Presbyterians, would foment disunion among disparate parties in the church in the years ahead. Yet, long term, the original subscription principles of 1729 would stand the test of time as a prudent path for peace among American Presbyterians devoted to both a common creed and liberty of conscience.[48]

Hemphill Trial: Deism versus Presbyterian Orthodoxy," *William & Mary Quarterly* (July 1953): 422–40.

46. According to Will Barker, members of the Commission of Synod also likely contributed to the *Vindication of the Reverend Commission*; see Barker, "The Heresy Trial of Samuel Hemphill (1735)," 98, 99.

47. Barker, "The Heresy Trial of Samuel Hemphill (1735)," 105.

48. For the Westminster Confession's historic role within Presbyterianism, see Alexander C. Cheyne, "The Place of the Confession through Three Centuries," in *The Westminster Confession in the Church Today*, ed. Alasdair I. C. Heron (Edinburgh: Saint Andrew Press, 1984), 17–53.

CHAPTER 7

A Great Awakening Shapes the Church

The historic roots of the eighteenth-century evangelical awakenings in America and Britain lay in Continental Pietism (Lutheran and Reformed) and English Puritanism. At their core, these movements were about "religion of the heart"—genuine conversion wrought by the Holy Spirit, and holiness of life that, of necessity, followed such regeneration by the Spirit. In seventeenth-century Germany, Lutheran pastor Jacob Spener (1635-1705) had called for the revival of the cold state church by a return to the biblical piety of "our sainted Luther." Spener had been influenced by a book by fellow German Johann Arndt (1555-1621), *True Christianity* (1606), and was also aware of similar emphases in the Reformed churches.[1] Spener's proposals for reform were articulated in his book *Pia Desideria* (1675), in which he outlined his *collegia pietatis* concept of small group meetings devoted to prayer, Scripture study, and personal spiritual growth. August Hermann Franke (1663-1727), a protégé of Spener, would advance these ideas through the Pietist University of Halle, founded in 1694. From the University of Halle, students spread the Pietist message through world missions, evangelism, care for the poor, medical care, and publishing.[2]

Conversion and holiness of life were emphases also found among the English Puritans; a leader among them was the Reformed pastor and prolific writer Richard Baxter. Widely known for evangelism, discipleship, social ministry, and ecumenism, Baxter was the foremost English clergyman of his

---

1. Arndt was a disciple of Philip Melanchthon, having studied in Wittenberg.

2. For a history of Pietism, see Roger E. Olson and Christian T. Collins, *Reclaiming Pietism: Retrieving an Evangelical Tradition* (Grand Rapids: Eerdmans, 2015), 38–80; see also Dale W. Brown, *Understanding Pietism*, rev. ed. (Nappanee, IN: Evangel Publishing House, 1996).

generation and leader of the Presbyterian party after the Restoration in 1660. His chief concern for reforming England was always the conversion of "dead-hearted" souls: "Alas! Can we think that the reformation is wrought, when we cast out a few ceremonies, and changed some vestures, and gestures, and forms! Oh no, sirs! It is the converting and saving of souls that is our business. That is the chiefest part of reformation, that doth most good, and tendeth most to the salvation of the people."[3] In America, the Puritan accent on conversion and holiness was pervasive in the noteworthy ministry of Cotton Mather of Boston. At North (Second) Church, the largest congregation in New England, Mather accentuated the necessity of new birth, "making it the first and principal application of nearly all his sermons," constantly calling for repentance. He was likewise concerned for the people's sanctification, urging daily times of prayer and Bible reading, as well as pursuing the practice of piety in one's vocation. Mather enjoyed an annual itinerant preaching ministry, spreading this message in New England.[4] Another New England minister known for his evangelical preaching was Solomon Stoddard, pastor of the Congregational church in Northampton, Massachusetts. During his forty-seven-year ministry, he witnessed several "harvests" of souls. Stoddard's grandson Jonathan Edwards succeeded him as pastor of the Northampton church.[5]

Reformed Roots of the Awakening

The initial stage of the great eighteenth-century awakening in America is typically considered to be the preaching of Dutch Reformed minister Theodorus Jacobus Frelinghuysen (1691–1747), who was deeply influenced by the Dutch Pietism of Wilhelmus à Brakel (1635–1711). Frelinghuysen was an advocate of "experimental divinity," insisting upon faith and repentance for conversion, with subsequent joy and obedience as fruit of new birth. He developed a reputation for being judgmental in his outspoken critique of those who opposed his message. Frelinghuysen immigrated to America in 1720 and began preaching the necessity of genuine conversion in the Raritan Valley of New Jersey, with

3. Richard Baxter, *The Reformed Pastor* (1656, reprint, Carlisle, PA: Banner of Truth Trust, 1974), 211. Baxter is often considered a prototype of evangelicalism.

4. Richard Lovelace, *The American Pietism of Cotton Mather: Origins of American Evangelicalism* (Grand Rapids: Eerdmans, 1979), 73–109; Rick Kennedy, *The First American Evangelical: A Short Life of Cotton Mather* (Grand Rapids: Eerdmans, 2015), 87–98.

5. See Harry S. Stout, *The New England Soul: Preaching and Religious Culture in Colonial New England* (New York: Oxford University Press, 1986).

significant results in the Dutch communities. George Whitefield (1714–1770) met Frelinghuysen in America and described him as "a worthy old soldier of Jesus Christ, and the beginner of the great work which I trust the Lord is carrying on in these parts."[6]

The writings and ministry of Mather and Frelinghuysen represent two of the historic streams behind the rushing waters of the eighteenth-century American awakening: New England Puritanism and Continental Pietism. There was a third stream, the heart religion of Scots-Irish Presbyterianism with its tradition of "holy fairs," or communion seasons where persons were revived or converted as a result of multiday preaching festivals associated with the celebration of the Lord's Supper.[7]

The traditional Scottish pattern for a sacramental season was adopted by Presbyterian preachers in America. The weekend services would begin on Friday with a time of fasting and prayer; Saturday included further preparations and exhortations by the ministers; Sunday was the day for the sermon and the Lord's Supper; on Monday, time was afforded to praise, thanksgiving, and encouragement to persevere in Christian living.[8] These communion seasons would become a staple of the American revivalists. Large crowds would gather to hear fiery preaching urging them to examine their souls, experience the new birth, and commit their lives to serious Christian discipleship. When the awakening arrived in America, Presbyterian support centered around a group of ministers associated with William Tennent Sr. (1673–1746) in Pennsylvania.

Tennent was an Ulster immigrant who had been educated at Edinburgh and ordained as an Anglican in 1704. Due to a change in convictions, when he came to the New World he sought out the Presbyterians for membership. He was received by the Synod in 1718 and served pastorates in New York. In 1726 he moved to the Presbyterian congregation on Little Neshaminy Creek in Bucks County, near Philadelphia. Tennent was troubled by the shortage of

---

6. *George Whitefield's Journals* (London: Banner of Truth Trust, 1969), November 20, 1739, 352.

7. Thomas Kidd, *The Great Awakening: The Roots of Evangelical Christianity in Colonial America* (New Haven: Yale University Press, 2007), 30. The rationale for the introduction of these outdoor communion celebrations has been explored in his chap. 5, pp. 57, 58. Leigh Eric Schmidt, *Holy Fairs: Scotland and the Making of American Revivalism*, 2nd ed. (Grand Rapids: Eerdmans, 2001), 21–32. Schmidt observes: "From at least the 1730s, the evangelical movement had been gaining momentum in the middle colonies; the sacramental season, a traditional source of revitalization for the Presbyterians, provided a notable portion of that impetus" (54); see also Marilyn J. Westerkamp, *Triumph of the Laity: Scots-Irish Piety and the Great Awakening, 1625–1760* (New York: Oxford University Press, 1988); see above, chap. 5.

8. Schmidt, *Holy Fairs*, 55.

Presbyterian ministers in the middle colonies and began training several of his sons for ministry, eventually opening his own private ministerial academy. Eventually, he built a log structure near his home where he instructed ministerial candidates.[9] Tennent's "Log College," as detractors referred to it, prepared twenty-one men for ministry, including four sons of Tennent during its existence up through the early 1740s. Students at the Log College received traditional training in biblical languages, theology, and preaching, but Tennent also emphasized "experimental orthodoxy" (piety), stressing that godly character was crucial for effective gospel ministry.[10]

Tennent's academy was no innovation; the pattern of older clergy tutoring young men to prepare them for Presbyterian ordination had been practiced in Scotland and Ireland. The minutes of Synod indicate that numerous options for theological training were acceptable to Presbyterians at the time. Ministerial students might receive individual tutoring, attend a private academy, or pursue collegiate classical studies (in Britain or America) supplemented with reading theology under a pastor/mentor to prepare for ordination. Other early eighteenth-century private academies led by Presbyterian ministers included those of Samuel Blair (1712–1751) at Faggs Manor, Pennsylvania; Jonathan Dickinson at Elizabethtown, New Jersey; and Samuel Finley (1715–1766) at West Nottingham, Maryland.[11]

REVIVAL COMES TO THE COLONIES

In 1726, William Tennent's oldest son, Gilbert (1703–1764), was ordained by the Presbytery of Philadelphia and began ministry to a Presbyterian congregation in New Brunswick, New Jersey. Young Tennent knew of Frelinghuysen's

9. Archibald Alexander, *Biographical Sketches of the Founder and Principal Alumni of the Log College, Together with an account of the revivals of religion under their ministry* (Philadelphia: Presbyterian Board of Publication, 1851; originally published in 1846 as *History of the Log College*). Alexander's account is one of the key sources on the Log College. He would be the first professor of Princeton Seminary in 1812, and he viewed the old Log College as a model for the new seminary.

10. See David C. Calhoun, "The Log College," in *Colonial Presbyterianism: Old Faith in a New Land*, ed. S. Donald Fortson III (Eugene, OR: Pickwick, 2007).

11. Jack C. Whytock, *An Educated Clergy: Scottish Theological Education and Training in the Kirk and Secession, 1560–1850* (Milton Keynes, UK: Paternoster, 2007); this work describes the Scottish ministerial academies used outside of the Church of Scotland by dissenting Presbyterians. Similar academies were created in America, serving the church's educational needs until more formal colleges and seminaries were established. Kidd, *The Great Awakening*, 31–32.

fruitful labors in the Dutch community, and would become frustrated with his own ineffectiveness in converting souls in contrast to the elder Frelinghuysen. During a severe sickness, he made a decision to direct his own preaching toward revival. Gilbert Tennent began urging his congregation to serious spiritual examination and explaining to them the necessity of the new birth. Frelinghuysen and Tennent started conducting worship services together in Dutch and English; this drew criticism from the Dutch, who complained of collaboration with an "English Dissenter." A mark of Frelinghuysen's ministry was his willingness to cross ecclesiastical boundaries, participating in the work of revival with Presbyterians, the German Reformed, and Anglicans in the early years of the Great Awakening. Gilbert Tennent and his Presbyterian pro-awakening brethren would share this same ecumenical spirit. Partnership in evangelistic preaching, and the resulting harvest of souls across denominations, brought spiritual unity to the colonies through the shared religious experience of the new birth.[12]

Tennent's preaching was transformed, and his congregation in New Brunswick responded with new spiritual life and conversions. He recalled the situation: "Frequently at Sacramental Seasons in New-Brunswick, there have been signal Displays of the divine Power and Presence: divers have been convicted of Sin by the Sermons then preached, some converted, and many much affected with the Love of God in JESUS CHRIST. O the sweet Meltings I have often seen on such Occasion among many!"[13] In addition to ministry among his flock, he regularly did pulpit supply on Staten Island; describing one occasion in 1728, he said the people "fell upon their Knees in the Time of the Sermon, in order to pray to God for pardoning Mercy."[14]

After his own dramatic conversion experience, Gilbert's brother John practiced the passionate preaching style of his brother during his short three-year pastorate at the Presbyterian church in Freehold, New Jersey. He died prematurely in 1732, and his brother William Jr. (1705–1777) took over pastoral responsibilities at Freehold the next year. Like his brothers, William Jr. witnessed revival in the congregation under his care. A relative reported that on one Lord's Day, during the evening service at Freehold, William Jr. experienced a remarkable joy in his soul and preached with great solemnity. That evening

---

12. James Tanis, *Dutch Calvinistic Pietism in the Middle Colonies: A Study in the Life and Theology of Theodorus Jacobus Frelinghuysen* (The Hague: Martinus Nijhoff, 1967), 67–79.

13. Thomas Prince, *Christian History*, November 10, 1744, quoted in Kidd, *The Great Awakening*, 30.

14. Milton Coalter, *Gilbert Tennent, Son of Thunder: A Case Study of Continental Pietism's Impact on the First Great Awakening in the Middle Colonies* (Westport, CT: Greenwood, 1986), 40.

"proved the happy means of the conversion of about thirty persons. This day he spoke of ever afterwards as his harvest day." Pastoral visitation was a very important part of his long ministry at Freehold; he was sure "to carry the riches of Christ to every house," including preaching to children and slaves.[15]

Samuel Blair, a Log College graduate licensed by New Castle Presbytery, took a call to the New Londonderry church in Faggs Manor, Pennsylvania, and there witnessed a remarkable revival in the summer of 1740. In his "faithful narrative" recounting the awakening, he described the "sabbath assemblies," which drew large crowds from the surrounding areas, in which people sobbed and fainted, and occasionally a few experienced some "strange, unusual bodily motions," as the people were "brought into deep distress of soul about their perishing state." Blair would exhort the congregation to restrain their emotional displays so as not to distract from the sermon, "but not so as to resist or stifle convictions." During that summer the theme of his preaching was the "awful condition of such as were not in Christ" and the "nature and necessity of faith in Christ, the Mediator." In his sermons he emphasized that a "right peace" was not found in their repentings, reformations, visions, or dreams, "but by an understanding view and believing persuasion of the way of life, as revealed in the gospel, through the surety, obedience and sufferings of Jesus Christ.... Thereupon freely accepting him for their Saviour." Blair described how many were converted "with satisfying evidence that the Lord had brought them to closure with Jesus Christ . . . they were enabled to believe in Christ with unspeakable joy and full of glory."[16]

In the 1730s, other pastors in the middle colonies began experiencing revival, and reports of revival also surfaced in New England. Congregational minister Jonathan Edwards witnessed revival in his Northhampton, Massachusetts, congregation in 1734–1735 and wrote about it in *A Faithful Narrative of the Surprising Work of God in the Conversion of Many Souls in Northhampton* (1737). When church authorities criticized the emotional excesses popularly associated with the revivals, Edwards ably defended the awakening in his essay "Distinguishing Marks of a Work of the Spirit of God" (1741). In it he argued that despite incidents of heightened affections, the "extraordinary influence that has lately appeared on the minds of people abroad in this land, causing in them an uncommon concern and engagedness of mind about the things

15. Alexander, *Biographical Sketches*, 109, 110, 112.

16. Blair to Thomas Prince Jr., August 6, 1744, published in *The Christian History containing accounts of the revival and propagation of religion in Great Britain & America* (no. 1-104, March 5, 1743–February 23, 1744), ed. Thomas Prince Jr. (Boston: S. Kneeland and T. Green, 1744–1745), quoted in Alexander, *Biographical Sketches*, 155-73.

of religion, is undoubtedly, in the general, from the Spirit of God."[17] Edwards maintained close ties with Presbyterians over the years, serving a Presbyterian congregation in New York when he was a young minister and finishing his ministry as president of the College of New Jersey.

The great evangelist of the American awakening was the Anglican George Whitefield, a close associate of the Wesley brothers, who led the revival in Britain during this period. Whitefield was a gifted orator who zealously preached the new birth from Georgia to Maine during seven tours of the colonies. When Whitefield came to Philadelphia in 1739, he aligned himself with the work of the Tennents. The Log College impressed young Whitefield, who wrote of the "gracious Youths" being trained there for work in the "Lord's Vineyard . . . to me it seemed to resemble the Schools of the old Prophets."[18] When Whitefield heard Gilbert Tennent preach, he wrote in his journal: "I never before heard such a searching sermon. He convinced me more and more that we can preach the Gospel of Christ no further than we have experienced the power of it in our own hearts. Being deeply convicted of sin, by God's Holy Spirit, at his first conversion, he has learned experimentally to dissect the heart of a natural man. Hypocrites must either soon be converted or enraged at his preaching. He is a son of thunder, and does not fear the faces of men."[19] After a 1740 preaching tour of New England, Whitefield asked Gilbert Tennent to follow up and revisit the preaching points to encourage converts. Yet, Presbyterian association with Whitefield would prove problematic.[20]

Debate and Schism

As a leader of the New Side ("New Lights") pro-awakening party in the middle colonies, Gilbert Tennent advocated "preaching of the terrors" (wrath of God) to awaken secure sinners to their plight before a holy God. According to Tennent, the Holy Spirit used this kind of preaching to convict lost souls, and clergymen who did not preach the terrors were hindering God's work. Concerned about the spiritual decline of Presbyterian congregations, he had presented an overture to the 1734 Synod urging special care in refusing admission to the ministry any that lacked "a work of sanctifying grace in their

17. Jonathan Edwards, "Distinguishing Marks of a Work of God," in *Works of Jonathan Edwards*, vol. 4 (New Haven: Yale University Press, 1972), 260.

18. *George Whitefield's Journals*, November 22, 1739, 354.

19. *George Whitefield's Journals*, November 14, 1739, 347, 348.

20. Whitefield's ministry was also condemned in Scotland by Ebenezer and Ralph Erskine of the Secession Church. The Erskine brothers and Whitefield eventually reconciled.

hearts."[21] Tennent and his colleagues in New Brunswick Presbytery came into further tension with the brethren by preaching outside the bounds of their own presbytery without permission. This itinerant ministry included encouraging church members to separate from unconverted ministers and seek out congregations where they received the most good. The Old Side ("Old Lights") anti-awakening ministers objected to this emotional preaching style and bitterly resented Tennent's judgmental attitude toward them.

William Tennent Sr.'s academy began falling into disfavor because of its association with the awakening and Whitefield. Revivalist demands for a godly ministry, and willingness to call into question the spirituality of fellow clergy not supporting the revival, would become intensely divisive. In 1736, two presbyteries raised concerns about the adequacy of a Log College education, and an "examining act" was passed that called for an examining committee to test privately educated candidates. The newly established New Brunswick Presbytery defiantly licensed a Log College graduate, John Rowland (who had been rejected by New Castle Presbytery), just three months after the new rule was adopted.

In May of 1740 Gilbert Tennent and Samuel Blair exacerbated an already tension-filled meeting of Synod when they publicly read a list of complaints against their fellow ministers. Blair charged his colleagues with preaching works righteousness and ignoring the doctrine of the new birth. Tennent added that ministers were leaving sinners in deadly security, and he rebuked his brethren for attacking revivals.[22] He also accused the Synod of "Great stiffness in Opinion, generally in smaller Matters where good Men may differ." Four months after the Synod meeting had adjourned, several members of New Castle Presbytery presented a list of defects in Whitefield's theology. Blair, who was present at the meeting, attempted to answer the accusations, but the presbytery authorized the printing of the accusations anyway. Whitefield's Calvinism was questioned on several points, and he was particularly criticized for ecumenical cooperation.[23] Acrimony reached a new low when Gilbert Tennent publicly rebuked the antirevival ministers in a sermon, "The Danger of an Unconverted Ministry" (1740), comparing clergy naysayers to Pharisees who "deserve the wrath and curse of a sin-avenging God."[24]

21. Guy S. Klett, *Minutes of the Presbyterian Church in America, 1706–1788* (Philadelphia: Presbyterian Historical Society, 1976), 122, 123.

22. Coalter, *Gilbert Tennent*, 70.

23. *The Querists, Or An Extract of Sundry Passages taken out of Mr. Whitefield's printed Sermons, Journal and Letters: Together With Some Scruples propos'd in proper Queries raised on each Remark. By some Church-Members of the Presbyterian Persuasion* (Philadelphia, 1740); the work is credited to David Evans of New Castle Presbytery.

24. "The Danger of an Unconverted Ministry," in *Sermons That Shaped America*, ed. William S. Barker and Samuel T. Logan (Phillipsburg, NJ: P&R, 2003), 130.

In 1741 the situation reached a crisis point when a conservative "protest" to the Synod announced that continued ecclesiastical union with the New Brunswick ministers had become intolerable. The protesters declared that the New Side "have at present no right to sit and vote as Members of this Synod," because of their "unwearied, unscriptural, antipresbyterial, uncharitable divisive Practices." A central objection was the awakening ministers' "Preaching the Terrors of the Law" in an unbiblical fashion that has "no Precedent in the word of God." The Old Side protesters also asserted that the awakening preachers had abandoned principles of Presbyterian government and doctrines of the Confession. A majority signed the protest, thereby proclaiming themselves the true Synod. Believing they had been unjustly excised, the ejected New Side men withdrew as the meeting adjourned, organizing themselves the next day as the conjunct presbyteries of New Brunswick and Londonderry.[25]

Members from the New York Presbytery, who were absent from the 1741 meeting, would eventually join with the conjunct presbyteries when early attempts at reconciliation failed. The New York Presbytery in 1742 and 1743 protested the illegal exclusion and put forward a compromise overture attempting to reconcile the two groups. In 1745 the Old Side offered its own proposal for union, asking that seven grievances be addressed. Each side rejected the ideas of the other, and division endured for seventeen years. In 1745 New York joined with New Brunswick, Londonderry, and New Castle to establish the Synod of New York. The Old Side henceforth referred to itself as the Synod of Philadelphia, having previously been known simply as "the Synod."[26]

THE SYNOD OF NEW YORK

The work of revival and church planting did not dissipate in the years following the 1741 schism. In 1744 William Tennent Jr. officiated during a sacramental season at a new congregation in the towns of Maidenhead and Hopewell, New Jersey. According to his account, the people were refreshed, and "some who had been distressed with Doubts about their State, received Soul-satisfying Sealings of God's everlasting Love: Others were supported and quickened, so that they returned Home rejoicing and glorifying GOD."[27] Gatherings for communion could be quite large. In summer 1745 Charles Beatty was assisted by fellow Presbyterian David Brainerd in leading a sacramental season in Ne-

25. "A Protestation Presented to the Synod June 1, 1741," in Klett, *Minutes*, 186–91.

26. For the protest and overture from the presbytery in New York, see Klett, *Minutes*, 177, 178, 181–83.

27. Quoted in Schmidt, *Holy Fairs*, 54.

shaminy, Pennsylvania, which included a crowd of three thousand to four thousand people. So impressed was Brainerd with the spiritual fruit of these services that he brought fifty Indians, whom he had been evangelizing, to the next communion assembly in the fall. Brainerd would eventually lead his own sacramental season in 1746, following the Scottish pattern. He recorded significant conviction and awakening during this "Season of divine Power among us." When the people participated in the Lord's Supper, they "seemed to be affected in a most lively Manner, as if Christ had been really crucified before them."[28]

Along with prolonged revival came more disorder and excess in a few corners. One notorious example was the case of Rev. James Davenport of Southold, Long Island. Davenport had collaborated with Gilbert Tennent in revival meetings in Philadelphia in 1740, but in the summer of 1741 he traveled on his own to Connecticut and Rhode Island for a preaching mission. A significant number of persons were converted over several months, but erratic behavior associated with his ministry discredited his labors. In emotional public worship services, Davenport attacked local ministers by name and allowed lay exhorting and prayer. He encouraged congregations to parade through the streets singing, and in one scandalous incident publicly burned his clerical vestments, showing disdain for unregenerate clergy. In 1742 he was arrested in both Hartford, Connecticut, and Boston and tried for itinerant preaching and questionable methods. Tennent was opposed to his methods but respected his piety.[29]

As there was no established church in the middle colonies, a variety of groups coexisted with rather equal status. Presbyterians competed on a level playing field with the other Christian sects, all of whom vied for the people's allegiance and a place at the social table. This interdenominational rivalry was intense between the Baptists and Presbyterians. In New England the Baptists had been persecuted by Congregationalists, thus the religious toleration practiced in the middle colonies would attract Baptists, who established a Philadelphia Baptist Association in 1707, just a year after the Presbyterians had organized themselves. In 1742 the Calvinist Baptists adopted their own statement of faith, the Philadelphia Confession, a modified version of the Westminster Confession.[30]

The catalyst for controversy between the Baptists and Presbyterians was a 1742–1743 revival among the people of Cape May, New Jersey. Ministers from

28. Jonathan Edwards, *Life of David Brainerd*, ed. Norman Pettit, in *Works of Jonathan Edwards*, vol. 7 (New Haven: Yale University Press, 1985), 383–89.

29. Coalter, *Gilbert Tennent*, 94–96, 107, 108.

30. See "The Baptist Confession of 1688 (The Philadelphia Confession)," in Philip Schaff, *The Creeds of Christendom*, vol. 3 (reprint, Grand Rapids: Baker Books, 1993), 738–41.

both denominations had participated in the spiritual harvest, but tensions emerged when some of the awakened departed the Presbyterian fold and joined the Baptists. Samuel Finley, a Log College graduate, distraught over this defection, observed that Baptist preachers were advocating the imperative of believer's baptism, and some Presbyterians had renounced their baptism as infants and were being rebaptized as adults. Finley resented what he considered an intrusion into his ministry to awakened souls. In response, Finley challenged Baptist minister Abel Morgan to a public debate on the issue of baptism.[31]

After the debate, Finley wrote *A Charitable Plea for the Speechless: Or the Right of Believers-Infants to Baptism Vindicated; And the Mode of It by Pouring or Sprinkling, Justified* (1746). Finley addressed two major questions: Do children of members of the visible church have a right to baptism? Is pouring water upon a person properly administering Christian baptism? Morgan wrote a rebuttal to Finley, and the debate continued in print for several years. Jonathan Dickinson entered the fray in 1746 with his own defense of Presbyterian baptismal practice—*A Brief Illustration and Confirmation of the Divine Right of Infant Baptism*.[32] Dickinson's work, intended for the lay reader, was written in the form of a conversation between a minister and a church member who was considering joining the Baptist church due to changing views on baptism. The Presbyterians, in addition to arguing from biblical texts, appealed to the uninterrupted practice of infant baptism since the ancient church, in contrast to the baptistic "madmen of Munster," a reference to sixteenth-century Anabaptists. The Baptists replied that Presbyterians could not fairly accuse the Baptists of being sectarian when the New Side Presbyterians were in schism with their Old Side Presbyterian brethren.[33]

Presbyterians also viewed Moravians as a threat to their ministry. Moravian roots lay in the *Unitas Fratrum* movement in Bohemia and Moravia after the

---

31. Bryan F. Le Beau, "The Acrimonious, Controversial Spirit among Baptists and Presbyterians in the Middle Colonies during the Great Awakening," *American Baptist Quarterly*, September 1990, 171, 172.

32. Dickinson's book got so much attention in the colonies that it was sent to London for a rebuttal by Baptist Dr. John Gill. Gill wrote *The Divine Right of Infant Baptism Examined and Disproved*, to which American Congregationalist Peter Clark of Salem responded in 1752 with a 485-page book, *A Defense of the Divine Right of Infant Baptism*, to vindicate Dickinson's book.

33. Le Beau, "The Acrimonious, Controversial Spirit," 172–79. Le Beau argues that the Baptist/Presbyterian debates in the middle colonies were not as acrimonious as those between Baptists and Congregationalists in New England. He also points to shared evangelical experiences that unified Baptists/Presbyterians, and that many Baptist ministers were theologically trained under Presbyterians, e.g., the College of New Jersey.

death of Jan Hus in the fifteenth century. The small group survived the Thirty Years' War, moving to the German estate of Count Nikolaus Ludwig Graf von Zinzendorf (1700–1760) in 1722.[34] Moravians were known for their serious piety and missions, but they had unique theological views that clashed with both the Methodists in Britain and the Presbyterians and Dutch Reformed in America. The Moravian version of Pietism was very ecumenical; they sought renewal by providing meeting places for Scripture study and prayer, and appealing to folks from many denominations to participate in the meetings. Zinzendorf's vision was for a "Congregation of God in the Spirit" that would ignore differences in creed while providing spiritual renewal within the church. This made people suspect that the Moravians' real goal was to make more Moravians, and to encourage people to leave their current denominations. There were also objections to specific Moravian doctrines. For Presbyterians, Moravians taught serious errors in their rejection of predestination in favor of universal salvation, in their teaching on perfectionism, in the diminished place they assigned the law in Christian life, and in their doctrine of "stillness"—the idea that one should cease from outward works and merely wait for God to provide salvation. Gilbert Tennent met with Zinzendorf during his one visit to the colonies in 1741–1742, and as a result Tennent published a treatise against him and the Moravian movement.[35]

Presbyterian conflict with Anglicans was especially intense in the southern colonies, where the Church of England was supported by the colonial government. The Virginia and Carolina Piedmont areas were unoccupied before 1730; Scots-Irish settlers, coming down the Great Philadelphia Wagon Road, began to populate the backcountry. By 1750, they had moved into the South Carolina Piedmont and north Georgia. Scots had already entered South Carolina by the 1680s, and by 1722 had formed a presbytery in the Charleston area.[36] Scottish Highlanders settled along the North Carolina seaboard and in coastal areas of Georgia, where an independent Presbyterian church was organized in Savannah in 1755.[37]

The Synod of New York sent missionaries into the southern colonies. William Robinson entered Virginia, preaching in the Shenandoah Valley and

34. Zinzendorf's estate, which he called Hernhutt, was intended to replicate Franke's orphanage and compound in Halle.

35. See Coalter, *Gilbert Tennent*, 96–104. Tennent's anti-Moravian work was titled *The Necessity of Holding Fast the Truth*. Coalter observed, "Although Tennent shared Zinzendorf's pietistic concern for spiritual rebirth, practical piety, and interdenominational cooperation, these interests were strictly circumscribed by his confessional allegiance to Calvinism" (102–3).

36. See above, chap. 6.

37. Ernest Trice Thompson, *Presbyterians in the South*, vol. 1, *1607–1861* (Richmond, VA: John Knox, 1963), 29–51. The congregation was originally known as the Independent Meeting in Savannah and later as Independent Presbyterian Church.

along the James River, in 1742–1743. He was arrested for preaching without a license and eventually had to leave Virginia permanently. New Side evangelist Samuel Davies (1723–1761) began his Virginia mission in 1747, establishing seven preaching points. Davies was harassed by the Virginia Anglican establishment but continued pressing the case for dissenters' religious liberty, appearing before the authorities on numerous occasions over several years to plead his case. The major issue was whether or not the 1689 Toleration Act, granting rights to English dissenters, was applicable in Virginia. The extended legal battle began in 1747 when Davies first entered Hanover County and was granted licenses to preach in four meetinghouses. The next year he attempted to acquire a license for fellow Presbyterian John Rogers but was denied by the governor; this was the first of multiple denials of licenses in the years that followed. Eventually, Davies was able to get the Anglican-controlled colonial government to grant the religious rights established by the Toleration Act.[38]

As Presbyterian numbers in Virginia grew, more freedom was granted. There were also concerns about physical safety on the Virginia frontier. When settlers in Virginia suffered from Indian attacks, Davies recruited troops to fight "the heathen savages and French papists" in the Seven Years' War (French and Indian War, 1756–1763). Davies took special interest in African slaves, teaching them to read the Bible, regularly preaching to several hundred and baptizing about a hundred. The famous Virginia patriot Patrick Henry (1736–1799), whose mother was Presbyterian, said Davies was the greatest orator he had ever heard. By 1755, Davies and six other ministers had organized Hanover Presbytery in Virginia, which became the mother presbytery of the Southern Presbyterian church.[39]

REUNION OF THE SYNODS

Jonathan Dickinson, the first moderator of the Synod of New York, pursued reuniting the synods in the early years after the schism. He was an intellectual leader among Presbyterians, defending Reformed commitment to Presbyterian government and Calvinism in numerous widely circulated publications.[40] And he had been a leading voice for moderation, calling for restraint of re-

38. George William Pilcher, *Samuel Davies: Apostle of Dissent in Colonial Virginia* (Knoxville: University of Tennessee Press, 1971), 119–21.

39. James H. Smylie, "Samuel Davies—Preacher, Teacher and Pastor," in *Colonial Presbyterianism: Old Faith in a New Land*, ed. S. Donald Fortson III (Eugene, OR: Wipf & Stock, 2007), 189–96.

40. See the list of Dickinson's published works in Bryan F. Le Beau, *Jonathan Dickinson and the Formative Years of American Presbyterianism* (Lexington: University Press of Kentucky, 1997), 226–28.

vivalist censoriousness and emotional excess.[41] When the Synod of New York had first convened in 1745, its initial act was to reaffirm the Adopting Act of 1729 with its allowance of scruples and its affirmation of the "essential and necessary" criteria.[42] The New Side had been under suspicion from the Old Side, who favored a more strict interpretation of confessional subscription.

When Dickinson died in 1747, a more temperate Gilbert Tennent assumed leadership of the reconciliation discussions on the New York side, having toned down his censorious spirit.[43] Observing "a Spirit of Moderation increasing between many of the Members of both Synods," the New York Synod approached Philadelphia with peaceable terms to resolve the impasse. The new 1749 proposal on union called for the two bodies to address "that paragraph about essentials," referring to the original subscription principles of 1729.[44] New York recommended that the two synods unite on consent to the Confession "according to the Plan formerly agreed to by the Synod of Philadelphia in ye Year 1729." The proposed articles further stipulated that all should stop publicly accusing brothers of immorality or errors in doctrine unless these charges were formally presented according to the rules of discipline. To avoid future division, the New York proposal recommended "That every Member promise, that after any Question has been determined by the Major vote, he will actively concur or passively submit to the Judgment of the Body: But if his Conscience permit him to do neither of these that then he shall be obliged to peaceably withdraw from our Synodical Communion without any Attempt to make a Schism or Division among us: Yet this is not intended to extend to any Cases but those which the Synod Judges essential in Matters of Doctrine or Discipline" (270).

A commission of both synods met in Trenton, with some heated interaction and no resolution to New York's demand that the "protest" excluding the New Brunswick Presbytery be nullified. The two groups agreed that a way forward must address three issues: the protest, presbytery boundaries, and "That Paragraph about Essentials" (270). As negotiations continued, it became clear that the Synod of Philadelphia did not want to affirm the essentials paragraph because it "has a bad Aspect & opens a Door for unjustifiable Latitude both in Principles & practices." New York also asked for a joint testimony of the two synods, that "a glorious Work of God's Spirit was carried on in the late religious

41. Le Beau, *Jonathan Dickinson*, 104–64.

42. Klett, *Minutes*, appendix, 322.

43. See Gilbert Tennent, *Irenicum Ecclesiasticum, or a Humble Impartial Essay upon the Peace of Jerusalem* (Philadelphia, 1749).

44. Klett, *Minutes*, 271, 272. Hereafter, references from the work will be given in parentheses in the text.

Appearances; (tho we doubt not but there were several Follies & Extravagancies of People, & Artifices of Satan intermixed therewith)" (274, 275). The Synod of Philadelphia was unwilling to concur in a joint public statement on the awakening. A turning point in reunion discussions occurred when a letter from Philadelphia clarified the meaning of the 1741 protest: "we declare, & do assure you, that we neither adopted nor do adopt sd. Protestation, as a term of ministerial Communion." The Philadelphia letter added, "We only Adopt & design to adhere to our Standards, as we formerly agreed when united, in one Body. We adopt no other" (252).

After seventeen years, the breach was finally healed in 1758, with Gilbert Tennent chosen as moderator of the reunited Synod of New York and Philadelphia. The Plan of Union retained much from the earlier proposals of New York reflecting New Side concerns about piety, the revival, and subscription. By the time of reunion, seventy-three of the ninety-six ministers had been members of the New Side Synod of New York. In the seventeen years of their separate existence, the Old Side Synod of Philadelphia had lost five ministers while the New Side had added fifty ministers; the number of New Side congregations was also much larger.[45] One of the articles of agreement was a balanced statement on the Awakening as a "gracious work of God" while pointing out where there had been "dangerous Delusion" in some aspects of it. Old Side minister Francis Alison was asked to preach on the occasion of reunion. He exhorted the two groups with these words: "We must maintain union in essentials, forbearance in lesser matters, and charity in all things. . . . In a church like ours in America, collected from different churches of Europe, who have followed different modes and ways of obeying the 'great and general command of the gospel,' there is a peculiar call for charity and forbearance."[46]

---

45. Leonard J. Trinterud, *The Forming of an American Tradition* (Philadelphia: Westminster, 1949), 151.

46. Trinterud, *The Forming of an American Tradition*, 148. The Evangelical Presbyterian Church (est. 1981) adopted a version of Alison's statement as its motto: "In essentials unity, in non-essentials liberty, in all things charity"; see below, chap. 19.

CHAPTER 8

American Independence and a National Assembly

The most remarkable spiritual event to shape Presbyterians in the generation preceding the Revolutionary War was the Great Awakening. New Side Presbyterians had supported the great revival, which deepened American passion for freedom to worship God according to the dictates of one's conscience. One fruit of the Awakening was a revitalized Christian piety, which many American clergy viewed as central to God's blessing on the colonies. There were also millennial overtones to this fresh movement of the Spirit as an inferred sign of America's providential destiny.[1] These factors helped create fertile soil for the American Revolution, and numerous Presbyterian ministers utilized these themes in sermons leading up to independence. Disdain for British policies swelled, and war with Britain seemed increasingly inevitable.

PRELUDES TO REVOLUTION

The hostilities that led to the French and Indian War began in 1754, with British regulars and colonial forces losing early battles to the French. The war spread to Europe as Great Britain declared war on France in 1756. In a sermon that same year, Gilbert Tennent declared, "My heart bleeds for this ravaged Country, especially for our poor Brethren in the back Parts of it, many of whom have been mercilessly sacrificed by the Pagan Savages, and the Remainder reduc'd

---

1. See Alan Heimert, *Religion and the American Mind: From the Great Awakening to the American Revolution* (Cambridge, MA: Harvard University Press, 1966); Nathan O. Hatch, *The Sacred Cause of Liberty: Republican Thought and the Millennium in Revolutionary New England* (New Haven: Yale University Press, 1977); Thomas S. Kidd, *God of Liberty: A Religious History of the American Revolution* (New York: Basic Books, 2010).

to such Circumstances of Destress and Woe, as are enough to pierce a Heart of Iron." Tennent was outspoken in his anger against the French for stirring up Indian rebellion against the British colonists, advocating defensive war for the "Publick Good."[2] When the tide turned in the American phase of the war, the French surrendered Canada in 1760, and the 1763 Treaty of Paris officially ended the conflict.

Not all interaction with Native Americans during this era was combative. In 1759 the Presbytery of Suffolk County on Long Island ordained Samson Occom (1723–1792), a Mohegan Indian, to the gospel ministry. Occom had been converted during the Great Awakening, attending school in Connecticut under Eleazar Wheelock. He initiated missionary work among several Indian tribes on Long Island and in Connecticut, preaching to them in their own language. To raise funds for his evangelistic work and Wheelock's school, he traveled to England with the Reverend Nathanial Whitaker, preaching there for two years. Substantial funds were raised, but he was disappointed with the response of English bishops. After his return to America in 1768, he reflected on his experience in England: "I waited on a number of Bishops, and represented to them the miserable and wretched situation of the poor Indians, who are perishing for lack of spiritual knowledge, and begged their assistance in evangelizing these poor heathen. But if you can believe me, they never gave us one single brass farthing. It seems to me that they are very indifferent whether the poor Indians go to Heaven or Hell." Occom continued his itinerant ministry in America among the Indians and spent the final decade of his life helping relocate remnants of Indian tribes to a safe haven in western New York.[3]

COLLEGE OF NEW JERSEY

As the number of Presbyterian churches proliferated, the pressing need for more ministers became urgent, and educating them became a priority. Frustrated with the negative attitude of Yale faculty toward the Awakening, a group of New Side ministers conceived a plan for establishing their own college,

---

2. Gilbert Tennent, "The Happiness of Rewarding the Enemies of Our Religion and Liberty," *Journal of Presbyterian History, Presbyterians and the Revolution: A Documentary Account*, Winter 1974, 322–24.

3. William B. Sprague, *Annals of the American Presbyterian Pulpit*, vol. 1 (New York: Robert Carter and Brothers, 1856; reprint, Birmingham: Solid Ground Christian Books, 2005), 192–95. See H. W. Blodgett, *Samson Occom* (Hanover, NH, 1935); *The Collected Writings of Samson Occom, Mohegan: Leadership and Literature in Eighteenth-Century Native America*, ed. Joanna Brooks (New York: Oxford University Press, 2006).

which would be the fourth college in America, following Harvard, Yale, and William and Mary. These ministers, along with a group of laymen, received a charter in 1746 to start the College of New Jersey (later Princeton University) for collegiate studies and training ministers. The majority of the new college trustees were either Yale or Log College graduates, all of whom were committed to the integration of academic study and experimental piety. The first president was the Synod of New York's Jonathan Dickinson, who opened the school in his home in Elizabethtown, New Jersey, with eight or ten students. Sadly, Dickinson died within five months of opening the school. Pastor Aaron Burr, of Newark, New Jersey, was willing to assume leadership of the college, so the handful of students packed up and moved to Newark for study under Burr.[4]

In 1752, Aaron Burr married Esther Edwards, daughter of New England's famous Congregational minister Jonathan Edwards.[5] Esther and Aaron welcomed the students into their home in Newark, where they also enjoyed occasional visits from both Esther's father and Aaron's friend George Whitefield. In the fall of 1748, the first class of six graduated, five of whom would become Presbyterian ministers, and one a signer of the Declaration of Independence, New Jersey lawyer and legislator Richard Stockton. Under Burr's leadership the college prospered; it acquired property in Princeton for a permanent campus with a building. To raise funds for construction, the college trustees sent Gilbert Tennent and a young Samuel Davies on a fund-raising tour of Britain that lasted for two years. Tennent and Davies secured several thousand pounds for their efforts, and construction of the new building began. The new Georgian building, named Nassau Hall in honor of King William III, included a classroom, a dormitory, a library, and a chapel with a pipe organ—the first organ used in Presbyterian worship in the colonies. When Nassau Hall opened in 1756, there were seventy students at the college. The next year Aaron Burr died at forty-one, and within a few months his twenty-six-year-old wife would pass away.[6]

Esther's father, Jonathan Edwards, was chosen by the trustees to be the next president, but he died three months after taking office from a smallpox inoculation; so again the office was vacant. Samuel Davies succeeded Edwards the next year, but he also died, of pneumonia, within eighteen months, at age thirty-seven. During his time as president, the college had 150 students and

4. Varnum L. Collins, *Princeton* (New York: Oxford University Press, 1914); Thomas J. Wertenbaker, "The College of New Jersey and the Presbyterians," *Journal of the Presbyterian Historical Society* 36 (December 1958): 209–16.

5. Edwards was much beloved by the New Side Presbyterians and would attend Synod of New York meetings when visiting his daughter.

6. Leonard J. Trinterud, *The Forming of an American Tradition: A Re-examination of Colonial Presbyterianism* (Philadelphia: Westminster, 1949), 124ff.

about 1,500 books in the library. Log College graduate Samuel Finley was chosen as the fifth president of the college and served for five years. Immediately preceding his arrival in Princeton, Finley had served a Presbyterian congregation in Nottingham, Maryland, where he had earlier established his own private academy for training clergy. Similar to previous presidents, his time at the college was abbreviated by death in 1766.

The next presidential candidate selected by the trustees was a Presbyterian minister from Scotland, John Witherspoon (1723–1794). Witherspoon's notoriety in America was tied to his popular book *Ecclesiastical Characteristics* (1753), wherein he had lampooned the latitudinarian "moderate party" in the Scottish church: "All ecclesiastical persons that are suspected of heresy are to be esteemed men of great genius, vast learning, and uncommon worth . . . and when any man is charged with loose practices or tendencies to immorality, he is to be screened and protected as much as possible."[7] Due to his bold stand for orthodox faith and practice, he had become the leader of the evangelical party in the Church of Scotland. His impressive Scottish education, ministry experience, piety, and orthodoxy inclined the trustees to think he could be a most useful bridge builder in America between the former Old Side and New Side parties. Witherspoon's wife, Elizabeth, was hesitant about moving to the colonies, but hearing pleas from the college trustees, she relented. The Witherspoons, with five children, boarded the ship *Peggy* in Glasgow for the twelve-week voyage to America. Arriving in summer 1768, they received a joyful welcome from the Princeton community.

As president, Witherspoon had his hands full managing the affairs of the fledgling school, giving significant effort to increasing enrollment and funding. He traveled throughout the colonies, from New England to the South, seeking support for the college, and under his leadership the school advanced. He upgraded the curriculum, encouraging additional studies in science, history, French, and "moral philosophy," which included ethics, political science, and law. As professor of divinity, he taught many of these subjects himself, including the senior course on moral philosophy. Witherspoon introduced his students to Scottish commonsense realism, a philosophy developed by Thomas Reid (1710–1796) of Glasgow.[8] Reid reasoned that humanity both had an accurate

---

7. John Witherspoon, "Ecclesiastical Characteristics," in *The Works of Rev. John Witherspoon*, ed. Ashbel Green, 9 vols. (Philadelphia, 1802; reprint, Harrisonburg, VA: Sprinkle Publications, 2007), 5:190, 193.

8. Mark Noll argues that the sentimentalist ethics of Francis Hutcheson, also a professor at Glasgow, were of greater influence on Witherspoon than Reid. Mark Noll, *America's God: From Jonathan Edwards to Abraham Lincoln* (New York: Oxford University Press, 2002), 93–113. For the debate over the degree to which Enlightenment philosophy influ-

knowledge of the real world and possessed an innate knowledge of basic morality. Scottish realism's opposition to skepticism, which questioned any certitude,
resonated with Witherspoon, for he was convinced that Christianity was reasonable and compatible with common sense. Witherspoon believed that Christian
liberal arts should foster both piety and duty, preparing students for civic affairs,
Christian ministry, and scholarship. Enlightenment-inspired theological error
and Deism were gaining popularity in the eighteenth century, but Witherspoon
encouraged perseverance in defense of truth. He asserted: "Let no Christian,
therefore, give way to desponding thoughts, though infidelity unresisted spread
its poison . . . though there are few to support the interest of truth and righteousness . . . let us not be discouraged. We plead the cause that shall prevail."[9]

The long-term legacy of Witherspoon the professor would be the impressive public careers that emanated from among the almost five hundred
students he taught over his twenty-five years at the college. These students
included a president of the United States (James Madison),[10] a vice president
(Aaron Burr Jr.), twelve members of the Continental Congress, five delegates
to the Constitutional Convention, forty-nine US representatives, twenty-eight
senators, and three Supreme Court justices. Added to this impressive list were
114 ministers of the gospel, 19 of whom became presidents of institutions of
higher learning.[11]

ROAD TO REVOLUTION

Responding to the huge debt incurred from the French and Indian War,[12] as
well as ongoing maintenance of an army in America, the British Parliament

---

enced Witherspoon's thought, see Mark A. Noll, Nathan O. Hatch, and George M. Marsden,
The Search for Christian America (Westchester, IL: Crossway, 1983); Kevin DeYoung, *The
Religious Formation of John Witherspoon: Calvinism, Evangelicalism, and the Scottish En-
lightenment* (London: Routledge, 2020).

9. Varnum Lansing Collins, *President Witherspoon: A Biography*, 2 vols. (Princeton:
Princeton University Press, 1925; reprint, New York: Arno, 1969), 53.

10. James H. Smylie, "Madison and Witherspoon: Theological Roots of American Polit-
ical Thought," *Princeton University Library Chronicle* 22, no. 3 (Spring 1961): 118–32; Gideon
Mailer, *John Witherspooon's American Revolution* (Chapel Hill: University of North Carolina
Press, 2017), 327–64.

11. Jeffry H. Morrison, *John Witherspoon and the Founding of the American Republic*
(South Bend, IN: University of Notre Dame Press, 2005), 4. For an early biographical sketch
of Witherspoon's life by one of his students, see Ashbel Green's *The Life of the Rev. John
Witherspoon* in the Sprinkle edition of *Works*, vol. 9.

12. The French and Indian War was the regional manifestation of a global conflict fought

began taxing the colonies to raise funds for the Crown. A host of trade laws followed, the most notorious being the Stamp Act of 1765, the first direct tax levied by Parliament on the colonies. There was almost universal opposition to this new tax imposed during a sluggish American economy, and fears were voiced about future "taxation without representation." Nonimportation of British goods followed, and colonial representatives to the Stamp Act Congress issued a "Declaration of Rights and Grievances" protesting that taxation without consent violated their rights as the king's subjects. The Stamp Act was repealed the next year, to great rejoicing in America, but the road to rebellion had begun. The 1767 Townshend Acts imposed import duties, and colonial nonimportation resumed. Again Parliament relented in 1770 but left duties on imported English tea in place. Skirmishes between British troops and colonists surfaced, resulting in soldiers killing five citizens in the 1770 Boston Massacre. Committees of correspondence were organized to encourage resistance to British policies across the thirteen colonies. The 1773 Tea Act, giving unfair economic advantage to the British East India Company, resulted in the Boston Tea Party, where 342 chests of tea were dumped into the harbor. A series of Coercive Acts to punish Massachusetts only further strained the situation. By the fall of 1774, the first Continental Congress had convened in Philadelphia.

Sensing that war was imminent, the Synod of Philadelphia and New York wrote a "pastoral letter" in May 1775 and sent it to Presbyterians throughout the colonies. The Synod observed that the colonies "seem determined to defend their rights by force of Arms," thus it would be prudent to offer its advice. While encouraging "respect to our sovereign King George," the letter counseled Presbyterians on how they should carry themselves during the tumult of war. There was a call for unity in the colonies, including that "a spirit of candour, charity and mutual esteem be preserved, and promoted towards those of different religious denominations."[13] Congregations should "watch over the morals of their several members" because "profligacy makes a nation ripe for divine judgments." Synod recommended the pursuit of order and peace for those who may be called into the conflict, urging them to practice "a spirit of humanity and mercy," noting "that man will fight most bravely, who never fights till it is necessary, and who ceases to fight, as soon as the necessity is over." The letter concluded with a call "to continue habitually in

---

between France and Britain. Battle theaters also included New France (today's Atlantic Canada), the Caribbean, and the Indian subcontinent.

13. William Harrison Taylor, *Unity in Christ and Country: American Presbyterians in the Revolutionary Era* (Tuscaloosa: University of Alabama Press, 2017); Taylor argues that Presbyterian interest in Christian ecumenism was driven by political concerns for national unity.

the exercise of prayer, and to have frequent occasional voluntary meetings for
solemn intercession with God on the important trial."[14]

Witherspoon weighed in on the crisis, preaching his first political sermon
in Nassau Hall in May 1776. The sermon, published as "The Dominion of
Providence over the Passions of Men," was dedicated to the president of the
Continental Congress, John Hancock. Based upon Psalm 76:10, the sermon
urged resistance to tyranny as obedience to God and encouraged trusting
God to bring good out of evil.[15] The sermon drew praise for Witherspoon
as a patriot, but British loyalists hated him, burning him in effigy. A member of the British Parliament exclaimed, "Cousin America has run off with
a Presbyterian parson." Witherspoon served as a delegate to the Continental
Congress and signed the "Unanimous Declaration" of the colonies for independence on July 4, 1776—the only clergyman to sign the document. Eleven
other Presbyterians signed the Declaration of Independence. During the war,
over two hundred students from the College of New Jersey would serve in
some capacity. Graduates of the college included eleven captains, six majors,
four colonels, ten lieutenant colonels, and eleven chaplains. Classes were dismissed in December 1776 when the British turned Nassau Hall into barracks
and stables. After George Washington won the Battle of Princeton, classes
resumed in July 1777. Witherspoon would pay dearly for supporting the revolution, losing two sons at the Battle of Germantown. He continued to serve the
new nation throughout the war, and beyond. He signed the Articles of Confederation (1778), participated in ratifying the Constitution (1787) as a member
of the New Jersey convention, and served on the Board of War and Board of
Foreign Affairs. He was keenly aware of God's providence in the conflict and
helped draft a proclamation on behalf of the Confederation Congress, calling
on Americans to thank the Almighty for his mercy.[16]

Presbyterians almost universally supported separation from Britain, earning
them the reputation of being a primary culprit behind the American rebellion.
In 1776, an Englishman wrote from New York: "Presbyterianism is really at the
Bottom of this whole Conspiracy, has supplied it with Vigour, and will never

14. Minutes of the Synod of New York and Philadelphia, May 22, 1775, as printed in
Guy S. Klett, ed., *Minutes of the Presbyterian Church in America, 1706–1788* (Philadelphia:
Presbyterian Historical Society, 1976), 543–46.

15. Witherspoon, "The Dominion of Providence over the Passions of Men," in *Works*,
5:17–42.

16. See "Proclamation" of the Confederation Congress, October 26, 1782, for "setting
apart a day of public thanksgiving and prayer," in *The Journals of the Continental Congress*,
1774–1789, vol. 21, 1781, ed. Gaillard Hunt (Washington, DC: Government Printing Office,
1912), 1074–76.

rest, till something is decided upon it." Presbyterian clergymen preached on aspects of the crisis regularly. At least thirty-seven Presbyterian ministers served as chaplains in the militia and Continental army.[17] Widespread Presbyterian patriotism prompted a New England loyalist to call Scots-Irish "the most God-provoking democrats on this side of Hell." Scots-Irish filled the ranks of General Washington's army for the duration of the Revolutionary War. At Valley Forge, when hundreds had deserted, many of the Scots-Irish remained, enduring the cold and hunger. During the war, the Continentals fought not only redcoats but also thirty thousand mercenary German (Hessian) troops, a quarter of the soldiers Britain sent to America. In 1778, one Hessian officer wrote home: "Call this war by whatever name you may, only call it not an American rebellion; it is nothing more or less than a Scotch Irish Presbyterian rebellion."[18]

Very few Scots-Irish moved to Canada or the West Indies during the war, unlike numbers of the English and Scots. By the 1770s, the strongest concentrations of Scots-Irish settlers were in Pennsylvania, Virginia, and the two Carolinas. While Pennsylvania and Virginia Scots-Irish were patriots, there were loyalists among the Highland Scots and Scots-Irish that had settled in the North Carolina Piedmont, between the mountains and the coast. The situation was complex due in part to the history behind the "Regulators" movement. Animosity between the plantation region of the coast and the Piedmont backcountry, with its heavily Scots-Irish population, had produced the Regulators mob, which had taken the law into their own hands. Frustrated with unequal representation in the legislature and extortion by tax agents, the Regulators turned to violence, and the colonial government finally crushed the movement, executing several leaders in 1771. The rest of the Regulators were pardoned if they took an oath to the Crown. The Regulator movement had included not only Scots-Irish but also Highland Scots, many of whom would remain loyal to George III. It has been suggested that once hostilities with Britain began, the new conflict gave loyalist ex-Regulators an opportunity to settle old scores with the colonial government. In parts of both Carolinas, Presbyterians would end up fighting one another. Presbyterians in the middle colonies were concerned about loyalists in the Carolinas, so they dispatched several ministers to bolster patriotic support among the Highland Scots.[19]

17. For a list of Presbyterian chaplains in the American Army, see *Presbyterians and the American Revolution: A Documentary Account, Journal of Presbyterian History* 52, no. 4 (1974): 406, 407.

18. Cited in James G. Leyburn, *The Scotch-Irish: A Social History* (Chapel Hill: University of North Carolina Press, 1962), 305.

19. Joseph Tiedemann, "Presbyterians and the American Revolution in the Middle Colonies," *Church History*, June 2005, 315.

The Scots-Irish in Mecklenburg County, North Carolina, were fixed supporters of the patriot cause. In 1764, the Synod of New York and Philadelphia commissioned two ministers to organize new congregations among the Scots-Irish in the Piedmont region. A cluster of seven churches in Mecklenburg County (Sugaw Creek, Steele Creek, Hopewell, Centre, Poplar Tent, Rocky River, and Providence) would become among the oldest Presbyterian congregations in the Charlotte area. When Presbyterians on the Committee of Safety got word about the skirmishes at Lexington and Concord in April 1775, they gathered at the Charlottetown Courthouse on May 31 and issued the "Mecklenburg Resolves." An elder at Sugaw Creek Presbyterian Church, Abraham Alexander, and Rev. Hezekiah Balch of Poplar Tent Presbyterian presided at the meeting. The resolves declared, "all laws and commissions confirmed by or derived from the authority of the King and Parliament are annulled and vacated," and called for the eight militia companies in the county to "provide themselves with proper arms" and maintain readiness.[20]

Many Carolina Presbyterians heeded the call to fight. Having learned to use a musket in the backcountry against Indians, the southern Scots-Irish frontiersmen were adept fighters. After Charleston surrendered in 1780, British general Cornwallis began to march through the Carolinas hoping to join forces with the Scottish loyalists. British troops battled American soldiers at Kings Mountain in North Carolina, where the redcoats were defeated. American forces at Kings Mountain were predominately Scots-Irish, led by five colonels who were Presbyterian elders in the region. Likewise at the South Carolina Battle of Cowpens in 1781, the commander of patriot troops was a Presbyterian elder, General Daniel Morgan, whose men routed the British forces under Tarleton's command.[21]

Backing of the patriot cause was not unanimous among clergy who served Presbyterian churches. One notorious loyalist was the pastor of the Presbyterian Church of Savannah (Independent Presbyterian Church), Rev. John Joachim Zubly, who began his ministry as the congregation's first pastor in 1755. Known throughout the colonies, he was awarded the doctor of divinity degree

---

20. Quoted in *Presbyterians and the American Revolution*, 373, 374. Another document purported to have been written eleven days earlier (May 20, 1775), the "Mecklenburg Declaration," proclaimed colonial independence, bearing a striking resemblance to Jefferson's Declaration of Independence written the following year. While many historians hold the "Mecklenburg Declaration" suspect, the date "May 20th 1775" was emblazoned on the North Carolina state flag in 1861. For history and text of these documents, see William Henry Foote, *Sketches of North Carolina* (New York: Robert Carter, 1846), 33–45.

21. Foote, *Sketches of North Carolina*, 264–71.

by the College of New Jersey in 1770. Zubly was beloved by his congregation and respected by the colonial government of Georgia, serving as a member of the Provincial Congress of Georgia and elected by them to the Continental Congress in July 1775. While Zubly believed that colonial complaints against the British Parliament were justified, he cautioned against rebellion, arguing from Scripture that Christians had no right to wage war against ordained British authority. In a 1775 sermon preached before the Provincial Congress of Georgia, published as "The Law of Liberty," he advocated a moderate approach toward Britain: "Let me intreat you, Gentlemen, think cooly, and act deliberately. . . . Consider how much lies at stake, how greatly your religion, your liberty, your property, your posterity, is interested. Endeavor to act like freemen, like loyal subjects, like real Christians."[22] As a member of the Continental Congress, Zubly spoke out against independence, but realizing that his views were becoming unacceptable, he left Philadelphia after a couple of months and returned to Georgia. He was jailed in Georgia and banished from the colony in 1778. When the British captured Savannah the next year, he returned, only to find that his property had been destroyed, along with his library. He died in South Carolina in 1781, not living to see the final victory of the American forces and the ratification of the Articles of Peace in 1783.[23]

A Presbyterian Constitution

After the Revolutionary War concluded, Presbyterians recognized the imperative of restructuring their polity if they were to function effectively in the new nation. Wartime had made attendance at Synod's annual meetings especially difficult; this was in addition to the perennial difficulty remote presbyteries had sending persons to Synod meetings in New York, Philadelphia, or Elizabethtown. Poor attendance at Synod had been a long-term issue needing to be addressed. Synod meetings from the 1758 reunion until 1774 had less than half of the clergy attending any given year; at times fewer than one-third of

22. John J. Zubly, "The Law of Liberty: A Sermon on American Affairs," in *Presbyterians and the American Revolution*, 398. See also Randal M. Miller, ed., *A Warm and Zealous Spirit: John J. Zubly and the American Revolution; A Selection of His Writings* (Macon, GA: Mercer University Press, 1982).

23. For the contrasting views of Zubly and Witherspoon on American independence, see Daryl C. Cornett, "The American Revolution's Role in the Reshaping of Calvinistic Protestantism," *Journal of Presbyterian History*, Winter 2004, 244–57. Noll, Hatch, and Marsden, in *The Search for Christian America*, question the moral argument for rebellion against Britain.

ministers were present. Some years, a few presbyteries sent no representatives to Synod, and attendance by elders was always minuscule. These patterns persisted after independence. The 1785 meeting of Synod was illustrative of the problem: out of over 150 ministers, only 30 were present; six of the thirteen presbyteries had no one present; and only six elders attended.[24]

Despite the anxiety over nonattendance at Synod meetings, the American Presbyterians resolved to design a constitution for themselves. The 1785 Synod appointed a committee (ten ministers, three elders) to consider the "constitution of the Church of Scotland and other Protestant churches, and agreeably to the general principles of Presbyterian government, compile a system of genuine rules for the Government of the Synod & the several Presbyteries under their inspection; & the People in their communion."[25] When Synod reconvened in May 1786, the committee presented a report that was not agreed upon. Professor Samuel Stanhope Smith of the College of New Jersey argued for adopting the entire Scottish system of government, which also proved unacceptable. Synod appointed a new committee to produce a book of government and discipline "accommodated to the state of the Presbyterian Church in America." The committee was tasked with printing three hundred copies of their work, *Draught of a Plan of Government and Discipline*, and sending it to all presbyteries, who were asked to respond in writing to the next Synod.[26]

When May 1787 arrived, Synod was poorly attended again, with only 69 of 177 ministers and fourteen elders showing up; three of the sixteen presbyteries were not represented at all. Debate on the *Draught* took up six days as the Synod worked through each section of the document. At one point the Synod voted to reconsider the Church of Scotland documents alongside the committee's draft, but this idea was ultimately rejected. After the committee had deliberated for a week on government and discipline, it was ordered that one thousand copies of the *Draught* be printed and sent to the presbyteries for their review.[27] The Synod also discussed revising the Westminster Confession. In light of the American church/state context, the body decided to amend paragraphs in chapters 20, 23, and 31, removing any references to state interference in church affairs. The Westminster Larger and Shorter Catechisms were adopted as part of the Presbyterian constitution; only the Confession had been adopted in 1729. The Book of Government standardized requirements for

24. Trinterud, *The Forming of an American Tradition*, 279–82; Klett, *Minutes*, 589, 590.
25. Klett, *Minutes*, 597.
26. Klett, *Minutes*, 611.
27. Trinterud, *The Forming of an American Tradition*, 288, 289.

presbyteries in ministerial preparation, licensure, and ordination. Two years of study in theology were a prerequisite for examinations before a presbytery. After adequate preparation, students would be tested on knowledge in Latin, Hebrew, and Greek; the arts and sciences; and theology and church history; also, inquiry would be made "with regard to the real piety of such candidates, to examine them respecting their experimental acquaintance with religion." After candidates sustained all their examinations, their vows consisted of answering four questions: "1. Do you believe the Scriptures of the Old and New Testament, to be the word of God, the only infallible rule of Faith and Practice? 2. Do you sincerely receive and adopt the Confession of Faith of this church as containing the system of doctrine taught in holy Scriptures? 3. Do you promise to study the peace, unity and purity of the church? 4. Do you promise to submit yourself, in the Lord, to the government of this presbytery, or of any other presbytery in the bounds of which you may be?"[28]

A committee had been appointed in 1786 to revise the 1644 Westminster Directory for Worship, chaired by John Rogers, pastor of First Presbyterian Church in New York City. By 1787, the committee had produced a draft new directory. The preface in this draft (which was later deleted) iterated some of the committee's initial concerns about Presbyterian public worship—"persons going in and out during divine services"; some people not singing; inattention during the pastor's prayers; neglect of Scripture reading; and sleeping, whispering, and laughing during the sermon. Included in the draft were pattern prayers in lieu of the list of topics from the original Westminster Directory. This was an attempt to encourage "regularity of worship" among American Presbyterians. The Synod voted against set prayers, favoring the minister's discretion to lead public prayer as he saw fit, although the final version included advice that prayers should include "adoration, thanksgiving, confession, supplication for pardon, pleading and intercession." The draft had recommended using the Lord's Prayer in public worship, but that was excised from the final version; apparently some perceived this as a vestige of the old mandated Anglican liturgy.[29]

On the topic of preaching, the final version encouraged ministers to use simple language in sermons and "not to make their sermons too long so as to interfere with, or exclude the more important duties of prayer and praise; but preserve a just proportion between the several parts of worship." Concerning

28. *Draught of the Form of Government and Discipline of the Presbyterian Church in the United States of America* (New York: S. and J. Loudon, 1787), 19.

29. Julius Melton, *Presbyterian Worship in America: Changing Patterns Since 1787* (Richmond, VA: John Knox, 1967), 17–27.

observance of the Lord's Supper, the committee's draft had wanted to minimize the use of "sacramental seasons" and its gathered crowds in favor of a more regular quarterly communion in congregations. The final version of the American directory encouraged frequent communion but did not specify quarterly observance. And warnings about overuse of sacramental seasons in the draft were dropped in the Synod's revised edition of 1788.[30]

The Presbyterian Constitution was officially adopted by the Synod of New York and Philadelphia in 1788. It included provisions for future alterations or amendments to the documents. The intrinsic fallibility of the constitutional documents was embedded in the recognition that, in contrast to Holy Scripture, these documents could be modified. The first General Assembly met in Philadelphia in 1789, just four blocks away from the US Constitutional Convention, which was in session at the same time. George Washington had been inaugurated as the first president of the United States three weeks earlier. The Assembly wrote a letter of congratulation to Washington, telling him, "We shall consider ourselves as doing an acceptable service to God in our profession when we contribute to render men sober, honest and industrious citizens, and the obedient subjects of a lawful government." Washington sent a letter of reply to the Presbyterians, reminding them that "all men within our territories are protected in worshipping the Deity according to the dictates of their consciences," and asking for their "prayers to almighty God for his blessings on our common country."[31] A national American government, and newly organized Presbyterian church, would work for the common good in the new republic. The 1789 General Assembly of the Presbyterian Church in the United States of America consisted of four synods and sixteen presbyteries encompassing four hundred churches and 177 ministers.

Reformed and Associate Presbyterians

Among the waves of Scottish Presbyterians who had come to America in the eighteenth century, some had declined to unite with the Synod of New York and Philadelphia. Recent history in Scotland had conditioned them to seek independent ecclesiastical affiliations in America. The Covenanters had re-

30. Melton, *Presbyterian Worship in America*, 17–27. For eighteenth-century Presbyterian discussions on frequency of the Lord's Supper, see Kenneth J. Stewart, *In Search of Ancient Roots: The Christian Past and the Evangelical Identity Crisis* (Downers Grove, IL: InterVarsity Press, 2017), 109–20.

31. Both letters are quoted by W. P. Breed in *Presbyterians and the Revolution* (Philadelphia, 1876; reprint, Decatur, MS: Issacharian, 1993).

sisted the imposition of episcopacy in Scotland during the Restoration, maintaining their commitment to the Solemn League and Covenant (1638) and its affirmation of a national covenanted Presbyterianism. Brutal repression under Charles II during the "killing times" had strengthened their resolve. The story of Covenanter immigration to America begins with a handful of Scots who made their way to the New World in 1685 during the "killing times." As more Covenanters arrived, they organized themselves into "praying societies" throughout the colonies. In 1743, these societies had their first significant gathering in Pennsylvania. They were led in renewing the covenants by Alexander Craighead (1705–1766), although he eventually affiliated with the Associate Presbyterians.[32] The American societies called upon the Reformed Presbytery of Scotland to send them ministers. In 1752, John Cuthbertson arrived from Scotland, serving the American societies until his death. Three more Scottish clergy joined him in 1774, and within a few months the four ministers formed the first American Reformed Presbytery in Paxton, Pennsylvania. The Reformed Presbyterians were supportive of American independence.[33]

The Seceders (Associate Presbyterians) were another group that pursued a distinct presence in the colonies. The Secession church was born out of several disputes—theological disagreements (including the Marrow controversy),[34] differences over closed communion, and a debate over psalm singing. There were also political issues related to the diluting of Presbyterian government in Scotland and oppressive laws of patronage. Under the leadership of Ebenezer Erskine, a group separated in 1733 from the Church of Scotland, referring to themselves as the Associate Presbytery. On behalf of the New Brunswick Presbytery, Gilbert Tennent wrote to the Associate Presbyterians in 1738 affirming the Seceders as allies. Whitefield noted in his journal, "He [William Tennent Sr.] is a great friend of Mr. Erskine, of Scotland, and as far as I can learn, both he and his sons are secretly despised by the generality of the synod as Mr. Erskine and his friends are hated by the judicatories of

32. Alexander Craighead had been expelled by Donegal Presbytery (Synod of Philadelphia) due to his participation in the revival. He was considered a radical for his association with Covenanters; however, he would rejoin the Synod of New York, serving as a missionary to North Carolina until his death.

33. On Covenanter immigration to America, see J. D. Douglas, *Light in the North: The Story of Scottish Covenanters* (Grand Rapids: Eerdmans, 1964), 179–87.

34. William Vandoodewaard, *The Marrow Controversy and Seceder Tradition: Atonement, Saving Faith, and the Gospel Offer in Scotland, 1718–1799* (Grand Rapids: Reformation Heritage Books, 2011). The Marrow controversy was an extended Church of Scotland debate over the book *The Marrow of Modern Divinity* (1645), which was alleged to advocate antinomianism (freedom from the need to obey the moral law).

Edinburgh, and, as Methodist preachers are by their brethren in England."[35]
In 1747 the Seceders divided again: the conflict concerned taking the king's
"Burgher oath" (citizen's oath), which included affirming the "true religion
presently professed within this realm and authorized by the laws thereof."
The meaning of this phrase was contested. Some argued that it referred to the
Presbyterian Church of Scotland, from which the Associate Presbytery had
recently separated, while others insisted that the expression merely referred to
the Presbyterian church without its corruptions, and in opposition to Roman
Catholicism. The Burghers (fourteen ministers) signing the oath retained the
name Associate Synod; the Anti-Burghers (nineteen ministers) designated
themselves the General Associate Synod.

Seceder societies in the 1740s had a very small footprint in America, and
finally the Anti-Burgher Synod secured two ministers for the colonies in
1753—Alexander Gellatly and Andrew Arnot. The two ministers, upon arrival, organized the Associate Presbytery of Pennsylvania under the oversight
of the Anti-Burgher Synod in Scotland. Additional Associate ministers came
to America, including Rev. Thomas Clark of the Burgher church, who joined
with the Anti-Burghers in 1765. The American Associates divided into the
Associate Presbytery of Pennsylvania and the Associate Presbytery of New
York, independent presbyteries but both accountable to the Scottish Anti-
Burgher Synod. In 1777, union discussions in America were initiated between
the Reformed Presbyterians and Associate Presbyterians, which produced a
ten-point "Basis of Union," which concluded "That both parties, when united,
shall adhere to the Westminster Confession of Faith; Catechism, Larger and
Shorter; Directory for Worship, and Propositions concerning Church Government. That they shall claim the full exercise of church discipline without
dependence on foreign judicatories."[36] The Basis of Union was approved by
the Associate Presbytery of New York, and the Reformed Presbytery unanimously. The decision process in the Associate Presbytery of Pennsylvania
was extended, and final approval of union came by a tie-breaking vote of the
moderator. In the fall of 1782, the three presbyteries, meeting in Philadelphia, established themselves as the Associate Reformed Church with a total
of fourteen ministers.[37]

35. *George Whitefield's Journals* (London: Banner of Truth Trust, 1960), November 10,
1739, 344.

36. Ray A. King, *A History of the Associate Reformed Presbyterian Church* (Charlotte, NC:
Board of Education of the Associate Reformed Presbyterian Church, 1966), 71.

37. For histories of the Reformed and Associate Presbyterians in America, see William
Melancthon Glasgow, *History of the Reformed Presbyterian Church in America* (Baltimore:
Hill & Harvery, 1888; reprint, Grand Rapids: Reformation Heritage Books, 2007); Robert

By the time of the early republic, Presbyterians were already separated into several denominations and had suffered division even within the distinct groups. Despite the absence of ecclesiastical unity, on the whole they had supported the War for Independence and pledged themselves to be virtuous citizens in a nation promising religious liberty and representative government. At the end of the century, Presbyterians were scattered across the breadth of the new nation and continued to expand their mission work as the nation's frontier moved westward.

Lathan, *History of the Associate Reformed Synod of the South, To Which is Prefixed A History of the Associate Presbyterian and Reformed Presbyterian Churches* (Harrisburg, PA, 1882).

CHAPTER 9

Missions and Revivals in the Early Republic

On a stormy summer's afternoon in 1806, a small group of Williams College students gathered not far from campus for conversation and prayer. Surprised by a sudden thunderstorm, the students sought refuge in a nearby haystack. There, sheltered from rain and wind, the little band of fervent Christians—including Luther Rice, James Richards, John Seward, Ezra Fisk, and Samuel John Mills—prayed for people they had yet to meet and committed themselves to go as missionaries to lands they had yet to visit. The fascinating story of the Society of Brethren and their "Haystack Prayer Meeting," as it is commonly known, serves as a convenient starting point for what historian Kenneth Scott Latourette, writing in the mid-twentieth century, famously labeled "the Great Century" of missionary expansion.[1]

At the center of the story was Mills. Considered by many the father of the foreign missionary movement in America, Samuel John Mills Jr. played a central role in igniting interest in overseas missionary service among college and seminary students throughout the Northeast, in enlisting the support of many of New England's leading pastors in support of the missionary cause, and in the establishment of the American Board of Commissioners for Foreign Missions (ABCFM), America's first overseas missionary organization.[2] Born on April 21, 1783, in Torringford, Connecticut, where his father was a respected Con-

1. Yale historian Kenneth Scott Latourette famously coined the phrase "the Great Century" to emphasize the unusual growth of worldwide Christianity during the period from 1792 until 1910. His descriptions of that remarkable expansion can be found in volumes 4, 5, and 6 of his seven-part *History of the Expansion of Christianity*, first published by Harper & Brothers in the late 1930s.

2. Clifford Putney and Paul T. Burlin, *The Role of the American Board in the World: Bicentennial Reflections on the Organization's Missionary Work, 1810–2010* (Eugene, OR: Wipf & Stock, 2012).

gregational minister, Mills committed his life to missionary service in 1801; was educated at Morris Academy, Williams College, and Andover Theological Seminary; and was ordained to the gospel ministry on June 21, 1815, at "Old South" Presbyterian Church in Newburyport, Massachusetts.[3]

Under the provisions of the Plan of Union, an ecumenical initiative approved by the General Assembly of the Presbyterian Church and the Congregational Association of Connecticut in 1801, Presbyterians were encouraged to cooperate with Congregationalists in the appointment of pastors for the dozens of new congregations that were springing up not only throughout New England and the mid-Atlantic states but also in western New York, Ohio, Indiana, Illinois, Kentucky, Tennessee, Alabama, Mississippi, Louisiana, and Texas.[4] Furthermore, such cooperation between Presbyterians and Congregationalists extended to their missionary outreach through such organizations as the American Home Missionary Society, founded in New York in 1826. Nowhere was such cooperation more clearly demonstrated, however, than through the work of the ABCFM. The Congregationalists who had established the missionary organization in 1810 were joined by Presbyterians, who became energetic supporters. Ashbel Green, Samuel Miller, and Elias Boudinot joined the board in 1812, and "by 1831 a majority of board members and missionaries of the ABCFM were Presbyterian, and the vast majority of churches planted by the board were of a Presbyterian stripe."[5]

The growth of population around the globe, to say nothing of the growth and population migrations within the new nation itself, made it increasingly apparent to members of the Society of Brethren that organizations such as the ABCFM were needed. Mills and his friends could not have known, of course, that an American population of less than four million in 1790, when the new nation's first census was taken, would expand to more than thirty million by 1860. As passionate students of global geography and demographics, however, they were well aware that the need for missionaries was increasing at an alarming rate. Indeed, Mills and his colleagues had not only read the great missionary sermon Edward Dorr Griffin preached at the Presbyterian

3. Gardiner Spring, *Memoir of Samuel John Mills* (Boston: Perkins & Marvin; New York: J. Leavitt and J. P. Haven, 1829); David B. Raymond, "The Legacy of Samuel J. Mills, Jr.," *International Bulletin of Missionary Research* 38, no. 4 (October 2014): 207–10; and Thomas C. Richards, *Samuel J. Mills: Missionary Pathfinder, Pioneer, and Promoter* (Boston: Pilgrim, 1906). A plaque on the wall of "Old South" commemorates the ordination of Mills.

4. James H. Smylie, *A Brief History of the Presbyterians* (Louisville: Geneva, 1996), 71–73; see chap. 10 below.

5. Bradley J. Longfield, *Presbyterians and American Culture: A History* (Louisville: Westminster John Knox, 2013), 83.

General Assembly in Philadelphia in 1805, "The Kingdom of Christ: A Missionary Sermon," but they had reproduced and circulated the message among missionary-minded students at colleges all over the Northeast.[6] Griffin, who would later become pastor of Boston's historic Park Street Church and the Professor of Pulpit Eloquence at Andover Theological Seminary, along with other missionary-minded pastors such as Samuel Worcester of Salem, Jedediah Morse of Charlestown, and Daniel Dana of Newburyport, deeply appreciated the students' growing interest in missions. "If I have played any role in establishing the ABCFM," he liked to say, "it is only because I was first encouraged to do so by Samuel John Mills!"[7]

The Rise of World Missions

By February 6, 1812, the remarkable coalition between established pastors and missionary-minded students had produced one of the most significant events in the history of modern missions. The historic gathering took place in Tabernacle Congregational Church in the heart of Salem, Massachusetts. It was bitterly cold that day as nearly fifteen hundred people made their way through the freshly fallen snow to attend the special service. The five young men who were about to be commissioned included Adoniram Judson, Gordon Hall, Luther Rice, Samuel Nott, and Samuel Newell. Since all were graduates of Andover Theological Seminary, literally dozens of their fellow students walked the considerable distance between Andover and Salem to attend the service that day.[8] Seated side by side on a small wooden bench at the front of the sanctuary, these young graduates would later be remembered as America's first foreign missionaries.

The atmosphere inside the beautiful old sanctuary that day, we are told, was "electric," charged by enormous emotion and anticipation. "At times the entire assembly seemed moved as the trees of the wood are moved by a mighty wind." Authorized and overseen by the ABCFM, the service opened with prayer by

6. Edward D. Griffin, "The Kingdom of Christ: A Missionary Sermon, Preached Before the General Assembly of the Presbyterian Church in Philadelphia, May 23, 1805" (Philadelphia: Aitken, 1805). For the context of this story, see Garth M. Rosell, *Boston's Historic Park Street Church: The Story of an Evangelical Landmark* (Grand Rapids: Kregel, 2009), 55–80.

7. Spring, *Memoir of Samuel John Mills*, 24–26.

8. Andrew P. Peabody, *History of the Missions of the ABCFM* (Boston: Crosby and Nichols, 1862); *View of the Missions of the American Board of Commissioners for Foreign Missions* (Boston: Crocker and Brewster, 1823); and Gordon Hall and Samuel Newell, *The Conversion of the World* (Andover, MA: Flagg & Gould, 1818).

Griffin, who joined colleagues such as Jedediah Morse, Gardiner Spring, and Samuel Worcester in leading the service. "If the Tabernacle in London is entitled to be called 'the cradle of the London Missionary Society,'" remarked Worcester, "the Tabernacle in Salem is entitled to be called 'the cradle' both of the Massachusetts Missionary Society and the American Board of Commissioners for Foreign Mission." Had "that single ordination scene" on a snowy February day been the only gathering ever held in this building, he continued, it alone would be "enough to hallow the memory of this revered and endeared old sanctuary."[9]

Men were not alone, of course, in their interest in overseas missionary service. On February 5, 1812, just a day before the famous gathering at Tabernacle Congregational Church in Salem, Ann Hasseltine and Harriet Atwood were commissioned as "assistant missionaries" in what historian Dana L. Robert believes may have been the first service held in America for the specific purpose of setting women apart for "a ministerial role." In that service, held at Harriet's home church in Haverhill, Massachusetts, and conducted by the Reverend Jonathan Allen, pastor of the First Congregational Church in Bradford, Massachusetts, where Ann was a member, not only were two remarkable young women commissioned for their new overseas service but, as Professor Robert has suggested, the seeds were planted that during the next century would grow "into a distinctive woman's mission theory."[10]

Ann Hasseltine (who married Adoniram Judson the day before the famous February 6 service at Tabernacle Congregational Church in Salem) and Harriet Atwood (who married Samuel Newell a few days after that service) were only the first of what would soon be a flood of women, both married and single, who followed the call of God into missionary service.[11]

Some of these new missionaries, like Ann and Harriet, joined hands with their husbands on mission outposts around the world. Others, like the amazing pioneer missionaries of the Woman's Union Missionary Society, went

9. J. Herbert Kane, *A Concise History of the Christian World Mission* (Grand Rapids: Baker Books, 1987), 88. The "Tabernacle in London" referred to would have been Surrey Tabernacle, host to many gatherings of the London Missionary Society.

10. Dana L. Robert, *American Women in Mission* (Macon, GA: Mercer University Press, 1997), 1. Robert points out that Leonard Woods's commission to the five men the following day was to "go" and "preach," whereas Allen's commission to the two women was to "go" and "teach" (3n4). For background information on these two notable women, see James D. Knowles, *Memoir of Mrs. Ann H. Judson* (Boston: Lincoln & Edmonds, 1831), and *The Life and Writings of Mrs. Harriet Newell* (Philadelphia: American Sunday School Union, 1831).

11. See Amanda Porterfield, *Mary Lyon and the Mount Holyoke Missionaries* (New York: Oxford University Press, 1997).

as teachers, nurses, medical doctors, and evangelists to some of the most difficult locations on the face of the globe.[12] While the names of missionaries like William Carey, Adoniram Judson, and David Livingston might come more easily to mind than those of Eliza Gillett, Harriet Newell, and Lillian Chipley, the story of modern missions would scarcely be recognizable without them all.

Two weeks after the service in Salem, Adoniram and his new bride, Ann Hasseltine Judson, along with newly married Samuel and Harriet Atwood Newell, left for British India from Derby Wharf in Salem on the *Caravan*. A few days later, on February 24, Samuel and Rosanna Nott, along with Gordon Hall and Luther Rice, set sail for India from Philadelphia on the *Harmony*. Although the passages took about four months and involved enormous hardships, they helped launch a movement that eventually circled the globe. "Such was the humble beginning of the American foreign missionary movement," observed missiologist Herbert Kane, a movement that within a century and a half was providing "almost 70 percent of the worldwide Protestant missionary force and about 80 percent of the finances."[13]

Most of the initiative for overseas missions during those early years came from the student population. The leadership of the older generations was essential, to be sure, but the explosive energy at the center seemed to come invariably from young men and women—including growing numbers of Presbyterian students. From Williams and Brown to Middlebury and Yale, missionary outreach in the "Great Century" seemed dominated primarily by young men and women.[14]

---

12. For their stories, see Judith MacLeod, *Woman's Union Missionary Society: The Story of a Continuing Mission* (Upper Darby, PA: InterServe USA, 1999).

13. Kane, *A Concise History*, 87. For studies of the five who were ordained, see Courtney Anderson, *To the Golden Shore: The Life of Adoniram Judson* (Valley Forge, PA: Judson, 1987); Benjamin C. Meigs, "Memoir of the Rev. James Richards, American Missionary in Ceylon," *Missionary Herald*, 1823, 241–47; Horatio Bardwell, *Memoir of Gordon Hall* (New York: J. Leavitt, 1834); James B. Taylor, *Memoir of Rev. Luther Rice* (Baltimore: Armstrong and Berry, 1841); Henry Clay Trumbull, *Old Time Student Volunteers* (New York: Revell, 1902); and William B. Sprague, *Annals of the American Pulpit* (New York: Robert Carter and Brothers, 1857), 2:538–42, 596–601, 531–38.

14. About seven years after the commissioning of America's first foreign missionaries at Tabernacle Congregational Church in Salem, the Sandwich Islands Mission was launched at Park Street (Congregational) Church in Boston. On October 15, 1819, three native Hawaiians, seven couples, and five children gathered to officially "constitute the Sandwich Islands Church in preparation for their imminent departure for the Hawaiian Islands." See David W. Forbes, Ralph Thomas Kam, and Thomas A. Woods, *Partners in Change: A Bi-*

Not all these missionary efforts were as successful as their supporters had hoped. Missionary outreach to America's native populations proved especially difficult.[15] In 1817, for example, the ABCFM, in partnership with the Union Presbytery of East Tennessee—with "the permission of the Cherokee leaders and support from the federal government"—began an evangelistic and educational outreach among the Cherokees in Tennessee. Despite some early success, however, Samuel Worcester, head of the mission, had to admit that few conversions had taken place. By 1830, in fact, "only 180 Cherokees had become Presbyterian."[16] Among the most interesting missionary efforts was the establishment in Cornwall, Connecticut, of a school for "indigenous youth" from around the world. During its relatively brief history, the missionary school welcomed dozens of students from places like China, India, Polynesia, and Europe. The institution's purpose was fourfold: to educate, civilize, convert, and send these students back to their home countries as missionaries. Among the most prominent students were Elias Boudinot (editor of the first newspaper published for and by Native Americans), "Henry" Obookiah (the close friend of Samuel Mills and the one who inspired the establishment of the Sandwich Islands Mission), and "Thomas" Hopoo (an early missionary to Hawaii). Although the school "prospered" and even "became quite famous," as historian John Demos has argued, the grand experiment was brought to a premature end by "bitter controversy."[17]

THE SECOND GREAT AWAKENING

As impressive as were the student contributions to worldwide missionary outreach, it seems doubtful that the movement could have been sustained for very long had it not been for the powerful religious revivals that swept concurrently across the new nation. Beginning in the southern states of Kentucky and Tennessee and spreading northward into the mid-Atlantic and New England states, what has often been called the "Second Great Awakening" provided the

---

ographical *Encyclopedia of American Protestant Missionaries in Hawaii and Their Hawaiian and Tahitian Colleagues, 1820–1900* (Honolulu: Hawaiian Mission Children's Society and Hawaiian Mission Houses Historic Site and Archives, 2018), and Rosell, *Boston's Historic Park Street Church*, 62–71.

15. See Longfield, *Presbyterians and American Culture*, 81–86.

16. Longfield, *Presbyterians and American Culture*, 84.

17. John Demos, *The Heathen School: A Story of Hope and Betrayal in the Age of the Early Republic* (New York: Knopf, 2014). Quotations are taken from the prologue, 3–6.

young missionary movement with fresh energy, a growing sense of urgency, and an abundance of new recruits.[18]

The South

"It is in no way derogatory to sister denominations," wrote Princeton Seminary historian Lefferts A. Loetscher, to say that by the opening of the nineteenth century the Presbyterian church "was the most influential" denomination in America. With "the efficient central government supplied by [its] new General Assembly," its twenty-six presbyteries, its 419 congregations, its cadre of well-trained ministers, and its record of sustained growth, the Presbyterian church seemed well positioned to provide spiritual leadership for the young nation. Perhaps most importantly, Loetscher believed, the religious revivals sweeping across America and the voluntary organizations they generated were helping to undergird Presbyterianism's vitality and growth.[19]

In 1787, a revival led by John Blair Smith at Hampden-Sydney College in Virginia marked the beginning of a fresh awakening in America. The college revival soon spread to churches in western Virginia, North Carolina, and Kentucky.[20] James McGready (1763–1817), the Presbyterian pastor at Gaspar River, Kentucky—who had himself been converted during the Hampden-Sydney revival—not only witnessed an outbreak of revival in his own congregation but also became one of the key leaders for the most famous of all the Kentucky revivals at Cane Ridge.[21] Following the tradition of Scottish and Scots-Irish Presbyterianism,[22] revival broke out once again in 1801. In these services, "long preparatory sermons [were] followed by communicants gathering around long

18. For background to the Second Great Awakening, see John Wolffe, *The Expansion of Evangelicalism: The Age of Wilberforce, More, Chalmers, and Finney* (Downers Grove, IL: InterVarsity Press, 2007); *The Memoirs of Charles Grandison Finney: The Complete Restored Text*, ed. Garth M. Rosell and Richard A. G. Dupuis (Grand Rapids: Zondervan, 1989); Charles E. Hambrick-Stowe, *Charles Grandison Finney and the Spirit of American Evangelicalism* (Grand Rapids: Eerdmans, 1996); and Nathan O. Hatch, *The Democratization of American Christianity* (New Haven: Yale University Press, 1991).

19. Lefferts A. Loetscher, *A Brief History of the Presbyterians*, 4th ed. (Philadelphia: Westminster, 1983), 80–81.

20. Longfield, *Presbyterians and American Culture*, 55.

21. Paul K. Conkin, *Cane Ridge: America's Pentecost* (Madison: University of Wisconsin Press, 1990), and John B. Boles, *The Great Revival: 1787–1805* (Lexington: University Press of Kentucky, 1972).

22. Leigh Eric Schmidt, *Holy Fairs: Scotland and the Making of American Revivalism*, 2nd ed. (Grand Rapids: Eerdmans, 2001).

tables to partake of 'platters of bread' and 'flagons or cups of wine.' In Scotland these communion services had developed into 'holy fairs,' which lasted for days and attracted thousands of participants."[23]

Although the nearly ten thousand that gathered at Cane Ridge included Presbyterians, Methodists, Baptists, and others, leadership seemed to be drawn largely from Presbyterian ranks. Presbyterian pastors such as McGready and Barton Stone (1772–1844) not only preached regularly to those who had gathered but also helped to oversee the Sunday communion services. With such large crowds, however, discipline and order were difficult to maintain, and "hundreds of participants fainted, groaned, laughed, or fell into convulsions" during the services. Such excesses soon created discord and division among clergy and laypersons alike. As a result, Presbyterians increasingly withdrew from participating in such "camp meeting" gatherings and (perhaps as an unintended consequence) the Presbyterian church in Kentucky, likely the "strongest denomination in Kentucky" in 1805, watched its numbers stagnate. Between 1800 and 1820, Kentucky Methodists grew from 2,000 to 21,000 while Presbyterians during those years only grew from 2,000 to 2,700.[24]

The North

A second major phase of the Second Great Awakening, differing markedly in style and tone from the revivals of Kentucky and Tennessee, was soon sweeping through the mid-Atlantic states and New England. One of the most notable of these early northern revivals broke out in 1801 at Yale College in New Haven, Connecticut.[25] Concerned about the rise of infidelity among the students, President Timothy Dwight (1752–1817) (a grandson of Jonathan Edwards) launched a remarkable counteroffensive. Yale "was in a most ungodly state" before the arrival of Dwight, wrote Lyman Beecher (1775–1863) (himself a student at the college). "The college church was almost extinct. Most of the students were skeptical, and rowdies were plenty. Wine and liquors were kept in many rooms," Beecher continued, and "intemperance, profanity, gambling, and licentiousness were common."[26]

23. Longfield, *Presbyterians and American Culture*, 55–57.

24. Longfield, *Presbyterians and American Culture*, 56. These controversies also contributed to the formation of the Cumberland Presbyterian Church in 1810; see chap. 10 below.

25. J. Edwin Orr, *Campus Aflame: A History of Evangelical Awakenings in Collegiate Communities*, rev. ed. (Wheaton, IL: International Awakening Press, 1994).

26. *The Autobiography of Lyman Beecher*, ed. Barbara M. Cross, 2 vols. (Cambridge, MA: Belknap Press of Harvard University Press, 1961), 1:27.

Determined to meet the challenge directly, President Dwight urged the students to build as strong a critique of "the truth of the Scriptures" as they were able to mount and as strong a defense of their intellectual heroes—including Tom Paine, Jean-Jacques Rousseau, and Voltaire—as they could establish. Then, in a series of powerful chapel sermons, he grappled with the issues they had raised and provided a carefully reasoned response. He met "ridicule with quiet argument," as historian J. Edwin Orr has observed. By the close of the academic year, in a memorable baccalaureate address, he "exhorted his beloved students to 'embrace Christianity.'" Slowly but inexorably "the tide began to turn at Yale and came in full flood in 1802. One third of the student body made profession of faith that year."[27] Lyman Beecher was among those most deeply affected by Dwight's "polished, disciplined and logical" approach. The light "did not come in a sudden blaze," Beecher explained, "but by degrees." And throughout the process, as a guide through the darkness, there was always Dr. Dwight. Later, during his pastoral ministry in Litchfield, Connecticut, Beecher told his old teacher that everything he had he owed to him. "Then," Dwight responded, "I have done a great and soul-satisfying work. I consider myself amply rewarded."[28] Early in 1817, having suffered for many months with "a painful form of cancer," Timothy Dwight died.[29]

Support for such spiritual awakening was nothing new for America's Presbyterians. Indeed, Presbyterian ministers like William and Gilbert Tennent, Samuel Blair, Jonathan Dickinson, and Samuel Davies had all played prominent roles in the spiritual awakenings and evangelistic efforts of the eighteenth century.[30] Such efforts were renewed and encouraged once again among Plan of Union pastors during the early years of the nineteenth century. Dirck Lansing, Lyman Beecher, Asahel Nettleton, Nathan S. S. Beman, Samuel Clark Aikin, and a host of others became increasingly active in the cause of revival, reform, and missionary outreach.[31]

27. Orr, *Campus Aflame*, 40. Yale was not alone, of course. Amherst, Dartmouth, Princeton, and Williams were among the colleges that "reported the conversion to God of a third to a half of their total student bodies, which in those days usually numbered between a hundred and two hundred fifty" students. See pp. 39–44 for Orr's more detailed descriptions.

28. *The Autobiography of Lyman Beecher*, 1:27–31.

29. Jack Fitzmier, *New England's Moral Legislator: Timothy Dwight, 1752–1817* (Bloomington: Indiana University Press, 1998), 76–77.

30. See chap. 7 above; Smylie, *A Brief History of the Presbyterians*, 46–56; and Loetscher, *A Brief History of the Presbyterians*, 82–103.

31. For a helpful summary of the Plan of Union, see Longfield, *Presbyterians and American Culture*, 57–59.

Western Revivals

None played a more prominent role, however, than Charles G. Finney (1792–1875).[32] As an aspiring young lawyer, Finney was apprenticed to Judge Benjamin Wright in Adams, New York, where he not only practiced law but also attended the local Presbyterian church and served for a time as the director of its choir. It was there that Finney met George Gale, pastor of the Adams congregation and a graduate of Princeton Theological Seminary. After Finney's dramatic conversion in 1821 and his subsequent call to preach, described in some detail in his memoirs, the Oneida Presbytery assigned Gale to serve as Finney's theological mentor.[33] And when Finney was ordained to the gospel ministry in 1824, it was the Oneida Presbytery that examined Finney and conducted his ordination.[34]

Equally important, it would seem, Finney conducted some of his earliest revivals in Presbyterian churches that were connected to the Oneida Presbytery.[35] In the autumn of 1825, for example, Finney launched what came to be known as his Western Revivals in a small Presbyterian church in the village of Western in upstate New York. His old pastor, George Gale, had recently had to leave his pastorate at Adams due to bad health and had moved to Western with the hope of recovery. Anxious to attract Finney on a preaching mission to his new town, Gale traveled to the Synod meetings with the express purpose of convincing Finney to come. "The Presbyterian house of worship," Gale told Finney, is "respectable for size and appearance," but it is much in need of repair. The membership is small, and the congregation is currently without a pastor.[36]

Finney accepted Gale's invitation, and he lodged with his old mentor while he was there. "Brother Finney," the wife of one of First Presbyterian Church's three elders remarked after Finney had been in town for a short time, "the Lord has come! This work will spread over all this region! A cloud of mercy over-

---

32. Hambrick-Stowe, *Charles G. Finney and the Spirit of American Evangelicalism*; Garth M. Rosell, "Charles G. Finney: His Place in the Stream of American Evangelicalism," in *The Evangelical Tradition in America*, ed. Leonard I. Sweet (Macon, GA: Mercer University Press, 1984), 131–47; and *The Memoirs of Charles G. Finney*.

33. *The Memoirs of Charles G. Finney*, 16–43.

34. For a fuller introduction to Finney's life and ministry, see James E. Johnson, "The Life of Charles Grandison Finney" (PhD diss., Syracuse University, 1959).

35. John Frost, Moses Gillett, and Noah Coe, *A Narrative of the Revival of Religion in the County of Oneida; particularly in the Bounds of the Presbytery of Oneida, in the year 1826* (Utica: Hastings and Tracy, 1826; reprint, Princeton: D. A. Borrenstein, 1827), 9.

36. *Autobiography of George Washington Gale (1789–1861), Founder of Galesburg, Illinois, and Knox College* (New York: privately printed, 1964), 263.

hangs us all; and we shall see such a work of grace as we have never yet seen."[37]
Her predictions proved accurate. The revival that broke out in Western caught
the attention of churches throughout the county, but soon other pastors were
showing up at the meetings. Moses Gillett of Rome, New York, for example,
having heard about "what the Lord was doing in Western," came with one of
his members to see firsthand "the work that was going on" and declared, after
hearing Finney, that they "were both greatly impressed with the work of God."
As a result, they invited Finney to come to Rome. The subsequent revival at
Rome proved to be even more impressive than the meetings at Western. So
much so, in fact, that Samuel Clark Aikin (1790–1879), the noted pastor of the
First Presbyterian Church in Utica, invited Finney to come and preach for his
congregation.[38] While Finney was preaching in Utica, Dr. Dirck Cornelius
Lansing (1785–1857), the distinguished pastor of the First Presbyterian Church
at Auburn and lecturer at Auburn Theological Seminary, came to see the Utica
revival for himself and soon invited the evangelist to conduct a preaching
mission at his church in Auburn.[39]

This pattern was to be repeated dozens of times in the coming years as word
of Finney's remarkable ministry spread across county and state boundaries,
across denominations, across barriers of class or race or gender or social standing, and eventually across national boundaries. Finney, quite simply stated, became "an immensely important man in American history," as historian Sydney
Ahlstrom phrased it, "by any standard of measure."[40]

While Finney's successful meetings were attracting a growing number of
supporters, they were also generating a substantial outpouring of opposition.
Among the active critics of Finney and his methods were the Unitarians and
Universalists, who had themselves been targets of Finney's criticism. Concerns
about Finney, however, were not limited to those widely considered as outside
the evangelical ranks. Three congregational ministers in Oneida County, for
example, constituting themselves as the Oneida Association, were among the
first to publish a "pastoral letter" warning readers against the Finney revivals.[41]
Widely circulated throughout the county, the letter warned readers of twenty-
nine "evils to be guarded against." A careful reading, however, indicates that

37. The Memoirs of Charles G. Finney, 147.

38. The Memoirs of Charles G. Finney, 172–92.

39. The Memoirs of Charles G. Finney, 193–202.

40. Sydney E. Ahlstrom, A Religious History of the American People (New Haven: Yale
University Press, 1972), 461.

41. William R. Weeks, A Pastoral Letter of the Ministers of the Oneida Association to the
Churches Under Their Care on the Subject of Revivals of Religion (Utica: Ariel Works, 1827).

the letter was concerned about five of the "new measures" in particular: the use of inquiry meetings, the holding of protracted meetings, the use of colloquial language in the pulpit, the hasty admission of converts to church membership, and the practice of women praying in public meetings.[42]

While the influence of this letter was largely confined to readers within Oneida County, Asahel Nettleton and Lyman Beecher's criticism of Finney's "New Measures," as they were called, quickly caught the attention of the entire country.[43] "That those brethren were grossly deceived by information that they received from some source, we were sure," wrote Finney in response to the criticisms. "We regarded them as good men, and true"; he continued, "but we knew that somebody was giving them most unreliable information."[44] More telling than Finney's response, perhaps, was the fact that an overwhelming majority of the pastors and members of the churches in which the revivals were actually held immediately voiced their support for Finney and the measures he was using. So strong were these sentiments, in fact, that the Oneida Presbytery published its own *Narrative of the Revival of Religion in the County of Oneida; particularly in the Bounds of the Presbytery of Oneida, in the Year 1826*, dealing with the very revivals it had witnessed firsthand. "More than three thousand are indulging hope that they have become reconciled to God through the Redeemer," the *Narrative* confirmed. "About half this number have already united with the Presbyterian and Congregational churches, and a large portion of the remainder with the Baptist and Methodists churches. Never before have the churches in this region been blessed with so great a shower of divine grace."[45]

To their lasting credit, many who were involved in the debates over the conduct of the Western revivals were willing to meet during the summer of 1827 to discuss their differences. The New Lebanon Convention, named for the little New York village near the border of Massachusetts, was held in mid-July of 1827. Meeting, as their official minutes phrased it, "to see in what respect

42. For a discussion of the growing opposition see Keith J. Hardman, *Charles Grandison Finney, 1792–1875: Revivalist and Reformer* (Syracuse: Syracuse University Press, 1987), 78–149.
43. *Letters of the Rev. Dr. Beecher and Rev. Mr. Nettleton, on the "New Measures" in Conducting Revivals of Religion* (New York: Carvill, 1828); *Autobiography, Correspondence, etc. of Lyman Beecher, D. D.*, ed. Charles Beecher, 2 vols. (New York: Harper, 1863/1865). For Finney's discussion of the "new measures" controversy, see *The Memoirs of Charles G. Finney*, 141–92. For Beecher's discussion of the controversy, see his two-volume autobiography.
44. *The Memoirs of Charles G. Finney*, 141. See also Rosell, "Charles G. Finney," in Sweet, *The Evangelical Tradition in America*, 131–47.
45. Frost, Gillett, and Coe, *A Narrative*, 41.

there is an agreement between brethren from different sections of the country, in regard to principles and measures in conducting and promoting revivals of religion," the Plan of Union clergy rediscovered the basic unity they shared in the work of revivals and benevolence.[46] The group of eighteen prominent Presbyterian and Congregational ministers that gathered for about a week in that small village were "considered the most representative of the clergy in New England and New York."[47]

Historians have generally interpreted New Lebanon in terms of conflict between east and west, the tidewater and the frontier, or between Connecticut Congregationalism and New York Presbyterianism.[48] Viewed from a different angle, however, the unexpected outcome of New Lebanon seemed to have been overwhelming agreement on nearly all the points of difference. Four years after the conference, in fact, Beecher wrote a letter to Finney admitting, as he phrased it, that "you and I are, as much, perhaps even more, *one* than almost any two men whom God has been pleased to render conspicuous in his Church."[49]

It would be claiming too much to say that all eighteen delegates agreed at every point during the meetings. Yet, of the twenty-seven resolutions considered during those four days, only one issue of substance permanently divided the delegates. It was an issue that deeply exercised Asahel Nettleton: the practice of allowing women to pray in public meetings. Even after agreement had been reached on such matters as the propriety of specifically referring to individuals by name in public prayer, the kind of guidelines to be used in reporting about revivals, and the proper attitudes to be maintained concerning such phenomena as "audible groanings" and "violent gestures" in a service of worship or prayer, the female prayer issue remained unresolved.[50]

Aiken, Beman, Churchill, Finney, Frost, Gale, Gillett, Lansing, and Smith maintained that there were indeed occasions, given proper limits, on which

46. Minutes of the New Lebanon Convention, *New York Observer*, August 4, 1827.

47. Charles C. Cole Jr., *The Social Ideas of the Northern Evangelists, 1826–1860* (New York: Columbia University Press, 1954), 390. Those that gathered at New Lebanon were Lyman Beecher, Justin Edwards, Heman Humphrey, Caleb Tenney, Joel Hawes, Asahel Nettleton, Silas Churchill, Nathan S. S. Beman, Henry Weed, William Weeks, Henry Smith, Asahel Norton, Moses Gillett, John Frost, Samuel C. Aiken, George Gale, Dirck Lansing, and Charles Finney.

48. William G. McLoughlin Jr., *Modern Revivalism* (New York: Ronald, 1959), 36–37; Charles C. Cole Jr., "The New Lebanon Convention," *New York History* 31 (October 1950): 395; and Robert Hastings Nichols, *Presbyterianism in New York State* (Philadelphia: Westminster, 1963), 101.

49. Beecher to Finney, August 2, 1831; letter in the Finney Papers at the Oberlin College Archives.

50. See reports in the *Western Recorder*, August 7, 1827, and the *New York Observer*, December 15, 1827.

the practice might be allowed, while Beecher, Edwards, Hawes, Humphrey, Nettleton, Norton, Tenney, Weed, and Weeks could conceive of no circumstance in which it might be proper for a female to pray "in social meetings for religious worship." Other than that single issue, however, the convention ended with worship and prayer on Saturday with relative unanimity on all the issues that had troubled the critics. Less than a year later, many of the principal participants gathered in Philadelphia to sign an agreement to halt any further bickering over questions relating to the new measures.[51]

Meanwhile, Finney's evangelistic efforts not only were swelling the membership rolls of Presbyterian congregations across America but were also invigorating the need for missionary outreach and spiritual renewal. "I was bred a lawyer," Finney often remarked. "I came right forth from a law office to the pulpit and talked to the people as I would have talked to a jury." Indeed, Finney sought in his preaching to appeal to the intellect and the will rather than the emotions. "Animal feelings," he argued, are "boisterous and unintelligent," whereas "spiritual feelings," those produced by a genuine encounter with reason and truth, are the "free and unembarrassed action of both the intelligence and the will."[52] While some like William B. Sprague, pastor of the Second Presbyterian Church in Albany, dismissed Finney's revivals as "mere animal excitements," other Presbyterian pastors like John Frost, Noah Coe, and N. S. S. Beman labeled such criticisms "misrepresentations" at best and outright "lies" at worst. Indeed, as the Oneida Presbytery's report had concluded, there was less "excitement of the passions" and more "wisdom and discretion" than any could recall having been exhibited in any prior revival within memory.[53] Preaching that appeals primarily to the emotions, Finney was convinced, is bad preaching. Rather, as he often urged his students, "Read, study, think and read again"—you were "made to think," he told them. "It will do you good."[54]

In addition to bringing an intellectual edge to the resurgence of evangelical Christianity, Finney urged the church to actively apply biblical Christianity to every arena of life. Far from abandoning its long-standing commitment to missionary outreach and spiritual awakening, Finney argued that it is precisely

51. The Philadelphia agreement was signed by Beecher, Lansing, Aiken, Finney, Holmes, Cheever, Frost, Beman, Coe, Gilbert, and Parker. See *The Memoirs of Charles G. Finney*, 223.

52. *The Memoirs of Charles G. Finney*, 168.

53. Frost, Gillett, and Coe, *A Narrative*, 35–39.

54. Charles G. Finney, *Lectures on Systematic Theology* (Oberlin, OH: James M. Fitch, 1846), v; Charles G. Finney, *A Sermon Preached in the Presbyterian Church at Troy, March 4, 1827* (Troy, NY: Tuttle and Richards, 1827), 10–14; and Charles G. Finney, *Revival Fire: Letters on Revivals* (Waukesha, WI: Metropolitan Church Association, n.d.), 7–53. For a fuller development of this line of thought, see Rosell, "Charles G. Finney," in Sweet, *The Evangelical Tradition in America*, 137–40.

because of those commitments that the church was obligated, to borrow the words of the prophet Micah, to "act justly and to love mercy and to walk humbly" with God. Indeed, it was their love for the Bible—with its repeated instructions to care for the poor and needy, to be honest in business dealings, to look after widows and orphans, to treat the neighbor as one might wish to be treated—that made so many evangelical Christians willing to risk their lives and their fortunes in the quest to fight injustice, to reform prisons, to care for the needy, and to rid the nation of the scourge of slavery. Christians have suffered mightily over the centuries in their efforts to preserve the Bible and obey its teachings. Their love for the Bible, as historian Timothy L. Smith argued so persuasively in *Revivalism and Social Reform*, has been a powerful engine for change and an enormous motivation for social reform.[55]

Since Smith's basic thesis is now widely accepted in the academy, it is surprising that so few general readers seem to be aware of evangelicalism's long history of social reform. Throughout the eighteenth and nineteenth centuries, literally tens of thousands of evangelical Christians on both sides of the Atlantic sought to apply the teachings of the Bible to every area of life. With uncommon passion, they threw themselves into the task of cleaning up the hospitals, reforming the prisons, securing the rights of women, providing food and clothing for the poor, protecting children from the brutal practices of the workplace, promoting Christian missions at home and abroad, translating and distributing the Bible to a needy world, and helping to bring an end to the tragic evil of slavery.[56] Many Presbyterians became enthusiastic participants in those efforts, and some, to their eternal credit, endured great hardship and loss because of their commitment. "If your heart is full of love, it will find vent and then you will find or make ways enough to express your love in deeds," wrote Jonathan Edwards. "When a fountain abounds in water, it will send forth streams."[57]

55. Timothy L. Smith, *Revivalism and Social Reform* (Eugene, OR: Wipf & Stock, 2004), and Donald Dayton, *Rediscovering an Evangelical Heritage: A Tradition and Trajectory of Integrating Piety and Justice* (Grand Rapids: Baker Academic, 2014).

56. Norris Magnuson, *Salvation in the Slums* (Eugene, OR: Wipf & Stock, 2004).

57. Jonathan Edwards, "Charity and Its Fruits" (1749), in *Ethical Writings*, ed. Paul Ramsey, vol. 8 of *The Works of Jonathan Edwards* (New Haven: Yale University Press, 1989), 147–48.

CHAPTER 10

American Reformed Theology

The early decades of the nineteenth century were an energetic time of Presbyterian growth as the new nation expanded westward. Americans crossed the Appalachians into western New York and began to populate the old Northwest. Soon after the turn of the century, a number of new states came into existence—Ohio (1803), Indiana (1816), and Illinois (1818). A significant number of these westward pilgrims were New England Congregationalists who started new churches as they settled in the west. Presbyterians would join with Congregationalists in evangelizing the old Northwest. The church-planting movement in the west coincided with frontier revivals, the growth of home and foreign mission agencies, the founding of Princeton Seminary (1812), and the proliferation of Presbyterian publications. Each of these endeavors shaped Presbyterianism in fresh ways.

Sadly, this was also a time of deep division between two parties in the church—the Old School and the New School. Conflict between the two groups intensified in the period leading up to the mid-1830s and caused a major schism. A chief culprit of the rising dissension was the so-called New Divinity, or New England theology, terms used for the Edwardsean party within Congregationalism. This school of thought was identified with several of Jonathan Edwards's students—Joseph Bellamy, Jonathan Edwards Jr., and Samuel Hopkins. The New Divinity men stressed piety, supported the revivals, and restated Calvinism in the Edwardsean theological framework, which included several innovations. The terms "Consistent Calvinism" and "Hopkinsianism" were also used for this group of theologians.[1] Within Presbyterianism, the controversy

---

1. For introductions to these authors and excerpts from their writings, see Douglas A. Sweeney and Allen C. Guelzo, eds., *The New England Theology: From Jonathan Edwards to Edward Amasa Park* (Grand Rapids: Baker Academic, 2006); see also Mark A. Noll, *Amer-*

concerned the degree to which the New England theology had permeated the Presbyterian church. Congregationalists and Presbyterians had a long history together in America. Presbyterian ministry candidates had studied under Congregational pastors and professors since early colonial days, and the two groups had collaborated during the First Great Awakening. Since they shared a common commitment to Calvinism, it seemed a natural progression when Connecticut Congregationalists and Presbyterians officially joined forces in the 1801 Plan of Union. It was a union with good intentions, but it sowed destructive seeds. The persistent query over New England theology resurfaced the old issue of confessional subscription as Presbyterians argued over defining faithfulness to the Westminster Confession.

New England Theology

Congregational minister Jonathan Edwards of New England was without American theological peer in the first half of the eighteenth century. Two of his major treatises, *Freedom of the Will* (1754) and *Original Sin* (1758), would be especially significant in ongoing nineteenth-century debates among Congregationalists and Presbyterians.[2] While all Calvinists maintained that human nature had been polluted by sin prior to actual sinning, they disagreed on how to explain this phenomenon called "original sin." In his work *Original Sin*, Edwards explained that depravity of the human heart comes from Adam's sin, due to a "constituted oneness" of Adam with the entire human race. Out of this "constituted union of the branches and the root" came universal human moral depravity, and man is guilty as a consequence of union with Adam. This was a "mediate imputation" of Adam's sin to humanity—man's guilt is mediated through his inheritance from Adam of a corrupt nature. This exposition differed from the Westminster Confession's explanation of "immediate imputation," wherein the guilt of Adam's sin is immediately imputed to his posterity, who therefore become corrupt in nature.[3] In *Freedom of the Will*, Edwards distinguished between "natural ability" and "moral ability," asserting

---

ica's God: From Jonathan Edwards to Abraham Lincoln* (New York: Oxford University Press, 2002), 227–316; E. Brooks Holifield, *Theology in America: Christian Thought from the Age of the Puritans to the Civil War* (New Haven: Yale University Press, 2005), 102–56.

2. *Works of Jonathan Edwards*, vol. 1, *Freedom of the Will*, ed. Paul Ramsey (New Haven: Yale University Press, 1957); vol. 3, *Original Sin*, ed. Clyde A. Holbrook (New Haven: Yale University Press, 1970).

3. See Elwyn A. Smith, "The Doctrine of Imputation and the Presbyterian Schism of 1837–1838," *Journal of the Presbyterian Historical Society* 38 (September 1960).

that post-Fall humanity retained all natural faculties (ability) to do God's will but no longer had the moral ability because of innate moral depravity. The distinction between natural and moral ability was commonplace among New School Presbyterians, while some Old School Presbyterians rejected Edwards's position as giving away too much. On the other hand, some Congregationalists believed Edwards's view was insufficient for safeguarding human freedom.

Congregational pastor Samuel Hopkins (1721–1803), who had been personally tutored by Edwards, reiterated the concept of "natural ability" but went a step further by arguing that human moral corruption comes through actual sin, that is, the first moral acts of a person define participation in Adam's sin.[4] This understanding was controversial, and several Presbyterian ministers would be accused of "Hopkinsianism." In 1811 Ezra Stiles Ely, a pastor in Philadelphia, published *A Contrast between Calvinism and Hopkinsianism.* Ely charged Hopkinsianism with being a dangerous threat to Presbyterians, pointing to the doctrines of original sin, human ability, and the atonement as examples of why "the system of Hopkinsianism is repugnant" to the confession of faith.[5] In 1817, the Hopkinsian question came before the Presbyterian General Assembly. The Synod of Philadelphia had adopted a pastoral letter, written by Ely, in which "Hopkinsian heresies" were condemned. The letter declared, "May the time never come in which our ecclesiastical courts shall determine that Hopkinsianism and the doctrines of our Confession of Faith are the same thing." A General Assembly committee, chaired by Princeton professor Samuel Miller (1769–1850), responded to the Synod with a resolution commending the Synod's zeal "to promote a strict conformity to our public standards," but warned that Synod's zeal would "introduce a spirit of jealousy and suspicion against ministers in good standing which is calculated to disturb the peace and harmony of our ecclesiastical judicatories." The resolution was adopted by the majority, but a minority opposed the Assembly's unwillingness to concur in the denunciation of Hopkinsianism. The protesters believed teaching these doctrines would place one "in violation of ordination vows."[6]

A more serious threat to traditional Reformed theology was "Taylorism," also known as New Haven theology, identified with professor Nathanial Taylor of Yale, who became the Dwight Professor of Didactic Theology in 1822. His

4. *The Works of Samuel Hopkins with a Memoir of His Life and Character*, ed. Edward Parks (Boston: Doctrinal Tract and Book Society, 1854); J. A. Conforti, *Samuel Hopkins and the New Divinity Movement* (Grand Rapids: Christian University Press, 1981).

5. Ezra Stiles Ely, *A Contrast between Calvinism and Hopkinsianism* (New York: S. Whiting and Co., 1811), 278.

6. *Minutes of the General Assembly in the United States of America, 1789–1837* (Philadelphia, 1817), 653–56.

elevated use of human reason as an infallible guide to truth caused him to jettison historically Calvinist understandings of original sin, human inability, and regeneration. Taylor believed that the depravity of the human heart was the result of one's own choices. He rejected the Edwardsean distinction between natural ability and moral ability, arguing for the origin of moral inability in a voluntary act of a free agent, not a depravity of nature inherited from Adam.[7] New Haven theology was especially worrisome because a number of Presbyterian ministers were graduates of Yale. Presbyterian professors weighed in on Taylorism through a series of journal articles in 1830–1831.[8] The articles appeared in the *Biblical Repertory*, one of the oldest quarterly journals in the United States, founded by young Princeton Seminary professor Charles Hodge (1797–1878) in 1825. Hodge argued that the doctrine of original sin was a vital doctrine of Christianity; he insisted that the imputation of Adam's sin and the imputation of Christ's righteousness to the sinner are inseparably connected.[9] It was in the context of challenging New England theology that the terms "Old School" and "New School" came into usage as labels for two distinct parties in the Presbyterian church.

OLD SCHOOL AND NEW SCHOOL

While the Old School was committed to traditional Calvinism, the New School practiced a broader version of Reformed theology that included a robust ecumenical spirit and more tolerant perspectives on revivalism. Clear party distinctions were obvious, for example, in the array of responses to the revivals of Charles Finney, who had been ordained as a Presbyterian minister in 1824. The Old School associated Finney's "New Measures" with doctrinal error, while the New School took a more nuanced approach. New School minister Lyman Beecher wrote in 1829, "There is such an amount of truth and power in the

---

7. Nathaniel Taylor, *Concio ad Clerum, A sermon delivered in the chapel of Yale College September 10, 1828* (New Haven: Hezekiah Howe, 1828), 6, 28, 29; see Douglas Sweeney, *Nathaniel Taylor, New Haven Theology, and the Legacy of Jonathan Edwards* (New York: Oxford University Press, 2002), and Earl A. Pope, *New England Calvinism and the Disruption of the Presbyterian Church* (New York: Garland, 1987).

8. Most of these articles have been reprinted in *Princeton versus the New Divinity* (Edinburgh: Banner of Truth Trust, 2001).

9. Charles Hodge, "Review of an Article in the June Number of *The Christian Spectator* Entitled 'Inquiries Respecting the Doctrine of Imputation,'" *Biblical Repertory and Theological Review* 2 (October 1830): 429. For an overview of this prolonged debate, see George P. Hutchinson, *The Problem of Original Sin in American Presbyterian Theology* (Phillipsburg, NJ: P&R, 1972).

preaching of Mr. Finney, and so great an amount of good hopefully done, that if he can be so far restrained as that he shall do more good than evil, then it would be dangerous to oppose him, lest at length we might be found to fight against God; for though some revivals may be so badly managed as to be worse than none, there may, to a certain extent, be great imperfections in them and yet they be, on the whole, blessings to the Church."[10]

Presbyterians and Congregationalists had cooperated in joint frontier missions since the 1801 Plan of Union,[11] an ecclesiastical arrangement that allowed for sharing ministers and accommodating one another's polity. A Congregational church could call a Presbyterian minister, or a Presbyterian church could call a Congregational minister, and in each situation local church polity would remain in force, whether Presbyterian or Congregational. If a congregation was comprised of both Presbyterians and Congregationalists, a standing committee would be chosen to supervise the flock. Members of this standing committee could vote in a presbytery like any Presbyterian elder. With a prevailing ecumenical spirit at the time, the 1801 Presbyterian General Assembly unanimously adopted the Plan of Union. This cooperative arrangement served the churches well for a season, but inherent problems surfaced in the "Presbygational" system. The Old School was vexed that "committee men," who had not taken ordination vows to the Westminster Confession, were voting in presbyteries.[12]

By the 1830s, irritation intensified in presbyteries, synods, and the General Assembly as the two parties sparred in church courts. Many Presbyterians, both Old School and New School, were certain that Taylor and his disciples had crossed the line into heterodoxy by their denial of doctrines essential to the Westminster Confession. The Princeton professors, as moderate Old School men, were convinced that the majority of the New School were orthodox and had not succumbed to Taylorism. However, conservative Old School men were persuaded that Arminian/Pelagian errors were more pervasive in the New School and tolerated in their presbyteries. The Old School answer was to enforce strict subscription to the Westminster Confession in the courts of the church. Professor Hodge believed this was a mistake, arguing that the ministerial ordination vow did not require adherence to every doctrine in

---

10. Beecher to Asahel Nettleton, quoted in George Marsden, *The Evangelical Mind and the New School Presbyterian Experience* (New Haven: Yale University Press, 1970), 77, 78.

11. See chap. 9 above.

12. *Minutes of the General Assembly*, 1801, 224, 225; Williston Walker, *A History of the Congregational Churches in the United States*, American Church History Series, vol. 3 (New York: Christian Literature Co., 1894), 316-19; Frederick Kuhns, "New Light on the Plan of Union," *Journal of the Presbyterian Historical Society* 26 (1948): 19-43.

the Confession, but to the "constituent doctrines of the Calvinistic system contained in the Confession of Faith." While this stance allowed a certain amount of liberty, it also meant that "no man, who denied original sin, efficacious grace, personal election, decrees, or perseverance of the saints," could honestly profess to affirm the Calvinistic system. Writing in 1831, Hodge argued that disagreement over subscription was the crucial issue separating the parties: "In the present agitated state of our Church, we are persuaded that this, of all others, is the subject of the most practical importance. If it could be once clearly ascertained and agreed upon, where the line was to be drawn, there would be an end to a great part of the contention and anxiety which so unhappily exists."[13]

CUMBERLAND, REFORMED, AND
ASSOCIATE REFORMED PRESBYTERIANS

In the South, theological tensions surfaced in the wake of frontier revivals in Kentucky and, within a few decades, produced new denominations. In 1796, Presbyterian minister James McGready, who was serving three congregations on the Kentucky frontier, began to stir these congregations through his preaching. The revival expanded, and by the end of 1800 thousands were attending "camp meetings." An 1801 camp meeting at Cane Ridge under Presbyterian minister Barton Stone drew thousands, but it was tainted with immoderate physical manifestations.[14] Two parties developed among the Presbyterians in the area: a New Light revivalist party and those opposed to the frontier revivalists' methods and doctrines. In 1803, the Synod of Kentucky became involved when the Presbytery of Washington refused to reexamine two of her ministers accused of Arminianism. As the Synod met, five of the New Light preachers protested the review of their presbytery's proceedings and announced their withdrawal from Synod to form their own Springfield Presbytery. The revivalists contended that the doctrines of the Confession of Faith were a hindrance to preaching the free offer of the gospel to all men, whom they believed could receive the gospel without a prior work of regeneration by the Spirit. The departed pastors rejected the use of creeds, which they viewed as divisive. The new Springfield Presbytery dissolved in less than a year, as the New Lights began referring to themselves only as "Christians." Under the lead-

---

13. Charles Hodge, "Remarks on Dr. Cox's Communication," *Biblical Repertory and Theological Review* 3 (October 1831): 524, 525.

14. See chap. 9 above.

ership of Barton Stone, the Christian Church was founded, and in the 1830s Stone joined with Alexander Campbell and the Disciples of Christ. Eventually, a number of the New Light ministers recanted their errors and returned to the Presbyterian church.[15]

With the Kentucky revival's success came petitions for more ministers to continue the work. The cries of the people for more preaching came from many parts of the extensive frontier. To meet this pressing demand, a plan was proposed by the Reverend David Rice for "encouraging such amongst us as appeared to be men of good talents, and who also discovered a disposition to exercise their gifts in a public way, to preach the Gospel, although they might not have acquired that degree of human education which the letter of discipline requires." This plan found general acceptance among the people, who began to earnestly pray for God to raise up these ministers, and in time several young men were presented as potential preachers. Transylvania Presbytery waived educational requirements, licensing or ordaining a number of young men as catechists, exhorters, and ministers. A rationale for waiving educational requirements was given: "They were men in a matrimonial state, and could not consistently with those relative duties, by which they were bound to their families, go and acquire the knowledge of all those forms of literature required in the Book of Discipline." A minority in the presbytery protested, and the Synod of Kentucky divided Transylvania Presbytery, creating a Cumberland Presbytery with a prorevival majority. Cumberland Presbytery "continued from time to time to license and ordain such men, both learned and unlearned"; meanwhile, some members of the Synod complained about these irregularities. A commission of Synod was sent to investigate and charged Cumberland with two "irregularities"—the candidates were not "examined on the learned languages" and had only partially adopted the Confession "as far as they believed it to agree with the Word of God." A number of revivalists with irregular credentials had objected to the doctrine of predestination as "fatalism." Two men were suspended from the ministry, and Cumberland Presbytery was dissolved by the Synod in 1806, with the ministers being transferred back to Transylvania Presbytery.[16]

A majority of Cumberland Presbytery objected to these actions by Synod, believing they were "competent judges of the faith and abilities of their own candidates." The 1807 General Assembly considered the protest, asking Synod to

---

15. Ernest Trice Thompson, *Presbyterians in the South*, vol. 1, *1607–1861* (Richmond, VA: John Knox, 1963), 155–64.

16. *The Cumberland Presbyterian Digest* (Memphis: Board of Publication and Christian Education of the Cumberland Presbyterian Church, 1957), 1–5.

review its proceedings. The review took place, and the 1809 General Assembly confirmed that Synod's actions were in order. After an unsuccessful attempt at reunion with the Synod of Kentucky, several ministers from the previously dissolved Cumberland Presbytery reconstituted themselves as Cumberland Presbytery in 1810, with three ministers, Finis Ewing, Samuel King, and Samuel M'Adow. The new Cumberland Presbytery added congregations and in 1813 formed their own synod with three presbyteries—Cumberland, Elk, and Logan. The new synod affirmed that "the Presbyterian confession is their confession except the idea of fatality," and they produced a list of "essential doctrines," which included a section on "dissent from the Confession." Objections included the doctrines of eternal reprobation, limited atonement, and the salvation of only elect infants. In 1814, the synod went through the Confession, modifying a number of chapters and adopting others verbatim. Fourteen additional presbyteries were created in the next fifteen years, and in 1829 a General Assembly of the Cumberland Presbyterian Church had its first meeting in Princeton, Kentucky.[17]

The Cumberland schism in 1810 was just the beginning of division among the Presbyterian denominations in America during the early decades of the nineteenth century. The Reformed and Associate Reformed Presbyterians likewise experienced separation during this period. In 1833, the Reformed Presbyterian Church divided into two groups—the Reformed Presbyterian Church in North America, General Synod, and the Reformed Presbyterian Church of North America (Old Lights). The separation occurred as a result of unresolved differences over the relation of the church to the civil government. The Old Lights, affirming their historic Covenanter heritage, stood aloof from participation in civil government since the United States did not recognize Jesus Christ as sovereign and his law as the foundation for government. The General Synod believed it was not sinful for its members to vote as citizens under the US Constitution. By 1804, the Associate Reformed Church had grown to four regional synods and a General Synod had held its first meeting.

Controversy in the Associate Reformed Church surrounded one of her ministers, John Mitchell Mason. For three decades he was pastor of two As-

---

17. *The Cumberland Presbyterian Digest*, 7–24. For Cumberland Presbyterian history, see William Warren Sweet, ed., *Religion of the American Frontier*, vol. 2, *The Presbyterians, 1783–1840* (New York: Harper & Brothers, 1936); Robert V. Foster, "A Sketch of the History of the Cumberland Presbyterian Church," in American Church History Series, vol. 11 (New York: Christian Literature Co., 1894); Louis B. Weeks, *Kentucky Presbyterians* (Atlanta: John Knox, 1983); Thomas H. Campbell, *Good News on the Frontier: A History of the Cumberland Presbyterian Church* (Memphis: Frontier, 1965). Cumberland educational institutions include Bethel College in McKenzie, Tennessee, and Memphis Theological Seminary of the Cumberland Presbyterian Church.

sociate Reformed congregations in New York City, where the General Synod established a training school for pastors in 1805, with Dr. Mason as the lone professor. Mason had studied at Edinburgh and used contacts there and in the Associate Church in Scotland to secure money and books for the school.[18] He had helped start the New York Missionary Society in 1790, and later the American Bible Society in 1816. Two issues would generate charges against him: his use of unapproved psalms in public worship and his advocacy of open communion.[19] A resolution came before the 1811 General Synod to censure Mason and two others for taking communion across denominational lines and charged Mason with using an unapproved version of the Psalter. The General Synod did not pass the resolution but pursued peace, acknowledging "diversity of judgment and practice" and exhorting all to "exercise mutual forbearance . . . and brotherly love."[20] Two synods, not happy with the perceived negligence of the General Synod as well as the challenges of distance, decided to go their own way. The Synod of Scioto departed in 1820, taking the name Associate Reformed Synod of the West; the Synod of the Carolinas requested permission for independence, which was granted in 1822, and became the Associate Reformed Synod of the South. In 1837, Erskine Seminary was founded in South Carolina, and Erskine College opened its doors in 1839. Mason and the Synod of Pennsylvania united with the Presbyterian Church in the United States of America (PCUSA), and the small New York seminary merged with Princeton Seminary.[21]

PRINCETON SEMINARY

In the eighteenth century, Presbyterians educated their ministers through tutors, private academies, British universities, New England colleges, and the College of New Jersey. With congregations spreading throughout the new republic in the early nineteenth century, the need for Presbyterian theological

18. Some consider this school the first theological seminary in America. The school library was later given to Pittsburgh Theological Seminary; most of the volumes are in Latin.

19. John Mason, *A Plea for Sacramental Communion on Catholick Principles* (1816).

20. Ray A. King, *A History of the Associate Reformed Presbyterian Church* (Charlotte, NC: Board of Education of the Associate Reformed Presbyterian Church, 1966), 77; Robert Lathan, *History of the Associate Reformed Synod of the South, To Which is Prefixed A History of the Associate Presbyterian and Reformed Presbyterian Churches* (Harrisburg, PA, 1882), 225–37.

21. King, *A History of the Associate Reformed Presbyterian Church*, 72–80; Lathan, *History of the Associate Reformed Synod of the South*, 238–52.

schools was paramount. Rev. Archibald Alexander (1772–1851) addressed the
1808 General Assembly: "We shall not have a regular and sufficient supply
of well-qualified ministers of the Gospel until every Presbytery, or at least
every Synod, shall have under its direction a seminary." Alexander's plan for
regional seminaries, while originally rejected, was eventually viewed as the
only workable solution. Princeton Theological Seminary was established in
1812, with Archibald Alexander as the first professor (1812–1851). Alexander, a
Virginian of Scots-Irish descent, was licensed to preach at nineteen. After serving two congregations in Virginia, he became president of Hampden-Sydney
College, then pastor of the Pine Street Church in Philadelphia. In 1807, he was
moderator of the Presbyterian General Assembly. He was a man of deep piety,
having been converted under the revival preaching of William Graham as a
young man, and led revivals himself as a minister. At Princeton, Alexander
attempted to steer a middle course between an overemphasis on objective doctrinal correctness as the essence of Christianity and an exclusively subjective
emotionalism often associated with some forms of revivalism. Fervent piety
and moral character in ministers were equally important to sound doctrine at
old Princeton Seminary. This emphasis came from Alexander, who was a role
model for the young preachers.[22]

The influence of the old Log College was visible in "The Plan of a Theological Seminary" (1811), the blueprint for the new seminary in Princeton.
According to the Plan, the institution's mission was "to unite, in those who
sustain the ministerial office, religion and literature; that piety of the heart
which is the fruit only of the renewing and satisfying grace of God, with solid
learning." The goal of the seminary was to "furnish our congregations with
enlightened, humble, zealous, laborious pastors, who shall truly watch for
the good of souls" and are willing "to make every sacrifice, to endure every
hardship, and to render every service which the promotion of pure and unde-
filed religion may require."[23] The academic regime of the seminary included a
curriculum covering three years of study. Alexander, and the second Princeton
professor, Samuel Miller, developed the curriculum in line with the seminary
goals stipulated in the Plan. In the first year, students took biblical studies,
which included courses in English Bible, Hebrew, Greek, biblical criticism,
and Bible history and geography. Second-year students continued study of the

22. Andrew Hoffecker, *Piety and the Princeton Theologians* (Phillipsburg, NJ: P&R, 1981),
1–43.
23. *The Plan of a Theological Seminary Adopted by the Presbyterian Church in the United
States of America* (Philadelphia: Jane Aitken, 1811), 5–7.

biblical languages, adding courses in systematic theology and church history. In the final year, more courses in church history and systematics were added, as well as studies in polity, pastoral care, and homiletics.[24] Alongside academic studies and devotional exercises, the seminary encouraged commitment to missions though the Concert of Prayer and the Society of Inquiry on Missions. The monthly Concert of Prayer consisted of prayer, Scripture reading, singing, a collection for missions, and a missionary address by a student, professor, or guest. The Society of Inquiry on Missions was likewise a monthly gathering for keeping current on information about foreign and domestic missions and for encouraging students to consider how they might become involved in missions. Society activities included hearing reports on revivals and letters from missionaries, as well as corresponding with missionaries and student mission organizations at other schools.[25]

Princeton professors were expected to "adopt, receive and subscribe [to]" the Westminster Confession and catechisms as a "just exhibition of that system of doctrine and religious belief which is contained in the Scriptures." There was no provision for scruples, but rather, a solemn promise was required: "I do solemnly promise and engage, not to inculcate, teach, or insinuate anything which shall appear to me to contradict or contravene either directly or impliedly, anything taught in said Confession of Faith or Catechism."[26] The Princeton pledge was clearly Old School in its strict subscription to Westminster Calvinism, but this meticulous vow was not required of other Presbyterian seminary professors. At New School Auburn Seminary, organized in 1820 by the Synod of Geneva in New York, professors took essentially the same vow as all Presbyterian ministers, that is, "to receive and adopt the system of doctrine" in the Confession.

Other New School–oriented seminaries were Southern and Western Seminary in Tennessee (1819, later Maryville College); Lane Seminary in Cincinnati (1832), whose president was revivalist Lyman Beecher; and Union Seminary in New York (1836). In addition to Princeton, Old School seminaries included Union Seminary in Virginia (1824); Western Seminary (1827, later Pittsburgh

24. David B. Calhoun, *Princeton Seminary*, vol. 1, *Faith and Learning (1812–1868)* (Carlisle, PA: Banner of Truth Trust, 1994), 83–89.

25. Calhoun, *Princeton Seminary*, 1:141–59.

26. *The Plan of a Theological Seminary*, 10. Samuel Miller acknowledged that the Princeton faculty pledge was a higher standard than that expected of Presbyterian ministers; Samuel Miller Jr., *Life of Samuel Miller D. D., LL. D.: Second Professor in the Theological Seminary of the Presbyterian Church in Princeton, New Jersey* (Philadelphia: Claxton, Remsen and Haffelfinger, 1869), 357.

Seminary); Centre College in Kentucky (1828), out of which came Danville
Seminary (1853, later Louisville Seminary); and the Theological Seminary of
South Carolina and Georgia (1831, later Columbia Theological Seminary).

Additional Presbyterian seminaries were started to provide ministers for
growing regions of the country. The Theological Seminary of the Northwest
(1859, later McCormick Seminary) in Chicago had its roots in Hanover Seminary of Indiana (1829); Dubuque Theological Seminary was founded in 1852
to reach German settlers moving into the Midwest. California's San Francisco
Seminary began in 1871, and in Texas, Austin Presbyterian Seminary was established in 1902 to serve the Southwest frontier. The Freedmen's Institute
of North Carolina, founded in 1867, was the beginning of Johnson C. Smith
University in Charlotte, which also included a seminary. Relocated to Atlanta
in 1969, Johnson C. Smith Seminary is the only historically black seminary of
the Presbyterian church.[27]

Road to Schism

The 1831 General Assembly was a substantial turning point in the Old School/
New School rivalry, as open conflict between the two parties was publicly displayed. The case of a prominent New School minister, Albert Barnes, came before the Assembly, and the lines were drawn. Barnes had been called as pastor
of First Presbyterian Church of Philadelphia, but members of the Presbytery
of Philadelphia had raised objections to this call based on a sermon he had
preached the previous year, "The Way of Salvation." His call was confirmed
21 to 12, but the minority entered a complaint to the Synod of Philadelphia,
claiming the content of Barnes's sermon was "opposed to the doctrinal standards of the Presbyterian Church." Barnes defended himself before the Synod,
which referred the case back to the presbytery.[28] After the presbytery was unable to reach consensus, the case was appealed to the General Assembly. The
case was handed to a committee, chaired by Samuel Miller, which determined
that there were "a number of unguarded and objectionable passages" in the
sermon but advised that all proceedings against Barnes should be suspended.
The Assembly voted 158 to 33 in support of the committee's recommendation,

27. For more on black Presbyterians after the Civil War, see chap. 12 below.
28. Albert Barnes, *The Way of Salvation: A Sermon Delivered at Morristown, New Jersey,
February 8, 1829 Together With Mr. Barnes's Defense of the Sermon, read Before the Synod of
Philadelphia, at Lancaster, October 29, 1830; and His "Defense before the Second Presbytery
of Philadelphia in Reply to the charge of the Rev. George Junkin,"* 7th ed. (New York: Leavitt,
Lord and Company, 1836), 59–85.

but conservatives complained about error being tolerated in the Presbyterian church.[29] To relieve strains within the Presbytery of Philadelphia, the Assembly instructed the Synod of Philadelphia to divide the presbytery; Barnes and fourteen other ministers were assigned to the new Second Presbytery of Philadelphia.

The Princeton professors, dubbed the "peace men" by Old School conservatives, attempted to build bridges between the two parties. Observing the ever-rising turbulence in the church, Samuel Miller attempted to pacify the situation through sixteen open "Letters to Presbyterians" that were published in the *Presbyterian* from January to May 1833 and printed together in a book. Miller's letters addressed the scope of issues dividing Presbyterians: voluntary societies versus church boards, revivals, requirements for ministerial candidates, Presbyterian government and adherence to the Confession and catechisms. He called for calm and charity, chastising both groups for the strife. The Old School should not be "overly rigorous in their demands; . . . they should not be perpetually and vexatiously occupied in the work of 'heresy hunting.'" The New School, for its part, must not "persist in the public, habitual use of a theological language which impartial judges consider Pelagian in its obvious import." The New School should cease to "license and ordain men who give too much reason to fear that they do not, *ex animo*, receive the doctrines and order of our Church," and be careful not to "always sustain and acquit lax theology, to whatever extreme it may go," when questions come in the higher judicatories. Miller bemoaned the fact that some ministerial candidates turned down by Old School presbyteries were readily received in New School presbyteries, which practice was "adapted to destroy mutual confidence" among brethren. He was convinced that if these practices continue, "it requires no spirit of prophecy to foresee that growing alienation, strife, and eventual rupture must be the consequence."[30]

Conservative Old School men, continually frustrated with what they perceived as the toleration of doctrinal errors, decided to enter "protests" at the General Assemblies. The first protest, known as the "Western Memorial," listed aberrant doctrines and named Presbyterian clergy, including Albert Barnes, who were considered the primary source of New School errors. Charles Hodge decried the document, pointing out that a number of the alleged errors had been "held and tolerated" by American Presbyterians "since its very organization." Hodge lectured, "Is it to be expected that, at this time of the day,

---

29. *Minutes of the General Assembly*, 1831, 329.

30. Samuel Miller, *Letters to Presbyterians in the Present Crisis in the Presbyterian Church in the United States* (Philadelphia: Anthony Finley, 1833), 126.

the Assembly would condemn all who do not hold to the doctrine of limited atonement?" The Assembly reprimanded the protesters for publicly defaming ministers without trial. Repulsed by the Assembly, conservatives revised the document and presented it again the next year. The new document, the "Act and Testimony," was distributed widely and was eventually endorsed by 374 ministers, five synods, and thirty presbyteries.[31] Hodge censured the new protest as inciting division by putting itself forward as "a test of orthodoxy." He argued that only a small minority would countenance the errors as described in the "Act and Testimony." The protest's call for a pre-Assembly Old School convention in 1835 was condemned by Hodge as a "revolutionary proceeding" that would bring schism to the church.[32] The pre-Assembly convention occurred, and Old School delegates secured a majority at the 1835 Assembly. Using this advantage, they strategically passed declarations on the duty of supporting Presbyterian missions and the necessity of examining ministers transferring from one presbytery to another, and initiated a process to annul the 1801 Plan of Union. Southern Presbyterians, who had been mostly spectators of northern Old School–New School battles, suddenly became animated when the 1835 Assembly received a petition from Ohio calling for immediate abolition of slavery. The Ohio overture troubled Southerners in the Assembly, who now looked more favorably upon Old School partisans inclined to keep abolition agitation out of General Assembly business. The 1835 General Assembly commissioned a Committee on Slavery, chaired by Samuel Miller, to report back to the Assembly the next year. Southerners feared they were about to be "unchurched" by their denomination for slaveholding.[33]

At the same time as abolition agitation reemerged, Albert Barnes again became the target of Old School conservatives. In 1835, Barnes published a commentary on the book of Romans, intended as a resource for Sunday school teachers. Immediately, Old School papers and periodicals began attacking *Barnes' Notes on Romans* as "unsound and dangerous." Hodge offered a balanced review, acknowledging erroneous statements but arguing that there was much good in the book and Barnes was not a heretic. Conservatives, determined to prosecute Barnes, brought charges against him for doctrines

31. For the full text of the two protest documents, see Samuel J. Baird, *A Collection of the Acts, Deliverances, and Testimonies of the Supreme Judicatory of the Presbyterian Church from its Origin in America to the Present Time* (Philadelphia: Presbyterian Board of Publication, 1856), 659–75.

32. Charles Hodge, "Act and Testimony," *Biblical Repertory and Theological Review* 6 (October 1834): 506, 509, 510, 517.

33. Bruce Staiger, "Abolition and the Presbyterian Schism of 1837–38," *Mississippi Valley Historical Review* 36 (December 1949): 391–414.

"contrary to the Standards of the Presbyterian Church." Barnes was acquitted by his presbytery in the summer of 1835, but when the Synod reversed this decision and suspended him from the ministry, Barnes appealed to the General Assembly. A final showdown appeared imminent, as conservatives viewed the Barnes case coming before the 1836 Assembly as a referendum on New School doctrine. The New School likewise viewed the upcoming Assembly as a test case for confessional boundaries in the Presbyterian church. Determined to exonerate Barnes, whose convictions were shared by a number of New School ministers, the New School was irritated with the censorious spirit of Barnes's Old School attackers and was in no mood to negotiate.[34]

The New School majority at the 1836 Assembly pushed through their agenda, completely alienating Old School conservatives. The Assembly cleared Barnes of all charges, refusing to censure any of his writings, and backed the American Board of Commissioners for Foreign Missions, opposing a separate Assembly Board of Missions. Samuel Miller attempted to broker moderate concessions to the Old School by proposing a censure of portions of Barnes's commentary. He also recommended a compromise on missions that would have endorsed both cooperative missions and Presbyterian missions. Both of Miller's attempts to offer the Old School a palm branch failed. On the slavery question, a motion to "indefinitely postpone" any discussion passed, but vociferous New School protests to postponement sealed in the Southern mind a connection of abolition with the New School. As soon as the 1836 General Assembly concluded, Old School leaders began to organize for a response. They were now convinced that ecclesiastical separation was the only option left, since their efforts at discipline in the church courts had failed. The perception among conservatives was that ministers from Plan of Union presbyteries had cast the deciding votes to exonerate Barnes. Hodge was dismayed by New School unwillingness to find middle ground, but he firmly asserted that this was inadequate justification for schism. He exhorted his fellow Old School men to trust New School claims of fidelity to the Westminster Standards. Princeton's influence was waning, and her pleas for peace went unheeded by resolute Old School conservatives, who chided Princeton to get on board for an inevitable schism.[35] In 1837, the conservative Old School party held a pre-Assembly convention where they adopted a hands-off strategy on slavery and

---

34. Albert Barnes, *Notes, Explanatory and Practical on the Epistle to the Romans* (New York: Leavitt, Lord & Co., 1835); Charles Hodge, "Barnes on the Epistle to the Romans," *Biblical Repertory* 7 (April 1835): 285–340.

35. S. Donald Fortson III, *The Presbyterian Creed: A Confessional Tradition in America, 1729–1870* (Milton Keynes, UK: Paternoster, 2008), 111–23.

issued a declaration of errors in the church that were "virtually sanctioned" by the 1836 Assembly: "hostility to the doctrines of the confession," toleration of the "heresies of Taylor" and the "policies of Finney."[36]

By this time Charles Finney had already departed the Presbyterian church. In 1835, he became a professor of theology at the new Oberlin College in Ohio; he also served as pastor of the First Congregational Church of Oberlin, eventually becoming president of the college in 1851. Finney's revivalist theology was more Wesleyan than Calvinist, stressing the ability of humans to repent and make a new heart, and he taught holiness doctrine (perfectionism) at Oberlin.[37] In the fall of 1835, thirty-two antislavery students left Lane Seminary in Cincinnati (president, Lyman Beecher) and joined Finney at Oberlin College, which would become renowned for its abolitionism. The "Lane Rebels" insisted that black students be admitted to Oberlin; it was also the first college in America to admit women students.[38]

When the 1837 General Assembly convened, an Old School moderator was elected on a close ballot. The Old School proceeded to systematically dismantle the church by officially abrogating the 1801 Plan of Union—which was interpreted as exscinding four New School synods—and ordering the investigation of errors in several presbyteries. An Assembly Board of Missions was appointed with a request that several voluntary societies cease operations in the Presbyterian church. After the Old School–dominated Assembly finished its ecclesiastical surgery, the New School members of the Assembly reconvened the next day at Albert Barnes's church. The New School challenged the accusations of heresy and condemned the Assembly's "unconstitutional measures." They directed all New School presbyteries to send delegates to the next year's Assembly, in 1838, including those presbyteries exscinded by the dissolved Plan of Union. At a late summer convention in Auburn, New York, New School delegates officially responded to an Old School list of sixteen alleged errors by producing their own statement of "true doctrines" reflecting their genuine views. This "Auburn Declaration," as it came to be known, cited the 1729 Adopting Act with its allowance of "scruples" to substantiate New

---

36. Charles G. Finney, *Lectures on Revivals of Religion* (New York: Revell, 1868). These 1835 lectures were a manual on how to conduct revivals.

37. Finney's "Lectures on Systematic Theology" (1846) have been described as "arminianized Calvinism." Charles Hodge critiqued these lectures as Pelagian; see Charles Hodge, review of *Lectures on Systematic Theology*, by Charles Finney, *Biblical Repertory and Princeton Review* 19 (April 1847): 237–77.

38. See Donald W. Dayton with Douglas M. Strong, *Rediscovering an Evangelical Heritage* (Grand Rapids: Baker Academic, 2014), 61–73, 85–93, 138–39.

School claims of Presbyterian orthodoxy.[39] When the 1838 General Assembly opened, New School commissioners from the four excluded synods were not recognized; accordingly, these delegates and those from twenty-nine other New School presbyteries elected their own Assembly officers and adjourned to another location.[40]

The first act of the Presbyterian Church (New School) was a resolution decrying the unconstitutional excision of the four synods and declaring the legal standing of the excluded synods. Declarations were issued in support of the voluntary societies; Lane, Auburn, and Union (New York) seminaries were endorsed; and the rule requiring presbyteries to examine transferring ministers was rescinded. The New School Assembly also recommended the Confession of Faith and Form of Government for greater circulation among the presbyteries. A "Pastoral Letter" to the churches, explaining the schism and affirming commitment to the Presbyterian doctrinal standards, stated: "We love and honor the Confession of Faith of the Presbyterian Church as containing more well-defined, fundamental truth, with less defect, than appertains to any other human formula of doctrine, and as calculated to hold in intelligent concord a greater number of sanctified minds than any which could now be framed; and we disclaim all design past, present or future to change it."[41]

39. "The Auburn Declaration," in *The Presbyterian Enterprise: Sources of American Presbyterian History*, ed. Maurice Armstrong, Lefferts Loetscher, and Charles Anderson (Philadelphia: Westminster, 1956), 166–71.

40. Fortson, *The Presbyterian Creed*, 123–27.

41. *Minutes of the Presbyterian Church in the United States of America* (New School) (New York: Published by Stated Clerks, 1838–1858; reprint, Philadelphia: Presbyterian Board of Publications and Sabbath-School Work, 1894), 35–42.

CHAPTER 11

Debate on the Question of Slavery

The year 1831 is considered a turning point of popular opinion in America on the issue of slavery. In January of that year, William Lloyd Garrison published the first issue of the abolitionist journal the *Liberator*. Later that year, Nat Turner, a slave preacher from Virginia, led an uprising that killed sixty whites, including women and children. Abolitionists began to saturate the nation with their materials, and the threat of more slave uprisings sent fear throughout the South. Northern abolitionists stepped up their campaign to free the slaves immediately, and without compensation to the owners. Abolitionist literature unleashed bitter and vindictive attacks on slave owners, which caused hardened attitudes from parts of the South. While the Old School/New School division of 1837–1838 had other theological matters in the forefront, slavery was an underlying, unresolved issue in the division.[1] There was a long history behind the Presbyterian struggle with slavery that erupted in the 1830s.

In the colonial era, some Presbyterians had accepted slavery as a part of God's providential plan for ordering society while others viewed it as an evil upon which God would bring judgment. Samuel Davies was not concerned with liberating the Africans from bondage; his chief interest was the soul of the slaves. In a 1757 sermon, Davies challenged Virginia masters to teach Christianity to their slaves. He chastised Christian masters for neglecting the spiritual care of slaves entrusted to them, exhorting them to evangelize their servants. In the midst of his indictment of masters' neglect, he acknowledged that slavery was an appointment of Providence "that there should be distinc-

---

1. Bruce Staiger, "Abolition and the Presbyterian Schism of 1837–38," *Mississippi Valley Historical Review* 36 (December 1949): 391–414; Elwyn A. Smith, "The Role of the South in the Presbyterian Schism of 1837–38," *Church History* 29 (1960): 44–63.

tions among mankind; that some should be Masters, and some Servants. And Christianity does not blend or destroy Distinctions, but establishes and regulates them, and enjoins every Man to conduct himself according to them." But, argued Davies, "as to the affairs of religion and eternity, all men stand upon the same footing," with immortal souls in need of salvation.[2]

Other Presbyterians in the prerevolutionary period viewed the Atlantic slave trade as wicked and feared God's judgment on the colonies for it. John Witherspoon, a slave owner and president of the College of New Jersey, declared the slave trade unjust in his *Lectures on Moral Philosophy* under his discussion of "politics." Men may become slaves by their consent or for punishment of a crime, "but it is certainly unlawful to make inroads upon others, unprovoked and take away their liberty by no better right than superior power." He noted that the practice of ancient nations in making slaves of prisoners of war was "altogether unjust and barbarous." Witherspoon told his students, "I do not think there lies any necessity on those who found men in a state of slavery, to make them free to their own ruin. But it is very doubtful whether any original cause of servitude can be defended, but legal punishment for the commission of crimes."[3] In 1768, Francis Alison, a professor at the College of Pennsylvania, wrote, "I am assured ye Common father of all men will severely plead a Controversy against these Colonies for Enslaving Negros, and keeping their children born British subjects, in perpetual slavery—and possibly for this wickedness God threatens us with slavery [British oppression of colonies]."[4] It is noteworthy that Alison and Witherspoon, both of whom taught political philosophy, would encourage their students to support American independence and its quest for human liberty. The duplicity of seeking freedom from British oppression while keeping Africans in bondage would not be lost on the revolutionary generation.

Liberty for All

From the time of the American Revolution, most of the country and most Presbyterians were in favor of gradual and peaceful emancipation of slaves.

2. Samuel Davies, *The Duty of Christians to propagate their Religion among Heathens, Earnestly recommended to the Masters of Negro Slaves in Virginia. A Sermon Preached in Hanover, January 8, 1757* (London: J. Oliver, 1757), 18–27.

3. John Witherspoon, "Lectures on Moral Philosophy," in *The Works of Rev. John Witherspoon*, ed. Ashbel Green, 9 vols. (Philadelphia, 1802; reprint, Harrisonburg, VA: Sprinkle, 2007), 6:107, 108, 116.

4. Francis Alison, quoted in Leonard Trinterud, *The Forming of an American Tradition* (Philadelphia: Westminster, 1949), 207.

The institution of slavery was viewed as inconsistent with the republican spirit that had given birth to the nation. Eighteenth-century Presbyterians affirmed the antislavery public mood and consistently favored gradual emancipation of the slaves. In 1787, the Northwest Ordinance, providing a plan for governing the vast area north of the Ohio River, was adopted unanimously by the Confederation Congress. In article 6, the ordinance prohibited involuntary servitude in the Northwest Territory, except as punishment for a crime, but it also included a fugitive slave provision for runaway slaves that might be reclaimed. That same year, the Committee of Overtures of the Synod brought forth an overture on slavery, affirming that "The Creator of the World having made of one flesh all the children of men, It becomes them as Members of the same family . . . to extend the blessings of equal freedom to every part of the human race." In reply, the Synod issued a joint statement on slavery:

> The Synod of New York & Philadelphia do highly approve of the general principles in favor of universal Liberty that prevail in America; and the interest which many of the States have taken in promoting the abolition of Slavery . . . they earnestly recommend it to all the members belonging to their communion, to give those persons who are at present held in servitude such good education as to prepare them for the better enjoyment of freedom . . . and finally, they recommend it to all their people to use the most prudent measures consistent with the interests & the state of civil Society in the countries where they live, to procure eventually the final abolition of slavery in America.[5]

This strong antislavery position and its principled commitment to gradual abolition would serve as bedrock for future Presbyterian pronouncements on slavery in the nineteenth century.[6]

In 1795, the General Assembly received an overture from the Transylvania Presbytery concerning Christian communion among those who differed on the issue of slavery. The question of fellowship with slaveholders had been pressed by the Reverend David Rice of Kentucky. The presbytery had debated the question and determined that they lacked "sufficient authority from the

---

5. Guy S. Klett, ed., *Minutes of the Presbyterian Church in America, 1706–1788* (Philadelphia: Presbyterian Historical Society, 1976), 627, 629.

6. For analysis of the 1787 declaration on slavery, see William Harrison Taylor, *Unity in Christ and Country: American Presbyterians in the Revolutionary Era, 1758–1801* (Tuscaloosa: University of Alabama Press, 2017), 105–12.

Word of God" to exclude slave owners from the church. The presbytery sent up an overture asking the Assembly to make a ruling on the question. The General Assembly responded by saying that "difference of opinion with respect to slavery" permeated the Presbyterian church, and it encouraged those with differing views to live "in charity and peace according to the doctrine and practice of the apostles." The Assembly also referred those concerned to its statement of 1787 and reiterated its position: "the General Assembly assure all the churches under her care, that they view with the deepest concern, any vestiges of slavery which may exist in our country." The Bills and Overtures Committee, which drafted the Assembly resolution, had nineteen members, of whom seven were from the South, and at least seven members were themselves slaveholders.[7]

Presbyterians in the southern states supported this position on slavery. In 1800 the Synods of the Carolinas and Virginia both made public statements affirming the Assembly's 1787 judgment on the issue. The Synod of Virginia asserted, "That so many thousands of our fellow creatures should in this land of liberty, and asylum for the oppressed, be held in chains, is a reflection to us peculiarly afflictive . . . that it was wrong in the first instance to reduce so many of the helpless Africans to their present state of thralldom, will be readily admitted, and that it is a duty to adopt proper measures for their emancipation, will it is presumed, be universally conceded."[8] The pretense of eighteenth-century America enslaving fellow human beings during and after its own struggle to establish liberty was a prominent theme among Presbyterian leaders.

Benjamin Rush (1746–1813), Presbyterian physician, trustee of the College of New Jersey, and signatory of the Declaration of Independence, wrote in 1773, "The plant of liberty is of so tender a nature, that it cannot thrive long in the neighbourhood of slavery." Rush declared, "Slavery is a Hydra sin, and includes in it every violation of the precepts of the Law and Gospel. . . . Let such of our countrymen as engage in the slave trade, be shunned as the greatest enemies of our country."[9] In 1774, Rush helped establish the first American abolition society—"Pennsylvania Society, for promoting the Abolition of Slavery; the Relief of free Negroes unlawfully held in bondage, and for improving the Condition of the African Race." Rev. Jacob Green, a Presbyterian pastor in New Jersey,

---

7. Ernest Trice Thompson, *Presbyterians in the South*, vol. 1, *1607–1861* (Richmond, VA: John Knox, 1963), 325.

8. Manuscript Minutes, Synod of Virginia, vol. 2, 1800, cited in Thompson, *Presbyterians in the South*, 326, 327.

9. Benjamin Rush, *An Address to the Inhabitants of the British Settlements on the Slavery of Negroes in America*, 2nd ed. (Philadelphia: John Dunlap, 1773), 13–26.

told his congregation this in a 1778 Fast Day sermon: "Supporting and encouraging slavery, is one of the great and crying evils among us . . . our liberty will be uncomfortable, till we wash our hands from the guilt of negro slavery."[10]

A young Samuel Miller, who later served as professor at Princeton Seminary (1813–1850), was a member of the New York Manumission Society. Speaking to the society in 1797, Miller told his audience, "in this country, from which has been proclaimed to distant lands, as the basis of our political existence, the noble principle, that 'ALL MEN ARE BORN FREE AND EQUAL,'—in this country are slaves!—men are bought and sold! Strange indeed!" Miller was convinced that "emancipation in a Gradual Manner" that would provide intellectual preparation "to exercise the rights and discharge the duties of citizens" was preferred to the "mischiefs attending an universal and immediate emancipation." He pointed to the "noble example" of Massachusetts and New Hampshire, where all slaves had been emancipated. "When shall a similar wisdom pervade the union, and rescue our national character from disgrace?"[11]

AMELIORATION AND ABOLITION

The emerging sense of the American public was that the liberties of freemen ought to extend to Africans as well. This societal trend is evidenced in the congressional action that made the transatlantic slave trade illegal in 1808. When the foreign slave trade was outlawed, many hoped this was the beginning of the end for American slavery. In 1815, the General Assembly reaffirmed previous Presbyterian declarations on liberty for the enslaved population, urging preparations be made for freedom:

> The General Assembly have repeatedly declared their cordial approbation of those principles of civil liberty which seem to be recognized by the Federal and State Governments in the United States. They have expressed their regret that the slavery of the Africans and their descendants still continues in so many places, and even among those within the pale of the church, and have urged the presbyteries under their care to adopt such measures as will secure, at least to the rising generation of slaves within the bounds of

10. Jacob Green, "A Sermon Delivered at Hanover, (in New Jersey) April 22d, 1778, Being the Day of public Fasting and Prayer Throughout the United States of America," in *Presbyterians and the American Revolution, Journal of Presbyterian History* 52, no. 4 (1974): 451–55.

11. Samuel Miller, *A Discourse, Delivered April 12, 1797, at the Request of and before the New York Society for Promoting the Manumission of Slaves, and Protecting Such of Them as Have Been or May be Liberated* (New York: T. and S. Swords, 1797), 9–11, 28–32.

the church, religious education, that they may be prepared for the exercise and enjoyment of liberty, when God in his providence may open a door for their emancipation.[12]

The Assembly also addressed specific crimes associated with slavery, calling on the church to address these reprehensible practices: "Although in some sections of our country, under certain circumstances, the transfer of slaves may be unavoidable, yet they consider the buying and selling of slaves by way of traffic, and all undue severity in the management of them, as inconsistent with the spirit of the Gospel. And they recommend to the Presbyteries and Sessions under their care, to make use of all prudent measures to prevent such shameful and unrighteous conduct."[13]

The occasion for the Assembly's statement in 1815 was a response to the antislavery activism of the Reverend George Bourne of Virginia. Bourne had made public statements at the Assembly criticizing the evils of slavery in Virginia among church members and ministers. Asked to name the alleged perpetrators, he declined. Returning home to Virginia, Bourne continued his vehement attack on slave owners, asserting that slaveholding and church membership were incompatible. In 1816, Bourne wrote *The Book and Slavery Irreconcilable*, one of the earliest American works advocating the immediate abolition of slavery.[14] Charges were brought against Bourne by members of the Lexington Presbytery, accusing him of making "unwarranted and un-christian charges against many of the members of the Presbyterian church in relation to slavery." The presbytery deposed Bourne, who appealed to the General Assembly. The Assembly ordered a retrial, and the presbytery found him guilty, removing him from the Presbyterian ministry. The 1818 General Assembly upheld the presbytery's decision and issued its strongest antislavery statement:

We consider the voluntary enslaving of one part of the human race by another, as a gross violation of the most precious and sacred rights of hu-man nature; as utterly inconsistent with the laws of God, which requires us to love our neighbour as ourselves, and as totally irreconcilable with the spirit and principles of the gospel of Christ . . . it is manifestly the duty of

12. 1815 Minutes, cited in Thompson, *Presbyterians in the South*, 328.
13. 1815 Minutes, cited in Thompson, *Presbyterians in the South*, 328.
14. Full text of Bourne's book is included in John W. Christie and Dwight L. Dumond, *George Bourne and "The Book and Slavery Irreconcilable"* (Wilmington: Historical Society of Delaware, 1969), 101–206.

all Christians who enjoy the light of the present day, when the inconsistency of slavery, both with the dictates of humanity and religion, has been demonstrated, and is generally acknowledged, to use their honest, earnest, and unwearied endeavours to correct the errors of former times, and as speedily as possible to efface this blot upon our holy religion, and to obtain the complete abolition of slavery throughout Christendom, and if possible throughout the world.[15]

The Assembly's unanimous adoption of the 1818 statement on abolition seemed to reflect the majority spirit of the country at the time, North and South.[16] One observes evidence for this in legislation, manumissions, and the proliferation of antislavery societies, especially in the South. In 1827, the number of abolition societies in the United States was 130; of these, 106 were located in southern states. There were four abolition papers in the South in 1819–1828.[17] In 1834, a Synod of Kentucky committee recommended to its presbyteries that all slaves under twenty years of age, and those yet to be born, be emancipated when they turn twenty-five.[18] One approach for addressing the plight of freed slaves was colonization to Africa, which Thomas Jefferson had proposed as early as 1776. The American Colonization Society was established in 1817, sending free and manumitted blacks to Sierra Leone, and then to the Republic of Liberia. The 1817 Presbyterian General Assembly approved supporting that organization.[19]

15. Quoted in Albert Barnes, *The Church and Slavery* (Philadelphia: Parry & McMillan, 1857), 54–56. See James H. Moorhead, "Between Hope and Fear: Presbyterians and the 1818 Statement on Slavery," *Journal of Presbyterian History* 96, no. 2 (Fall/Winter 2018): 49–61; Moorhead argues that the 1818 statement was a compromise enabling Presbyterians to maintain unity.

16. E. T. Thompson observed: "there was at this time a widespread feeling among churchmen in the South as well as the North that slavery was an evil for which a solution must be found. The General Assembly's 1818 declaration was not regarded at this time or later as a mild indictment of slavery." *Presbyterians in the South*, 1:332.

17. Alice Dana Adams, *The Neglected Period of Anti-Slavery in America, 1801–1831* (Williamstown, MA: Corner House Publishers, 1973), 34–37; see also Gilbert Hobbs Barnes, *The Antislavery Impulse, 1831–1844* (Gloucester, MA: Peter Smith, 1973), which underscores the important role of Finney's western revivals for abolitionism.

18. Transylvania Presbytery adopted the plan, ordering that it be it read before every congregation once a year. *Minutes of the Transylvania Presbytery*, April 2, 1836, cited in William Warren Sweet, *Religion on the American Frontier*, vol. 2, *The Presbyterians, 1783–1840* (New York: Harper & Bros., 1936), 278.

19. Some abolitionists favored colonization, believing blacks would likely experience more liberty in Africa.

Other Presbyterian bodies also addressed the pressing questions about slavery. The Associate Reformed Church was formed by the 1782 union of the Associate Presbytery and the Reformed Presbytery. A few defiant Covenanters reconstituted themselves as the Reformed Presbytery of America in 1798. In 1800, this group unanimously declared that "no slaveholder should be allowed the communion of the Church." The matter came before them through the refusal of a minister to take a call to a congregation in New York because slaveholders belonged to the church. Representatives were sent to Covenanters in South Carolina, who were "delighted to find with what alacrity those concerned came forward and complied with the decree of Presbytery." A number of Reformed Presbyterians were supporters of the Underground Railroad. In 1849, a memorial came before the synod, asking the body "to reassert their position in regard to excluding slave-holders from her fellowship." The committee to which the memorial was referred gave this response: "No slave-holder can have privileges in the Reformed Presbyterian Church. . . . Covenanters have not sworn, and do not swear oaths to the institutions of the country, among other reasons, because the Constitution of the United States contains compromises with slaveholding interests, and guarantees for the institution itself protection so long as it exists in the slave-holding States."[20]

Members of the Presbytery of Pennsylvania (Associate Presbytery), which had protested the union of 1782, constituted themselves as the continuing Presbytery of Pennsylvania, eventually taking the name Associate Synod of North America in 1800. In 1811, the synod pronounced slavery a moral evil, directing church members to free their slaves. If state laws prohibited this, members were to treat slaves as freedmen in terms of food, clothing, instruction, and wages. Those who failed to comply with these directives were not worthy of church fellowship. In 1831, an additional act excluded all slaveholders from communion, which resulted in the Presbytery of the Carolinas separating from the Synod.[21] The Associate Reformed Presbytery of the South, which had separated in 1822 to form its own distinct church, never directly addressed

20. William Melancthon Glasgow, *History of the Reformed Presbyterian Church in America* (Baltimore: Hill & Harvery, 1888; reprint, Grand Rapids: Reformation Heritage Books, 2007), 79–80, 114–15. See also William J. Roulston, "The Reformed Presbyterian Church and Antislavery in Nineteenth-Century America," in *Faith and Slavery in the Presbyterian Diaspora*, ed. William Harrison Taylor and Peter C. Messer (Bethlehem, PA: Lehigh University Press, 2016), 149–74; Joseph S. Moore, *Founding Sins: How a Group of Antislavery Radicals Fought to Put Christ in the Constitution* (New York: Oxford University Press, 2016).

21. Gross Alexander et al., *A History of the Methodist Church, South, the United Presbyterian Church, the Cumberland Presbyterian Church, and the Presbyterian Church, South in*

slavery, but in 1828 it urged members of the Synod to oppose a proposed South
Carolina law that would have prohibited teaching slaves to read, because "such
a law would be a serious infringement of their rights of conscience."[22]

FREE BLACK PRESBYTERIAN MINISTERS

There were several free black Presbyterian ministers during the early decades
of the nineteenth century, several of whom left a significant legacy. The first
licensed black Presbyterian minister was John Chavis of North Carolina, who
was licensed and commissioned as a "riding missionary" in 1800 under the
oversight of the Lexington, Hanover, and then Orange Presbyteries. Chavis
served in the Revolutionary army and was tutored by John Witherspoon at the
College of New Jersey, finishing his studies at Washington College in Virginia.
Preaching to whites and blacks in his itinerant ministry, Chavis also opened in
1805 a classical school in Raleigh, North Carolina, which served both blacks
and whites. Chavis's work declined after Nat Turner's murderous rebellion in
1831, when Southern legislatures began to restrict black preachers' freedom to
speak in public.[23]

Samuel Eli Cornish of Delaware was licensed and commissioned in 1819,
having been tutored by ministers of Philadelphia Presbytery. Organizing the
first black Presbyterian congregation in New York City, First Colored Presbyterian Church, he became its pastor in 1824. He also served as pastor of the
First African Presbyterian Church in Philadelphia before returning to New
York City to serve at Emmanuel Church. In 1827 Cornish became coeditor
of *Freedom's Journal*, the first black newspaper in America. Cornish managed several other black papers (the *Rights of All*, the *Colored American*) with
limited success, was a member of the American Bible Society, and became a
founding member of the American Anti-Slavery Society in 1833. A vocal abolitionist, Cornish also used his voice in print and pulpit to advocate for the
free black population.[24]

---

the United States, American Church History Series, vol. 9 (New York: Christian Literature
Co., 1894), 174–79.

22. Robert Lathan, *History of the Associate Reformed Synod of the South, To Which is
Prefixed A History of the Associate Presbyterian and Reformed Presbyterian Churches* (Harrisburg, PA, 1882), 359–62.

23. Darryl Williamson, "John Chavis," in Collin Hansen and Jeff Robinson, *12 Faithful Men: Portraits of Courageous Endurance in Pastoral Ministry* (Grand Rapids: Baker
Books, 2018).

24. Jane H. Pease and William H. Pease, "The Negro Conservative: Samuel Eli Cornish,"

Theodore Sedgwick Wright, ordained as a Presbyterian clergyman in 1829, was the first black graduate of Princeton Seminary in 1828. Wright had attended the African Free School in New York City—established by members of the New York Manumission Society in 1787, providing education for children of slaves and free blacks—and was mentored as a young man by Samuel Cornish. Wright succeeded Cornish as pastor of New York City's First Colored Presbyterian Church, remaining there until his death in 1847. Wright was a very effective pastor; under his leadership, his congregation grew to over four hundred members, making it among the largest black churches in the United States at the time. Wright joined Cornish as a founding member of the American Anti-Slavery Society, but due to the radical abolitionist influence of William Lloyd Garrison within the society, Wright withdrew, helping to establish another abolitionist association, the American and Foreign Anti-Slavery Society, in 1840. That same year, Cornish and Wright spoke out against the American Colonization Society's work of repatriating blacks to Africa in their coauthored book, *The Colonization Scheme Considered, In Its Rejection by the Colored People.*[25]

New School and Old School

A Presbyterian martyr for the abolitionist cause was Princeton graduate Rev. Elijah Parish Lovejoy. Lovejoy, editor of the *Observer* of Alton, Illinois, had struggled with his duty on the slavery issue, but eventually he advocated immediate abolition in 1835, considered a radical position at the time. The abolitionist cause was agitating the country, resulting in the suppression of antislavery discussions, confiscation of abolitionist documents, a gag rule in Congress, and riots in Washington, Philadelphia, and Baltimore. Lovejoy's press in Alton was destroyed three times by his opponents. This muzzling of abolitionist papers denied constitutional civil rights, according to Lovejoy, who defended his views: "I can make no compromise between truth and error." Lovejoy was present at the summer 1837 General Assembly meeting in Philadelphia, witnessing an Old School majority eject four northern New School synods; these synods all held strong abolitionist sentiments. The Alton press was destroyed

---

in *Bound with Them in Chains: A Biographical History of the Anti-Slavery Movement* (Westport, CT: Praeger, 1972).

25. David E. Swift, "Black Presbyterian Attacks on Racism: Samuel Cornish, Theodore Wright and Their Contemporaries," *Journal of Presbyterian History* 51, no. 4 (Winter 1973): 433–70; David E. Swift, *Black Prophets of Justice: Activist Clergy before the Civil War* (Baton Rouge: Louisiana State University Press, 1989).

for the fourth time in the evening of November 7, 1837. Sometime after 10:00 p.m., Elijah P. Lovejoy was shot five times and died attempting to protect his warehouse from a mob intending to burn it down. His death would help animate the abolitionist cause in the United States.[26]

The 1818 General Assembly had declared it a Christian duty "as speedily as possible to efface this blot on our holy religion, and to obtain the complete abolition of slavery throughout Christendom, and, if possible, throughout the world." After the schism, the New School church never backed away from that pronouncement and repeatedly reaffirmed its commitment to emancipation of all slaves. The New School would typically have free discussion of the matter for multiple days at each General Assembly meeting in the 1840s and 1850s. Albert Barnes, writing in 1857, observed, "No one subject, from the time of the division of the church in 1838, has been so frequently before the Assembly. . . . If there has been at any time, and from any quarters, a disposition to suppress discussion and action, it has been resisted by a strong and unambiguous voice of the church demanding that the subject should *not* be suppressed." Barnes believed the New School Presbyterians had been a role model to the other American denominations, who had generally tended to exclude the agitating subject from ecclesiastical discussion.[27]

When the New School Assembly convened in 1846, prolonged discussion of slavery took up twelve sessions. The minutes indicate that the roll was called so "that each member may have opportunity of expressing his opinion on the general subject." As a result of this open discussion, a significant paper was adopted, 92 to 29, that addressed the complexities of slavery "as it exists in these United States." The paper began with a declaration that slavery in America "is intrinsically an unrighteous and oppressive system, and is opposed to the prescriptions of the law of God, to the spirit and precepts of the gospel, and to the best interests of humanity." It reaffirmed the testimonies of 1787 and 1818 as "the recorded testimony of the Presbyterian church of these United States

26. Robert Merideth, "A Conservative Abolitionist at Alton: Edward Beecher's Narrative," *Journal of Presbyterian History* 42, no. 2 (March 1964): 39–53; see also part 2 of this essay in the June 1964 issue. Merideth recounts the Lovejoy story as told by his close friend Edward Beecher, son of Lyman Beecher; Edward Beecher, *Narrative of the Riots at Alton: in connection with the Death of Rev. Elijah P. Lovejoy* (Alton, IL, 1838). See also Merton L. Dillon, *Elijah P. Lovejoy, Abolitionist Editor* (Urbana: University of Illinois Press, 1961).

27. Barnes, *The Church and Slavery*, 68–70. For a survey of the New School church and slavery, see Leo P. Hirrel, *Children of Wrath: New School Calvinism and Antebellum Reform* (Lexington: University of Kentucky Press, 1998), 134–54, and Harold M. Parker, *The United Synod of the South: The Southern New School Presbyterian Church* (Westport, CT: Greenwood, 1988), 111–35.

against it [slavery], from which we do not recede." Regretting that slavery is "continued and countenanced" by some members of the church, the paper read, "we do earnestly exhort them, and the churches among whom it exists, to use all means in their power to put it away from them." The paper admitted there were obstacles to emancipation in the slaveholding states and recognized "the social influence affecting the views and conduct of those involved in it." In light of these realities, "we cannot pronounce a judgment of general or promiscuous condemnation . . . which should exclude from the table of the Lord all who stand in the legal relation of masters to slaves." This matter must be left to sessions, presbyteries, and synods, "to act in the administration of discipline as they may judge it to be their duty, constitutionally subject to the General Assembly only in the way of general review and control."[28]

An abolitionist denomination was established in 1847, the Free Presbyterian Church Synod of the United States, originally organized as the Free Synod of Cincinnati. The organizer was John Rankin, a New School pastor in Ripley, Ohio, who had tried unsuccessfully to get the New School to bar slaveholders from church membership. Rankin influenced the abolition movement in America through his 1826 *Letters on Slavery*[29] and by his involvement with the American Anti-Slavery Society and the Underground Railroad. By the 1850s the Free Presbyterian Church had grown to seventy-two congregations in seven presbyteries from Pennsylvania to Iowa. It started a newspaper, the *Free Presbyterian*, as well as Iberia College in 1854. The Free Presbyterian Synod did not meet after 1863, and many congregations reunited with the northern Presbyterian church after the war.[30]

The 1850 New School Assembly was explicit in its condemnation of the whole system of slavery in "the slave-holding States, as fraught with many and great evils to the civil, political, and moral interests of those regions where it exists." The same assembly made explicit its understanding that slaveholding was an "offense" subject to the Book of Discipline, "except in those cases where it is unavoidable, by the laws of the State, the obligations of guardianship, or

28. *Minutes of the General Assembly of the Presbyterian Church in the United States of America* (New School) (New York: Stated Clerk of the General Assembly, 1846), 15-31.

29. John Rankin, *Letters on American Slavery Addressed to Mr. Thomas Rankin, Merchant at Middlebrook, Augusta Co., VA*, 2nd ed. (Newburyport, MA: Charles Wipple, 1836). The series of letters to his brother Thomas, who had purchased slaves in Virginia, was first published in William Lloyd Garrison's abolitionist paper, the *Liberator*, and later printed together as a book in 1826.

30. See Larry G. Willey, "John Rankin, Antislavery Prophet, and the Free Presbyterian Church," *American Presbyterians*, Fall 1994, 157-71. Charles Finney served a Free Presbyterian congregation in New York City in the 1830s.

the demands of humanity." The whole subject, as it exists in the church, is to "be referred to the sessions and presbyteries, to take such action thereon as in their judgment the laws of Christianity require."[31] The new element in 1850 was the recognition of exceptions in specific cases that might exempt a slave owner from church discipline. This appears to be a bit of an olive branch to the South, but the Northern New School men were not offering an off-ramp on the issue. Albert Barnes, commenting on the 1850 New School caveat about "exceptions," noted that "the holder of the slave should be able to show that in that particular case it is proper that the slave should not be emancipated, or that it is an impractical thing to do it. . . . If this cannot be done, he is presumed to be guilty of an 'offence'; that is, an act which subjects him to the proper discipline of the church."[32]

New School strains finally reached crisis levels by 1856 when abolitionists pushed harder for disciplining slave owners. Political tensions in the country by this time had reached fever pitch in the wake of bloody conflict between proslavery and antislavery settlers in Kansas and the *Dred Scott* case. Southern New School leaders pushed back, believing their constant pleas to let the South deal with the issue in its own way were now falling on deaf ears. Southern delegates to the 1857 Assembly, responding to demands for church discipline, presented an "Address of Protest" against the "political agitation" and "ultra-abolitionist sentiments" within the New School church. The protestors argued that there was nothing in the church's constitution about slaveholding, thus discipline would be "ecclesiastical despotism" violating the spirit and letter of the constitution. The Southern plan was to form a new ecclesiastical body "in which the agitation of the Slavery question will be unknown." A key principle of the new denomination would be "an understanding that, however, we may differ in our views respecting Slavery, the subject is never to be introduced into the Assembly either by Northern or Southern men."[33]

Typical New School Southern perspectives were expressed by minister Fred A. Ross of Alabama in his 1857 book, *Slavery Ordained of God*. Ross wrote, "Let the Northern philanthropist learn from the Bible that the relation of master and slave is not sin per se. . . . Let him learn that slavery like all evil has its corresponding greater good; that the Southern slave, though degraded compared with his master, is elevated and ennobled compared with his breth-

31. *Minutes of the General Assembly* (New School), 1850, quoted in Barnes, *The Church and Slavery*, 85. The General Assembly statement was approved 87 to 16.

32. *Minutes of the General Assembly* (New School), 1850, quoted in Barnes, *The Church and Slavery*, 86, 87.

33. "The United Synod of the South," in *Presbyterian Historical Almanac and Annual Remembrancer of the Church for 1858–1859* (Philadelphia: Joseph M. Wilson, 1859), 135, 136.

ren in Africa." And to the Southerner, Ross issued a challenge: "Let him believe that slavery, although not a sin, is a degraded condition,—the evil, the curse of the South,—yet, having blessings in its time to the South and the Union. Let him know that slavery is to pass away in the fullness of Providence. Let the South believe this, and prepare to obey the hand that moves their destiny."[34] In 1857, Southern churches (285 congregations) withdrew from the New School, establishing themselves as the United Synod of the South at their first assembly, which convened in Knoxville, Tennessee, the following year.[35]

Old School Presbyterians escaped schism over slavery by purposefully avoiding the topic at Assembly meetings. Assuring slave-owning Southerners that they would not face church discipline, the 1845 Old School Assembly declared,

> The General Assembly of the Presbyterian Church in the United States was originally organized, and has since continued the bond of union in the church upon the conceded principle that the existence of domestic slavery, under the circumstances in which it is found in the southern portion of this country is no bar to communion . . . the Assembly are not to be understood as denying that there is evil connected with slavery. Much less do they approve those defective and oppressive laws by which, in some of the States, it is regulated. . . . Nor is this Assembly to be understood as countenancing the idea that masters may regard their servants as mere property, and not as human beings . . . the Assembly intend simply to say that since Christ and his inspired Apostles did not make the holding of slaves a bar to communion, we, as a court of Christ, have not authority to do so.[36]

An overriding concern was to maintain harmony in church and state; the Assembly believed threats of discipline for slaveholding tended toward "the dissolution of the union of our beloved country, and which every enlightened Christian will oppose as bringing about a ruinous and unnecessary schism between brethren who maintain a common faith."[37] The 1845 statements on slaveholding were sustained by subsequent Assemblies, a significant factor aiding Old School unity up until the secession crisis hit the nation.

34. Fred A. Ross, *Slavery Ordained of God* (Philadelphia: J. B. Lippincott & Co., 1857), 1.
35. Parker, *United Synod of the South*, 157–94.
36. *Minutes of the General Assembly of the Presbyterian Church in the United States of America* (Old School) (Philadelphia: Presbyterian Board of Publication, 1846), 16–18. This statement was approved 168 to 13.
37. *Minutes of the General Assembly* (Old School), 1846, 18.

Some Old School Southern Presbyterians began moving toward a more hardened defense of slavery. In 1840, Robert Lewis Dabney of Virginia admitted Southern recalcitrance in the face of abolitionist abuse: "I do believe that if these mad fanatics had let us alone, in twenty years we should have made Virginia a Free State. As it is, their unauthorized attempts to strike off the fetter of our slaves has but riveted them on the faster. Does this fact arise from the perversity of our natures? I believe that it does in part. We are less inclined to that which we know is our duty because persons, who have no right to interfere, demand it of us."[38] James Henley Thornwell of South Carolina, writing in 1851, defended the Southern institution by appealing to the Bible: "The Scriptures not only fail to condemn slavery, they as distinctly sanction it as any other social condition of man. The Church was formally organized in the family of a slaveholder; the relation was divinely regulated among the chosen people of God; and peculiar duties of the parties are inculcated under the Christian economy. These are facts which cannot be denied."[39] In a published sermon, Thornwell described slavery as a blessing: "Slavery may be a good, or, to speak more accurately, a condition, from which, though founded in a curse, the Providence of God extracts a blessing."[40]

Despite hardening Southern perspectives in response to militant abolitionist rhetoric, Southern Presbyterians continued ministry to the slave population. Charles Colcock Jones, a Princeton seminary graduate, committed much of his pastoral ministry to evangelizing blacks through his circuit preaching on plantations when he returned home to Georgia. He established church schools to teach English, and in the 1840s wrote both a catechism and a manual for instructing blacks, which were widely used.[41] In 1854, John L. Girardeau of South Carolina became pastor of the predominately black Zion Presbyterian

38. Quoted by Frank Bell Lewis in "Robert Lewis Dabney, Southern Presbyterian Apologist" (unpublished thesis, Duke University, 1946), 40; cited by Thompson, *Presbyterians in the South*, 1:535.

39. James H. Thornwell, "The Relation of the Church to Slavery" (1851), in *The Collected Writings of James Henley Thornwell*, ed. John B. Adger and John L. Girardeau, vol. 4 (Richmond, VA: Presbyterian Committee on Publication, 1873; reprint, Edinburgh: Banner of Truth Trust, 1974), 385. This essay was adopted by the Synod of South Carolina.

40. James H. Thornwell, "The Christian Doctrine of Slavery" (1850), in *The Collected Writings of James Henley Thornwell*, 4:421. The sermon was given in Charleston, South Carolina, at the dedication of a building erected for blacks to worship. For a survey of debate on the Bible and slavery, see Mark A. Noll, *The Civil War as a Theological Crisis* (Chapel Hill: University of North Carolina Press, 2006), 31–94.

41. Works by C. C. Jones on ministry to slaves: *A Catechism of Scripture, Doctrine and Practice for the Oral Instruction of Colored Persons* (1837; 1843) and *The Religious Instruction of Negroes in the United States* (1842). See Wayne C. Tyner, "Colcock Jones: Mission

Church in Charleston. The congregation experienced a multiweek revival in 1858, where hundreds of blacks and whites were converted, and by 1860 fifteen hundred (90 percent black) were attending weekly Sunday services. Girardeau established "class" meetings in the congregation under black leadership, to provide fellowship, to care for the sick, and "to further growth in Christian knowledge and experimental religion." During the war, Girardeau served as a chaplain in the Confederate army, and afterward he was a theology professor at Columbia Seminary.[42]

There were strident Old School abolitionists such as John J. Breckinridge of Kentucky; Thomas D. Baird, editor of the *Pittsburgh Christian Herald*; John W. Nevin, a professor at Western Seminary;[43] and Joshua Wilson of Cincinnati, but the majority Old School opinion, North and South, advocated a peaceful, gradual emancipation as the way forward for the United States. A widely respected representative of this perspective was Princeton professor Charles Hodge,[44] who wrote in 1849, "The old school Presbyterians . . . have stood up as a wall against the flood of abolitionism, which would have overwhelmed the church and riven asunder the State. But at the same time, they have been the truest friends of the slaves and most effectual advocates of emancipation."[45] In 1836 Hodge had explained his Old School position as follows: "The question is not about the continuance of slavery and of the present system, but about the proper method of effecting the removal of the evil. . . . We think, therefore, that the true method for Christians to treat this subject, is to follow the example of Christ and his apostles. . . . Let them enforce as moral duties . . . the great principles of justice and mercy, and all the specific commands and precepts of the Scriptures." If this is done, then emancipation will follow: "If it be asked what would be the consequence of thus acting on the principles of the gospel, of following the example and obeying the precepts of Christ? We answer, the gradual elevation of the slaves in intelligence, virtue, and wealth; the peaceable and speedy extinction of slavery. . . . It may be objected that if

---

to Slaves," *Journal of Presbyterian History* 55, no. 4 (Winter 1977): 363–80; Erskine Clarke, *Wrestlin' Jacob: A Portrait of Religion in the Old South* (Atlanta: John Knox, 1979), 3–81.

42. Douglas Kelly, *Preachers with Power: Four Stalwarts of the South* (Edinburgh: Banner of Truth Trust, 1992), 121–70.

43. John W. Nevin, a Princeton Seminary graduate, served at Western Seminary for a decade, then took a position at Mercersburg Seminary of the German Reformed Church.

44. Hodge purchased a sixteen-year-old slave girl in 1828 to assist his wife; she was freed at age twenty-one, consistent with an 1804 emancipation law in New Jersey.

45. Charles Hodge, review of *The Question of Negro Slavery and the New Constitution of Kentucky*, by Robert J. Breckinridge, *Biblical Repertory and Princeton Review*, October 1849, 586.

the slaves are allowed so to improve as to become freemen, the next step in their progress is that they should become citizens. We admit that it is so."[46] Hodge's gradual emancipation position resonated with the majority of the Old School and held their branch of Presbyterianism together until the war forced the issue of sectional separation.

---

46. Charles Hodge, review of *Slavery*, by William E. Channing, *Biblical Repertory and Princeton Review*, April 1836, 302–5. Allen Guelzo views this statement as Hodge's "anti-slavery moment"; he places Hodge into a proslavery category. Others reckon Hodge as a centrist who voiced a "repeated rejection of the indefinite perpetuation of slavery" (Peter Wallace). See Allen C. Guelzo, "Charles Hodge's Antislavery Moment," in *Charles Hodge Revisited: A Critical Appraisal of His Life and Work*, ed. John W. Stewart and James H. Moorhead (Grand Rapids: Eerdmans, 2002), 299–325; Peter J. Wallace, "The Defense of the Forgotten Center: Charles Hodge and the Enigma of Emancipationism in Antebellum America," *Journal of Presbyterian History* 75, no. 3 (Fall 1997): 174.

CHAPTER 12

Presbyterianism, Civil War, and Reunions

The 1840s and '50s was a period of American national expansion—statehood for Texas (1845), the Oregon Territory coming under United States jurisdiction (1846), and the California Gold Rush (1849). The nation went to war with Mexico (1848), and fresh waves of immigrants from Ireland, Germany, and China arrived on American shores. By midcentury Presbyterians had built churches and mission stations across the newly populated territories, with established congregations giving faithfully to support home missions. This was a time of increased strain between slave and free states. The Fugitive Slave Act of 1850, the publishing of *Uncle Tom's Cabin* in 1851 by Harriet Beecher Stowe (daughter of the New School's Lyman Beecher), and the Supreme Court's 1857 *Dred Scott* decision each added to the swelling tide. The 1850s mayhem in "bleeding Kansas" became an armed contest between proslavery and antislavery settlers. In 1859, militant abolitionist John Brown tried to initiate a slave insurrection at Harpers Ferry, Virginia, but was stopped by soldiers under Colonel Robert E. Lee. All these factors exacerbated sectional strife, and churches were not exempted from grappling with the gathering storm. Many denominations, including the Old School and New School churches, could not avoid schism as the divided nation approached war.

What Is Presbyterianism?

For the New School church, the 1840s was an era of developing its identity and organizational structures. Property litigation with the Old School denomination was abandoned as the New School concentrated on its own mission, with annual reports of local revivals and increasing church membership. The New School established its own boards and publishing house but remained on the defense against attacks in the Old School press. In 1852 the Presbyterian Church (New School) established its own journal, the *Presbyterian Quarterly Review*.[1] A chief goal of the periodical was both to justify the New School church's existence and to defend her distinctives. The editors of the *Review* deemed it their mission to defend "old fashioned, Catholic, American Presbyterianism," which they described under four principles: religious liberty, living Calvinism, cooperative Christianity, and an aggressive Christianity. "Living Calvinism" was understood as the "true line of succession" from the Log College and the New Side, which emphasized the element of piety. The robust theology of Calvin needed to be infused with inward piety. Between the years 1852 and 1855, the *Presbyterian Quarterly Review* carried a series of five articles entitled "The Spirit of American Presbyterianism."[2]

From the other side, Charles Hodge defended Old School perspectives in his *Constitutional History of the Presbyterian Church*, written in the years following the 1837 schism.[3] Hodge also defended his Old School views on Presbyterianism against other Protestants. In nineteenth-century Britain, the Oxford Movement, also known as "Tractarianism," which derived its name from *Tracts for the Times*, written by several Anglican theologians, was calling for a return to the values of dogma, holiness, apostolic succession, and catholicity. In the 1850s, Hodge weighed in on the debate, arguing against the "Romanizing party" (Tractarians) in the Church of England. Summarizing his own views on church government, he listed the principles he observed in the Bible: (1) The right of the people to take part in the government of the church. Hence, the divine right of the office of ruling elders, who appear in all church courts as representatives of the people. (2) The appointment and perpetual continuance of presbyters as ministers of the Word and sacraments, with authority to rule, teach, and ordain, as the highest permanent officers of the church. (3) The unity of the church, or the subjection of a smaller to a larger part and of a larger part to the whole.[4]

Hodge was drawn into intra–Old School polity debates with John B. Adger and James Henley Thornwell, professors at Columbia Seminary in South Caro-

1. The editor of the *Presbyterian Quarterly Review* was Ben J. Wallace; associate editors included Albert Barnes and the professors at Union (New York), Auburn, and Lane theological seminaries.

2. "The Spirit of American Presbyterianism," *Presbyterian Quarterly Review*, December 1852, 475–77.

3. Charles Hodge, *The Constitutional History of the Presbyterian Church in the United States of America*, 2 vols. (Philadelphia: William S. Martien, 1840).

4. See Charles Hodge, "The Church of England and Presbyterian Orders," *Princeton Review*, April 1854, 377–404, and "What Is Presbyterianism?" (Philadelphia: Presbyterian Board of Publications, 1855).

lina. Hodge affirmed certain prescribed principles of government in Scripture, but beyond these, discretion in details was allowed. Thornwell countered that the Bible provided more than mere general principles of polity, and any ecclesiastical action without specific warrant from the Word of God was unlawful. In 1860, the Old School Assembly debated the legitimacy of church boards, and whether boards should be replaced by committees more directly tied to church courts. After Thornwell's impassioned speech for committees, Hodge gave a forty-minute rebuttal, convincing the Assembly, which overwhelmingly voted to keep the church boards. Another issue that surfaced was the relationship between ministers and ruling elders. Adger and Thornwell argued that elders and ministers are one order/office in the church, while Hodge advocated a clear distinction between clergy and lay elders. For Hodge, clergy have distinct gifts, training, ordination, and duties in church life, whereas lay elders have unique roles as chosen representatives of the congregation. Elders rule in the church through the exercise of government and discipline; professional ministers conversely have a special calling to preach and administer the sacraments. Hodge believed his position safeguarded lay leadership in the local church and represented the views of historic Presbyterianism.[5]

Presbyterian worship had been shaped by revivalism to include more extempore prayer, praise songs, and more informal preaching. Over time revivalist worship practices became more formalized, and there was renewed interest in more accepted formal patterns. Some Presbyterians, desirous of more formal worship, departed and affiliated with the Episcopal Church. Albert Barnes, who had lost some of his own members, attacked historic liturgical worship as incompatible with the free spirit of American worship, calling it the "folly of the past." Charles W. Baird, who was exposed to the rich Reformed liturgical heritage while in Europe for a number of years, advocated a return to Reformation-era liturgies. Baird wrote *Eutaxia, or the Presbyterian Liturgies: Historical Sketches*, in 1855.[6] The name *Eutaxia* came from the Greek words translated "decently and in order" in 1 Corinthians 14:40. His collection of classical Protestant sixteenth- and seventeenth-century liturgies was impressive in its historical research and drew extensive attention in the church. Charles Hodge concurred with Baird's call for liturgical reform, asserting that the use

5. Charles Hodge, "Presbyterianism," *Princeton Review*, July 1860, 546–67, and "Theories of Eldership," *Princeton Review*, October 1860, 702–59; John B. Adger, "Princeton Review on Theories of Eldership," *Southern Presbyterian Review*, October 1860, 578–623; James H. Thornwell, "Princeton Review on Presbyterianism," *Southern Presbyterian Review*, January 1861, 757–810.

6. Charles W. Baird, *Eutaxia, or the Presbyterian Liturgies: Historical Sketches* (New York: M. W. Dodd, 1855), republished as *The Presbyterian Liturgies: Historical Sketches* (Grand Rapids: Baker Books, 1960; reprint, Eugene, OR: Wipf & Stock, 2006).

of a set liturgy was not the exclusive domain of Episcopalians; indeed, all Protestants of the Reformation era had adopted their own liturgies, including Presbyterians. He acknowledged that abandonment of these worship patterns by many Protestants had been detrimental to the life of the church. While he agreed with historic resistance to imposing the Anglican Book of Common Prayer, he thought providing optional liturgies for the sacraments, ordination, marriage, and burial could be useful to Presbyterian congregations.[7] The New School generally was not so favorable to Baird's proposals, believing the Directory of Worship had been sufficient; however, a couple of New School ministers in 1861 collected contemporary compositions into a book of forms and prayers, *The Presbyterian's Handbook of the Church*.[8]

Presbyterians shared the growing national anxiety over increasing numbers of Roman Catholics immigrating to the United States. Most Americans perceived their nation as Protestant, and many viewed Catholicism as a threat to both Protestantism and political liberty. Three million European immigrants made their way to America in the 1840s and '50s, and the vast majority of them were Roman Catholics from Germany or Ireland. By the time of the Civil War, Catholics would be the largest denomination in America.[9] There was organized political animosity; for example, the Know-Nothing movement (American Party), which was pledged to protect America from foreigners and Catholics, got seventy-five persons elected to Congress in 1854.[10] Intense Protestant animosity toward Catholics had a long history, and identifying the papacy with the antichrist had been common Protestant teaching since the sixteenth century. Many Presbyterians interpreted the "Beast" of the book of Revelation as the Roman Church and the "Whore of Babylon" as the papal antichrist. In his commentary on Revelation 17, Albert Barnes offered his interpretation of the woman sitting on the beast: "The image here is that of papal Rome, represented as an abandoned woman in gorgeous attire, alluring by her arts the nations of the earth and seducing them into all kinds of pollution and abomination."[11] A practical issue concerned whether or not Roman Catholics

7. Charles Hodge, "Presbyterian Liturgies," *Biblical Repertory and Princeton Review* 27 (July 1855): 445–67.

8. Julius Melton, *Presbyterian Worship in America: Changing Patterns Since 1787* (Richmond, VA: John Knox, 1967), 59–92; Joel Parker and T. Ralston Smith, *The Presbyterian's Handbook of the Church* (New York: Harper & Bros., 1861).

9. Sydney E. Ahlstrom, *A Religious History of the American People*, vol. 1 (Garden City, NY: Image Books, 1975), 627, 649–50.

10. For an overview of anti-Catholicism, see Ray A. Billington, *The Protestant Crusade, 1800–1860: A Study of the Origins of Nativism* (New York: Macmillan, 1938).

11. Albert Barnes, *Notes, Explanatory and Practical on the Book of Revelation* (New

should be rebaptized if they joined a Presbyterian congregation. In 1845, the Old School Assembly voted overwhelmingly to require it. This was a reversal of its historic practice, and Hodge chastised his Old School brethren for this novelty: "Are we to suggest that Luther, Calvin and untold thousands of other Protestants who only had 'Romish baptism' (no rebaptism) were actually unbaptized persons? What new light has been shed on this question to overturn the custom of the Protestant Reformers?" He asserted that Roman Catholics profess "the essentials of the true Christian religion" despite corruption and abuses. Catholics affirmed the ecumenical creeds and so should be considered part of the visible church. Hodge took heat for his articles in the *Princeton Review*; on the other side, Thornwell wrote several articles supporting the Assembly's position.[12]

Reform and Revival

Many Americans believed that inculcating Christian virtues in the people was essential for the republic to survive. Vice among the populace would destroy the country, and one critical social vice was desecration of the Christian Sabbath. Historically, Americans had made Sunday sacrosanct by refraining from work and commerce in order to allow the public to attend Christian worship. This commitment would decline in the nineteenth century, and Presbyterians protested these changes along with other Christians involved in the Sabbatarian movement. In 1810 Congress had passed a law requiring all post offices to remain open seven days a week, which precipitated protests in the nation. In 1828 the General Union for Promoting the Observance of the Christian Sabbath was organized by Lyman Beecher and others. Sabbatarians argued that keeping the Sabbath was required by man's nature and the need for rest. In addition, the religious education that took place on Sundays was impor-

---

York: Harper & Bros., 1852; reprint, Grand Rapids: Baker Books, 1958), 384; see also George Duffield, *Dissertation on the Prophecies Relative to the Second Coming of Christ* (New York: Dayton & Newman, 1842). In 1903 the Westminster Confession, chap. 25, was modified by the Presbyterian Church in the United States of America (PCUSA) to remove language about the pope being the antichrist.

12. Charles Hodge, "The General Assembly of 1845," *Biblical Repertory and Princeton Review* 17 (July 1845): 444–71, and "Is the Church of Rome Part of the Visible Church," *Biblical Repertory and Princeton Review* 18 (April 1846): 320–44. Thornwell's articles appeared in the *Watchman Observer* of Richmond in 1846; they are included in *Collected Writings of James Henley Thornwell*, vol. 3 (Richmond, VA: Presbyterian Committee of Publication, 1871; reprint, Carlisle, PA: Banner of Truth Trust, 1974).

tant for teaching the values needed in society. Presbyterian minister George Duffield argued that it was "impossible that our public morals can flourish, or be preserved without religion. And it is further impossible that religion can long exist without a Sabbath." Albert Barnes asserted, "If the institution of the Sabbath is abolished, the Christian religion will be abolished with it."[13] This battle would continue in American society for decades.

Excessive alcohol consumption was a serious social problem in the United States, and multitudes of Christians committed themselves to alleviating this problem, which they believed was overwhelming the country with crime, poverty, and family issues. Initially, opposition was focused on distilled hard liquor, but eventually fermented drinks also became targets of the temperance movement, which insisted on abstinence as the ultimate solution to the intoxication crisis. The American Temperance Society began in Boston in 1826, spreading to local societies in all the states. Organizations like the Washingtonians (1840) and the Sons of Temperance (1842) sought to support sobriety and encourage abstinence. New School ministers were consistently supportive of the temperance movement and calls for total abstinence.[14] Lyman Beecher opposed the licensing of liquor sales in the states, declaring in published sermons that "intemperance is the sin of our land."[15] The Old School, with some exceptions, tended to take a more nuanced approach to drinking alcohol, supporting abstinence as prudent but unwilling to condemn all drinking as sinful. In 1842 the Old School Assembly went on record that abstaining from intoxicating drink was not a prerequisite for taking communion.[16] By the 1850s, twelve states had passed prohibition laws of some kind, all based upon a model law passed in Maine in 1851, though most were repealed or declared unconstitutional by the end of the decade. Despite setbacks, the prohibition movement would press forward into the early twentieth century.[17]

The year 1857 witnessed immigrant gang riots in New York, a stock market crash, bank failures, and the *Dred Scott* decision by the Supreme Court. In

13. George Duffield and Albert Barnes, *Discourses on the Sabbath* (Philadelphia: George W. Donohue, 1836), 85, 105, cited in Leo Hirrel, *Children of Wrath: New School Calvinism and Antebellum Reform* (Lexington: University of Kentucky Press, 1998), 83, 84.

14. For example, George Duffield, *The Bible Rule of Temperance* (New York: National Temperance Society, 1866).

15. Lyman Beecher, *Six Sermons on the Nature, Occasions, Signs, Evils, and Remedy of Intemperance* (Boston: T. R. Marvin, 1828).

16. *Minutes of the General Assembly of the Presbyterian Church in the United States of America* (Old School) (Philadelphia: Presbyterian Board of Publication, 1842), 16.

17. Ian Tyrrell, *Sobering Up: From Temperance to Prohibition in Antebellum America, 1800–1860* (Westport, CT: Greenwood, 1979).

the midst of widespread despair, prayer meetings began to spring up across the country, and America experienced one of its greatest revivals, the Prayer Meeting Revival of 1857–1858. It was led by laymen who daily gathered at noon for prayer in cities all over the nation and resulted in thousands of conversions, renewal in churches, and a fresh spirit of ecumenism among denominations. The American population stood at around 30 million, and between 1856 and 1859 the Protestant churches gained about half a million members, Presbyterians being one of the beneficiaries. The lay-led prayer times began with the efforts of Jeremiah Calvin Lanphier, a businessman turned home missionary who worked in New York City evangelizing the lower classes. Lanphier had been assigned to this ministry by the North Dutch Church on Fulton Street, near Wall Street. In September of 1857, Lanphier initiated a lunchtime prayer meeting for businessmen at the North Dutch Church, which began small but rapidly grew. Other prayer meetings spread throughout the city, and other parts of the country began to emulate these lay-led prayer meetings.[18] In New York City, the pastor of Fifth Avenue Presbyterian Church, James W. Alexander (son of Princeton's Archibald Alexander), wrote, "You may rest assured there is a great awakening among us. . . . The best token I have seen of revival was our meeting of Presbytery. I never was at such a one. Brethren seemed flowing together in love, and reported a great increase of attention in all their churches."[19] Another Presbyterian New Yorker, Rev. Samuel Irenaeus Prime, editor of the *New York Observer*, wrote several books on the ongoing results of the prayer revival, including an account of the Fulton Street meetings.[20]

In Philadelphia, the prayer revival so transformed the city that a group of fifteen, supported by the Young Men's Christian Association, published an account of the revival in 1859—*Pentecost or the Work of God in Philadelphia*. The group consisted of representatives from a dozen denominations, including both Old and New School Presbyterians, Reformed Presbyterians, and Associate Presbyterians. The Philadelphia revival included a keen spirit of unity among the Christians, including preachers sharing pulpits across denominations. The authors observed that there was no famous name or

---

18. See Kathryn Teresa Long, *The Revival of 1857–58: Interpreting an American Religious Awakening* (New York: Oxford University Press, 1998). Long argues that the nascent railroads and telegraph lines were the links that facilitated the spread of the awakening.

19. James W. Alexander to John Hall, April 2, 1858, cited in Ian H. Murray, *Revival and Revivalism: The Making and Marring of American Evangelicalism, 1750–1858* (Carlisle, PA: Banner of Truth Trust, 1994), 344.

20. Samuel Irenaeus Prime, *The Power of Prayer, Illustrated in the Wonderful Displays of Divine Grace at the Fulton Street and Other Meetings in New York and Elsewhere, 1857 and 1858* (New York: Charles Scribner, 1859).

eloquent voice leading the revival as in previous times. In March 1858, a twenty-nine-year-old Episcopalian minister, Dudley Tyng, preached to five thousand at a noon meeting held at the downtown YMCA, with over one thousand committing to follow Christ. Tyng was fatally injured the following week in an accident, and as he died surrounded by friends, he uttered, "Let us all stand up for Jesus." A group of ministers in the city led the funeral service for Tyng, and among them was George Duffield, pastor of Philadelphia's Temple Presbyterian Church. Duffield publicly read a poem he had written for the occasion that began, "Stand up, stand up for Jesus, ye soldiers of the Cross; lift high His royal banner, it must not suffer loss." The four stanzas that Duffield penned would become the popular hymn "Stand Up, Stand Up for Jesus."[21]

Foreign and Domestic Missions

One outcome of the prayer revival was a fresh burst of domestic and foreign missions by Americans. The most famous missionary converted during the revival was Baptist Lottie Moon, missionary to China.[22] Princeton graduate Ashbel Green Simonton became the first missionary to Brazil under the auspices of the Presbyterian Board of Foreign Missions. Simonton moved to Rio de Janeiro in 1859; he held his first worship service in Portuguese the next year and led the struggle for Protestant toleration in this predominately Roman Catholic country. The first Presbyterian church in Brazil was established in 1862. Three years later the first presbytery in Brazil was organized, with an ex-Catholic priest becoming the first native Brazilian pastor. Just before his death in 1867 from yellow fever at age thirty-seven, Simonton founded the first Presbyterian seminary in Brazil.[23]

21. Young Men's Christian Association, *Pentecost or the Work of God in Philadelphia* (Philadelphia: Parry & McMillan, 1859); J. Edwin Orr, *The Event of the Century: The 1857–1858 Awakening*, ed. Richard Owen Roberts (Wheaton, IL: International Awakening Press, 1989).

22. Charlotte Diggs "Lottie" Moon (1840–1912) was converted in 1858 college revival meetings led by John Broadus (a founder of the Southern Baptist Theological Seminary). Moon departed for China in 1873, where she was a missionary for forty years. Though a schoolteacher by training, she was an effective evangelist and church planter in China. Lottie Moon initiated the first Southern Baptist Christmas offering for missions in 1888. For information on Lottie Moon, consult H. Leon McBeth, *The Baptist Heritage: Four Centuries of Baptist Witness* (Nashville: Broadman, 1987), 416–19.

23. Robert E. Speer, *Presbyterian Foreign Missions: An Account of the Foreign Missions of the Presbyterian Church U.S.A.* (Chicago: Revell, 1901), 273–80. Speer's book includes chapters that cover Presbyterian missions in Africa, India, Siam and Laos, China, Japan,

In these years before the Civil War, Texas Presbyterians were taking the initiative to reach Mexican Americans. A handful of missionaries took the lead in this ministry: Sumner Bacon, W. C. Blair, John McCullough, and Melinda Rankin. They all had a vision to reach the Mexican people in their homeland, but Mexico was closed to Protestants before 1860; thus they focused on the Mexican immigrants to the republic of Texas (state of Texas after 1845). As Protestant missionaries were permitted to move into Roman Catholic Mexico, many Presbyterian bodies—PCUSA, Presbyterian Church in the United States (PCUS), Cumberland Presbyterian Church (CPC), and the Associate Reformed Presbyterian Church (ARP)—were involved. The PCUS had the most success in Mexican American ministry, organizing its first Mexican Presbyterian congregation in Brownsville, Texas, in 1877. By 1902 there were eleven churches with 618 communicants and 292 baptized noncommunicants. In 1908, the PCUS established the Texas-Mexican Presbytery, with seventeen churches, four ordained ministers, and four candidates, under the Synod of Texas.[24] From these early mission efforts in the Southwest among Mexicans up to the present day, Presbyterian denominations have continued their ministry to Hispanic immigrants from Central and South America coming to the USA.

There was also ministry among Native American tribes. Old School Presbyterians pursued mission work among five Indian tribes (Creeks, Seminoles, Cherokees, Choctaws, and Chickasaws) after their relocation into "Indian Territory" west of the Mississippi River. Indian Presbytery was organized in 1840, and by the time of the Civil War it had twelve missionaries, two Indian ministers, and seventeen churches. A Presbytery of the Creek Nation (1848) served the Creeks and Cherokees with seven ministers. In the Far West, the first Chinese Presbyterian church was organized in California in 1853.[25]

In the decades after the Civil War, Korea would become a significant Presbyterian foreign missions endeavor. Horace Underwood arrived in Korea in 1885, building an orphanage and school for Korean children. He helped translate the Bible, and by 1889 had organized a church.[26]

Korea, Syria, Persia, North America, South America, and the Philippines. Today the *Igresia de Presbyteriana de Brasil* (IPB) has a membership of about one million.

24. R. Douglas Brackenridge and Francisco O. Garcia-Treto, *Iglesia Presbiteriana: A History of Presbyterians and Mexican Americans in the Southwest*, 2nd ed. (San Antonio: Trinity University Press, 1987), 1–31.

25. E. T. Thompson, *Presbyterian Missions in the Southern United States* (Richmond, VA: Presbyterian Committee of Publication, 1934), 155–57.

26. Samuel Hugh Moffett, *A History of Christianity in Asia*, vol. 2, *1500–1900* (Maryknoll, NY: Orbis, 2005), 528–53. In South Korea today there are between nine and ten million Presbyterians, about half of the Christian population.

During this era, Sheldon Jackson became a successful pioneer in Presbyterian church planting. At one point Jackson had oversight of all Presbyterian mission work between Canada and Mexico and from Nebraska to Nevada, serving as editor of the *Rocky Mountain Presbyterian* from 1872 to 1882. His untiring ministry to the Eskimos of Alaska included providing education and economic assistance and starting new churches. Under his leadership, eight synods were established in the Northwest and over 150 churches were organized.[27]

War between the States

In the years immediately preceding the war, there were both Presbyterian division and a new union. The New School had split over slavery in 1858, but in that same year two other Presbyterian bodies united. The new denomination was formed by a union of the Associate Reformed Church and the Associate Synod, with a combined total of over 650 congregations. Negotiations over potential union among the American Presbyterian bodies with Scottish Dissenter roots had been initiated in the 1830s, had continued through the 1840s with little progress, and eventually the Reformed Presbyterians had withdrawn. Undeterred, the Associate Synod offered a "Basis of Union" to the Associate Reformed Church in 1856, which they adopted the next year. The Basis of Union included a modification to the Westminster Confession on the power of the civil magistrate and a "Judicial Testimony" with eighteen declarations on contemporary topics not fully addressed in the Confession. Declaration 14 condemned slavery: "That slaveholding—that is, the holding of unoffending human beings in involuntary bondage, and considering and treating them as property, and subject to be bought and sold—is a violation of the law of God, and contrary both to the letter and spirit of Christianity." The declarations also forbade participation in secret societies or communion with those outside their profession of faith and affirmed public social covenanting as a duty "in times of great danger to the church." The final declaration addressed use of the Psalter: "That it is the will of God that the songs contained in the Book of Psalms be sung in his worship, both public and private, to the end of the world; and in singing God's praise these songs should be employed to the exclusion of the devotional compositions of uninspired men." The Associate Synod and Associate Reformed accepted the "Testimony" as a term of communion. In a

---

27. J. Arthur Lazell, *Alaskan Apostle: The Life Story of Sheldon Jackson* (New York: Harper, 1960).

joint session at Pittsburgh City Hall on May 26, 1858, the two churches officially constituted themselves as the United Presbyterian Church of North America (UPCNA).[28]

With the election of Abraham Lincoln in 1860—a man whom the South considered an antislavery radical—the dissolution of the Union appeared imminent. As hard as the peacemakers tried, they could not stem the rising tide of sectional division engulfing America. During the early morning of April 12, 1861, South Carolinians opened fire on Fort Sumter from shore batteries in Charleston. The Old School Assembly convened the next month in Philadelphia with very few Southern commissioners in attendance. An amiable spirit prevailed among the brethren, yet the inevitable question had to surface. After twelve days and much debate, the moment of truth finally arrived when Gardiner Spring, pastor of the Brick Church in New York, offered a resolution affirming loyalty to the federal government. The resolution was approved 156–66, but immediately a protest was entered by fifty-eight commissioners that declared, "The General Assembly in thus deciding a political question, and in making that decision practically a condition of membership in the Church, has, in our judgment, violated the Constitution of the Church, and usurped the prerogative of its Divine Master." The protesters asserted that a church court had no right to require citizens in the seceding states to support the federal government. While Christians are taught to support the powers that be, "the Bible does not enable any man to decide whether these United States are a nation, or a voluntary confederacy of nations, the church has no voice in the decision of this question."[29] The protest was rebuffed, and Southern synods, believing they had been unconstitutionally debarred by the Old School Assembly, formally withdrew over the next few months. To have remained a part of the Northern Assembly would have been tantamount to treason in the Southern mind.

The Presbyterian Church in the Confederate States of America (PCCSA) was established in 1861 by representatives of forty-one Southern presbyteries assembled at First Presbyterian Church in Augusta, Georgia. The pastor of First Presbyterian was Dr. Joseph Wilson, father of Thomas Woodrow Wilson, future president of the United States. By 1861, both Old School and New School had divided into two bodies, North and South, each of the denominations loyal to the Union or the Confederacy, respectively.

28. James Brown Scouller, "History of the United Presbyterian Church of North America," in *American Church History Series*, vol. 11 (New York: Christian Literature Company, 1894), 225–32; W. N. Jamison, *The United Presbyterian Story: A Centennial Study, 1858–1958* (Pittsburgh: Geneva, 1958). The UPCNA merged with the PCUSA in 1958 to form the United Presbyterian Church in the United States of America; see chap. 18 below.

29. *Minutes of the General Assembly* (Old School, North), 1861, 339–41.

Revival in the Armies

During the war years, home missions dissipated—especially in the South. Yet there were significant conversions in the Confederate armies, often generated by PCCSA and Cumberland Presbyterian chaplains and missionaries. Some of the chaplains were also officers, leading the soldiers in battle and in prayer. Chaplains would spend months at a time embedded in the army ranks, preaching, praying, distributing Bibles and tracts, and providing pastoral care to the wounded. The total number of PCCSA ministers who served in the Confederate army was 130. General Thomas "Stonewall" Jackson, a pious Presbyterian deacon, was notable for his support of Christian ministry in the Army of Northern Virginia.[30] Army churches were organized with officers, the chaplains serving as moderators; sometimes soldiers built log churches in camps that could seat three hundred to five hundred. Many Southern denominations participated in the revivals throughout multiple brigades of the Confederate army, especially in northern Virginia and Tennessee. In 1864, the Committee on Domestic Missions reported to the PCCSA Assembly, "The whole number of conversions among soldiers during the past year have probably exceeded 12,000. Besides those numbered as converts there are probably hundreds and thousands in the army at the present time inquiring what they must do to be saved." Religious periodicals in the South carried stories of widespread awakening as well as eyewitness reports from soldiers' letters home and officers' accounts.[31]

In the Union army, Presbyterians supplied about one-quarter of the total number of military chaplains, second only to the Methodists. The Old School church provided 152 army chaplains, and the New School had 118 of its ministers serve as chaplains. In 1861, Reformed Presbyterian businessman George Stuart of Philadelphia helped organize the nondenominational United States Christian Commission, whose mission was to distribute supplies as

30. J. William Jones, *Christ in the Camp: The True Story of the Great Revival during the War between the States* (B. F. Johnson & Co., 1887; reprint, Harrisonburg, VA: Sprinkle, 1986), 82–101. General Jackson wrote to the PCCSA General Assembly, "Each branch of the Christian Church should send into the army some of its most prominent ministers who are distinguished for their piety, talents and zeal; . . . I would like to see no question asked in the army of what denomination a chaplain belongs to; but let the question be, Does he preach the Gospel?" (94).

31. Benjamin Rice Lacy Jr., *Revivals in the Midst of the Years* (Richmond, VA: John Knox, 1942; reprint, Presbyterian Evangelistic Fellowship, 1968), 115–45; see William W. Bennett, *A Narrative of the Great Revival which Prevailed in the Southern Armies during the Late Civil War between the States of the Federal Union* (Philadelphia: Claxton, Remsen & Haffelfinger, 1877).

well as provide religious literature and chapels for the troops. Prominent Presbyterian businessman John Wanamaker, known for the 1858 founding of the Bethany Sunday school in Philadelphia, participated in the Christian Commission's ministry to soldiers. As denominations, both the Old School and New School supported the Christian Commission. Revivals in the Union army were most intense from 1863 to 1865, alongside a growing sense that the war was a righteous crusade against slavery.[32] An ecumenical spirit pervaded the revivals as Presbyterians, Methodists, Baptists, and others shared communion together in camp. A number of Northern generals encouraged religious services and would not put their men into battle on the Sabbath. Estimates of conversions among Union soldiers range from one hundred thousand to two hundred thousand.[33]

REUNIONS AND RECONSTRUCTION

The war years shattered the nation, yet churches continued to carry on ministry in the midst of the conflict. As the bitter contest continued, Presbyterians in the South (Old and New School, South) reconnected, but in the North reunion discussions did not begin until the late 1860s. In both instances, the war had given Presbyterians a new perspective on ecclesiastical unity. The United Synod of the South (New School) had initiated interest in reunion as early as 1858, only to be rebuffed by the Old School church, which was still undivided. Just three years later things changed dramatically when the Old School South became a separate church. This time the subject of reunion was raised from the Old School side, which had expressed a desire for closer communion with other Reformed churches in the South as early as 1861. A Committee of Conference was appointed in 1863 to meet with representatives of the United Synod, and a meeting was set for Lynchburg, Virginia, with Professor Robert L. Dabney of Union Seminary in Virginia leading the Old School group and Dr. Joseph Stiles serving as chief spokesman for the New School. Dabney presented an opening speech with "entire fairness" and "the spirit of magnificent

32. Mark Noll has underscored the "theological crisis" of the Civil War, arguing that diverse interpretations of the Bible's teaching on slavery yielded vastly different understandings of God's purposes in the war. *The Civil War as a Theological Crisis* (Chapel Hill: University of North Carolina Press, 2006); see chap. 11, n. 40, above.

33. Gardiner H. Shattuck Jr., *A Shield and Hiding Place: The Religious Life of the Civil War Armies* (Macon, GA: Mercer University Press, 1987), 13-33, 73-93; Lewis G. Vander Velde, *The Presbyterian Churches and the Federal Union, 1861-1869* (Cambridge, MA: Harvard University Press, 1932), 467-75.

equity," according to Stiles, who declared that if Dabney's views represented those of the Old School, "the breach between us is healed."[34]

Dabney and Stiles later met as a subcommittee to draw up articles for union. After full discussion and amendment by the joint committee, the articles were unanimously endorsed. The doctrinal articles were counterbalancing statements that both honored New School emphases and affirmed traditional Old School theology. On the revivals, for example, one article declared,

> It is dangerous to ply the disordered heart of the sinner with a disproportionate address to the imagination and passions . . . and to employ with him such novel and startling measures as must tend to impart to his religious excitement a character rather noisy, shallow and transient, than deep, solid, and Scriptural. . . . But, on the other hand, we value, cherish, and pray for true revivals of religion, and wherever they bring forth the permanent fruits of holiness in men's hearts, rejoice in them as God's work, notwithstanding the mixture of human imperfection. And we consider it the solemn duty of ministers to exercise a Scriptural warmth, affection, and directness in appealing to the understanding, hearts, and consciences of men.[35]

A handful of Southern Old School men resisted the reunion, but Dabney ably defended the reunion agreements before the 1864 Old School General Assembly in Charlotte, North Carolina. Dabney told his Old School brethren: "A right cause can be advocated in a wrong spirit; . . . we should be willing to confess that part of the guilt [for the 1837 schism] is ours." The Southern Old School Assembly overwhelmingly adopted the Plan of Union with only seven dissenting votes; the Southern New School Assembly was unanimous in favor of union. After the war, the Southern body changed its name to the Presbyterian Church in the United States (PCUS).[36]

The South had been economically devastated by fighting a war in her backyard, and the Southern states were controlled by the US Army during a difficult Reconstruction period (1865–1877). Princeton's Charles Hodge disagreed

34. S. Donald Fortson III, "Old School/New School Reunion in the South: The Theological Compromise of 1864," *Westminster Theological Journal*, Spring 2004, 203–26. Both Dabney and Stiles ministered to Confederate troops during the war. Dabney was a chaplain under General Stonewall Jackson and wrote a biography of the general; Stiles was an evangelist, described by a contemporary as "one of the most successful laborers whom we had in the camps." Jones, *Christ in the Camp*, 524.

35. *Presbyterian Historical Almanac and Annual Remembrancer of the Church for 1865*, vol. 7 (Philadelphia: Joseph M. Wilson, 1865), 317.

36. Fortson, "Old School/New School Reunion in the South," 203–26.

with the government's oppressive Reconstruction policies imposed upon the South. He also differed with his denomination's "extreme measures of ecclesiastical reconstruction" driven by anger after the assassination of President Lincoln on April 14, 1865. The Presbyterian General Assembly, meeting in Pittsburgh a month after Lincoln's death, issued what came to be known as the "Pittsburgh orders," labeling secession a sin for which Southerners must repent before readmission to the Presbyterian church. Hodge protested this action as undermining peace: "Whatever therefore tends to alienation and division is contrary to the spirit of the gospel." The Pittsburgh orders were never implemented.[37]

It would take several years of postwar negotiations to consummate Presbyterian reunion in the North. From the beginning of the war, the Northern New School church was intensely loyal to the federal government; similarly, the Northern Old School church supported the Union and became more critical of slavery as the war years progressed. It became clear in early reunion discussions that the question of confessional subscription would be the principal obstacle along the road. Meetings of the joint committee revealed, however, that there was more accord on this issue than either side realized. Henry B. Smith, professor of theology at New York's Union Seminary, defended the New School's understanding of subscription against Old School critics by articulating a clear traditional view, which Old School Charles Hodge acknowledged as the same view he held. After much discussion, a Joint Committee of Reunion proposed a "Plan of Union" that was presented to the 1868 General Assemblies. Both Assemblies adopted the plan, but a protest was raised on the Old School side about an "explanatory clause" in one article that appeared to grant too much doctrinal latitude. New School men raised concern about a controversial provision for reexamining ministers that had been a sticking point for the New School, fearful that Old School presbyteries might refuse admission of transferring ministers. Taking into consideration these objections, a revised plan was resubmitted to both 1869 Assemblies, which were meeting in New York City within walking distance of one another. The Old School voted in favor of union, with only nine negative votes, while the New School vote was unanimous. The reunited church was now known as the Presbyterian Church in the United States of America (PCUSA).[38]

---

37. W. Andrew Hoffecker, *Charles Hodge: The Pride of Princeton* (Phillipsburg, NJ: P&R, 2011), 321–23. Hoffecker indicates that Hodge's love for Abraham Lincoln makes his charity toward the South impressive.

38. S. Donald Fortson III, *The Presbyterian Creed: A Confessional Tradition in America, 1729–1870* (Milton Keynes, UK: Paternoster, 2008), 213–29. The reunification process in the North and South displayed both moderation and compromise as Presbyterians sought

By 1870 there were two main branches of American Presbyterianism, which divided North and South rather than Old School and New School. There was continuous harassment of Southern sympathizers in Missouri and Kentucky, which finally drove the Synod of Kentucky to withdraw from the Northern Old School and unite with the Southern Presbyterian Church in 1869; the Synod of Missouri joined the Southern church in 1874. There were several unsuccessful attempts in the latter decades of the nineteenth century to reunite the Northern and Southern churches, but it would be more than one hundred years (1983) before the two major Presbyterian branches were reunited.[39]

Despite the ongoing sectional divide among Presbyterians, there was an ecumenical spirit among Christians in the postwar years. Charles Hodge eloquently expressed his Presbyterian solidarity with fellow Protestants at the fall 1873 General Conference of the Evangelical Alliance meeting in New York. The seventy-six-year-old Princeton professor was asked to bring a plenary address to the gathering. His speech, "The Unity of the Church based on Personal Union with Christ," emphasized the unity believers shared in Christ and with each other through the indwelling Spirit. Believers scattered over the globe were children of the same Father. The common religious experience of Christ's followers was a sure basis of Christian fellowship and evidence of the truth of Christianity. While outwardly Protestant groups articulate a diversity of creeds, they share the same life experiences through conversion, worship, and hymnody. By virtue of this union in Christ, denominational churches owe three duties to each other: mutual recognition, intercommunion, and recognition of each other's sacraments and order. If Christians really believed these things, said Hodge, churches would cease mutual incriminations and rivalry and instead practice "mutual respect" and "cordial co-operation." This kind of unity would present "an undivided front against infidelity and every form of Anti-Christian error."[40]

After the war, Presbyterians in the North approached the Southern church about joint efforts for ministry to the freedmen. Southern Presbyterians resented Northern whites treating the South as a mission field; they believed Southerners knew the situation better and already had a track record of work

---

the greater good of the whole church. In the end, the Old School and New School needed each other. The reunited strengths of the two groups shaped an evangelical Calvinism that curbed the excesses of either party.

39. E. T. Thompson, *Presbyterians in the South*, vol. 2 (Richmond, VA: John Knox, 1973), 156–94.

40. Charles Hodge, "The Unity of the Church Based on Personal Union with Christ," *Documents of the Sixth General Conference of the Evangelical Alliance, Held in New York October 2–12*, ed. Philip Schaff and S. Irenaeus Prime (New York: Harper & Bros., 1874), 139–44.

among the blacks. Northern missionaries moved into the South regardless and began starting schools and churches for blacks; typically the schools came first, as the need for educating former slaves was pressing. The PCUSA and UPCNA efforts combined were responsible for starting 157 Presbyterian schools for blacks in the years after the war up through the early decades of the next century. Black Northern Presbyterian membership in the South was around five thousand by 1870, but the congregations were typically isolated by distance. The first black presbytery was organized in 1866 by three white Southern ministers, Samuel Alexander, Sidney S. Murkland, and Willis C. Miller, who left the PCUS to establish Catawba Presbytery, which later aligned with the Northern church. In 1866, Alexander organized the Colored Presbyterian Church in Charlotte, North Carolina, which became the first site of the Biddle Institute (later Johnson C. Smith University), a training school for black pastors. The UPCNA organized a black Presbytery of Tennessee in 1866, which covered Tennessee, Alabama, North Carolina, and southwest Virginia. The black presbyteries had a few white members, usually ministers who served in black schools or congregations.

By 1861 there were only fourteen thousand black members in the PCCSA; there were far more black Methodists and Baptists. The Committee on Domestic Mission continued its work among slaves during the war, but many freedmen deserted the white churches after the war, starting their own independent black congregations or aligning with churches started by the Northern Presbyterians. Southern Presbyterians accepted the reality of separate black congregations but wanted them to be under the care of white pastors and sessions. These plans never materialized, as the majority of blacks had left the churches. There were a few exceptions—a handful of blacks in white churches or a small black body still connected to the PCUS.[41] The Southern church supported black education, founding Stillman College in Tuscaloosa, Alabama, in 1876.[42] The Cumberland Presbyterians had not divided as a result of the war, but black Cumberlands, wanting more autonomy, created their own ecclesiastical body during the Reconstruction era. Black ministers petitioned the 1869 Cumberland General Assembly to sanction the formation of "presbyteries of colored ministers." The Assembly concurred, and the first presbytery was formed in 1869, followed by a synod in 1871. By 1874 a separate

41. Thompson, *Presbyterian Missions in the Southern United States*, 177–94.

42. Darius L. Swann and James Foster Reece, "Perspectives on the Development of the Black Presbyterian Church in the South," *Journal of Presbyterian History*, Spring/Summer 2007, 49–56; Inez Moore Parker, *The Rise and Decline of the Program of Education for Black Presbyterians of the United Presbyterian Church U.S.A., 1865–1970* (San Antonio: Trinity University Press, 1977).

denomination with forty-six ministers was established: the Colored Cumberland Presbyterian Church, the only independent black Presbyterian denomination in America, later changing its name to the Cumberland Presbyterian
Church in America (1992).[43]

After the war, the federal government initiated the process of making freedmen citizens, establishing the Freedman's Bureau, setting up a free labor economy, and passing three new constitutional amendments establishing freedmen
rights. When Reconstruction ended in 1877, there were tragically numerous
setbacks for African American equality. An important black Presbyterian voice
challenging racial prejudice in the country and church was Francis James
Grimke, a graduate of Lincoln University in Pennsylvania, and of Princeton
Seminary in 1878. Grimke served as pastor of the Fifteenth Street Presbyterian
Church in Washington, DC, until he retired in 1925.[44] When the Cumberland
Presbyterians began reunion discussions with the Northern church (PCUSA)
in 1904, Grimke was outspoken in his opposition to the reunion proposal's call
for segregated presbyteries in the South. The predominately black Catawba
Presbytery in North Carolina also protested this introduction of the "color
line" into church polity. Reunion, with its inclusion of segregated presbyteries,
was approved by both denominations in 1906.[45]

43. Black and white Cumberlands have collaborated in educational efforts and pursued
formal reunion in the 1960s, but efforts failed when not enough black presbyteries approved
the merger plan. Ben W. Barrus, Milton Baughn, and Thomas H. Campbell, *A People Called
Cumberland Presbyterians* (Memphis: Frontier, 1972).

44. See Hugh T. Kerr, ed., "Francis James Grimke (1850–1937)," in *Sons of the Prophets:
Leaders in Protestantism from Princeton Seminary* (Princeton: Princeton University Press,
1963), 161–75; Justin Ferry, "Francis James Grimke: Portrait of a Black Puritan" (PhD diss.,
Yale University, 1970); *The Works of Francis J. Grimke*, ed. Carter G. Woodson, 4 vols. (Washington, DC: Associated Publishers, 1942).

45. For the controversy over segregated presbyteries, see Bradley J. Longfield, *Presbyterians and American Culture: A History* (Louisville: Westminster John Knox, 2013), 139–41.

CHAPTER 13

The Darwinian Challenge

The second half of the nineteenth century was indeed a challenge for the Presbyterian churches; there were internal divisions and the national turmoil of the Civil War. A long-lasting and profound challenge resulted from a book published in 1859 entitled *On the Origin of Species*, authored by Charles Darwin (1809–1882).[1]

While Darwin professed no desire to harm the Christian church and shied away from any speculation about the Bible or about God, his theory of evolution laid the foundation upon which new critical theories arose to counter Christian orthodoxy. The evolutionary model not only revolutionized the field of biology but also directly impacted the new disciplines of anthropology, Freudian psychology, sociology, biblical criticism, and neoliberal theology. In the words of Prof. Sydney Ahlstrom: "Darwin unquestionably became the 19th century's Newton, and his theory of evolution through natural selection became the century's 'cardinal idea.' In every discipline from physics to biblical criticism, myth and error were being dispelled, and the result of this activity was a world view which raised problems of the most fundamental sort."[2]

DARWIN'S EARLY LIFE

Charles Darwin was born in Shrewsbury, England, to Robert and Susannah Wedgwood Darwin. Robert was a medical doctor with a highly successful

---

1. See Adrian Desmond and James Moore, *Darwin: The Life of a Tormented Evolutionist* (New York: Norton, 1991).

2. Sydney Ahlstrom, *A Religious History of the American People* (New York: Doubleday, 1972), 2:225.

practice, and Susannah was an heiress to the Wedgwood pottery fortune. Charles grew up in the comfort of a wealthy home.

Although in his early years Darwin was an avid collector of beetles and developed considerable skill as a marksman, he was not a success in school. Darwin's parents wanted him to follow in his father's footsteps as a physician. His older brother, Erasmus, was a medical student at the University of Edinburgh, and Charles's father pulled some strings to get his younger son admitted to the same program. In medical school, Charles maintained his lackluster academic performance. He was especially averse to attending live surgery demonstrations.

Darwin quit his program after two years and returned home to Shrewsbury.[3] While he was pondering what to do next, a family member suggested that he consider becoming an Anglican clergyman. Once again, Robert Darwin proved the old adage "it's not so much what you know as who you know" and secured Charles a place at Christ's College, University of Cambridge, with a view to becoming an Anglican vicar. Darwin was eighteen years old when he enrolled at Cambridge in 1828, and he finished his course three years later.[4] He remembered his Cambridge years with great affection.[5]

During his Cambridge days, Darwin became a protégé to a professor of botany, the Reverend Dr. John S. Henslow. His mentor deepened his interest in natural history and theology by taking Darwin on regular collecting trips to nearby streams and the countryside of Cambridgeshire. In 1831, Darwin graduated tenth in a class of 178 students who took the ordinary degree. His best scores were in theology.

THE VOYAGE OF HMS *BEAGLE*

Henslow was instrumental in Darwin being accepted to serve aboard HMS *Beagle* as a privately funded ship's naturalist.[6] The *Beagle* was a Royal Navy ship beginning a voyage around the world, with a special focus on charting the Atlantic and Pacific coastlines of South America. The *Beagle* would then continue across the Pacific to the Indian Ocean, around the southern tip of

3. *The Autobiography of Charles Darwin and Selected Letters*, ed. Francis Darwin (New York: Dover, 1958), 11–16.

4. *Autobiography of Charles Darwin*, 18–26.

5. John van Wyhe, *Darwin in Cambridge: The Most Joyful Years* (London: World Scientific Publishing, 2009).

6. *Autobiography of Charles Darwin*, 26–27.

Africa, and back to England. This scheduled two-year voyage stretched to five long years. Once back in England, Darwin returned to Cambridge University to help organize whole rooms of fossils, stuffed animals, and artifacts he had collected and sent back to Henslow during the five-year voyage.

In 1839, he married his first cousin Emma Wedgwood. The two would become parents to ten children, three of whom died in adolescence. After living for a time in London, the Darwin family settled in the town of Downe, in Kent.

NATURAL SELECTION

Darwin's work on developing his theory of evolution was a long and slow process. He had been especially interested in the finches he had encountered and collected while visiting the Galapagos Islands. On the many small islands in the small British-controlled archipelago, the characteristics of individual finches varied widely from island to island. Darwin wondered how to account for the bird's differences, especially the size and shape of the finches' beaks. Gradually, over decades of work, the theory of evolution began to emerge.[7]

When the first edition of his work was published in 1859, the title *On the Origin of Species* was followed by the subtitle *Or the Preservation of Favored Races in the Struggle for Life*. This full title gives a preview of the direction Darwin would take as he pursued a theory known as "natural selection." In simple terms, (1) more individuals of a given species are born than can possibly survive due to limitations of space and food, the presence of predators, etc.; (2) this fact creates a struggle for existence, a concept popularized by the words "survival of the fittest"; (3) those individuals best adapted to their environments are able to survive and pass along their traits and characteristics to the next generation; (4) in this way, nature selects for survival in a rough approximation of what human animal breeders do when they select breeding pairs ' to produce a wanted trait or characteristic. The final and most controversial step in this evolutionary process was "speciation," the premise that over aeons of time groups of animals of the same species are so changed by adaptation to their environment that a new species emerges.[8]

7. See J. Bernard Cohen, *Revolution in Science* (Cambridge, MA: Harvard University Press, 1985), chap. 19, "The Darwinian Revolution," 283–300.

8. Desmond and Moore, *Darwin*, 265–74.

The Question of the Age of the World

Darwin's theory of natural selection was predicated on a radical reassessment of the Earth's age. While on the *Beagle* voyage, Darwin read a newly published book entitled *Principles of Geology* (1830), written by geologist Sir Charles Lyell.[9] Lyell articulated the thesis of the book in these words: "an attempt to explain the former changes of the Earth's surface by reference to causes now in operation."[10] Lyell's work was a rejection of "catastrophism," the idea that changes in the Earth's crust, like those that created Arizona's Grand Canyon, resulted chiefly from sudden violent events. In its place, he introduced the term "uniformitarianism." He saw the Earth as much older than previously imagined, shaped entirely by slow-moving forces of erosion still in operation in the present day. This work provided for Darwin a crucial element in the process of natural selection. The Earth, he reasoned, was much older than the standard ten thousand years accepted by many. This vast age was crucial for the process of natural selection to have produced the numerous plant and animal species on the planet today.

The Reception of *On the Origin of Species*

In Britain, the most noted public reaction to Darwin's theory of evolution occurred on June 30, 1860, at what has become known as the "Oxford Conference."[11] It was the annual meeting of the British Association for the Advancement of Science, when British scientists meet in Oxford at the University Museum. A large number of men of science were in attendance, as well as key members of the clergy, including Samuel Wilberforce, bishop of Oxford, and the Reverend Dr. John S. Henslow, who mentored Darwin in his Cambridge days. Interestingly, the *Beagle*'s captain, Robert Fitzroy, was among those who publicly spoke against Darwin. Darwin's key supporter was the English biologist Thomas Henry Huxley, who made an impassioned defense of *On the Origin of Species*, living up to his nickname "Darwin's Bulldog."[12]

Both highly positive and stingingly negative reviews of *On the Origin of Species* were written in leading British periodicals. The British public seemed

9. Charles Lyell, *Principles of Geology*, 3 vols. (London: John Murray, 1830–1833).

10. Lyell, *Principles of Geology*, 13.

11. Desmond and Moore, *Darwin*, 492–93.

12. Keith Stewart Thomson, "Huxley, Wilberforce and the Oxford Museum," *American Scientist* 3 (2000): 88.

to take the controversy in stride. Perhaps they had become inured by the anonymous publication of *Vestiges of the Natural History of Creation* (1844).[13] Much later it was revealed that this book was the work of Robert Chambers. The main theme of Chambers's work was that animals and plants and everything on Earth were the product of a cosmic theory of transmutation. Everything currently in existence developed from earlier forms. Life on Earth was explained by a form of spontaneous generation. This book became a best seller, and it was even reported that Prince Albert read it aloud to Queen Victoria. However, it was routinely panned by scholars and scoffed at by scientists.

In America, it was a Presbyterian botanist, Asa Gray (1801–1888), who functioned as the major promoter for and defender of Darwin's ideas, while at the same time holding staunchly to the premise that God was the designer and sustainer of nature. Gray is reputed to have been one of the most influential American botanists of the nineteenth century.

Gray was born in Souquait, New York, in 1810 into a family that traced its religious affiliation with Presbyterianism back to a grandfather who came to Boston from northern Ireland in 1718; the Grays were part of the large Scots-Irish Presbyterian immigrant group. A love for botany led Gray to become a teacher, first in high school, then in a small college. As his reputation grew, he accepted a position at the University of Michigan and finally rose to become the Howard Fisher Professor of Natural History at Harvard in 1842.[14]

Gray's relationship with Darwin began with an exchange of letters, and between 1855 and 1881 over three hundred letters were exchanged between the scientists. Their relationship is described by A. Hunter Dupree in a biography entitled *Asa Gray: American Botanist, Friend of Darwin*. The two men shared an empirical approach to science. As early as 1846, Gray had strongly opposed the idea of the transmutation of species, that simpler forms become more complex over time. Gray was convinced that there must be a genetic link that exists between all members of a species. He gladly became an advocate of Darwin's *On the Origin of Species* when it first arrived on American shores. He grew to function as an apologist for Darwin, explaining his ideas in journal articles and the popular press to those he felt were ill informed. At the same time, Gray, who described himself as a "devout Presbyterian" and served as a deacon in a local Cambridge congregation, repeatedly sought to convince Darwin that there was a design in nature that revealed an intelligent creator.

13. Robert Chambers and James A. Secord, *Vestiges of the Natural History of Creation* (1860; reprint, Chicago: University of Chicago Press, 1994).

14. A. Hunter Dupree, *Asa Gray: American Botanist, Friend of Darwin* (Baltimore: Johns Hopkins University Press, 1988), 110–15.

In Gray's words, "God himself is the very last, irreducible causal factor and, hence, the source of all evolutionary change."[15] He argued that the natural world is filled with "unmistakable and irresistible indicators of design."[16]

Gray recognized the purpose and value of natural selection while at the same time arguing that, for example, the mutual adaptation relationships between orchids and the insects that fertilize them cannot be due to chance alone. Gray believed that adaptations indicated the thought and intent of the Creator. In essence, God created the variations that allowed natural selection to choose which was best in the competition for survival. Gray authored an influential book entitled *Darwiniana*,[17] which served as a vehicle for explaining and defending Darwin's theory. Gray was perhaps the first noted American promoter of theistic evolution.

Darwinian Evolution and Presbyterian Seminary Education

There was another, and his name was James Woodrow (1828–1907). The Woodrow family roots reached back to England. James Woodrow would be remembered as the uncle of President Woodrow Wilson, but he was to play a key role in the American evolutionary drama as it unfolded in a Presbyterian seminary in the South.[18]

At the age of eight, Woodrow moved with his family to Canada and then shortly relocated to Ohio. After graduating from Jefferson College, he entered the Lawrence School of Science at Harvard in 1853, where he worked under the famous Louis Agassiz, before going on to the University of Heidelberg for a PhD, where he graduated *cum laude* in 1856. He was offered a teaching position at Heidelberg, a full professorship, but he chose to return to America. In 1859, Woodrow was ordained as a Presbyterian minister by the Hopewell Presbytery, then part of the PCUSA. He was one of the bright lights of the Presbyterian world, and he was destined to make his mark in academia.

Woodrow was appointed Perkins Professor of Natural History in Its Relation to Revealed Religion at Columbia Theological Seminary in South Carolina in 1860. From the beginning of his work at Columbia, the issue of academic

15. Randy Moore, *Evolution in the Courtroom: A Reference Guide* (Santa Barbara, CA: ABC-Clio, 2002), 125, 307.

16. Moore, *Evolution in the Courtroom*, 125.

17. Asa Gray, *Darwiniana: Essays and Reviews Pertaining to Darwinism* (Appleton, 1876; reprint, Cambridge: Cambridge University Press, 2008).

18. Robert K. Gustafson, *James Woodrow (1828–1907): Scientist, Theologian, Intellectual Leader* (Lewiston, NY: Mellen, 1995).

freedom was a key factor in his development. He had embraced the concept of the antiquity of the Earth and, with it, the geological doctrine of uniformitarianism; Woodrow saw no reason why holding those views would conflict with his complete confidence in the veracity of Holy Scripture. He argued before his students that the words of the Bible must not be forced to conform to traditional belief. He urged them to understand that the text of Genesis chapters 1 and 2 must not be read in the sense of a scientific textbook.

On Darwin's actual theory, however, Woodrow stayed quiet. It was highly unusual for a professor of natural science to be silent on the issue of evolution, and it led to rumors that he was secretly teaching the radical new view. Columbia Seminary's board of directors wrote a message to the 1883 General Assembly (Southern) that contained a statement from Woodrow: "The Bible teaches nothing as to God's method of creation, and therefore it is not teaching anything contradicting God's word to say that he may have formed the higher beings from the lower by successive differentiations; and as several series of facts, more or less independent of one another, seem to point this out as a method which he chose."[19]

When pressed to clarify his position, Woodrow explained that he had moved from doubting the truth of evolution to the position that it was possibly true in some aspects. He argued that the Bible and evolutionary theory can be seen as "noncontradictory." He explained, in an address to the Alumni Association, that the language of Genesis 1 and 2 was not explicit and therefore allowed for a variety of interpretations. It says, he went on, that God created Adam from dust, but it does not specify the type of dust and it could be interpreted as preexisting matter from the original creation of the Earth. Woodrow quickly added that he held that the soul of Adam was certainly created *ex nihilo*.[20]

The pressure on Woodrow to resign began to build from presbyteries of the Presbyterian Church in the United States (PCUS) and from Presbyterian periodicals. In 1884, Columbia Seminary released a statement indicating that while the board disagreed with Woodrow on his view of Adam's creation, it found none of his views incompatible with Christianity. Nevertheless, when his resignation from his chair was requested in 1884, Woodrow refused to step down. This tension led to an internal conflict within Columbia Seminary, and it actually was forced to close its doors from 1887 to 1888.

---

19. Ernest Trice Thompson, *Presbyterians in the South* (Richmond, VA: John Knox, 1973), 2:459–60.

20. James Woodrow, *Evolution, An Address Delivered May 7th, 1884, Before the Alumni Association of the Columbia Theological Seminary* (Columbia, SC: Presbyterian Publishing House, 1884), 4–30.

In 1886, Woodrow was tried for heresy by the Augusta Presbytery. The trial led to his exoneration. The following year, the Synod of Georgia overturned the heresy trial's exoneration. Eventually, Woodrow was removed from his chair but not from his role as a leader in the Presbyterian church. He remained a minister in good standing within the PCUS. He was elected president of South Carolina College in 1891, a position he held until 1897. To round off his years of service to the Presbyterian church, Woodrow was elected moderator of the Synod of Georgia in 1901.

CHARLES HODGE: APOLOGIST FOR ORTHODOXY

Charles Hodge (1797–1878), principal of Princeton Seminary, author of a classic systematic theology, founder of the influential journal *Princeton Review*, epitomized old school Princeton theology.[21] He became the most powerful critic of Darwinian evolution[22] in America in the late nineteenth century.

Hugh Hodge, Charles's father, was of Scots-Irish descent, having immigrated from northern Ireland; he practiced medicine in Philadelphia. When Charles was only seven months of age, his father died of yellow fever. His mother, Mary, raised Charles. Taking his religious education seriously, she schooled him using the Westminster Shorter Catechism. Hodge was steeped in the Presbyterian way. The family moved to New Jersey to allow Charles to enroll at Princeton College in 1812. Hodge joined a local Presbyterian church and decided to enter the ministry. He enrolled in Princeton Seminary in 1816 and graduated three years later.

Returning to Princeton Seminary for a one-year appointment to teach biblical languages, Hodge was ordained as a Presbyterian minister in 1821. His ministry, however, was not to be in a church but rather in a classroom. The next year his mentor and theology professor, Archibald Alexander, was instrumental in his appointment as assistant professor of Oriental and biblical literature.[23]

Feeling that he wanted to enhance his seminary education with study abroad in Europe, Hodge traveled to Paris and studied French, Arabic, and Syriac. In Germany he became acquainted with Friedrich Schleiermacher (1768–1834), a rising force in liberal theology. Unlike many Americans who

21. See A. A. Hodge, *The Life of Charles Hodge . . . Professor in the Theological Seminary, Princeton, N.J.* (New York: Charles Scribners, 1880).

22. See Bradley J. Gundlach, *Process and Providence: The Evolution Question at Princeton, 1845–1929* (Grand Rapids: Eerdmans, 2013), 55–57.

23. A. A. Hodge, *The Life of Charles Hodge*, 92–94.

studied in Europe, Hodge remained true to his Reformed theology and became a leading apologist for orthodoxy.[24]

In 1840 he became the professor of didactic theology. When Professor Archibald Alexander died in 1849, Hodge was the senior professor at the seminary. He was soon to be acknowledged as the leading architect of the "Princeton theology."

Deeply influenced by both John Calvin and the Westminster Confession, Hodge had a traditional view of God's revelation. He believed that the Word of God was inspired by the Holy Spirit and therefore infallible and authoritative in all things pertaining to faith and practice and free from error, whether in doctrine, fact, or precept. His view of the inspiration of Scripture was plenary, as he wrote in *Systematic Theology*, "and not confined to moral and religious truths, but also statements of facts, whether scientific, historical, or geographical."[25]

On harmonizing the Bible and contemporary science, Hodge based his argument on the premise that God was the author of both Holy Scripture and nature. As such, there would be no essential conflict between the text of the Bible and natural science. As he wrote in the *Princeton Review*, "there can be no contradiction between what God does and what he says."[26] He explained, "Because we are perfectly sure of ultimate agreement . . . we are content to allow the devotees of the former (natural science) to prosecute their researches and correct their deductions until agreement is reached."[27] In *Systematic Theology*, he urged Christians to not be dismayed by seeming contradictions between scientific theories and Christian doctrine. "Let science take its course assured that the Scriptures will accommodate themselves to all well-authenticated scientific facts in time to come as they have in times past."[28]

A key to Hodge's analysis was the distinction he made between fact and theory. In science there are two salient factors: facts and ideas. A fundamental principle of science is that theory has to be determined by facts, and not vice versa. Hodge insisted that facts cannot be denied. "To deny facts is to deny what God affirms to be true." Theories "are human speculations and can have no higher authority than their own inherent probability."[29]

24. Hodge's European studies are described in Paul Gutjahr, *Charles Hodge: Guardian of American Orthodoxy* (New York: Oxford University Press, 2011), chaps. 17–19.

25. Charles Hodge, *Systematic Theology* (1872–1873; reprint, Grand Rapids: Eerdmans, 1981), 1:181–82.

26. M. B. Hope, "On the Relation between the Holy Scriptures and Some Parts of Geological Science," *Biblical Repertory and Princeton Review* 13 (1841): 391–92.

27. "Short Notices," *Biblical Repertory and Princeton Review* 23 (1851): 556.

28. Charles Hodge, *Systematic Theology*, 1:1.

29. Charles Hodge, *Systematic Theology*, 1:13–14.

Facts are divine and cannot conflict with other facts, but theories, being of human origin, often do. Applying this to science and Scripture, Hodge wrote, "It is unwise for theologians to insist on an interpretation of Scripture which brings it into collision with the facts of science, and it may happen in the future, as it has in the past, that interpretations of the Bible long confidently received, must be modified or abandoned, to bring revelation into harmony with what God teaches in his works."[30]

At times science would put forward a theory that is clearly contrary to the revealed Word of God. One example of this furnished by Hodge is "polygenism," a minority view among biologists but one supported by Louis Agassiz at Harvard. Polygenism maintained that the various races represented within humanity are really separate species with unique origins. For Hodge, such a theory was clearly at odds with the biblical doctrine that all humanity shared a spiritual unity and universal depravity. All races were clearly fallen in orthodox theology. For Hodge, scientists who espoused polygenism were ignoring the scriptural "facts."

Hodge's strongest denunciation of evolution by means of natural selection was his work *What Is Darwinism?* (1874).[31] The title was motivated by a debate that occurred at Princeton College in which the president, James McCosh, a philosopher by training as well as a Presbyterian minister, speculated that biological evolution was not necessarily incompatible with Christian doctrine and therefore the Bible and science could be seen as parallel revelations. In his *Systematic Theology* Hodge made the case for incompatibility. The issue, said Hodge, was whether one believed intellectual process guided by God or material process ruled by chance. This was for him common sense. He argued, "to any ordinarily constituted mind it is impossible to believe that the eye is not a work of design."[32]

The theologian carefully scrutinized the text of *Origin of Species* and took into account later editions of the same book. He traced with great care Darwin's argumentation and carefully documented each of his points with a direct reference to Darwin's text. Hodge identified three crucial elements in Darwin's theory: evolution, natural selection, and natural selection without design. Everyone understood that there were evolutionary theories before Darwin. Hodge asserted that natural selection predated *On the Origin of Species*. Only

---

30. Charles Hodge, *Systematic Theology*, 1:56–59.
31. Charles Hodge, *What Is Darwinism?* (New York: Scribner, Armstrong and Co., 1874).
32. Charles Hodge, *Systematic Theology*, 1:60.

the third component, natural selection resulting from unintelligent causes, was peculiar to Darwin.

One crucial issue was that of speciation, the theory that given enough time and key differences in environment, a group of individuals within a species could change and adapt to the point where they became a new species. In his *Systematic Theology*, Hodge stated that only some species were originally created, leaving open the question of possible evolution. In *What Is Darwinism?* he distinguished between "species" and "primordial forms." He reserved the phrase "underived creation" only for "primordial forms."[33] Interestingly, Darwin had assumed that life had been "originally breathed by the creator into a few forms or into one."[34] The two views appear to have some common ground. But the fact that Darwin ruled out the possibility of divine intervention in the development of species seemed to Hodge to directly counter the doctrine of God's providence in nature. "Yes," he argued, "God works through secondary causes, but any theory of evolution which excluded God's control and or intervention must be by category unscriptural and really a form of Deism."[35]

For Hodge, a second impediment for the Christian in accepting evolution was the issue of design. Natural selection was directly challenged by the biblical claim that God is the creator not only of the universe but of the Earth, its plants and animals, and most especially humans. This was, in Hodge's words, "the grand and fatal objection to Darwinism."[36]

For Charles Hodge, the theory of natural selection as an explanation for all of life on planet Earth was an audacious claim in view of the clear teachings of the Bible. For most evangelical Christians in the late nineteenth century, Hodge's arguments made sense.

B. B. WARFIELD

Born and raised in Lexington, Kentucky, to wealthy parents who hailed from Virginia, Benjamin Breckinridge Warfield (1851–1921) succeeded Archibald Alexander Hodge (son to Charles Hodge) at Princeton Seminary in 1887; he

---

33. Charles Hodge, *What Is Darwinism?*, 153–54.

34. Charles Darwin, *On the Origin of Species by Means of Natural Selection, or the Preservation of Favoured Species in the Struggle for Life*, 5th ed. (London: John Murray, 1869), 579.

35. Charles Hodge, *What Is Darwinism?*, 119–23.

36. Charles Hodge, *What Is Darwinism?*, 169.

became another key Presbyterian voice raised against the dangers of Darwinian evolution. Yet his voice did not merely echo Hodge's but also sounded a new note of openness to the question of how evolution should be considered by Christians.

Like Hodge, Warfield grew up in a family that was steeped in Presbyterianism. His maternal grandfather was a Presbyterian minister. He was educated at the College of New Jersey (later to become Princeton University), earning a bachelor's degree in mathematics and science. At this point in his intellectual development, Warfield later admitted, he was very much taken with Darwin's theory of evolution.

While traveling in Europe after graduation, Warfield sensed God's call to devote his powerful mind and heart to theology. Returning home to the USA, he chose to continue his education at Princeton Theological Seminary (1873–1876). After postseminary studies in Germany and a brief pastorate, Warfield joined the faculty of Western Seminary, Allegheny, Pennsylvania, in 1879. Transitioning to Princeton Seminary in 1887 to become the Charles Hodge Professor of Theology, he eventually became the fourth principal of the seminary.

Warfield became, like his mentor Charles Hodge, a key defender of the authority of Holy Scripture against its critics, who were becoming known as "modernists." These wanted to place Christianity on a modern "scientific" foundation. Archibald Alexander Hodge, the son of Charles Hodge, and Warfield, aiming to defend the biblical text, popularized and supported the view that has come to be known as "biblical inerrancy." Yet, along with that major focus, Warfield continued to wrestle with and publish books, articles, and reviews on evolutionary theory. In 1888 he wrote "Charles Darwin's Religious Life," "Arguments against Christianity and against Religion," and "On the Antiquity and Unity of the Human Race."[37] His final study on the subject was published in 1915 and entitled "Calvin's Doctrine of Creation."[38] Evolution was clearly a very significant issue in Warfield's thinking.

In his lectures as a seminary professor and in his writings on issues dealing with Christianity and science, Warfield continually stressed the importance of distinguishing among three aspects of what is commonly meant by "evolution." The first and most basic meaning of the term was a series of explanations of

37. B. B. Warfield, "Charles Darwin's Religious Life," *Presbyterian Review* 9 (1888): 569–601; B. B. Warfield, "Arguments against Christianity and against Religion," *Homiletic Review*, January 1889, 9–16; B. B. Warfield, "On the Antiquity and Unity of the Human Race," *Princeton Theological Review* 9, no. 1 (January 1911): 1–25.

38. B. B. Warfield, "Calvin's Doctrine of Creation," *Princeton Theological Review* 13 (1915): 190–225.

general development in the natural world. That basic meaning of evolution, he cautioned his students, must not be confused with the (second) Darwinian theory of evolution based primarily on natural selection, the survival of the fittest, speciation, etc. Thirdly, Warfield urged that Charles Darwin himself must not be confused with theories that arose following the publication of his works, *On the Origin of Species by Natural Selection* (1859) and *The Descent of Man* (1871). The man Charles Darwin had a unique historical context in which his ideas developed, and that individual must not necessarily be identified with ongoing additions to evolutionary theory.

Warfield clearly believed that Darwin's view of evolution by natural selection proved to be injurious to his Christian faith. In 1888, he discussed Darwin's spiritual life and concluded, "Thus, the doctrine of evolution once heartily adopted by him gradually undermined his faith, until he cast off the whole of Christianity as an unproven delusion."[39] Such a rejection of faith by those who embraced evolution was not inevitable, Warfield noted. In a published review of *The Life and Letters of Charles Darwin* in 1889, he wrote: "There have been many evolutionists who have been and have remained theists and Christians."[40]

Warfield seemed to be open to the possibility that evolution in some general sense could have been involved as part of the Creator's work. He intimated that God might have worked in the formation of the physical world through an evolutionary process. The one crucial caveat in this speculation was that this argument would be valid if and only if it were directly linked to God's sovereignty over all nature and his providence in creating the Earth. These were issues that Darwin was unwilling to countenance. Darwin suggested that perhaps a "Creator" may have caused life to begin, but, once established, unmoderated natural selection was responsible for nature's vast diversity of life.[41]

Warfield speculated that perhaps God placed energy within the raw earthly matter that was created *ex nihilo* (out of nothing), as recorded in Genesis 1:1. God could have then predetermined and directed the developmental ends of that matter according to his sovereign will and purpose. The professor, in his

39. B. B. Warfield, "Charles Darwin's Religious Life: A Sketch in Spiritual Biography," *Presbyterian Review* 9 (1888): 569-601.

40. See Mark Noll, ed., *The Princeton Theology* (Grand Rapids: Baker Books, 1983), 293.

41. Charles Darwin, *On the Origin of Species by Means of Natural Selection, or the Preservation of Favoured Races in the Struggle for Life* (London: John Murray, 1859), final page. The passage reads: "There is a grandeur in this view of life, with its special powers, having been originally breathed by the Creator into a few forms or into one; and that, whilst this planet has gone circling on according to the fixed law of gravity, from so simple a beginning endless forms most beautiful and most wonderful have been, and are being evolved."

later writings on the subject, speculated that in that sense of the word "evolution," God could have used formerly created matter to fashion Adam's body. The first human soul, however, would have been an immediate unique creation by God, *ex nihilo*. In his work *Calvin's Doctrine of Creation*, Warfield wrote, "It should scarcely be passed without remark that Calvin's doctrine of creation is, if we have understood it aright, for all except the souls of men, an evolutionary one. The 'indigested mass,' including the 'promise and potency' of all that was yet to be, was called into being by the simple fiat of God. But all that has come into being since—except the souls of men alone—has arisen as a modification of this original world-stuff by means of the interaction of its intrinsic forces. Not these forces apart from God, of course."[42] Warfield continued, "What concerns us here is that he ascribed the entire series of modifications by which the primal 'indigested mass,' called 'heaven and earth,' has passed into the form of the ordered world which we see, including the origination of all forms of life, vegetable and animal alike, inclusive doubtless of the bodily form of man, to the second causes as their proximate account. And this, we say, is a very pure evolutionary scheme."[43]

Warfield used the phrase "mediate creation" or "secondary causes" to explain what he meant by "a modification of this original world stuff."[44] By those words he meant that perhaps the power of God could affect original matter in a way that something new would come into being, but once again, that the process could only work under God's direct superintendence and providential care.

Warfield also used the theological construct called "concursus,"[45] or conjoined spheres or domains, which seem on the surface to be in contradiction but actually work together and complement one another. "Concursus" was an important idea in the christological development of the early church's view of the "God-man," especially in the deliberations of the Council of Chalcedon of 451. Christ was affirmed to be both "undiminished deity" and "complete humanity," both seeming to contradict one another yet nevertheless existing simultaneously.

---

42. B. B. Warfield, "Calvin's Doctrine of Creation," in Noll, *The Princeton Theology*, 297.
43. Warfield, "Calvin's Doctrine of Creation," 298.
44. Warfield, "Calvin's Doctrine of Creation," 298.
45. "In philosophical theology, the relationship between God and human beings has been historically referred to as *concursus*: the concurrence, or cooperation, of more than one agent to cause a particular effect. In theological terms, *concursus* is the cooperation of God and humanity as the causal forces of some particular effect." Joshua Reichard, "Beyond Causation: A Contemporary Theology of Concursus," *American Journal of Theology and Philosophy* 34, no. 2 (May 2013): 117.

Another example of "concursus" was also evident, Warfield argued, in the teaching that the writings of the Old and New Testament canonical documents were the product of human authors. Those widely different prophets, evangelists, and apostles were not receiving dictation from on high in what they produced, and yet those writings were directly superintended by the Holy Spirit as described in the doctrine of inspiration.

To sum up, Warfield's position was that God may have used an evolutionary process, guided at every stage by divine providence, to bring about the creation of life on Earth. The one noted exception was the creation of human souls, which are created *ex nihilo*. Warfield never directly asserted that he was a theistic evolutionist. Nevertheless, he did not see the Genesis record to be in any way at odds with the possibility of God working in that way. In a lecture at Princeton Seminary in 1888, he said the following, according to a student's notes: "I do not think that there is any general statement in the Bible or any part of the account of creation, either as given in Genesis 1 and 2 or elsewhere alluded to, that need be opposed to evolution."[46] The fascination with the juxtaposition of evolutionary evidence and biblical revelation at Princeton Seminary continued to advance after Warfield's death in 1921.[47]

In the twenty-first century, the available data affecting the question of human origins has grown exponentially. The ongoing debate among American evangelical scholars on the possibility of theistic evolution as a means by which God created life on Earth continues.

---

46. This Warfield quotation comes from class lectures on evolution prepared in 1888, and the general content was used in his subsequent years of teaching that class into the next century. See Dennis Alexander, *Rebuilding the Matrix: Science and Faith in the 21st Century* (Grand Rapids: Zondervan, 2003), 177.

47. Gundlach, *Process and Providence*.

CHAPTER 14

Immigration, Urbanization, and Industrialization

The last two decades of the nineteenth century and the first two of the twentieth presented the Presbyterian churches with a challenge and an opportunity: to adjust ministry to the rapidly changing social dynamics in the United States. Many new trends indicated a period of unprecedented change at the national level. The dramatic rise in industrialization, European and Asian immigration, political corruption, and the need to regulate big business and monopolies seemed daunting. The new watchword in American culture was "modernization," giving science new authority when solving questions of production, economics, and politics.

The key stressors of the Progressive era were America's entry into World War I in 1917 and Prohibition. Prohibition was, simply put, the reality that the manufacture, transportation, sale, possession, and consumption of alcoholic beverages were prohibited by law. Another key political theme was the push for women's suffrage, an issue that would have great impact on all facets of American society.

IMMIGRATION

European immigrants flooded into the United States in the middle of the nineteenth century. Before that time, the high cost of traveling across the Atlantic in a sailing ship was prohibitive, drastically limiting the number of those who could undertake the voyage. The development of the iron-hulled steamship greatly reduced the cost and ushered in what is often called "the age of mass migration from Europe" (1850–1920).[1] During these years, the number

---

1. The time spent at sea in the era of sailing ships was reduced from one month in 1750

of immigrants leaving Europe for the New World was about 55 million, and of that number, 30 million arrived in the United States.[2] Due to that massive influx, the foreign-born percentage of the population of the USA grew from 10 percent in 1850 to 14 percent in 1870 and remained at that level until about 1920.[3]

In 1850, 90 percent of European immigrants were from northern and western Europe, particularly Germany, Great Britain, and Ireland. By 1890, the demographics of the immigrant population had shifted toward southern and eastern Europe, in large part because the cost of transatlantic travel was so greatly reduced. In 1920, 45 percent of migrants came from the northern areas while 41 percent arrived from the southern regions. Immigrants were predominantly single, male, and younger than those who had come forty years earlier.[4] As a group, migrants from Poland, Italy, and other southern and eastern countries did not assimilate quickly into the American culture due in large part to language difficulties. They tended to move to large cities such as Boston, New York, Philadelphia, Detroit, and Chicago. This had a profound effect on social dynamics in urban centers. As a case in point, Chicago had one hundred thousand immigrants in 1860 and two and a half million by 1900. Those new arrivals gravitated to the inner-city areas, where they hoped to find work and a community of immigrants who shared the same language, diet, and culture.

In his novel *The Jungle* (1906), Upton Sinclair raised the consciousness of Americans regarding working-class conditions and their impact upon recent immigrants from Europe. Sinclair chose the meat industry in Chicago as the setting for his fictional story of Jurgis Rudkus, a recent arrival from Lithuania. Rudkus and his family did not yet have a good command of the English language and chose to settle near the Chicago stockyards.

Rudkus encountered dangerous working conditions in the meatpacking plant and was chagrined to find very few social supports for the family. The pay for his job barely covered expenses, and the immigrants soon were caught in a downward spiral of poverty, which led to a breakdown in family life and eventually moral decay. Rudkus's father died of an accident in the meatpacking plant, and one of his children succumbed to food poisoning. Rudkus lost his

---

to eight days by 1870. Peter Hugill, *World Trade Since 1431: Geography, Technology, and Capitalism* (Baltimore: Johns Hopkins University Press, 1995), 10–12.

2. Timothy Hatton and Jeffrey Williamson, *The Age of Mass Migration: Causes and Economic Impact* (New York: Oxford University Press, 1998), 7.

3. Leah Platt Boustan and Katherine Eriksson, "Europe's Tired, Poor, Huddled Masses: Self-Selection and Economic Outcomes in the Age of Mass Migration," *American Economic Review* 102, no. 5 (August 2012): 1833.

4. Hatton and Williamson, *The Age of Mass Migration*, 11, 101–2.

job and was lured into neighborhood crime, finally serving time in jail. Shortly after his release, he met a socialist orator and found new hope for the future.

To give his novel a jolt of reality, Sinclair spent seven weeks working in meatpacking plants near the Chicago stockyards. His plan was to develop a newspaper serial that focused on the dangers inherent in the meatpacking industry. His reports came out in a socialist newspaper, *Appeal to Reason*, before their publication as a book.

Conditions like those described in *The Jungle* soon had an impact on the populations served by inner-city churches in Boston, Philadelphia, New York, Detroit, and Chicago. Many areas that once supported thriving middle-class congregations changed into immigrant neighborhoods. The new parishioners tended to speak in their native languages when not at work and were generally not attracted to worship with mainline Protestant congregations. Inner-city churches responded to these new challenges in two main ways. One way was by relocating to outlying districts inhabited by middle-class English-speaking parishioners.

The other approach was more radical: they adapted to the new social conditions of the neighborhood by finding creative new ways to minister. The traditional Sunday school and preaching services had to be tailored to meet the needs of a new generation of inner-city dwellers. In addition, many churches began to tailor social service programs to meet the needs of the poor, the uneducated, and often isolated people all around them. In this way, there emerged the concept of the "institutional church," that is, a congregation active on several levels within the communities.

THE SOCIAL GOSPEL

Both liberal and more conservative evangelical churches were part of this transition in ministry. This progressive approach also became known as the Social Gospel; in many cases, it combined innovative social reforms with theological adjustments. The earliest major figure to shape the Social Gospel movement was Washington Gladden (1836–1918). After losing his father when he was six, he had to leave his birthplace in Pennsylvania for a farm near Oswego, New York, in what was called the "Burned-Over District"; this name refers to the aftermath of a succession of revivals in that part of western New York State in connection with the ministry of Charles G. Finney during what came to be known as the Second Great Awakening.[5] In his eighteenth year, Gladden put

---

5. Whitney R. Cross, *The Burned-Over District* (Ithaca, NY: Cornell University Press, 1951).

his trust in the "Heavenly Father's love." For him, the concept of religion could be summed up by the word "friendship": friendship with "the Father above and with the brother by our side."[6]

Gladden's professional life involved pastoral ministry and journalism. Over a long and very active career, he pastored five churches while also achieving success in journalism, publishing in a variety of magazines and books. In 1860, at twenty-four years of age, Gladden was called and ordained by the State Street Congregational Church in Brooklyn, New York. Although he stayed at this calling for only one year, it was during that year that he married Jeannie Cohoon, a friend from school in Oswego. The couple were blessed with four children: two boys and two girls.

His next ministry position was in Morrisonia, New York, for five years, followed by another five-year stint in North Adams, Massachusetts. From 1871 to 1875, Gladden served as the religious editor of a weekly newspaper titled the *New York Independent*, which had a national following. His contributions included both news articles and editorials that dealt with social issues, which he deemed "practical theology."

Gladden turned next to writing; he published two major books: *Working People and Their Employers* and *The Christian Way: Whither It Leads and How to Go On*. These works helped to solidify his leadership in the Social Gospel movement. It was during this time that Gladden began to advocate for labor unions. A short time later, on a visit to Atlanta University[7] in Georgia, Gladden took note of how southern blacks were treated and began to speak out and preach against racism.

In 1882, the peripatetic Gladden became the pastor of the First Congregational Church in Columbus, Ohio, where he was to remain for thirty-six years. What made this post so important in his life was its close proximity to the state capitol. Among his parishioners were many legislators and people of political influence. He preached at two services on Sundays. The morning message dealt with living the Christian life; in the evenings, he turned his attention to Christianity and social issues. Membership at the First Congregational Church grew from about 500 in 1882 to 1,200 by the time he retired in 1914.

The second major American figure to help shape the Social Gospel movement was Walter Rauschenbusch (1861–1918), the fourth and youngest son of an immigrant. His father, August Rauschenbusch, was a Lutheran pastor from Germany who came to the United States to minister to immigrants. Shortly after his arrival, August connected with the American Tract Society;

6. Washington Gladden, *Recollections* (Boston: Houghton Mifflin, 1909), 40–41.
7. Today, Clark Atlanta University.

this new association led to his break from the Lutheran church, as his family embraced the North American (German) Baptist denomination. They then settled in Rochester, New York, where in 1855 the senior Rauschenbusch joined the faculty of Rochester Theological Seminary. Walter's parents were not at all convinced that high school education in America was equal to that which their son could receive in their homeland. From the age of eighteen to twenty-two, Walter studied in Germany. It is clear that during this time Rauschenbusch encountered a higher-critical view of the Bible.

When he returned home, the University of Rochester granted him three years' credit toward his BA and simultaneous admission to Rochester Theological Seminary. At this time, Rauschenbusch began to notice a loss of hearing in one ear that was to grow worse as the years passed. Rauschenbusch graduated first in his seminary class in 1866 and felt a strong calling to serve as a missionary. Later, he would equate the Social Gospel with being a missionary to the working-class immigrants of American inner cities. In that same year, he received a call from the Second Baptist Church of New York City, in an area dubbed by the police "Hell's Kitchen" (West Forty-Fifth Street and Tenth Avenue), because trouble always seemed to be cooking there. He began his work on June 1, and on October 21 was ordained for ministry by the Second Baptist Church, where he received the modest salary of $600 a year.[8]

At this point in his development, Rauschenbusch was thoroughly evangelical in his theology, and in the summers of 1887 and '88 he participated in evangelistic campaigns led by D. L. Moody. He remarked of this time, "I gave myself to God unreservedly and had a rich blessing."[9] Reflecting on that time, he also said, "My idea then was to save souls in the ordinary accepted religious sense."[10]

Ministry in Hell's Kitchen was a daunting and emotionally taxing endeavor. The area was marked by overcrowding, violence, prostitution, and an almost total lack of social programs to help the immigrants. Of all his pastoral duties, he found the funerals for little children the most difficult and emotionally wrenching. In 1892, Rauschenbusch convened a meeting of New York City Baptist ministers who were interested in developing a social justice program in the American church. This group was the beginning of a "kingdom theology" for Rauschenbusch. In the words of biographer Paul Minus, "The major

8. Melanie May, "Gender and the Kingdom of God: The Values of Walter Rauschenbusch," in *The Social Gospel Today*, ed. Christopher H. Evans (Louisville: Westminster John Knox, 2001), 53–66.

9. Paul M. Minus, *Walter Rauschenbusch: American Reformer* (New York: Macmillan, 1988), 5.

10. Minus, *Walter Rauschenbusch*, 56.

issue engaging him was how the Church could close the widening gap between itself and the urban masses. The issue presented itself as two questions: how far can Christians go toward embracing the aspirations of workers, especially those expressed in socialism, and how can Christians be made to care about the social revolution underway in their country."[11]

Rauschenbusch's life became more complete in April 1893 when he married a schoolteacher named Pauline Rother. His bride had been an immigrant; Pauline came to the United States from Silesia at the age of six. The couple had two children.

After eleven years of ministry at Second Baptist Church, the minister's hearing problem had worsened, making pastoral care more difficult. In 1897 the family left New York City for Rochester, and Rauschenbusch became a professor of New Testament interpretation at Rochester Theological Seminary. He flourished as an academic; in 1902 he was made the chair of the church history department, a position he held until his death in 1918. It was during this time that he turned his attention to writing and laying down the foundations of a theology for the Social Gospel.

The first work he produced was written in the summer of 1891 and entitled *Christianity Revolutionary*. It was not published until after his death, when it was retitled *The Righteousness of the Kingdom*.[12] Rauschenbusch was on sabbatical leave from his ministry in New York City and was enjoying a break in the Allegheny Mountains when the idea for this work came to him. He used this time to read widely from the works of German Protestant thinkers whom he admired, one of whom was Albrecht Ritschl (1822–1889). Ritschl was a highly influential theologian who was influenced by Hegelian thought, as well as by Immanuel Kant and Friedrich Schleiermacher. Ritschl became a professor of theology at the University of Bonn and subsequently at Göttingen. He wrote, among other books, major works on the doctrines of the atonement and justification and the history of Pietism.[13]

What captured the attention of Rauschenbusch was Ritschl's focus on the kingdom of God in the New Testament church. He argued that the kingdom of God had been central to the ministry of Jesus and therefore to the early mission of the church. According to Ritschl, the kingdom was a gradually de-

---

11. Minus, *Walter Rauschenbusch*, 59.

12. Walter Rauschenbusch, *The Righteousness of the Kingdom* (Nashville: Abingdon, 1968).

13. Albrecht Ritschl, *The Christian Doctrine of Justification: The Positive Development of the Doctrine* (1900; reprint, Sydney, Australia: Wentworth, 2019), and *Three Essays: Theology and Metaphysics; Prolegomena to the History of Pietism; Instruction in the Christian Religion* (Philadelphia: Fortress, 1972).

veloping social ideal by which God integrates both social and spiritual reality. Rauschenbusch worked this idea into his vision for a Social Gospel:

> Christ initiated his Kingdom on earth by establishing a community of spiritual men, an inward communion with God and an outward obedience to him. This was the living germ of the Kingdom. . . . Every such step forward, every increase in mercy, every obedience to justice, every added brightness of truth, would be an extension of the reign of God in humanity, an incoming of the Kingdom of God. The more men became saturated with the thoughts of Christ, the more they came to judge all actions from this point of view, the more they conformed the outward life of society to the advancing inward standard the more would Christ be the dominant force in the world.[14]

Christopher Evans maintained in *The Kingdom Is Always but Coming: The Life of Walter Rauschenbusch* that Ritschl's concept of the kingdom of God was crucial to Rauschenbusch's vision of addressing the terrible social problems that marked so many American inner cities. Evans writes, "In effect, German liberalism gave him the theological framework for articulating beliefs that he already had held for several years."[15]

In 1906, Rauschenbusch expanded upon his ideas developed in *The Righteousness of the Kingdom* by writing *Christianity and the Social Crisis*, and applied them to the current situation that he knew so well from his eleven years of parish ministry in Hell's Kitchen. This book was a challenge to connect again with the New Testament kingdom of God, which had become obscured in the medieval period and lay dormant. Christians, argued Rauschenbusch, needed to apply kingdom principles to reinvigorate the church and bring help to so many souls in need.

At the center of America's inner-city problems, he urged, was an unjust economic and social system that was the product of capitalism. Rauschenbusch wrote:

> During the great industrial crisis in the 90's, I saw good men go into disreputable lines of employment and respectable widows consent to live with men who would support them and their children. One could hear the hu-

---

14. Rauschenbusch, *The Righteousness of the Kingdom*, 87–88.
15. Christopher Evans, *The Kingdom Is Always but Coming: The Life of Walter Rauschenbusch* (Grand Rapids: Eerdmans, 2004), 94.

man virtues crackling and crumbling all around. Whenever work is scarce, petty crime is plentiful. But that is only the tangible expression of the decay in the morale of the working people on which the statistics can seize. The corresponding decay in the morality of possessing classes at such a time is another story but industrial crises are not inevitable in nature; they are merely inevitable in capitalism.[16]

Rauschenbusch envisioned a new American Christian culture built first and foremost upon an equitable distribution of wealth. He encouraged the middle class to catch a vision for improving the lives of everyone, and this had to begin with the local churches.

Perhaps the most influential book that Rauschenbusch wrote was his 1917 publication, *A Theology for the Social Gospel*. His thesis was crystal clear from the first page: "We have a Social Gospel. We need a systematic theology large enough to match it and vital enough to back it."[17] The structure for the book was simple: the first three chapters presented reasons for a "readjustment and expansion of theology," and the following nineteen chapters were meant to demonstrate how key Christian doctrines and practices could be "expanded and readjusted" (1).

The first key doctrine to be dealt with was sin. As a pastor and as a seminary teacher, Rauschenbusch never doubted the reality of sin. He began with a simple definition: "theology with remarkable unanimity has discerned that sin is essentially selfishness" (47). He stated that human beings sin both against God and against each other because all are interconnected. Classical theology had therefore failed to understand the nature and pervasiveness of social sin, often treating sin as a private matter between God and the sinner.

Rauschenbusch defended the reality of original sin, but he went on to reinterpret it. For example, the transmission of a sin nature was seen as biological through human reproduction from one generation to the next. He stated that "sin is transmitted along the lines of social tradition" (60). Such social sin is absorbed by the individual from his social group and is always marked by selfishness, a characteristic of the kingdom of evil (78) as opposed to the kingdom of God. How then is one saved? An individual or group can only be saved by turning away from self and selfishness to God and humanity and working with others to overcome evil (95).

16. Walter Rauschenbusch, *Christianity and the Social Crisis* (New York: Macmillan, 1907), 238.

17. Walter Rauschenbusch, *A Theology for the Social Gospel* (New York: Abingdon, 1917) 1. Hereafter, page references from this work will be given in parentheses in the text.

Rauschenbusch was very clear that the old individualist concepts of sin and salvation must be reconsidered in a more biblical and corporate sense proposed by the Social Gospel. He did not denigrate the value of individual salvation but saw it as a necessary part of the whole of God's redeeming work (95). He completely rejected the idea that individual salvation is of the utmost importance, for such a view failed to recognize the necessity of the redemption of social institutions and the creation of an environment that looked to the kingdom of God for models of righteousness. "The supreme purpose of God . . . is realized not only by redemption, but also by the education of mankind in the revelation of his life within it. It is for us to see the kingdom of God as always coming, always pressing in on the present, always big with possibility, and always inviting immediate action" (141–42).

In terms of ecclesiology, Rauschenbusch argued that the church must exist not just for itself but for the kingdom of God, and that this gives the church the power to save. The church is the social factor in salvation that brings social forces to bear on evil. "The Church offers Christ not only many human bodies and minds to serve as ministers of his salvation, but its own composite personality, with collective memory revealed and stored with great hymns and Bible stories and deeds of heroism, with trained aesthetic and moral feelings, and with the collective will set on righteousness" (119).

On the denominational level, Rauschenbusch was always a committed Baptist. He passionately favored congregational church government and was suspicious of hierarchy and creeds. Decisions in the local church, he felt, should be made democratically. The final chapter of *Theology for the Social Gospel* is perhaps the one that would most trouble evangelicals and other more traditional Christians. It deals with the theology of atonement and Christ's work on the cross.

For Rauschenbusch, the death of Christ changed everything. However, as with other doctrines, his view enlarged and reinterpreted key elements of the atonement. First, he argued that the sins that led to the crucifixion of Christ were social sins: class contempt, religious bigotry, abuse of political power, a mob spirit and a mob action, and militarism (267). In answering the question, "Why did Christ have to die?" Rauschenbusch rejected any view that presupposed a legal theory of imputation (259), that is, that the suffering and death of Christ on the cross bore the guilt of individuals who put their faith in the Savior. Rather, the death of Jesus on the cross inspired courage and defiance of evil. "The cross of Christ put God's approval on the sacrificial impulse in the hearts of the brave" (278). Atonement for Rauschenbusch was in essence "a conception of spiritual solidarity" (259). The cross promoted the cause and strengthened the redemptive power of the kingdom of God.

PRESBYTERIAN RESPONSE TO THE SOCIAL GOSPEL

In response to the dramatic increase of the immigrant population in America during the second half of the nineteenth century, Christians—both conservative and liberal—felt compelled to come to the aid of the poor and oppressed migrant populations flocking to large cities in the East and Midwest. The Social Gospel movement, although launched by theologically progressive leaders like Gladden and Rauschenbusch, was clearly aided by evangelical Christians who long had a tradition of social reform crusades.[18] From 1880 until the turn of the century, Protestant seminary professors, pastors, and laity joined forces to improve social conditions in the inner city.[19]

An ecumenical group called the Federal Council of Churches was established with offices in New York City and Washington, DC.[20] At its founding in 1908, it consisted of thirty-two denominations, including the Presbyterian and Reformed traditions. The goals of the council were to ameliorate injustice in the workplace, advocate for protection of the worker from occupational injuries and diseases, advocate against child labor, and provide for a fair living wage as a minimum for all workers.[21]

The PCUSA established the Department of Church and Labor under Charles Stelzle, the son of German immigrants; Stelzle became a Presbyterian early in life and studied at the Moody Bible Institute. Having been apprenticed as a machinist, he identified with the working man and felt drawn to ministry. Stelzle enrolled in a self-study program and became a lay worker in the Minneapolis Minnesota Hope Chapel, which ministered among an immigrant population. He moved to New York City and in 1900 was ordained as a Presbyterian minister. The Department of Church and Labor, established in 1901, was perhaps the earliest church program of its kind. By 1910, the PCUSA had developed over a hundred industrial training schools as well as forty social centers in immigrant communities.[22]

---

18. See Aaron Abell, *The Urban Impact on American Protestantism, 1865–1900* (Cambridge, MA: Harvard University Press, 1943), and C. Howard Hopkins, *The Rise of the Social Gospel in American Protestantism, 1865–1915* (New Haven: Yale University Press, 1967).

19. Gary Scott Smith, "Conservative Presbyterians: The Gospel, Social Reform, and the Church in the Progressive Era," *American Presbyterians* 70, no. 2 (Summer 1992): 107.

20. Gary Dorrien, *Economy, Difference, Empire: Social Ethics for Social Justice* (New York: Columbia University Press, 2010), 134.

21. *Federal Council of Churches of Christ in America* (Westerville, OH: American Issue Press, 1925).

22. Richard Poethig, "Urban/Metropolitan Mission Policies: An Historical Overview," *Journal of Presbyterian History* 57 (Fall 1979): 316–17.

In the second decade of the twentieth century, Presbyterian and other evangelical denominational leaders reacted negatively to the social programs that
had developed over the previous ten years. Opponents focused their criticism
on several aspects of the Social Gospel and the reliance of Christians on sociological theories and methods to solve social issues. These conservative leaders
were clearly concerned about the immigrant population and supported efforts
to ameliorate poverty, working conditions, unemployment, and housing problems, and they were especially concerned to allow a Sabbath rest. But they felt
that something important had been lost.

In 1909, a committee of ten (five clergy and five laymen) within the PCUSA
General Assembly presented a report, "The Christian Solution to the Social
Problem." While acknowledging the significant progress that had been made
due to the "demand for social justice," the committee urged that Presbyterians
recognize Jesus Christ as "the final authority over social as well as individual
aspects of life" and that the principles of the kingdom of God as taught by Jesus
Christ should be employed.[23]

A 1912 report to the General Assembly entitled "Safeguarding Social Service
in the Life of the Church" encouraged Presbyterians to follow Christ's example
in resolving social needs and conditions. The report clearly recognized once
again the enormity of the need. It called for more child welfare, better working
conditions, improved public health and housing, the need for more public
parks and recreational opportunities, the importance of mediation between
owners and workers, and the value of observing the Sabbath and fighting
liquor trusts.[24]

The focus of much of the criticism as delineated in the General Assembly's
report fell on Charles Stelzle. The Reverend Mark Matthews, pastor of the
ten-thousand-member First Presbyterian Church of Seattle, Washington, who
was very active in promoting inner-city reforms, argued that Stelzle's approach
had been too much influenced by socialism. In 1913, the General Assembly
proposed that the work of the Bureau of Social Service should be redesigned,
and its budget was cut.[25] Due to such criticism, Stelzle resigned from leadership that same year.

Several Presbyterian and Reformed groups established a joint committee
that produced the "United Declaration of Christian Faith and Social Service"

23. *Minutes of the General Assembly of the Presbyterian Church in the United States of
America* (Philadelphia: Presbyterian Committee of Publication, 1910), 230.

24. Smith, "Conservative Presbyterians," 95.

25. *Minutes of the General Assembly of the Presbyterian Church in the United States of
America* (Philadelphia: Presbyterian Committee of Publication, 1913), 188, 189.

in 1913. Their goal was "to make clear to the world the true place of Social Service in Christian life and work."[26] The report argued that because all the evils that affect human life are rooted in sin and selfishness, the church must continually work to be aware of conditions in the immigrant populations and strive to address them with Christian love and grace. However, such was not the primary role of individual congregations whose focus was on the spiritual life and were called to provide Christian nurture, evangelism, worship, Bible study, Christian missions, etc. A better approach, it was argued, would be for individual churches to encourage their parishioners to work through voluntary organizations that were specifically created to ameliorate social ills. Congregations should not identify with political or social positions and reforms.[27]

Two of the leading conservative Presbyterian critics of the Social Gospel movement in America and Christian socialism as an ideology were Charles R. Erdman and William B. Greene Jr., both professors at Princeton Seminary. Erdman was ordained in 1891 by the Presbytery of Philadelphia North, PCUSA. He served at Princeton as the professor of practical theology from 1905 until his retirement in 1936. In 1925, he was elected moderator of the General Assembly of the Presbyterian Church. During his career, he published over thirty popular biblical commentaries and works on pastoral theology.

Erdman was part of the joint committee that wrote the "United Declaration." As one of the contributors to *The Fundamentals* (1910–1917), he also penned "The Church and Socialism."[28] He also served as the chair of the Standing Committee on Home Missions that played a leading role in Presbyterian Home Missions ministry. In Erdman's estimation, the rise of socialism "was the most surprising and significant movement of the age."[29] Although acknowledging that socialists and Christians fought against many of the same social and economic evils, he felt the two movements were at cross purposes. Some, he suggested, even saw socialism as a substitute for religion. Other well-meaning individuals attempted to meld Christianity and socialism into Christian socialism in an effort to help change society.

For Erdman, the key idea to be repudiated was that "Jesus Christ was a socialist and that the Early Church as described in the book of Acts was built upon socialist principles."[30] He argued that Christ was in no way political.

26. *Minutes of the General Assembly of the Presbyterian Church in the United States of America* (Philadelphia: Presbyterian Committee of Publication, 1914), 52.

27. *Minutes of the General Assembly* (1914), 54–55.

28. Charles Erdman, "The Church and Socialism," in *The Fundamentals: Testimony to the Truth* (Chicago: Testimony Publishing Co., 1917), 4:97–108.

29. Erdman, "The Church and Socialism," 97.

30. Erdman, "The Church and Socialism," 99.

Jesus certainly was an advocate of brotherhood, love, and justice, but he was not in any way aligned with a political party. As for the common sharing of means and goods in Acts (4:32–35), Erdman believed that the narrative was in no way pointing to the creation of socialism. The sharing of early Christians was a unique situation in that it was "local, voluntary, occasional and temporary." A church member was of course free to either "adopt or reject socialism and to be at the same time an ardent and sincere Christian," or to be "a true Christian and a determined opponent of Socialism."[31] He urged ministers not to advocate for socialism, and he rejected altogether the phrase "Christian socialism."

Greene was a professor of apologetics, ethics, and philosophy at Princeton from 1893 to 1928. A strong critic of the Social Gospel movement, he emphasized that Christ had been misrepresented by the advocates of the Social Gospel, who saw Christ mainly as a social reformer. They tended to emphasize the example of Jesus and his ethical teachings more than his work in atonement for sin as the redeemer.[32] Christians, he urged, must "attack the causes not just the results of these conditions."[33] All of society, the family, church, and state, had an "important part to play in forming and reforming civilization." Church members should be involved and deeply interested in questions affecting society and the church and "should be the most potent agent for social regeneration."[34] Greene went further than Erdman in encouraging Christians to reject socialism and oppose it.[35] Socialism advocated "state control" in place of "divine providence" and put society in the role of almighty God.[36]

For evangelical Presbyterians, the Social Gospel movement and Christian socialism misunderstood the central mission of the church. The focus and zeal of the Christian churches must not be directed toward the changes needed in society but rather toward changing individuals. Congregations should do what they do best: worship, Bible study, Christian education, and evangelism. The crux of the social question, according to Erdman, was: "How can individuals be regenerated and perfected?"[37]

31. Erdman, "The Church and Socialism," 100.
32. William B. Greene Jr., "The Church and the Social Question," *Princeton Theological Review* 10 (July 1912): 513–14.
33. Greene, "The Church," 514.
34. Greene, "The Church," 515–16.
35. Greene, "The Church," 517.
36. William B. Greene Jr., "The Bible as the Textbook in Sociology," *Princeton Theological Review* 12 (January 1914): 22.
37. Erdman, "The Church and Socialism," 99.

Presbyterians, Immigration, and Ministry in California

Thus far, this chapter has focused on the challenges brought about by the intense immigration from Europe and the ministry of Christians to those immigrants, who often moved to inner cities in the East and Midwest. During the same period, especially the first two decades of the twentieth century, the Presbyterian church was faced with a similar challenge in the Far West. Historians who focus on the religion of the western states during this time note that the area west of the Rocky Mountains contained the highest percentage of unchurched people in America.[38]

The development of the Presbyterian church in California in the early twentieth century has been very carefully documented.[39] Research has demonstrated that California began to attract people in large numbers beginning with the Gold Rush in 1849. By the end of the 1860s, immigrants from Ireland, Germany, Italy, and China, when combined, constituted one-third of the residents of San Francisco.[40] Unlike other western states, California grew rapidly both in population and in economic development, with two key cities becoming centers of trade: San Francisco and Los Angeles. Presbyterians and other evangelical Protestant denominations played a crucial role in the evolution of California. Linked to their evangelistic work, conservative Christians stressed ministry programs in education and medical and social welfare. This desire to help had been there since Gold Rush days.[41]

The minutes of the annual meeting of the Synod of California in 1892 highlighted the special challenges of their work. Conditions in California "make carnality easy and attractive"; the minutes elaborated these conditions: "the absence of a Sabbath law, a climate favorable to Sabbath desecration, a cosmopolitan population most of whom prefer a holiday to a holy day one day in seven, and many other things too numerous to mention within the limits

---

38. Ferenc M. Szasz, *The Divided Mind of Protestant America, 1880–1915* (Tuscaloosa: University of Alabama Press, 1982), 5.

39. Douglas Anderson, "Through Fire and Fair by the Golden Gate: Progressive Era Protestantism and Regional Culture" (PhD diss., Graduate Theological Union, Berkeley, 1988).

40. Ferenc M. Szasz, *The Protestant Clergy in the Great Plains and Mountain West, 1865–1915* (Albuquerque: University of New Mexico Press, 1988); Carl Guarneri and David Alvarez, eds., *Religion and Society in the American West: Historical Essays* (Lanham, MD: University Press, 1987), x–xi; Sandra Frankie, *California's Spiritual Frontiers* (Berkeley and Los Angeles: University of California Press, 1988) .

41. See Eldon Ernst and Douglas Anderson, *Pilgrim Progression: The Protestant Experience in California* (Santa Barbara, CA: Fithian, 1993).

of this narrative."[42] The state synod organized permanent committees to deal with both temperance and Sabbath observance, issues it believed were clearly linked. Interestingly, the Presbyterian church had more success with temperance than it did with Sabbath observance.

There was a steady flow of immigrants after 1900 heading to the Golden State. The sheer numbers that poured into California cities year after year were seen by many as a threat to the church. By 1930, half the population of San Francisco was foreign born.[43] A 1905 Synod report read as follows: "California with a climate so much like that of southern Europe is bound to be a dumping ground for hundreds of thousands of the least desirable of Europe's population. Presbyterian churches in our Synod have gone down and are going down before this tide of foreign immigration. Help us to meet this army of invasion and the only way it can be met, with the sword of the spirit, which is the word of God."[44] As in Chicago and New York, Presbyterians saw the immigrant population of California as people who needed to know the gospel of Christ and at the same time needed help fitting into American life and embracing its values. "We grow discouraged here in the Far West, at times, because the bulwarks of sin seem too impervious to assault. But why should we be downcast? The wonder is not that California is so irreligious, but that it is as responsive to spiritual influences as it is."[45]

Asian Immigration

Immigrants from Asia, especially Chinese and Japanese, presented the Christian community with a unique challenge. The impact of the Gold Rush was especially significant for the Chinese. The first wave of Chinese immigration began in 1850. Two years earlier, there were fewer than four hundred native Chinese in California, but by 1852 the number had jumped to about twenty-five thousand.[46] These laborers were sought for their work in gold mines, factories, and especially on the transcontinental railroad (completed in 1869).[47]

---

42. *Minutes of the Annual Session of the Synod of California* (Los Angeles: Commercial Printing House, 1902), 33.

43. See Kenneth McDonald, "The Presbyterian Church and the Social Gospel in California: 1890–1910," *American Presbyterians* 72, no. 4 (1994): 244.

44. *Minutes of the Annual Session of the Synod of California* (Los Angeles: Commercial Printing House, 1905), 31.

45. *Minutes of the Annual Session of the Synod of California*, 1902, 34.

46. Geoffrey Ward, *The West: An Illustrated History* (Boston: Little, Brown, 1996), 147.

47. Ronald Takaki, *Strangers from a Different Shore: A History of Asian Americans* (Boston: Little, Brown, 1998).

Chinese immigrants encountered not only distrust from the general population but also outright racism. Special laws were enacted, like the Foreign Miners Tax Act of 1850, which prohibited Chinese men from marrying white European women and barring such men from United States citizenship.[48] In 1875 the Page Acts were passed by Congress to specifically control the number of Chinese immigrants admitted to the country. Asian women, presumably seen by lawmakers as potential prostitutes, could be barred from entry and were described as "undesirable people."[49] Some merchants were allowed to immigrate from China to open grocery stores and shops in areas where many Chinese immigrants lived. Such Chinese settlements soon were dubbed "China Towns," in which most Chinese were forced to live in poverty.[50]

Japanese immigration increased in California in the late 1890s to meet the need for agricultural laborers.[51] As their numbers increased, tension developed around the question of segregated education. In 1907, a riot led by anti-Japanese nativist protesters erupted in San Francisco; the rioters demanded that Caucasian and Japanese children be taught in separate schools.[52] Similar riots that same year occurred in Bellingham, Washington, and Vancouver, British Columbia.[53]

In the face of such discrimination, Presbyterians took up the issue of public rights for Asian immigrants. They advocated for Chinese and Japanese immigrants' rights in both print media and the political sphere. Presbyterian press articles publicly criticized the segregation of Japanese students in California public schools and took to task racist argumentation put forth by popular political candidates.[54]

The Women's Occidental Board of Foreign Missions of the Presbyterian Church[55] was directly responsible for organizing the first "Rescue Home" in San Francisco in 1876; the home had the goal of helping Chinese girls escape from the lure and evils of prostitution.[56] A similar refuge, the San Francisco

48. Thomas W. Chinn, ed., *A History of the Chinese in California* (San Francisco: Chinese Historical Society of America, 1969).

49. Kerry Abrams, "Polygamy, Prostitution, and the Federalization of Immigration Law," *Columbia Law Review* (Rochester, NY), 2005, 641.

50. Takaki, *Strangers*, 36–37, 91–93, and 118–19.

51. Takaki, *Strangers*, 197–211.

52. Erika Lee, "The Yellow Peril and Asian Exclusion in the Americas," *Pacific Historical Review* 76 (2007): 537–62.

53. Lee, "Yellow Peril," 551.

54. "The Japanese School Controversy," *Pacific Presbyterian*, 1907, 2–3.

55. This group united with six other societies to form the Presbyterian Church in the USA Women's Board of Foreign Missions.

56. Edward A. Wicher, *The Presbyterian Church in California, 1849-1927* (New York: Grafton, 1927), 289–90.

Presbyterian Orphanage, opened in a rented house in February of 1895. Three years later, needing more and better facilities, the group erected a three-story building on a twenty-acre parcel of land in San Anselmo; that facility served children for twenty-seven years before it was destroyed in a fire.

The Presbyterian church was also deeply concerned with the issue of labor relations and the exploitation of foreign workers. In 1901, the Narrative Committee of the State Synod delineated in a special report the key issues and hope for reconciliation between immigrant laborers and the captains of industry:

> Surely there never was an hour in the church's history when there was a greater need than this when our Church should seek to leaven with Gospel truth the army of humanity so largely untouched that swarms in our cities. The churches' wonderful opportunity for reaching the working man and becoming an arbiter of righteousness in the great battle that is now on between capital and labor are particularly to be realized at this time. The fact that the church is the only place where these two forces can meet on equal footing and recognize before God their common interests and common humanity, makes of the church a natural arbiter and peacemaker.[57]

One of the most successful and wide-ranging issues of social activism undertaken by the Presbyterian church was education. It is clear that Presbyterian leaders put a high value on early childhood education in an effort to inculcate into young children literacy and Christian values. Presbyterian ministers were very active in the creation of California's first schools, and in time they began to promote a state-sponsored public school system. They put great stock in placing the right kind of person in the schoolmaster's office.[58] Once a public-school system had been established, Presbyterians deferred to the state in terms of control and influence.

A leading local church in northern California was First Presbyterian of Berkeley, which offered Bible classes for Chinese speakers as well as Sabbath schools in Berkeley and in nearby towns.[59] First Berkeley set a standard in terms of mission to the immigrants and influenced many Presbyterian churches in northern California.

A much more extensive and significant role was played in higher education at least until the twentieth century. Presbyterians founded Occidental College

---

57. *Minutes of the Annual Session of the Synod of California* (Los Angeles: Commercial Printing House, 1901), 42.

58. Wicher, *The Presbyterian Church*, 249.

59. Wicher, *The Presbyterian Church*, 175–79.

in 1888 in the Los Angeles area; this school is still in existence and maintains a strong academic reputation, although it is no longer associated with the Presbyterian church. Presbyterian and Congregational ministers were also very active in the establishment and organization of the University of California.[60]

In the twentieth century, as it became clear that public schools would adopt a secular curriculum, it became clear that this trend would carry over to colleges and universities. Presbyterians were concerned that higher education would militate against religion. In the 1897 minutes of the state synod, the Aid for Colleges Committee urged that "our state system of public education, from bottom to top, should be absolutely free from all influences, potent or latent, that are prejudicial to the plain truths of the holy Bible. . . . If it must needs be that our schools shall not be distinctively Christian, it also must needs be that they shall not be in any sense anti-Christian."[61]

CONCLUSION

In the period defined in American history as the Progressive Era, the story of the American Presbyterian church was one of a broadening ministry to embrace a large immigrant population from Europe and Asia. All the clear Presbyterian strengths—preaching, evangelism, education, organization, record keeping, and commitment to social service programs—were employed in ministry to the newest Americans. Theirs was a serious commitment to Christ's words recorded in Matthew 10:42: "And if anyone gives even a cup of cold water to one of these little ones who is my disciple, truly I tell you, that person will certainly not lose their reward."

---

60. Wicher, *The Presbyterian Church*, 246–64; Nell Young, *William Stewart Young, 1859–1937: Builder of California Institutions* (Glendale, CA: Clark, 1967), 68–85.

61. *Minutes of the Annual Session of the Synod of California* (Los Angeles: Commercial Printing House, 1897), 19.

CHAPTER 15

German Universities and American Protestantism

I n the seventeenth century, a new view of authority was introduced by the French mathematician and philosopher René Descartes (1596–1650).[1] Although insisting that he was a devout Christian, a Roman Catholic, and arguing forcefully for the reality of God, Descartes also argued for the centrality of human reason as the final guide to truth.

Descartes is sometimes characterized as the "apostle of doubt." He challenged people to believe only in that about which they were certain. He was fond of asking, "How would you prove that you exist?" With such an approach, Descartes is seen as laying the foundation for modern Western philosophy, and especially rationalism,[2] and in time the Enlightenment of the eighteenth century. With Descartes, the final arbiter of truth shifted from God's revelation to the power of human reason.

THE AGE OF REASON AND THE ENLIGHTENMENT

The Enlightenment was inextricably connected with the scientific revolution of the seventeenth century. This revolution was rooted in the work of Nicholas Copernicus, who published *De revolutionibus orbium coelestium* (*On the Revolution of Celestial Spheres*) in 1543; this revolution of heliocentrism was fueled by the work of Galileo Galilei and Johannes Kepler, among others, and

1. See Stephen Gaukroger, *Descartes: An Intellectual Biography* (Oxford: Oxford University Press, 1995).

2. A seventeenth-century philosophical school that is usually traced back to Descartes and Baruch Spinoza; it postulated that reason is the chief source of knowledge and the means by which knowledge can be tested.

furnished with mathematical support by Sir Isaac Newton,[3] in his *Philosophiae naturalis principia mathematica* (*Mathematical Principles of Natural Philosophy*, 1687), most often abbreviated as *Principia Mathematica*. Newton's law of universal gravitation was viewed by intellectuals in Europe and America as an example of how reason could discover the laws of nature. These leaders of the Enlightenment, men like Immanuel Kant, Montesquieu, David Hume, Jean-Jacques Rousseau, Denis Diderot, Voltaire, and Thomas Jefferson, looked to reason in searching for laws governing humanity and social relationships and believed that when those laws were found, they would help enlightened leaders to create a better world.

Enlightenment ideas and ideals took root in the American colonies by the middle decades of the eighteenth century.[4] Many of the key leaders who would promote rebellion against Britain and later be acknowledged as "founding fathers" were also familiar with Enlightenment philosophy, Deism, and rationalist liberalism.

Jefferson, who served as the third president of the United States, from 1797 to 1801, and was one of the principal authors of the Declaration of Independence, was, like many in his generation, influenced by Deism.[5] Jefferson was a baptized Christian and became a member of the Episcopal Church in Charlottesville, Virginia. As a student at the College of William and Mary in Williamsburg, he began to question the basic doctrines of orthodox Christianity. For Jefferson, the essence of Christianity could be defined as the teachings of Jesus of Nazareth. He was clearly a theist who believed that God was the creator of the world and humanity and was perfect. He also expressed a belief in the afterlife. In his public life, Jefferson's references to God as the source of natural law and morality were numerous, as can easily be seen when a visitor scans the ceiling of the Jefferson Memorial.[6]

By contrast, one can see that, in his private life, the president's stance on the Christian religion reflects a much more progressive position reflecting Enlightenment tendencies. In his book *The Life and Morals of Jesus of Nazareth* (1804) (today often referred to as the *Jefferson Bible*),[7] he took a razor to his

3. See Gale E. Christianson, *In the Presence of the Creator: Isaac Newton and His Times* (New York: Simon & Schuster, 1984).

4. See Conrad Wright, *The Beginnings of Unitarianism in America* (Boston: Beacon, 1966).

5. For more on Jefferson, see Dumas Malone, *Jefferson and His Time* (Boston: Little, Brown, 1948).

6. Merrill D. Peterson, *The Jefferson Memorial: An Essay* (reprint, London: Forgotten Books, 2017).

7. Thomas Jefferson, *The Jefferson Bible: The Life and Morals of Jesus of Nazareth*, Smithsonian Books (New York: Random House, 2011).

King James New Testament and cut out all references to the miracles of Jesus, Christ's divinity, and his resurrection.

Benjamin Franklin was clearly an American "Renaissance man" influencing the culture of his day as an author, printer, politician, postmaster, scientist, inventor, statesman, and diplomat.[8] Franklin grew up in a Puritan home; yet in an autobiography published in 1771, he referred to himself as a Deist.[9] He also claimed he was Christian. Franklin was an admirer of the evangelist George Whitefield and published many of his writings.

One month before he died in 1790, the president of Yale University, Ezra Stiles, wrote to ask Franklin's views on religion. The ailing Franklin clearly expressed faith in God but also doubts as to the veracity of the Bible.

> As to Jesus of Nazareth, my Opinion of whom you particularly desire, I think the System of Morals and his Religion, as he left them to us, the best the world ever saw or is likely to see; but I apprehend it has received various corrupt changes, and I have, with most of the present Dissenters in England, some Doubts as to his divinity; tho' it is a question I do not dogmatize upon, having never studied it, and I think it needless to busy myself with now, when I expect soon an Opportunity of knowing the Truth with less Trouble.[10]

One of the leading lights in Boston's ministerial consortium who promoted and preached a rationalist liberal perspective on the Bible in the late eighteenth century was Jonathan Mayhew. Mayhew dealt extensively with the question of how the biblical text is to be interpreted. Called as minister to the Old West Congregational Church in Boston (1747), Mayhew was a 1744 graduate of Harvard College. His preaching focused on the unity of God, and thus he became anti-Trinitarian. He viewed Jesus Christ from an Arian perspective;[11] the Son was consequently subordinate to God the Father. Mayhew came into the ministry during the period of revival known as the Great Awakening and

8. Both Jefferson and Franklin served as American ambassador to France.

9. Benjamin Franklin, *Autobiography and Other Writings* (New York: Random House, 2008), 52.

10. Benjamin Franklin, https://www.constitution.org/primarysources/franklin-stiles .html, accessed February 26, 2019.

11. Arius was a fourth-century presbyter from the Christian church in Alexandria, Egypt, who was tried at the Council of Nicaea (325) and expelled from the church for teaching that Christ was not equal to the Father and in fact had been created in time; this was famously expressed in the words "There was a time when Christ was not."

became a leading critic of awakening preachers like George Whitefield and Jonathan Edwards. His rationalist liberal hermeneutic is described thus:

> The overarching principle that guided the proponents of the advanced views was that universal truths of reason and morality should be the standards by which to interpret Scripture. Mayhew himself made the point in a series of sermons preached in 1749. "Reason was a gift of God, and it would be wrong not to use it. The doctrine of total ignorance and incapacity to judge of moral and religious truth, brought upon mankind by the apostasy of our first parents, is without foundation. Human freedom to choose the good followed from the gift of reason. Exercise your reason and the liberty you enjoy, in learning the truth and your deity from it."[12]

This approach to the text was to become a mainstay for rationalist liberal hermeneutics: reason is the final arbiter in matters of interpretation of the passage under consideration. The Bible is God's word and infallible, provided that it is interpreted according to reason.

The power and impact of Enlightenment ideas in eighteenth-century America were also embraced and spread by evangelical Christians. One such was a Presbyterian farmer in rural New Jersey named Philip Fithian; he kept a detailed diary of his life and thoughts as he longed for a deeper and richer intellectual life. He became an active member of the "republic of letters," a multinational community of intellectuals from both Europe and America who communicated with handwritten letters in the late seventeenth and early eighteenth century.[13] Fithian's experience of the Enlightenment search for truth led to his sense of call to the Presbyterian ministry.

The Impact of the Modern University on Issues of Truth and Authority

To review: with the advance of the Enlightenment in the eighteenth century and especially with the philosophical system known as rationalism, various forms of Deism and liberal Protestantism began to emerge. As liberal Protestants developed in both Europe and North America, the concept of biblical

12. George M. Marsden, *Jonathan Edwards: A Life* (New Haven: Yale University Press, 2003), 27.

13. John Fea, *The Way of Enlightenment Leads Home: Philip Vickers Fithian and the Rural Enlightenment in Early America* (Philadelphia: University of Pennsylvania Press, 2013).

authority was radically revised, both in regard to divine revelation and as to the nature of the inspiration of the text. This process was enhanced and empowered by the development of the modern university, initially in Prussia, then elsewhere in western Europe and Great Britain.

The university in western European history developed out of the rise of cathedral schools in the eleventh century.[14] Our earliest known examples are in Mediterranean Europe, especially in the Italian city-states.[15] Each early university built its reputation on some academic specialty, whether medicine, law, or theology. One classic example of the latter was the cathedral school of Notre-Dame de Paris, begun in the 1100s; it existed before the great Cathedral of Notre Dame began to rise in the 1160s. It was originally designed as a Roman Catholic training center for priests and other church leaders, so the first and basic subject areas were Christian dogmatics, ecclesiastical Latin, and various aspects of applied ministry.

The French Revolution, which began in 1789 and lasted until 1799, had a profound influence on the social and political structure of France and its colonies. The revolution soon overthrew the monarchy and eventually established a republic. It was inspired by radical rationalist ideas. Reason became the guiding principle.

Napoleon Bonaparte was a product of the French Revolution and extended its impact through the conquest of major parts of western Europe. Beginning in 1793, many universities in conquered territories were suppressed by the revolutionary zeal spread by Napoleon's armies. Oftentimes the endowments of the universities were nationalized and the schools were taken over by the state. Theological faculties especially were jettisoned from universities.[16] By 1815, at least sixteen universities were no longer viable, including the famous schools of Halle, Wittenberg, and Louvain. It should be noted that Napoleon did support Protestant theological faculties after 1803 in Montaubon, France, and Geneva, Switzerland.[17]

To many progressive intellectuals in the eighteenth century, a revision of the nature and purpose of the university was long overdue. Many saw universities as outdated institutions, medieval in origin and therefore stilted, out of touch, and of very little use to society. The theological faculties were especially looked down upon. Denis Diderot, a French philosopher and writer, educa-

14. Charles H. Haskins, *The Rise of Universities* (Ithaca, NY: Cornell University Press, 1957).

15. Bologna claims the distinction of being first, in the year 1088.

16. Laurence Brockliss, *French Higher Education in the Seventeenth and Eighteenth Centuries* (Oxford: Oxford University Press, 1987), 125.

17. Kenneth J. Stewart, *Restoring the Reformation: British Evangelicalism and the Francophone 'Réveil,' 1816–1849* (Eugene, OR: Wipf & Stock, 2006), 41–53.

tional advisor to Empress Catherine the Great of Russia, founder and editor of the famous *Encyclopédie* (*Encyclopedia*), viewed the theological faculties of universities to be tainted with fanaticism and promoters of controversy.[18]

As one modern historian has written: "In his *Streit der Fakultaten* (1798), Immanuel Kant heaped scorn on the so-called 'queen of the sciences' (regina scientiarum), suggesting that theology could neither serve society nor true religion unless it first conformed to the universal dictates of reason, which, in Kant's view, were best embodied in the traditionally 'lower' philosophical faculty—or what in the English-speaking world we understand today as 'the arts and sciences.'"[19] With the fall of Napoleon in 1814, universities in Continental Europe regained a degree of stability that had been lost during the revolutionary period. The University of Berlin, founded in 1810, was to have a profound influence on the rise of the modern university. Not only in Germany and western Europe but also in Great Britain and North America, the University of Berlin became the "gold standard" for developing schools of higher learning in the West.

Interestingly, the modern university did not fully reject the academic structures and departments of the medieval past but rather adapted them to meet the new historical conditions of the modern era. This model of adaptation was at work in the founding of the University of Berlin and especially in the influence of theologian Friedrich Schleiermacher, one of the key founders of modern Protestant liberalism. Schleiermacher argued effectively for maintaining the fourfold structure of the modern university, that is, with faculties of theology, law, medicine, and philosophy—with philosophy's numerous subcategories such as mathematics, history, and philology coming to be elevated to a position of equality with the traditional faculties.[20] In this new model and structure, theology underwent a transition as it came to be dubbed "scientific theology," or, in German, *wissenschaftliche Theologie*.

Later in the nineteenth century, another theologian and church historian, Adolf von Harnack, continued to revise the structure of university curricula especially by emphasizing the importance of theological study being branded "*wissenschaftliche Theologie*." Theology, Harnack argued, can no longer be the product of church councils debating the meaning of the scriptural text; he forcefully argued that maintaining the old system would be injurious to true science.[21]

18. Denis Diderot, "Plan d'une université pour le gouvernement de Russie," in *Ouevres complètes*, ed. J. Assézat (Paris, 1875), 3:438.

19. Thomas A. Howard, *Protestant Theology and the Making of the Modern German University* (Oxford: Oxford University Press, 2006), 3.

20. Howard, *Protestant Theology*, 6.

21. See Alister E. McGrath, *A Scientific Theology*, vol. 3, *Theory* (London: T&T Clark, 2006), 279-83.

For a great number of devout Christian scholars in Germany and Prussia, this move away from the authority of the sacred text toward a more scientific or reasoned approach to the meaning of the Bible was not a healthy thing for the church. The noted Danish existentialist and Christian philosopher Søren Kierkegaard, who was a student at the University of Berlin, shared with other like-minded intellectuals the concern that "Christianity has so completely merged with science—that . . . Christianity no longer exists."[22]

The PhD, doctor of philosophy, was another innovation developed at the University of Berlin in the nineteenth century. "Philosophy" here is not to be confused with the formal subject of philosophy, but rather is connected with the original Greek meaning of the word, "a lover of wisdom." "Philosophy" in German universities was the term that described the arts curriculum that included history, philology, and mathematics. The faculty of philosophy and theology began to insist that students not only attend lectures but also engage in seminar-style learning, where students were encouraged to probe ideas as they interacted with one another in a dialectical way. A further innovation was the requirement that students research and write a dissertation in order to receive a doctorate, or PhD. These reforms proved to be so successful that they quickly spread to other European universities as well as to those of Great Britain and the United States. In the late nineteenth and early twentieth century, American students increasingly enrolled in German PhD programs to enhance their status as scholars and to gain academic advancement.[23]

HISTORICAL-CRITICAL METHOD

A key component of *wissenschaftliche Theologie* (scientific theology), which surfaced in German universities in the nineteenth century, was the historical-critical method, often referred to as "historical criticism." It is more popularly known as "higher criticism," in part to distinguish it from the history of the transmission of biblical and other ancient texts through time, which is usually referred to as "textual criticism" or "lower criticism."

Textual criticism is a necessary discipline because ancient texts had to be copied by hand since there was no mechanical printing until the 1450s. Therefore, handwritten manuscripts were the norm; these were prone to scribal

---

22. *Søren Kierkegaard's Journals and Papers*, ed. and trans. Howard V. Hong and Edna H. Hong (Bloomington: Indiana University Press, 1975), 4:463.

23. The preceding chapter has noted, for example, how the American Presbyterian James Woodrow received the Heidelberg PhD in 1856.

errors. A monk copying a page of sacred text would accidentally make a slip, a small mistake. When that text was itself copied, the error would be transmitted forward. Over time such mistakes added up. The textual critic sought to identify which is the oldest and thus the most accurate text of a given document.

Probably the most famous textual critic of the Reformation era was Erasmus of Rotterdam, who, in compiling and translating his famous 1516 edition of the New Testament,[24] critically compared several New Testament Greek biblical texts to establish which were the most accurate; this Dutch humanist added marginal notes for documentation. Lower criticism is not generally a controversial field of study; all scholars, whether liberal or conservative, want to work with the most accurate text.

Historical criticism, by contrast, works at a different level to critically examine and establish "the world behind the text."[25] The goal of historical criticism is to discover the meaning of the words in a given text in their historical context. To do so, the scholar must critically determine what the author intended as well as what the recipients understood by the written words. To arrive at that intended meaning, the origins of the text—that is, the time and place in which it was written, the words chosen, the potential sources used by the author and any key persons or places, events or dates, etc.—must be scrutinized.[26]

One of the early centers for historical criticism in Germany was Tübingen University. F. C. Baur was first a student and later a professor at Tübingen; he is often looked upon as the founder of the Tübingen School of Theology. Baur published a key work in 1825 entitled *Symbol and Mythology: The Natural Religion of Antiquity*.[27] This philosophical study of ancient religious myths and symbols was deeply influenced by Schleiermacher. On the basis of this publication, Baur was invited to Tübingen and assumed the title Professor of Theology.

It was at Tübingen that Baur began to analyze the early development of the Christian church in the first three centuries using the Hegelian dialectical approach.[28] He posited two rival schools of Christianity in conflict during the

24. Erasmus of Rotterdam, *Novum Instrumentum* (Basel: Johannes Froben, 1516). This important book presented, on facing pages, a Greek New Testament text and a fresh Latin translation with footnotes. This work allowed scholars and reformers to make vernacular translations of the New Testament from a Greek text. See Erasmus of Rotterdam, *Erasmus 1516 Greek and Latin New Testament* (Phillipsburg, NJ: Reformed Church Publications, 2015).

25. Richard N. Soulen and R. Kendall Soulen, *Handbook of Biblical Criticism* (Louisville: Westminster John Knox, 2001), 78.

26. Soulen and Soulen, *Handbook*, 79.

27. F. C. Baur, *Symbolik und Mythologie: Oder Die Naturreligion Des Alerthums* (n.p.: Ulan Press, 2012).

28. G. W. F. Hegel (1770–1831) was a highly influential German philosopher who was often cited in the twentieth century as inventing the thesis, antithesis, synthesis model to

first century, one described as "Jewish Christians," who were followers of Peter (often referred to as "Petrine"), and a more gentile-based church following Paul, dubbed "Pauline Christianity." According to this theory, the church in the second century represented a synthesis of the two opposing movements.

In his work *The So-Called Pastoral Epistles of Paul* (1835), Baur argued against Paul's authorship of the Pastoral Epistles and dated those writings to the second century AD. Further, in his *Paul the Apostle of Jesus Christ* (1845), Baur held that only four New Testament letters were authentically Pauline: Galatians, 1 and 2 Corinthians, and Romans. The Revelation of John he dated to the first century and the Acts of the Apostles to the late second century.[29]

The Tübingen School had reached its peak of influence by the 1840s. Its influence began to fade after 1860, as critical studies of the detailed use of the four Gospels by second-century church fathers Ignatius, Justin Martyr, and Papias demonstrated how deeply familiar with them these fathers already were. Baur's proposal of a late date for the four Gospels was not historically tenable.[30]

THE DOCUMENTARY HYPOTHESIS

Another major area for critical reevaluation of the biblical text was a close and careful examination of the Pentateuch, the first five books of the Old Testament. The traditional view, held by most Christian scholars until the mid-nineteenth century, was that Moses had received from God what he wrote in Genesis, Exodus, Leviticus, Numbers, and Deuteronomy.

Mosaic authorship had first been questioned during the Enlightenment, especially by philosophers Baruch Spinoza (1632–1677)[31] and Thomas Hobbes (1588–1679),[32] both of whom noted problematic issues like seeming contradictions in parallel accounts of the same event or narrative. Their objective was to cast aspersions on the reliability of the Bible.

---

explain the development of theories, movements in history, etc., although those terms were not the ones Hegel used. See Paul Redding, *Analytic Philosophy and the Return of Hegelian Thought* (Cambridge: Cambridge University Press, 2010), 200–219.

29. See Horton Harris, *The Tübingen School* (Oxford: Clarendon, 1975).

30. See Geoffrey R. Treloar, *Lightfoot the Historian: The Nature and Role of History in the Life and Thought of J. B. Lightfoot as Churchman and Scholar* (Tübingen: Mohr Siebeck, 1998), 340–46.

31. See Tremper Longman and Raymond Dillard, *An Introduction to the Old Testament* (Grand Rapids: Zondervan, 2006), 40.

32. See Frank M. Coleman, "Thomas Hobbes and the Hebraic Bible," *History of Political Thought* 25, no. 4 (2004): 642–69.

Another pioneer was a French medical scholar, Jean Astruc. Astruc, aiming to defend the Old Testament against critical attack from the likes of Hobbes and Spinoza, began a detailed study of the text of Genesis. In 1753 he anonymously published his findings in a work called *Conjectures on the original documents that Moses appeared to have used in composing the book of Genesis. With remarks that support or throw light on these conjectures.*[33] This text is commonly referred to as *Conjectures.*

Astruc produced a detailed and careful study of the book of Genesis. He noted that it contained several doublets, or second renditions of the same narrative often with distinctive differences, like the two creation accounts of humankind in Genesis 1 and 2. He also noticed that in parallel stories, often different Hebrew names for God were used in the text. Astruc nevertheless defended Mosaic authorship of the Pentateuch.

Astruc's speculations led another Old Testament scholar, Johan Eichhorn, a professor at the University of Jena, to designate these documents, based on the name for God used in them, as the J source and the E source, *J* standing for "Jahwist" (Yahweh) and *E* for "Elohist." At some later time, he conjectured, another writer had combined the four into one document, which produced the doublets. This idea of several sources or documents led to the name "Documentary Hypothesis," which is designated at present the "Older Documentary Hypothesis."[34]

The leading promoter and popularizer of what is now called the Documentary Hypothesis was the German scholar Julius Wellhausen,[35] who began his academic career as a professor of Old Testament at Greifswald University; he later was a professor of semitics at the Universities of Marburg and Göttingen. In 1878 he published *History of Israel.*[36] This book was reissued as *Prolegomena to the History of Israel* in 1883. In this work he incorporated theories on the composition of the Pentateuch by Hermann Hupfeld, who postulated two separate sources that used the name Elohim, the E source and the P, or

33. Jean Astruc published this work anonymously in fear of Roman Catholic reprisals for works critical of the Bible. The French title reads *Conjectures sur les mémoires originaux dont il paroit que Moyse s'est servi pour composer le livre de la Genèse. Avec des remarques qui appuient ou qui éclaircissent ces conjectures.* Reprint edition in French from Nabu Press, 2010.

34. Eddie Ruddick, "Elohist," in *Mercer Dictionary of the Bible*, ed. Watson E. Mills and Roger Aubrey Bullard (Macon, GA: Mercer University Press, 1990).

35. William A. Irwin, "The Significance of Julius Wellhausen," *Journal of Bible and Religion* 12 (August 1944): 160–73.

36. *Geschichte Israels*, vol. 1, the second edition he titled *Prolegomena zur Geschichte Israels* (*Prolegomena to the History of Israel*) (reprint, Cambridge: Cambridge University Press, 2013).

"Priestly," source, and Karl Graf, who hypothesized that the P source that includes Leviticus was the most recent addition to the Pentateuch. So influential
was the work of Graf that the Documentary Hypothesis is often referred to as
the Graf-Wellhausen Hypothesis.

In essence, the Graf-Wellhausen thesis on the composition of the Pentateuch is this: Early written and oral sources of what would later be called
Genesis, the J and the E sources, were written down in the late 900s BC.
Sometime in the late 700s the two documents were combined by a redactor, an
editor, and the two became a new document, the JE source. Shortly thereafter
the Deuteronomist, or D source, and the P, or Priestly source, were written.
Finally, in the 400s BC, a later redactor joined all four in what became known
as the JEPD document.

What made Wellhausen's *History of Israel* so influential was his explanation of the evolution of the religion of the Jews. He wove together the Graf-
Welhausen theory with a developmental explanation of Israel's history. The J
and E sources bore the marks of a primitive and rather personal creator God,
the earliest stage of Israel's history. In the D source, Wellhausen postulated
the impact of the prophets and the development of more ethical ideas, which
he saw as the high point of Jewish religion. Finally, the Priestly source, or P,
reflected a postexilic period (400s BC), with greater emphasis on ritual and
rule-oriented worship.

The Graf-Wellhausen Documentary Hypothesis had widespread support
in the late nineteenth and through much of the twentieth century; it had a
profound influence upon developing biblical scholars in Germany, Great
Britain, and America. An interesting anecdote regarding the impact of the
Documentary Hypothesis on the perceived authority of the biblical text came
from the professional life of Wellhausen. In 1872 he became a professor of Old
Testament at Greifswald University, where he would lecture to young men
preparing for the Lutheran ministry; but with his developing interest in the
textual criticism of the Old Testament, he decided to resign his post in 1882
due to pangs of conscience. As he wrote in his resignation letter: "I became
a theologian because the scientific treatment of the Bible interested me; only
gradually did I come to understand that a professor of theology also has the
practical task of preparing the students for service in the Protestant Church,
and that I am not adequate to this practical task, but that instead despite all
caution on my own part I make my hearers unfit for their office. Since then my
theological professorship has been weighing heavily on my conscience."[37]

---

37. Robert J. Oden Jr., *The Bible without Theology* (New York: Harper & Row, 1987), 20.
Oden quotes from Wellhausen's *Prolegomena to the History of Ancient Israel*.

The Bible in American Culture in
the Mid-nineteenth Century

When it came to biblical authority, the academic climate was far different in the America of the mid-1800s. One historian has described the period from the end of the Revolutionary War until the middle of the nineteenth century as "the democratization of American Christianity."[38] He elaborated several factors that shaped the view of American culture toward the Bible. The historian pointed out that unlike most of western Europe, there was no national church that was allied with the state; in fact, the American Constitution forbade any intermingling of church and state. He added that an important contextual factor to the American view of the Bible was the influence of the Second Great Awakening,[39] embodied in renewed efforts at foreign and domestic missionary outreach, frontier camp meeting revivals in the new states of Kentucky and Tennessee at the turn of the century, and urban revivals associated with Charles G. Finney. Because of the Second Great Awakening, it is quite clear that Americans began to take the Bible with new seriousness and apply it to social needs like prison reform, education, and the abolition of slavery.

Such a remarkably different approach to religion from that going on in Continental Europe was noted by the famous French chronicler Alexis de Tocqueville, who described the America of 1830 in these words: "religion in America takes no direct part in the government of society but nevertheless it must be regarded as the foremost of the political institutions of the country for if it does not impart a taste for freedom it facilitates the use of free institutions."[40]

Changes in Ministerial Education in America

Among the institutions of higher learning founded in colonial America was the Presbyterian-funded College of New Jersey (now Princeton University). Under the leadership of President John Witherspoon, the College of New Jer-

---

38. Nathan O. Hatch, *The Democratization of American Christianity* (New Haven: Yale University Press, 1989). Cf. Mark Noll, *America's God: From Jonathan Edwards to Abraham Lincoln* (New York: Oxford University Press, 2002), 161.

39. The Second Great Awakening (1800–1840s) is contrasted with the Great Awakening (1724–1776) for many reasons, including Arminian theology, camp meeting frontier revivals, big city revivals epitomized by the preaching of Charles G. Finney, who linked revival with the abolition of slavery.

40. Alexis de Tocqueville, *Democracy in America*, trans. George Lawrence (Garden City, NY: Doubleday, 1969), 287.

sey moved away from its identity as solely a Presbyterian school to a "broadly conceived intercolonial instrument of social integration and reformation."[41] The focus of instruction turned from primarily that of training clergymen to a broader general education for the laity. Witherspoon brought with him from Scotland openness to certain features of Enlightenment thought; in this, he was followed by his successor as president, the Princeton alumnus and his son-in-law, Samuel Stanhope Smith.[42] But by 1812, serious questions had been raised as to whether the college's stance on the relative roles of divine revelation and human reason were satisfactory. It was by now feared that the Enlightenment exaltation of reason had proved a corrosive influence.[43]

Princeton Theological Seminary

Such questions had already been raised in Boston; there, the orthodox wing of the Congregational Association, being unsatisfied with the orthodoxy of Harvard College, determined to launch an orthodox institution that aimed specifically at preparing trustworthy candidates for the ministry of their churches; thus Andover Seminary commenced operation in 1807. In the mid-Atlantic region, Ashbel Green, who succeeded Samuel Stanhope Smith as president of the College of New Jersey, was instrumental in establishing, adjacent to the college campus, the Theological Seminary of the Presbyterian Church in the United States of America at Princeton in 1812.[44] The name was soon shortened to Princeton Theological Seminary. The launch of the two seminaries, Andover and Princeton, symbolized disquiet after a century in which reason had been gradually permitted to encroach on the primacy of divine revelation. By 1820 Princeton had 67 students enrolled compared to Andover's 110. By 1860 the Princeton student body numbered 172 to Andover's 126; it was at that time the largest seminary in the country.[45]

Princeton Seminary had begun with a single faculty member: Archibald Alexander. The faculty soon grew to include Samuel Miller, Charles Hodge, and

41. Howard Miller, *The Revolutionary College: American Presbyterian Higher Education, 1707–1837* (New York: New York University Press, 1976), 67.

42. Mark Noll, *Princeton and the Republic, 1768–1822: The Search for a Christian Enlightenment in the Era of Samuel Stanhope Smith* (Princeton: Princeton University Press, 1989).

43. The career and legacy of Samuel Stanhope Smith are evaluated by M. L. Bradbury, "Samuel Stanhope Smith: Princeton's Accommodation to Reason," *Journal of Presbyterian History* 48, no. 3 (Fall 1970): 189–202.

44. James H. Moorhead, *Princeton Seminary in American Religion and Culture* (Grand Rapids: Eerdmans, 2012), chap. 1.

45. Peter Wallace and Mark Noll, "The Students of Princeton Seminary, 1812–1929: A Research Note," *American Presbyterians* 72, no. 3 (1994): 205.

other notable scholars; Princeton Seminary became known in the nineteenth century for its defense of Calvinistic Presbyterianism and the authority of the Bible. As such, Princeton greatly influenced the development of American evangelicalism through what became known as the "Princeton Theology."[46]

The Impact of the PhD Degree in America

Inevitably, American colleges and universities were influenced by the existence of European PhD programs, and especially those in Germany. It became quite common for university and seminary graduates in America to add one or two years of postgraduate study in Europe. Even from a seminary like Princeton, somewhat wary of Enlightenment influences, a number of its most distinguished graduates such as Hodge and Warfield augmented their education with study in Europe, including in Germany.[47] As no American university was providing doctoral study in the first half of the nineteenth century, future American scholars crossed the Atlantic to find what they could not obtain at home. Not until 1861 did Yale University graduate its first candidates for the PhD degree.[48] Five years later, Johns Hopkins University followed suit and added the seminar model of graduate education. The educational tide was turning in America in light of influence from both European and these American institutions. The dawn of the nineteenth century had confronted the churches with the dangers posed to Christianity by the expanded sway of reason; this current would by itself encourage the growth of liberalism in theology.[49] But by late in the century, the higher-critical views of the Bible, whose origin lay in European research universities, had begun to circulate. Conflict was not long in coming.

Controversies quickly erupted, centering on the origin and composition of biblical books; this in turn raised questions of their consequent authority.

46. See Thomas M. Lindsay, "The Doctrine of Scripture: The Reformers and the Princeton School," *Expositor*, 5th ser., 1 (1895): 278–93.

47. Paul Gutjahr, *Charles Hodge: Guardian of American Orthodoxy* (New York: Oxford University Press, 2011), chaps. 17–19, has detailed Hodge's study of Oriental languages at Paris and theology at Halle and Berlin. While in Europe, Hodge encountered future Andover professor Edward Robinson.

48. Ralph Rosenberg, "The First American Doctor of Philosophy Degree; a Centennial Salute to Yale," *Journal of Higher Education* 32, no. 7 (1961): 387–89.

49. William R. Hutchison, "Disapproval of Chicago: The Symbolic Trial of David Swing," *Journal of American History* 59, no. 1 (June 1972): 30–47, argued that this heresy trial of a Chicago Presbyterian minister in 1874 demonstrated that American religious liberalism did not necessarily emanate from eastern USA seminaries and universities but arose instead in settings where thoughtful individuals reflected on the Christian faith in rapidly changing cultural settings, in this case, the expanding American West.

The education and career of Charles Augustus Briggs (1841–1913) illustrate the impact that a German PhD program could have on a Presbyterian scholar. Briggs began his higher education at the University of Virginia, followed by study at Union Theological Seminary, in New York, from which he graduated. He then completed three years of postgraduate work at the University of Berlin (1866–1869), where he encountered higher-critical views of the Bible. After a brief New Jersey pastorate, in 1874 Briggs became professor of Hebrew and cognate languages at his alma mater. He was subsequently made professor of biblical theology in 1891. In conjunction with his appointment to that chair, Briggs made an inaugural address, "The Authority of Holy Scripture"; this was widely reported by the press. In a somewhat swashbuckling manner, Briggs dismissed the Mosaic authorship of the Pentateuch and rejected the attribution of the whole of Isaiah to that prophet.[50]

Long-simmering theological and ecclesial tensions within American Presbyterianism now reached a crisis point. Sixty-three presbyteries protested against Briggs's appointment to this chair, and the annual General Assembly (to which Presbyterian seminaries were subject) vetoed the appointment in 1891. At this point three things happened. His employer, Union Theological Seminary, removed itself from the jurisdiction of the General Assembly in 1892, opting instead for independence. The General Assembly, intending to deal by way of anticipation with future doctrinal challenges of a similar kind, endorsed a statement, the Portland Deliverance, which articulated the standard of orthodoxy it intended to see upheld. The Deliverance affirmed: "The General Assembly would remind all under its care that it is a fundamental doctrine that the Old and New Testaments are the inspired and infallible Word of God. Our Church holds that the inspired Word, as it came from God, is without error. The assertion of the contrary cannot but shake the confidence of the people in the sacred Books."[51] As for Briggs—while he kept his chair in Union Seminary—he was removed from the Presbyterian ministry by decision of the General Assembly of 1893.[52]

50. The inaugural address is paraphrased and analyzed in Lefferts Loetscher, ed., *The Broadening Church: A Study of the Theological Issues in the Presbyterian Church Since 1869* (Philadelphia: University of Pennsylvania Press, 1957), 50–62. Excerpts are provided in Maurice W. Armstrong, Lefferts A. Loetscher, and Charles A. Anderson, eds., *The Presbyterian Enterprise* (Philadelphia: Westminster, 1956), 251–53.

51. The Portland Deliverance, so-called because of the Assembly's meeting in Portland, Oregon, is reprinted in Armstrong, Loetscher, and Anderson, *The Presbyterian Enterprise*, 249–50. It is significant that seventy-three persons present in the General Assembly registered their dissatisfaction with this resolution.

52. Bradley Longfield, *The Presbyterian Controversy: Fundamentalists, Modernists, and Moderates* (New York: Oxford University Press, 1991), 23. Briggs was eventually received into the ministry of the Episcopal Church in 1899.

This conflict unfolding within the Presbyterian churches was unfolding also among Baptists, Methodists, and Episcopalians. A collaborative cross-denominational response to liberalism and the higher criticism was already in process of formation: eventually it would be known as fundamentalism, a movement that would fight to maintain biblical orthodoxy.

CHAPTER 16

Fundamentalism and Modernism

In the final quarter of the nineteenth century, devout Christians weathered a firestorm of controversy. New ways of thinking about science created challenges for American Presbyterians in general, and especially for those who were evangelical by conviction. We have already discussed the rapid development of the Darwinian evolutionary theory and the rise of biblical criticism in Europe, especially in German universities. Added to those powerful critiques of biblical authority were major developmental shifts in sociology and anthropology in American universities, especially in the field of comparative religion, and the rise of the uniformitarian understanding of geology. How different Christian groups responded to these challenges had profound implications for their future in the twentieth century.

SOCIOLOGY AND ANTHROPOLOGY

As the twentieth century began, courses in sociology and anthropology became popular in American colleges and universities. A key emphasis in these courses was the study of comparative religions. One book that promoted comparative religion as a discipline was J. F. Clarke's *Ten Great Religions: An Essay in Comparative Theology* (1872).[1] Clarke showed the similarities between Christianity and Confucianism, Brahmanism, Buddhism, Zoroastrianism, ancient Egyptian and Greek religions, the religion of Rome, Teutonic and Scandinavian religion, and Islam. Clarke was himself a liberal Christian; his book

---

1. J. F. Clarke, *The Ten Great Religions: An Essay in Comparative Theology* (Boston: James Osgood, 1872).

raised the question of Christianity's uniqueness. That in turn opened the way for the idea that perhaps religion was a social phenomenon that develops or evolves from primitive to complex forms over vast periods of time. Darwin's evolutionary model became highly influential in the social sciences.

A modern writer has argued that the universities' embrace of this new comparative religions approach accelerated a move that changed university departments of Christian theology into departments of religion. He argues: "In the end the university's disregard of religion may not only be a good thing for higher education but also for religion itself. . . . Because the university is incapable of evaluation of dogmatic claims and supernaturally inspired texts, the religion it tolerates tends to be the very thin variety."[2]

Uniformitarianism

A corollary to the idea that religion was a social phenomenon was called uniformitarianism, which began as an element in the study of geology. The basic premise is that uniform processes have shaped the surface of the Earth over aeons of time. This viewpoint was promoted by Charles Lyell, whose *Principles of Geology* was published in three volumes from 1830 to 1833. Lyell's works were written to overturn the long-held theory of catastrophism in shaping the Earth's surface; it postulated that cataclysmic events had left their mark on a landmass. A classic example of catastrophism was the impact of the biblical flood of the Genesis record in shaping geological landmarks such as Arizona's Grand Canyon. Lyell was a gradualist. He argued that the Earth is gradually being shaped in uniform ways by natural forces like earthquakes, weather, and erosion.[3]

The English anthropologist Sir Edward Burnett Tylor used the same principle of uniformitarianism in analyzing the development of human civilization, and especially the development of religion. Tylor's book *Primitive Culture* (1871) argued that the religion practiced by humans evolves in uniform ways.[4] For example, the polytheism of some cultures developed into monotheism over time. The basic premise was that religion was continually evolving to higher forms.

2. D. G. Hart, *The University Gets Religion* (Baltimore: Johns Hopkins University Press, 2002), 250–51.

3. See Charles Lyell, *Principles of Geology* (1830–1833; reprint, Harmondsworth: Penguin Classics, 1998). The influence of Lyell's writings on Charles Darwin has been described in chap. 13 above.

4. E. B. Tylor, *Primitive Culture*, vols. 1 and 2 (London: John Murray, 1871).

Modernism

Those Christian groups and individuals who sought to reconcile Christian dogma with current scientific advances, so as to put the church on a modern foundation, were known generally as "modernists," and their viewpoint as "modernism." Shailer Mathews provides a definition of modernism in his work *The Faith of Modernism* (1924). Though not all early modernists would fully agree with his formulation, it is helpful in describing the movement. Mathews writes: "It is not a denomination or a theology. It is the use of methods of modern science to find, state and use the permanent and central values of inherited orthodoxy in meeting the needs of a modern world. The needs themselves point the way to formulas. Modernists endeavor to reach beliefs and their application in the same way that chemists or historians reach and apply their conclusions. They do not vote in conventions and do not enforce beliefs by discipline. Modernism has no Confession."[5]

Modernism in theology was both a transatlantic and a cross-denominational phenomenon. The official reaction of the Roman Catholic Church toward modernism in the early twentieth century was illustrated by Pius X, whose pontificate extended from 1903 to 1914. In July of 1907, Pius issued the decree *Lamentabili sane exitu* (A Lamentable Departure Indeed); it openly condemned sixty-five propositions ascribed to modernism. The fourth condemned proposition read, "Even dogmatic definitions by the Church's magisterium cannot determine the genuine sense of the Sacred Scriptures," and the ninth read, "They display excessive ignorance who believe that God is really the author of the Sacred Scriptures."[6]

The Protestant response to the rise of modernism can be summarized in two general categories: (1) accommodation and (2) militant opposition. The accommodationist position appeared under several labels, including "New Theology," "Christo-centric liberalism," and "neoliberalism."[7] The goal

---

5. Shailer Mathews, *The Faith of Modernism* (New York: Macmillan, 1924), 15.

6. *Lamentabili sane exitu* (A Lamentable Departure Indeed), online at https://muse .jhu.edu/article/476893, accessed March 25, 2021. Mark S. Massa, in an essay, "'Mediating Modernism': Charles Briggs, Catholic Modernism, and an Ecumenical 'Plot,'" *Harvard Theological Review* 81, no. 4 (1988): 413–30, has shown how Union Seminary (New York) scholar Charles A. Briggs was in extensive consultation with European Roman Catholic modernists, with whom he shared a common vision.

7. The term "New Theology" was especially associated with a book of the same name authored by the British preacher R. J. Campbell (1867–1956). His espousal of theological modernism made him unacceptable within the Congregational Union; he was received into the Church of England in 1915.

of these approaches was to accommodate the interpretation of the Bible to the new revelations of science, sociology, psychology, and anthropology. The purpose of this accommodation was to preserve the church and present a way for Christians to feel comfortable with both scientific advances and the statements of Scripture. The militant opposition to this accommodating approach in time became known as "fundamentalism." George Marsden, in his work *Fundamentalism and American Culture*, defines the movement as "The demand for a strict adherence to certain theological doctrines, in reaction against Modernist theology."[8]

The Accommodationist Position

Those key leaders who embraced the accommodationist position that began in the 1850s had little in common with the American rationalist liberal exponents who were dominant at the time of the American Revolution. The rationalists had accepted the Bible as authoritative, provided that it was interpreted according to reason. This view was clearly influenced by the European Enlightenment,[9] which quickly took root in the American colonies and the fledgling United States of America. The Jefferson Bible, Holy Writ modified by the third president, was a prime example of this approach.

The "New Theology"—one of the common names for the late nineteenth-century accommodationist view—included progressive Protestants as well as some evangelicals in many denominations. Their stated goal was the "preservation" of the gospel through the harmonization of it with current insight. The latest developments in science that were so influential, beginning with Darwin's evolutionary model, called for a reformulation of basic doctrinal tenets of Christianity in ways that would appeal to the modern Christian thinker and, at the same time, put the faith on a sturdy foundation for sustained growth.

Within the USA, one influential leader promoting the "New Theology" was Henry Ward Beecher (1813–1887), the eighth child born to Presbyterian evangelist and pastor Lyman Beecher of Boston. Beecher graduated from Amherst College in 1834 and then matriculated at Lane Theological Seminary, a Presbyterian school in Cincinnati, Ohio. He served for a time as minis-

8. George M. Marsden, *Fundamentalism and American Culture* (New York: Oxford University Press, 2006), 4–5.

9. The Enlightenment, often called the "Age of Reason," was a philosophical movement of the seventeenth and eighteenth centuries that spread from Europe to America and beyond. See chap. 15.

ter of the Second Presbyterian Church of Indianapolis; there he developed
a reputation for a uniquely informal mode of preaching. Beecher became a
social reformer supporting women's suffrage, the abolition of slavery, and the
temperance movement. In the 1880s, he accepted Darwinian evolution and
claimed for himself the title "cordial Christian evolutionist"; he went on to
publish a book, *Evolution and Religion* (1885).[10] It was said of Beecher: "The
most prominent among those clergymen who developed a new, liberal theology was Rev. Henry Ward Beecher. Aware that the churches were in danger of
being left behind by 'the intelligent part of society,' Beecher maintained that
the church needed to adjust its theological system to take account of known
facts about the universe."[11]

Christian minister, social reformer, and prolific author Washington Gladden was another early advocate for the accommodationist approach.[12] Gladden
hailed from western New York State. Beginning as a newspaper apprentice, he
felt a strong call of God upon his life and became an ordained Congregationalist minister but felt the need for more training and graduated from Williams
College in 1859.[13] In his day, he was referred to as an "evangelical liberal" who
sought to "adjust Christianity to modern times."[14] Gladden's works on the
subject included *Burning Questions* (1890) and *Who Wrote the Bible?* (1891), in
which he wrote, "it is idle to try to force the narrative of Genesis into an exact
correspondence with geological science."[15]

An influential Presbyterian exponent of the accommodationist position
was William P. Merrill (1867–1954), a graduate of Rutgers University (BA 1887,
MA 1890). In 1890, Merrill gained the BD from Union Theological Seminary in
New York, at which school he was influenced by Professor Charles A. Briggs[16]
regarding historical criticism of the Bible. In two books, *Faith Building* (1886)
and *Faith and Sight* (1890),[17] Merrill showed that his theology displayed a
modernist bent. He wrote, "Theology must change as the science of man be-

10. Henry Ward Beecher, *Evolution and Religion: Eight Sermons Discussing the Bearings
of the Evolutionary Philosophy* (New York: Fords, Howard and Hulbert, 1885).

11. Winthrop S. Hudson, *Religion in American History* (1965; reprint, New York: Macmillan, 1987), 206.

12. Gladden's influence on the Social Gospel movement is explored in chap. 14 above.

13. Washington Gladden, *Recollections* (Boston: Houghton Mifflin, 1909), 56–57.

14. Timothy C. Ahrens, "Washington Gladden: Prophet of Truth and Justice," October 1,
2011, 12, http://www.first-church.org/Downloads/gladdengreenlawnspeech.pdf.

15. Washington Gladden, *Who Wrote the Bible?* (Boston: Houghton Mifflin, 1891), 352.

16. For biographical and theological background on Briggs, see pp. 243–44 above.

17. William P. Merrill, *Faith Building* (Philadelphia: Presbyterian Bd. of Publication,
1896); William P. Merrill, *Faith and Sight: Essays on the Relation of Agnosticism to Theology*
(New York: Charles Scribners, 1900).

comes more thoroughly understood. A conception of God which is true for one time may be far from adequate for another."[18] In his *Footings for Faith*, he argued along the same lines: "It is a simple fact that every advance in knowledge makes inevitable some change in the idea of God."[19]

After serving as pastor of Presbyterian churches in Pennsylvania and Illinois, he accepted a call to the Brick Presbyterian Church, one of the most prestigious pulpits in New York City. Merrill served that historic church from 1911 to 1936, during which time he "energetically promoted the advance of liberal Christianity against the opposition of militant conservatives such as J. Gresham Machen and Clarence E. Macartney. Merrill's efforts contributed significantly to the church's decision to tolerate liberalism in order to preserve the institutional unity of the church."[20]

Militant Opposition

Just as the phenomenon of theological modernism manifested itself as a transatlantic and transdenominational reality, so also were the militant responses to it. For the last half century, it has become popular to explain the rise of this widespread militant opposition by portraying it as a fusion of two influences that, in tandem, constituted fundamentalism.[21] The first was the emergence circa 1830 of dispensational premillennialism within the United Kingdom (a viewpoint transmitted to North America by the globe-trotting J. N. Darby). The second was the emergence of an increasingly conservative theology at Princeton Theological Seminary.

In the decades since this thesis was first advanced, further research has required substantial modifications to it. First among these is the recognition that forms of fundamentalism manifested themselves in the United Kingdom

18. Merrill, *Faith Building*, 4–5.

19. William P. Merrill, *Footings for Faith* (New York: Charles Scribner's Sons, 1915), 27.

20. Bradley J. Longfield, "William P. Merrill, the Brick Church, and the Fundamentalist-Modernist Conflict," *Journal of Presbyterian History* 97, no. 2 (Fall/Winter 2019): 61–62. It is evident that Longfield here uses "modernist" and "liberal" as interchangeable terms.

21. Ernest Sandeen, "Toward a Historical Interpretation of the Origins of Fundamentalism," *Church History* 36, no. 1 (1967): 66–83. Sandeen developed the argument more fully in his monograph *The Roots of Fundamentalism: British and American Millennialism: 1800–1930* (1970; reprint, Grand Rapids: Baker Books, 1978). Though it does not build upon Sandeen's foundation, affinities with his approach may be seen in David W. Bebbington's *Evangelicalism in Modern Britain: A History from the 1730s to the 1980s* (London: Unwin Hyman, 1989), chap. 3, where it is maintained that a "hardening" of evangelical Christianity occurred in the 1830s.

without any particular dependency on either of these named components.[22] These expressions of fundamentalism had in common primarily their opposition to the higher criticism of the Scriptures.[23] A second is that the Princeton theological tradition never embraced or encouraged a premillennial or dispensational understanding of Scripture. Princeton lent no assistance in any alleged fusing of these influences.[24] A third is that American fundamentalism in the late nineteenth century was—as in the United Kingdom—clearly cross-denominational, with no greater indebtedness to Princeton figures than to some in other institutions.[25]

Princeton as Nexus and Gatekeeper

With this affirmed, it is still necessary to recognize that Princeton Seminary in the post–Civil War era functioned as a kind of resource center in furnishing materials to those in the transatlantic world looking for leadership in the struggle against accommodation to modernism. In this, Princeton did not lack allies. Western (now Pittsburgh) Seminary furnished Princeton with a whole series of faculty members of note: Archibald Alexander Hodge (1823–1886) and Benjamin Warfield left the western Pennsylvania sister school to return to Princeton, where they had studied earlier. John

22. David W. Bebbington and David Ceri Jones, eds., *Evangelicalism and Fundamentalism in the United Kingdom in the Twentieth Century* (New York: Oxford University Press, 2013), shows that UK Baptist, Methodist, Presbyterian, and Church of England constituencies all generated fundamentalist responses to modernism without any particular connection to millennialism or Princeton theology.

23. A helpful example of this independence from either influence would be the opposition to higher criticism and modernism exerted by C. H. Spurgeon during what is called the "Downgrade Controversy" of the 1880s.

24. An observation clearly articulated by Bradley Longfield, *The Presbyterian Controversy: Fundamentalists, Modernists, and Moderates* (Louisville: Westminster John Knox, 1993), 220, and James Moorhead, *Princeton Seminary in American Religion and Culture* (Grand Rapids: Eerdmans, 2012), 342.

25. The Niagara Bible Conferences (1883–1897), though led by James H. Brookes (1830–1897) of St. Louis (who had only part of a seminary course at Princeton), drew in concerned theological conservatives who were graduates of other Presbyterian seminaries (Xenia, Western), Congregationalists, Baptists, and Episcopalians. One observes the same eclectic blend if one examines the list of contributors to a volume such as Nathaniel West, ed., *Premillennial Essays of the Conference Held at Holy Trinity Church, New York* (Chicago: Revell, 1879), or to R. A. Torrey, ed., *The Fundamentals* (1910–1915; reprint, Grand Rapids: Baker Books, 2003).

DeWitt returned to teach at Princeton after laboring at Lane Seminary, Cincinnati, and McCormick Seminary, Chicago. Francis Landey Patton, the Seminary's first president (from 1902), had also earlier taught at Mc-Cormick.[26] All Princeton graduates, their acceptability in the other institutions prior to returning illustrated that Princeton did not exist in isolation from sister institutions. On the contrary, Princeton—with an expanding graduate program—had become a preferred training ground for future faculty for sister institutions.

Princeton also served allies beyond the northern Presbyterian church (PCUSA). There were cordial relationships with the United Presbyterian seminary in Xenia, Ohio; with Pittsburgh Seminary; and with Columbia Seminary, Decatur, Georgia, that would live on into the twentieth century. The later-controversial professor of New Testament J. Gresham Machen (1881–1937) was still welcome to give the Sprunt Lectures in 1921 at Union Theological Seminary, Richmond, Virginia. In published form, these lectures appeared as *The Origin of Paul's Religion.*[27] When the era of definite theological polarization of the 1920s arrived, this preexisting network of collaborative relationships helped give rise to the League of Evangelical Students. This group aimed to unite students at various college, seminary, and university campuses in the advancement of sound biblical and theological teaching.[28]

However, it is also true that in the period following the 1870 reunion of the two northern "schools" of Presbyterianism (Old and New) that followed the Civil War, Princeton began to function in a way that made theological confrontation more likely. The Princeton Seminary faculty had not favored the reunion of the two factions, which had stood apart since 1837; the perception at Princeton had been that the New School—in such institutions as Lane Seminary, Cincinnati; Auburn Seminary, Auburn, New York; and Union Seminary, New York City—had embraced a loosened attitude toward the Westminster Standards. Yet, Princeton acquiesced when the two denominations determined to reunite.[29]

---

26. Moorhead, *Princeton Seminary*, biographical details furnished between pages 122 and 123.

27. Published by Macmillan, New York, 1921.

28. Jeffrey S. McDonald, "Advancing the Evangelical Mind: Melvin Grove Kyle, J. Gresham Machen, and the League of Evangelical Students," *Religions* 12, no. 7 (2021): 1–15. For further information on the League of Evangelical Students, see also Longfield, *The Presbyterian Controversy*, 52, 147, 162, 166, and Moorhead, *Princeton Seminary*, 363.

29. Paul Gutjahr, *Charles Hodge: Guardian of American Orthodoxy* (New York: Oxford University Press, 2011), chap. 53. See the treatment of the reunion of 1870 in chap. 12, above.

DISCUSSIONS ABOUT THE INERRANCY OF SCRIPTURE

Princeton Theological Seminary and Union Theological Seminary, New York, as the principal schools of theological study in the formerly separate denominations, made an attempt to provide for a common future of collaboration by agreeing, in 1880, to copublish a periodical, the *Presbyterian Review*. The periodical survived only until 1889, as its publication proved to be a failed experiment. By then, it had become clear that a single periodical could not accommodate the theological breadth that the recent reunion had encompassed. Published for the benefit of the recently united PCUSA constituency, with its multiple presbyteries and schools of theology, the periodical was edited by two professors: Archibald Alexander Hodge (representing Princeton) and Charles Augustus Briggs (representing Union, New York).[30] The periodical soon became a forum in which the views of accommodationists and militants were exchanged. Representatives of the Princeton theology laid down a "marker" with the publication of an essay in the spring of 1881. "Inspiration" was the joint production of *Review* coeditor Archibald A. Hodge and (then) Western Seminary, Pittsburgh, professor Benjamin B. Warfield. The essay was not, as is sometimes suggested, the first appearance of the notion of biblical inerrancy, but a setting forth of this existing conception with "new precision."[31] The authors were attempting to restate the existing concepts of inspiration and inerrancy in a way that took into adequate account the profusion of academic biblical studies in the nineteenth century. Hodge and Warfield faced an intellectual climate entailing even greater criticism of the text of the Bible than faced by Archibald Hodge's father, Charles Hodge, a half century earlier. Higher-critical views of the authorship, dating, and accuracy of the biblical text were proliferating in the last two decades of the nineteenth century.[32]

The Princeton theology of inspiration, as articulated by Hodge and Warfield, placed the work of divine revelation and the subsequent recording of that revelation in the context of God's ways of working in the world. They

---

30. Moorhead, *Princeton Seminary*, 234, 235. The jointly authored essay appeared in the *Presbyterian Review* 2, no. 6 (1881) and may be accessed online at https://commons.ptsem .edu/?toc=pts-journals/presr/18810206.

31. Moorhead, *Princeton Seminary*, 234. The existence of conceptions of an errorless Bible prior to the nineteenth century is explored by Kenneth J. Stewart, "Soundings in the Evangelical Doctrine of Scripture, 1650–1830: A Re-examination of David Bebbington's Theory," in *The Emergence of Evangelicalism: Exploring Historical Continuities*, ed. Michael A. G. Haykin and Kenneth J. Stewart (Leicester: IVP, 2008), 394–416.

32. As described in chap. 15 above.

acknowledged an obligation to recognize both the divine and human elements of God's revelation. The author is God,[33] and his message is communicated in a truly human style and expression. The Holy Spirit drew upon the unique personalities, intellects, backgrounds, and interests of the human authors of the Scriptures. God chose and used men as they were, across sixteen centuries in a divinely regulated "concurrence."[34]

The Hodge-Warfield essay was the first to make the point that the inerrancy of the text upon which the authority of the Bible rested was only truly present in the "original autographs" of Scripture; take, for example, the first copy of Paul's letter to the Romans. The science of textual criticism had long demonstrated that transcriptional errors had crept into the manual copying of biblical texts over time; the job of lower criticism[35] had been to ascertain the earliest and truest possible form of the text. Thus when Hodge and Warfield used the word "inerrancy," it was regularly followed by the phrase "in the original autographs."

But to this point we have concentrated on only one aspect of what might be called a "conversation" of views within the *Presbyterian Review*. Hodge and Warfield, as it turned out, saw their cautious perspective elaborated further by other writers who cautioned about the writings of particular German higher critics.[36] But from the other side came the determined and forceful perspective of Charles Augustus Briggs, Hodge's coeditor from Union Seminary, New York City. In the issue of the *Presbyterian Review* immediately following the "Inspiration" article, Briggs—making explicit reference to the views of the other authors—pursued the theme with an article entitled "Critical Theories of the Sacred Scriptures in Relation to Inspiration: I. The Right, Duty and Limits of Biblical Criticism."[37] In 1883, he followed up with "A Critical Study of the History of the Higher Criticism with Special Reference to the Pentateuch."[38] The *Review*, instead of being (as hoped) a peaceable forum in which the diverse views of the newly united denomination could be brought into conversation and dialogue, was proving to be a display case of two trajectories not likely to converge.

33. Archibald A. Hodge and Benjamin Warfield, "Inspiration," *Presbyterian Review* 2, no. 6 (April 1881): 225–60.

34. Hodge and Warfield, "Inspiration," 230.

35. "Lower criticism" is commonly referred to as "textual criticism." The goal of textual criticism is to get back to the earliest version of a given passage of the Bible.

36. So, for instance, "The Theory of Professor Kuenen," *Presbyterian Review* 1, no. 2 (1880).

37. *Presbyterian Review* 2, no. 7 (1881).

38. *Presbyterian Review* 4, no. 13 (1883).

As it turned out, a decade later, on account of his embrace of higher criticism of the Bible and dogmatic assertions of scriptural error, Briggs was removed from the Presbyterian ministry; and his employer, Union Theological Seminary, terminated its relationship with the PCUSA. As of 1893, it became an independent school. In the 1890s, far from being isolated from the Presbyterian mainstream, the Princeton theologians were standing in that mainstream and were widely supported. In 1893, the General Assembly, meeting at Portland, Oregon, declared that an affirmation of the inerrancy of the Bible was henceforth required of all who would be ordained to the ministry.[39] Yet, the pressure by advocates of theological accommodation was still growing with each passing decade.

Confessional Revision and Mergers

Meanwhile, Presbyterians had expressed reservations about parts of the Westminster Confession for decades, objecting to the alleged harshness of predestination in chapter 3 ("Of God's Eternal Decree") and the phrase "elect infants" in chapter 10 ("Of Effectual Calling"). An 1890 committee was appointed to draft a revision with the directions not to propose "any alterations or amendments that will in any way impair the integrity of the Reformed or Calvinistic system of doctrine taught in the Confession of Faith."[40] An 1892 presbytery vote on the proposed revisions failed to reach the two-thirds approval required for constitutional amendment. By 1900, thirty-seven presbyteries had requested revision or a new creed or both. A committee was appointed to survey the presbyteries; in addition to objections to phrases in chapters 3 and 10, concerns were raised about calling the pope "anti-Christ," the evident failure to affirm the universal love of God, an inadequate treatment of the Holy Spirit, silence on the worldwide mission of the church, and the need for updating seventeenth-century terminology. The proposed revisions received the two-thirds vote required by presbyteries, and the 1903 General Assembly completed the process of officially incorporating the changes into the church's constitution.

The approved revisions included a "Declaratory Statement," stating that the doctrine of election should be "held in harmony" with God's love for all

---

39. Excerpts of this Portland Affirmation are provided in Maurice Armstrong, Lefferts Loetscher, and Charles Anderson, eds., *The Presbyterian Enterprise* (Philadelphia: Westminster, 1956), 249. It is also true that eighty-seven delegates to the General Assembly protested the legality of adding this extraconfessional standard.

40. Lefferts Loetscher, *The Broadening Church: A Study of Theological Issues in the Presbyterian Church Since 1869* (Philadelphia: University of Pennsylvania Press, 1957), 46.

humankind. There was also a statement declaring that all dying in infancy are saved by Christ. Two new chapters—"Of the Holy Spirit" and "Of the Love of God and Missions"—were added to the Confession of Faith. The previous Assembly (1902) had also adopted a "Brief Statement of Faith" with sixteen short articles. Some Presbyterians expressed reservations about these new statements, but most embraced the additions, believing that the "generic Calvinism of the Standards" was still intact. In 1942, the Southern Presbyterian Church added essentially the same two chapters to the Confession.

One immediate by-product of the 1903 revisions was a reunion overture from the Cumberland Presbyterian Church. The overture heralded the new confessional revisions as removing the "fatalism" in the doctrinal standards to which the Cumberland movement had long objected. The Cumberland proposal was resisted by those opposed to compromise with Arminians (e.g., B. B. Warfield). Nevertheless, 194 of 241 presbyteries approved the reunion, which was officially consummated in 1906.[41] About a thousand Cumberland churches joined, but a remnant decided not to participate, preferring to maintain their distinct identity as the Cumberland Presbyterian Church. Another ecclesiastical addition was the Calvinistic Methodist Church in the USA (originally known as the Welsh Calvinistic Church, 1828–1869); it merged into the PCUSA in 1920. The Calvinistic Methodist Church had its roots in the eighteenth-century Welsh Revival led by Howell Harris. Welsh immigrants to New York brought the church with them in the 1790s.

THE FURTHER ADVANCE OF FORCES OF ACCOMMODATION

By 1910, the northern General Assembly needed to return to the issue of doctrinal integrity, and it specified five key "essential and necessary doctrines" that, while parts of the doctrinal standards of the church, were in process of being undermined in that concessive era. Included were the inerrancy of the Bible, the virgin birth of Christ, the importance of actual miracles in Jesus's earthly ministry, the death of Christ as a satisfaction for human sin, and Christ's bodily resurrection.[42] But actions like those of 1910 were turning into rearguard efforts that would prove unsustainable in the long run; those of traditional and conservative views were beginning to lose heart in the quest to uphold the church's doctrinal standards.

---

41. See Bradley J. Longfield, *Presbyterians and American Culture: A History* (Louisville: Westminster John Knox, 2013), 139–41; also chap. 12 above.

42. Armstrong, Loetscher, and Anderson, *Presbyterian Enterprise*, 281.

The next assault came in the 1924 circulation of the Auburn Affirmation, a document eventually signed by 1,234 Presbyterian ministers. It was a plea for the maintaining of unity within the Presbyterian church by permitting a distinction to be made between elements of the Christian faith and explanatory theories used to elaborate them. On this plan, one could affirm support for biblical inspiration without agreeing to any common understanding of what that meant or ensured. So strongly was this supported that, by 1927, the General Assembly agreed that it would no longer (as it had since 1910) attempt to specify "essential and necessary doctrines."[43] In the space of thirty years, an existing consensus of conservative orthodoxy had been reduced to being one option among others.

While this process unfolded in the 1920s, there was one small victory for orthodoxy and also a further sign of erosion. The first was the eventual removal of Harry Emerson Fosdick (1878–1969), a Baptist of modernist opinions, from the pulpit of First Presbyterian Church, New York; there he had served an extended interim ministry. The Presbytery of New York, after a very prolonged process, was required by the action of the 1923 General Assembly to either examine Fosdick as to his fitness for Presbyterian ministry in keeping with the doctrinal standards of the church, or dismiss him.[44] Fosdick was removed—only to shift the scene of his ministry to the newly built Riverside Church, constructed with Rockefeller wealth.

Also during this period, the General Assembly of 1925 sent a commission to investigate dissension within Princeton Theological Seminary. While all in the faculty held conservative theological positions, they no longer agreed on whether the unsettling trends of the denomination required militancy or tolerance. The investigation by this commission would lead, eventually, to the reorganization of the seminary, a reorganization intended to bring it to reflect the denomination's existing diversity.[45] That would lead to the departure of a committed element of the Princeton faculty led by Professor J. Gresham Machen and the founding of an independent seminary at Philadelphia.[46]

---

43. Armstrong, Loetscher, and Anderson, *Presbyterian Enterprise*, 284.

44. Loetscher, *The Broadening Church*, 113, 114. The conflict over Fosdick's questionable ministry at First Presbyterian Church, New York, has recently been explored by Paul Hunt in an article, "Closer Than They Appear: The Surprising Similarities between Clarence E. Macartney and Harry Emerson Fosdick," *Journal of Presbyterian History* 96, no. 2 (2018): 62–74.

45. Moorhead, *Princeton Seminary*, chap. 13. See also John W. Hart, "Princeton Theological Seminary: The Re-organization of 1929," *Journal of Presbyterian History* 58, no. 2 (1980): 124–40.

46. Westminster Seminary, Philadelphia.

It was therefore in those closing decades of the nineteenth and open-ing decades of the twentieth century that evangelical Presbyterians found themselves as cobelligerents with other theological conservatives in Baptist, Methodist, Episcopal, and Congregational churches. These same erosions of Christian orthodoxy had been propelling the growth of the nondenom-inational Niagara Bible Conferences, the launch of the Bible School Move-ment,[47] and the composition and publication of *The Fundamentals*. The latter project, first published in booklet form, was undertaken by two wealthy Presbyterian brothers of California, Lyman and Milton Stewart. Completed under three successive editors, A. C. Dixon, Louis Meyer, and R. A. Torrey, *The Fundamentals* were eventually distributed without cost to every English-speaking minister in the world. Over three million booklets were sent out.[48] Presbyterians from both Scotland and the USA presented the case for evan-gelical orthodoxy alongside Baptists, Episcopalians, Congregationalists, and Methodists.[49]

THE SCOPES TRIAL OF 1925

Although evangelical Presbyterians took more than one stance in their ap-praisal of Darwin's *Origin of Species*,[50] it can safely be said that evangelical Christianity in general suffered a major public relations setback in 1925 that affected the movement for decades to come in the eyes of many Americans. The catalyst for this was a court case in Dayton, Tennessee, known formally as *The State of Tennessee v. John Thomas Scopes*. The more common names were the Scopes trial and the monkey trial.[51]

The trial centered on the Butler Act, named after John W. Butler, a Ten-nessee state assemblyman who wrote the legislation. This law, enacted on March 25, 1925, made it unlawful to teach human evolution in any state-funded school in Tennessee. The American Civil Liberties Union (ACLU)

---

47. Virginia Brereton, *Training God's Army: The American Bible School, 1880–1949* (Bloomington: Indiana University Press, 1990).

48. George M. Marsden, *Fundamentalism and American Culture* (Oxford: Oxford Uni-versity Press, 2006), 118–19.

49. Character studies of some of the contributors to the collection are provided in Beb-bington and Jones, eds., *Evangelicalism and Fundamentalism in the United Kingdom in the Twentieth Century*, chaps. 1 and 2.

50. See chap. 13 above.

51. See Edward J. Larson, *Summer of the Gods: The Scopes Trial and America's Continuing Debate over Science and Religion* (New York: Basic Books, 2006).

agreed to finance a test case to determine the legality of this law. John T. Scopes, against whom a charge was laid, was a twenty-four-year-old high school science and math teacher at Dayton. He had substituted for the regular biology teacher and openly admitted that he had violated the Butler Act by discussing Darwinian evolution; he had employed a chart contained in the science textbook.

Leading the prosecution for the state of Tennessee were Tom Stewart and John R. Neal. The Baptist pastor William Bell Riley, founder of the World Christian Fundamentals Association, encouraged William Jennings Bryan to join the team as co-counsel in order to fortify the prosecution's position. Bryan was seen as raising the profile of the prosecution, as he had served the United States as a secretary of state and been the Democratic nominee for the presidency three times. Bryan, a Nebraskan, was also a lifelong Presbyterian.

The ACLU countered this recruitment of Bryan with Clarence Darrow, a highly respected attorney known for the intelligence and wit he employed in arguing several famous cases.[52] Darrow, in contrast to Bryan, was an outspoken agnostic who was aided in the defense of Scopes by Charles F. Potter, a Unitarian preacher and authority on the Bible. The two celebrity counsels in the trial were both nearing the end of their respective careers; Bryan was sixty-five years old and died within weeks of the trial's end. Darrow was sixty-eight.

In legal terms, the trial was very simple. Scopes, who never testified, was found guilty of breaking the law and was ordered to pay a fine of $100. The defense appealed the verdict on several grounds to the Supreme Court of Tennessee, which determined that the statute was constitutional.

The impact of the trial on Christians identifying with fundamentalism, however, was enormous. One historian reported: "The press coverage of the 'Monkey Trial' was overwhelming. The front pages of newspapers like the *New York Times* were dominated by the case for days. More than 200 newspaper reporters from all parts of the country and two from London were in Dayton."[53] The real drama of the trial, and the focus of most of the journalistic analysis, was found in the arguments and counterarguments presented by Bryan and Darrow. Darrow wished to focus on questioning the veracity of the Bible in matters of science. The defense had brought several scientists to Dayton, hoping that their testimony would prove the Butler Act to be flawed. The judge, however, insisted the issue was not whether the Butler Act was constitutional but rather whether it had been violated.

52. Joy Hakim, *War, Peace, and All That Jazz* (New York: Oxford University Press, 1995), 44.
53. Hakim, *War, Peace, and All That Jazz*, 211–13.

On the seventh day of the trial, the defense asked the judge if Bryan, who was prosecuting, could take the dock as a hostile witness and face questions from Darrow. It was argued that Bryan was reputed to be an expert on the Bible, and that belief in the truthfulness of the biblical record on matters of science was germane to the defense. Bryan had agreed, on the basis of Darrow's assurances that he would in turn take the dock and allow Bryan to cross-examine him. The pointed questions that Darrow posed came primarily from the book of Genesis. Examples include: "Was Eve actually created from a rib of Adam?" and "Where did Adam find a wife for Cain?"[54] Darrow's motive was to demonstrate that Bryan's interpretation of the Bible ran counter to virtually every finding of modern science. By prosecuting Scopes, urged Darrow in his critique of Bryan, "You insult every man of science and learning in the world because he does not believe in your fool religion."[55] Bryan's rejoinder was just as pointed: "The reason I am answering is not for the benefit of the Superior Court. It is to keep these gentlemen from saying I was afraid to meet them and let them question me, and I want the Christian world to know that any atheist, agnostic, unbeliever, can question me anytime as to my belief in God, and I will answer him."[56] Bryan never got his chance to cross-examine Darrow, because the judge ruled the whole hostile witness examination to be irrelevant and expunged it from the record.

The jury met for nine minutes before reaching its verdict. Scopes was found guilty, and the judge ordered him to pay a $100 fine. The verdict was later over-turned on a technicality; the fine was to be set by the jury and not the judge, and judges could not impose a fine greater than $50. However, the impact of the 1925 trial would last for decades. Fundamentalism was portrayed as a movement that was foolish, antiscience, and obscurantist. Thirty-five years later, a whole new generation of Americans would be influenced by a reenact-ment of the Scopes trial in the 1960 hit film *Inherit the Wind*.

Fundamentalist expressions of Christianity began to lose momentum in the interwar era, during which many forms of evangelicalism exiled them-selves from conventional forms of higher education. New colleges and semi-naries were eventually erected to provide alternatives to institutions that were perceived to be no longer trustworthy. Evangelical Presbyterians increasingly trained their ministers in alternative schools such as Dallas Seminary (founded as Evangelical Theological College in 1924), Westminster Seminary (1929),

---

54. Jeffrey P. Moran, *The Scopes Trial: A Brief History with Documents* (New York: Bed-ford/St. Martin's, 2002).

55. Moran, *The Scopes Trial*, 155.

56. Moran, *The Scopes Trial*, 157.

Fuller Theological Seminary (1947), Talbot Theological Seminary (1952), and Covenant Theological Seminary (1956). Later, these resources would be augmented by the founding of Reformed Theological Seminary (1966) and Gordon-Conwell Theological Seminary (1969). Fundamentalism, reconstituted in the 1940s as "new evangelicalism," continues into the twenty-first century as a movement of growing influence.[57]

---

57. Chaps. 17 and 18 of this volume describe the important postwar resurgence.

CHAPTER 17

Two World Wars and Reaching the World for Christ

The outbreak of two world wars profoundly influenced the story of the American Presbyterian churches in the twentieth century. Prior to World War I, American church culture reflected diverse values displayed in the Progressive Era. Some Americans, having seen the government intervene to curb unrestrained business trusts, were open to seeing this power focused abroad. Others, wary of the imperialist overtones of the Spanish-American War and the building of the Panama Canal, wanted an America that stayed at home; there was a strong antiwar movement. Presbyterians tended to favor American neutrality.

WOODROW WILSON, NEUTRALITY, AND AMERICA'S ENTRY INTO WORLD WAR I

Woodrow Wilson (1856–1924), the twenty-eighth president and a devout Presbyterian, hoped to keep the United States out of the conflict in Europe. He, like many others, pushed for a peaceful resolution. President Wilson's Presbyterian credentials were impressive. His father, John Ruggles Wilson, was a Presbyterian minister and stated clerk from 1865 to 1898 of the Presbyterian Church (PCUS). Young Woodrow was educated at Davidson College in North Carolina, an institution affiliated with the PCUS. In 1873, Wilson became a communicant member of the First Presbyterian Church of Columbia, South Carolina, and retained that membership throughout his life.[1]

Wilson embraced the idea of a career in academia in 1883, while still a student at Johns Hopkins University in Baltimore. He received his PhD there in

---

1. August Heckscher, *Woodrow Wilson* (Norwalk, CT: Easton, 1991), 23.

1886, and, having taught a variety of courses in history and political science, earned a reputation as an excellent lecturer. He then became a professor at Princeton University, where he was elected by the university trustees to the Chair of Jurisprudence and Political Economy in 1890. Two years later, those same trustees promoted him to president of Princeton.[2]

His destiny was to fill a different office and a higher calling, however, as he was first elected governor of New Jersey in 1911 and then president of the United States in 1913. In April 1917, five months after winning reelection on a platform of American neutrality, Wilson asked Congress to declare war against Germany due to aggressive new tactics in submarine warfare and a German diplomatic effort to turn Mexico against the United States.[3] Most Protestant denominations supported Wilson's new tack. This was especially true for Presbyterians, as prominent evangelists and intellectuals sided with their Presbyterian president. One notable exception was William Jennings Bryan, Wilson's secretary of state in his first administration; this devout Presbyterian resigned his office to protest the president's response to the sinking of the RMS *Lusitania*. German U-boats torpedoed the ocean liner on June 9, 1915. Over 1,100 passengers and crew perished, yet Bryan did not wish to offend the Germans.[4]

EVANGELIST BILLY SUNDAY

By contrast, Presbyterian evangelist Billy Sunday (1862–1935) was one of President Wilson's most loyal, outspoken, and flamboyant supporters in the cause of defeating the Central Powers[5] in the war. Born in a log cabin in Iowa, Sunday endured childhood poverty, a broken family unit, and a short stint in an orphanage. At the age of fourteen, he was making his way in the world by working at various odd jobs in Nevada, Iowa. In high school, things began to look up as coaches noticed that Sunday was an exceptionally fast runner. He was to make his mark in life initially as a baseball player and then as an evangelist. Because of his ability to steal bases, Sunday was given a chance to try out for the Chicago White Stockings (known since 1900 as the Chicago

2. Heckscher, *Woodrow Wilson*, 110.

3. Barbara W. Tuchman, *The Zimmerman Telegram*, 2nd ed. (London: Macmillan, 1966); Christopher Andrew, *For the President's Eyes Only* (New York: HarperCollins, 1996), 42.

4. Diana Preston, *Lusitania: An Epic Tragedy* (Waterville, ME: Thorndike, 2002), 216–17. Bryan did not support the president's strongly worded diplomatic communication with Germany.

5. Germany, Austria-Hungary, the Ottoman Empire, and Bulgaria.

White Sox); they signed him in 1883. He moved to the Pittsburgh Pirates and, in 1890, to the Philadelphia Athletics. Sunday astonished baseball fans with his speed; he could run the bases of a major league diamond in fourteen seconds; in the 1890 season he stole eighty-four bases.[6] However, his life's trajectory had changed course in 1886 when he became a Christian at Chicago's Pacific Garden Mission.[7] Five years later, he retired from baseball.

After a short time working with the YMCA, Sunday joined an evangelistic team led by J. Wilbur Chapman (1859–1918), the Presbyterian evangelist.[8] Sunday worked with him for two years, and when Chapman returned to urban pastoral ministry, Sunday launched his own career as a freelance evangelist. Seeking to be ordained, he approached the PCUSA and, in 1903, was examined by the Presbytery of Chicago. They found that he knew very little theology but had "an amazing capacity to win souls." He was ordained at the Jefferson Park Presbyterian Church, where he held membership.[9] His ability to move people with his flamboyant preaching was extraordinary. Though Sunday continued his evangelistic crusades into the 1930s, his years of greatest influence were in the century's second decade.

A Revival of Pacifism in the Buildup to World War II

World War I, also known as "the Great War," raged from 1914 to 1918. It has been estimated that 70 million combatants met in battle; this conflict qualifies as one of the deadliest in all of history.[10] In the United States, President Wilson confidently called World War I "the war to end all wars," and the phrase became associated with him even though he only used it once.[11] The victors—Great Britain with her empire, the United States, France, Italy, and Japan—imposed their will upon the Central Powers in 1919 at the Paris Peace Confer-

---

6. Wendy Knickerbocker, *Sunday at the Ballpark: Billy Sunday's Professional Baseball Career* (Lanham, MD: Scarecrow, 2000), 2–3, 135–37; Lyle Dorsett, *Billy Sunday and the Redemption of Urban America* (Grand Rapids: Eerdmans, 1991).

7. Elijah P. Brown, *The Real Billy Sunday* (New York: Revell, 1914), 70–78.

8. Ross A. Purdy, "The Development of John Wilbur Chapman's Life and Thought: 1859–1918" (PhD diss., University of Stirling, 2016).

9. William McLoughlin Jr., *Billy Sunday Was His Real Name* (Chicago: University of Chicago Press, 1955), 1–9.

10. Anthony Pagden, *Worlds at War: The 2,500-Year Struggle between East and West* (Oxford: Oxford University Press, 2008), 407.

11. Kathleen H. Jamieson, *Eloquence in an Electronic Age: The Transformation of Political Speechmaking* (Oxford: Oxford University Press, 1990), 99.

ence. Individual treaties were made with specific countries, the best known being the Treaty of Versailles, which imposed reparations upon Germany.[12]

During the twenty-year interwar period (1919–1939), a renewed Christian pacifist program gained momentum in many Protestant denominations. It was modeled on the liberal ideal of a reconstruction of society,[13] yet few endorsed an absolute pacifist position. Once again, the campaign for peace was undermined by German military aggression. In March 1936, Germany began a military reoccupation of its Rhine Valley region; by 1938 Germany had absorbed Austria and forcibly occupied a German-speaking region of Czechoslovakia. There followed the "lightning war" (*der Blitzkrieg*), as Nazi armies overran Poland. The rapid conquest of France quickly followed.

Sympathy for America's greatest ally, Great Britain, tugged at American hearts during the evacuation of British troops from the beaches of Dunkirk in early June 1940 and throughout the heroic Battle of Britain from August through October of that year. Then the war came home to Americans with the Japanese air raid on Pearl Harbor on the morning of December 7, 1941. This cascade of events ended all hope for a peaceful resolution to the conflict. The United States would enter World War II and declare war on Japan and Germany with its allies.

At the start of the war, the issue of Christian pacifism was already in flux. American evangelicals and social conservatives in mainline denominations, including the Presbyterian church, tended to hold pacifism suspect, as if it were an outgrowth of modernism and liberal theology. However, there was also a growing nonpacifist movement embraced by liberals.[14] This movement was championed in the United States by the German Reformed scholar Reinhold Niebuhr (1892–1971) of Union Theological Seminary in New York City.

Niebuhr developed a response to pacifism and war known as Christian realism. He insisted that the church must be involved in resolving critical social issues. Christians must condemn and resist the reality of a world in which powerful nations exercised naked coercion toward neighboring countries in Asia and Europe.[15] Such a position began to emerge in the official documents of the Presbyterian church. In the 1940 General Assembly of the PCUSA, we

12. See Michael S. Neilberg, *The Treaty of Versailles: A Concise History* (Oxford: Oxford University Press, 2017).

13. See Umphrey Lee, *The Historic Church and Modern Pacifism* (New York: Abingdon-Cokesbury, 1943), 203–9. See also Vernon Holloway, "A Review of American Religious Pacifism," *Religion in Life* 19 (Summer 1950): 372.

14. See Donald B. Meyer, *The Protestant Search for Political Realism, 1919–1941* (Berkeley: University of California Press, 1960).

15. See Arthur M. Schlesinger Jr., "Reinhold Niebuhr's Role in American Political

find the issue of the morality of war discussed: "Good and honest men differ violently upon what is the right and the Christian thing to do."[16] The following year, the same body began to distinguish between "aggressive" and "defensive" war in their annual report.[17]

REASSESSING MISSIONS AND PEARL BUCK

With the financial backing of John D. Rockefeller Jr., a reevaluation of the effectiveness of American foreign missions was begun in 1930. Seven major denominations participated: Presbyterian Church in the USA, United Presbyterian Church of North America, the Reformed Church in America, the Baptist church (Northern), the Congregational Church, the Episcopal Church, and the Methodist church. Five representatives from each denomination were invited to be directors for the Laymen's Foreign Missions Inquiry. Their investigation focused on missionaries in Burma, China, India, and Japan. The Institute for Social and Religious Research was organized to interview these missionaries and was led by Harvard professor William Ernest Hocking. The resulting seven-volume report with recommendations was published under the title *Re-thinking Missions: A Laymen's Inquiry after One Hundred Years.*[18]

Re-thinking Missions strongly suggested that in light of the "many changes in the world during the past century," three crucial areas had to be addressed: (1) the theological outlook of missions; (2) a new world culture that demanded a reorientation of Protestant missions; and (3) the rise of nationalism in the East as a reaction against Western domination and cultural control.[19] As to theological shifts, the authors argued that Western missionaries should move away from "traditional claims about the everlasting torments of hell, God's punitive justice, or similar realities which had provided the original mo-

---

Thought and Life," in *The Politics of Hope*, rev. ed. (Princeton: Princeton University Press, 2007), 123–58.

16. *Minutes of the General Assembly of the Presbyterian Church in the United States of America* (Philadelphia: Office of the General Assembly, 1940), 180.

17. *Minutes of the General Assembly of the Presbyterian Church in the United States of America* (Philadelphia: Office of the General Assembly, 1941), 167.

18. William E. Hocking, *Re-thinking Missions: A Laymen's Inquiry after One Hundred Years* (New York: Harper & Bros., 1932), 18. See also John Fitzmier and Randall Balmer, "The Hocking Report and Presbyterian Missions," in *The Diversity of Discipleship: Presbyterians and Twentieth-Century Christian Witness*, ed. Milton Coalter, John Mulder, and Louis B. Weeks (Louisville: Westminster John Knox, 1991), 105–25.

19. Hocking, *Re-thinking Missions*, 18.

tive of Protestant missions much of its urgency."[20] A fundamental change in worldview had taken place. The report claimed, "There is little disposition to believe that sincere and aspiring seekers after God in other religions are to be damned."[21]

By means of reorientation, a new missions approach should emphasize "a simpler, more universal, less contentious and less expressive religion coming into human consciousness which might be called the 'religion of modern man,' or the 'religious aspects of the coming world culture.'"[22] In view of rising nationalism, the commission summarized: "We believe that the time has come to set the educational and other philanthropic aspects of missions work free from organized responsibility to the work of conscious and direct evangelism. . . . We must work with greater faith in invisible successes, be willing to give largely without any preaching, to cooperate wholeheartedly with non-Christian agencies for social improvement, and to foster the initiative of the Orient in defining the ways in which we shall be invited to help."[23]

Many Presbyterians were not pleased with the report. One of the most controversial general conclusions was that Christian missionaries should join with other religions rather than struggle against them. The publication of *Re-thinking Missions* resulted in the seven sponsoring denominational bodies distancing themselves from this project and its findings. The Presbyterian Board of Foreign Missions, for example, quickly affirmed the board's commitment to evangelism and to Jesus Christ as the only Lord and Savior.[24]

Presbyterian leaders were surprised and chagrined to discover that, two weeks before the release of *Re-thinking Missions*, their missionary Pearl Buck (1892–1973) had spoken to an audience of two thousand women at New York City's Astor Hotel on the theme "Is there a case for foreign missions?" They were chagrined that the most notable Presbyterian missionary of the time seemed very guarded in her answer to that question. Although she did give a qualified yes, in many ways Buck seemed to echo the findings put forth in *Re-thinking Missions*. A gifted speaker, Pearl Buck was then forty years old and furloughing in America. She had grown up in China as the daughter of Presbyterian missionaries and was now the wife of a Presbyterian missionary

20. Hocking, *Re-thinking Missions*, 19.
21. Hocking, *Re-thinking Missions*, 326–27.
22. Hocking, *Re-thinking Missions*, 19–22.
23. Hocking, *Re-thinking Missions*, 326.
24. Fitzmier and Balmer, "The Hocking Report and Presbyterian Missions," 111. See also Grant Wacker, "Second Thoughts on the Great Commission: Liberal Protestants and Foreign Missions, 1890–1940," in *Earthen Vessels: American Evangelicals and Foreign Missions, 1880–1940*, ed. Joel Carpenter and Wilbert Shenk (Grand Rapids: Eerdmans, 1990), 281–300.

to China. Over a long career, Buck had changed; by the 1920s and 1930s she had "displayed increasingly liberal attitudes . . . from the 1940s to the end of her life, [she] reflected post-Christian if not anti-Christian feelings."[25]

Buck was a popular speaker and writer, due in part to her second novel, *The Good Earth*, for which she had been awarded the Pulitzer Prize for Literature. In an article in *Cosmopolitan* magazine in 1933 entitled "Supernaturalism," Buck addressed the problem of trying to preach about the supernatural aspects of the gospel story in the modern age.[26] In her 1954 autobiography, *My Several Worlds*, she indicated that she no longer supported conversionary mission work. "I have never been an evangelical missionary, and indeed abhor the general notion." In fact, she discounted all types of overseas missionary work, including evangelistic, educational, and medical work, characterizing them all as essentially imperialistic. She wrote, "The effrontery of all this still makes my soul shrink."[27]

There were both immediate and longer-term consequences arising from the recommendations of the Hocking Report and the unguarded disclosures of Pearl Buck. An immediate consequence was that numerous conservative northern Presbyterians, whose Board of Foreign Missions had distanced itself from the Hocking Report but still supported Pearl Buck, reacted by launching the Independent Board for Presbyterian Foreign Missions in 1933.[28] Though its operations were small by comparison and represented no sizable threat to the denominational agency, the challenge it posed led, ultimately, to the expulsion from the ministry of the northern church a group of notable conservative ministers in March 1935 and the creation of a small rival denomination, the Orthodox Presbyterian Church, in June 1936.[29]

The longer-term implications became more obvious in the second half of the twentieth century.[30] Presbyterian missions clearly began to move steadily

25. Grant Wacker, "Pearl Buck and the Waning of the Missionary Impulse," *Church History* 72, no. 4 (December 2003): 852–74; note especially 856.

26. "Supernaturalism," *Cosmopolitan*, May 1933.

27. Pearl S. Buck, *My Several Worlds* (New York: Pocket Books, 1956), 96–97.

28. See chap. 16 above.

29. Among the Presbyterian leaders removed from the ministry in this controversy were J. Gresham Machen and J. Oliver Buswell. Machen biographer D. G. Hart, in *Defending the Faith: J. Gresham Machen and the Crisis of Conservative Protestantism in Modern America* (Baltimore: Johns Hopkins University Press, 1994), 147–56, allows that Machen's persistent involvement in this scheme unduly jeopardized the future usefulness of Westminster Theological Seminary, Philadelphia (founded 1929). Until the removal of Machen and supporters from the ministry of the PCUSA, the seminary's graduates were themselves eligible to serve in the PCUSA.

30. Paul A. Varg, "Motives in Protestant Missions, 1890–1917," *Church History* 23 (1954),

away from a traditional emphasis on evangelism and discipleship and toward the promotion of education, health, medical care, reconciliation, etc. The change of missionary philosophy was spelled out in a 1961 United Presbyterian Church in the United States of America (UPCUSA) document, *An Advisory Letter*; the denomination's mission board was henceforth known as the Commission on Ecumenical Missions and Relations. Facing similar challenges, concerned southern Presbyterians (PCUS), led by Clayton Bell (of Highland Park Presbyterian Church, Dallas) and former missionary to Brazil Jules Spach, established the Outreach Foundation; this attempted to maintain earlier denominational missionary initiatives. Another such initiative was the Frontier Missionary Fellowship, launched by Presbyterian missionary Ralph Winter. This missionary initiative gave rise, in turn, to the establishing of the US Center for World Mission at Pasadena, California. [31]

Evangelistic and missionary work was falling more and more to such nondenominational agencies. British missionary Hudson Taylor (1832–1905), the founder of the China Inland Mission, is often referred to as creator of the model for faith missions.[32] Interdenominational mission agencies such as Latin American Mission USA (LAM), Sudan Interior Mission (SIM), The Evangelical Alliance Mission (TEAM), Wycliffe Bible Translators, and the Bible and Medical Missionary Fellowship (now Interserve) were widely supported by evangelical Presbyterian congregations. Evangelical Presbyterians saw these mission organizations as alternatives to denominational agencies, which had forfeited their trust.

PRESBYTERIANS AND THE POST-1940S EVANGELICAL RESURGENCE

"God has come to town," wrote the pastor of Boston's historic Park Street Church in 1950, and "if New England can receive such a shaking of God under the stripling who like David of old went forth to meet the giant of the enemy, then we believe that God is ready to shake America to its foundations in revival."[33] The "stripling" was a young evangelist by the name of Billy Graham, baptized and raised by his parents in the Associate Reformed Presbyterian

---

reprinted in *Modern American Protestantism and Its World*, ed. Martin E. Marty, vol. 10, *Fundamentalism and Evangelicalism* (Munich: K. G. Saur, 1993), 6–15.

31. Scott W. Sunquist and Caroline N. Becker, *A History of Presbyterian Missions, 1944–2007* (Louisville: Geneva, 2008), 13–35, 115–21.

32. Hudson Taylor, *A Retrospect* (London: Morgan & Scott, 1906).

33. Harold John Ockenga, "Boston Stirred by Revival," *United Evangelical Action*, January 15, 1950, 4.

Church of Charlotte, North Carolina.[34] The "pastor," trained at Princeton Theological Seminary and Westminster Theological Seminary and ordained in 1931 by the Presbytery of Pittsburgh, was Harold John Ockenga.[35] And the "shaking of God," as Graham and Ockenga were both convinced, was the remarkable spiritual awakening that seemed to be sweeping across North America and around the globe during the 1940s and 1950s.[36]

Indeed, the largest auditoriums and stadiums across the country—and increasingly around the world—were being filled again and again by young women and men hungry for the gospel. In Chicago, Orchestra Hall was packed to the rafters in May of 1944 to hear Billy Graham, and in October of that same year over twenty-eight thousand jammed into Chicago Stadium to hear another evangelist named Merv Rosell. Moreover, by the following spring, a reported seventy thousand eager listeners had gathered at Soldier Field to hear yet another evangelist named Percy Crawford.[37] To the astonishment of many, similar gatherings were breaking out in cities like Philadelphia, Denver, Oakland, Tacoma, Dallas, and New York.[38] Furthermore, reports of revival were beginning to arrive from places such as Japan, Belgium, Ireland, New Zealand, Spain, India, Czechoslovakia, Italy, Guatemala, Finland, Holland, Germany, Sweden, Wales, Switzerland, and Austria.[39] What had started during the early 1940s as a youth movement—encouraged largely by groups such as Youth for Christ, InterVarsity Christian Fellowship, Young Life Campaign, and Voice of Christian Youth—was by the 1950s beginning to touch virtually every denomination, demographic, and region of the world.[40] "A year ago," wrote evangelist Merv Rosell late in 1950, "I was able to write with conviction and assurance" that I was "expecting revival." Now he was seeing with his own

---

34. See Grant Wacker, *America's Pastor: Billy Graham and the Shaping of a Nation* (Cambridge, MA: Harvard University Press, 2014) and *One Soul at a Time: The Story of Billy Graham* (Grand Rapids: Eerdmans, 2019).

35. J. Gresham Machen preached Ockenga's ordination sermon at First Presbyterian Church in Pittsburgh, where he had served as an assistant to Clarence Macartney. For a study of Ockenga, see Garth M. Rosell, *The Surprising Work of God: Harold John Ockenga, Billy Graham, and the Rebirth of Evangelicalism* (Grand Rapids: Baker Academic, 2008).

36. William G. McLoughlin, *Modern Revivalism: From Charles Grandison Finney to Billy Graham* (New York: Ronald, 1959), 8, and Rosell, *The Surprising Work of God*, 127–47.

37. See Dan D. Crawford, *A Thirst for Souls: The Life of Evangelist Percy B. Crawford, 1902–1960* (Plainsboro, NJ: Susquehanna University Press, 2010). Crawford, like Ockenga, was a Westminster Seminary graduate.

38. See Rosell, *The Surprising Work of God*, 127–59.

39. See *Youth for Christ* magazine, October 1950, 8–71.

40. See Bruce Shelley, "The Rise of Evangelical Youth Movements," *Fides et Historia*, January 1986, 47–63, and Billy Graham, *Just as I Am* (San Francisco: HarperSanFrancisco, 1997).

eyes that an "avalanche of blessing is gathering force to thunder into every valley of our nation."[41]

While growing numbers of Presbyterians were active participants in these mid-twentieth-century revivals, the movement was far larger than any single denomination or region of the world. Nonetheless, the surprisingly ecumenical and increasingly international nature of the midcentury spiritual awakening should not obscure the large and influential Presbyterian presence that was at its very core. Presbyterians joined hands with growing numbers of Christians from other denominations in cooperative efforts to spread the gospel to every woman, man, boy, and girl on the face of the planet.

Hollywood Presbyterian Church

At the First Presbyterian Church of Hollywood (California), for example, the remarkable ministry of Henrietta Mears inspired thousands of young men and women to commit themselves to lives of service as disciples of Jesus Christ.[42] Born in Fargo, North Dakota, in 1890, the youngest of seven children, Mears graduated from the University of Minnesota in 1913 and was appointed director of Christian education and teacher of the College Department at Hollywood's First Presbyterian Church in 1928.

For the next thirty-five years, from her base at "Hollywood Pres" (as it was known), the "Teacher" (as she came to be identified) inspired a generation of leaders throughout the denomination and within the larger evangelical world. Expanding the congregation's Sunday school from 400 to 6,500 active members during the first decade of her tenure at the church, Henrietta became a significant influence in shaping the thought of young men and women such as Louis Evans Jr., who subsequently served as pastor of the National Presbyterian Church in Washington, DC; Bill and Vonette Bright, the founders of Campus Crusade for Christ; Jim Rayburn,[43] the founder of Young Life; L. David Cowie, who later served as pastor of University Presbyterian Church in Seattle; Robert

---

41. Merv Rosell, "Revival Can Come to Your Town," *Youth for Christ*, October 1950, 51, 76–79.

42. For a fuller account of Henrietta Mears's life and work, see Earl O. Roe, ed., *Dream Big: The Henrietta Mears Story* (Ventura, CA: Regal Books, 1990); Arlin C. Migliazzo, *Mother of Modern Evangelicalism: The Life and Legacy of Henrietta Mears* (Grand Rapids: Eerdmans, 2020); Andrea Van Boven, *A Little Drop of Love: Henrietta Mears; How She Changed a Generation and You Can Too* (Eugene, OR: Wipf & Stock, 2020); and Wendy Murray Zoba, "The Grandmother of Us All," *Christianity Today*, September 16, 1996, 44–46.

43. Jim Rayburn's brother, Robert, was one of the founding faculty and later president of

Boyd Munger, Presbyterian pastor and professor at Fuller Theological Seminary; Frederick Dale Bruner, a biblical scholar and professor at Whitworth College in Spokane, Washington; Donn Moomaw, senior minister of Bel Air Presbyterian Church; and Billy Graham himself, the young evangelist who later came to be known as "America's Pastor."[44]

"I doubt," Graham later commented, "that any other woman outside of my wife and mother has had such a marked influence [in my life]." "There is simply no way to exaggerate her effectiveness as a teacher, communicator and inspirer," remarked United States Senate Chaplain Richard C. Halverson. "There is not an area of my life that her influence has not touched with great significance." "The best thing I ever did for Hollywood Presbyterian Church," added Stewart P. MacLennon, the congregation's pastor from 1921 to 1941, "was to get Miss Mears as Director of Christian Education."[45]

Many who never knew Henrietta Mears by name or visited the congregation in which she served were still influenced by her strategic leadership. In 1933—when economic depression was afflicting the USA—Mears helped to launch a new publishing venture: Gospel Light Publications. This publisher sought to meet the need for creative and biblically faithful Sunday school curricula. Many evangelical Presbyterian congregations (with others) preferred these materials over denominationally produced materials.[46]

CHRISTIAN CONFERENCE CENTERS

In addition to the work of mentors like Mears, a network of Bible conferences and renewal centers was springing up across America. From Forest Home and Westminster Woods in California; to Maranatha Bible Conference in Michigan; to Green Lake in Wisconsin and Winona Lake in Indiana; to Word of Life in New York, Camp Peniel in Texas, and Glen Erie in Colorado, Christian camps and conference centers began attracting thousands of families seeking Christian fellowship, biblical training, and spiritual inspiration. Among

---

Covenant Seminary in St. Louis; Covenant College and Seminary was started in 1956 by the Evangelical Presbyterian Church (later, Reformed Presbyterian Church, Evangelical Synod).

44. Wacker, *America's Pastor*.

45. The quotations are all taken from the early pages of Roe, *Dream Big*. In addition to serving on the staff of Hollywood Presbyterian Church, Mears was the founder of Forest Home Christian Conference Center (1938) and founder of Gospel Literature International (1961). She died March 20, 1963.

46. Since 2015, Gospel Light has been associated with the David C. Cook publishing group.

Presbyterians in the South, none were more important than two conference grounds in the North Carolina mountains—the Bonclarken Conference Center (Associate Reformed Presbyterian Church), established in 1921,[47] and the Montreat Conference Center (PCUS). The Mountain Retreat Association (Montreat) was purchased in 1905 by the Presbyterian Synod of North Carolina, the group that sponsored the first Presbyterian conference in 1907. In addition to serving as the geographical site for both the Historic Foundation for the Presbyterian and Reformed Churches at Montreat and Montreat College, the Montreat Conference Center (as it officially came to be known in 1983) has hosted dozens of conferences, retreats, academic gatherings, concerts, and special events across the years in its 1,500-seat Anderson Auditorium.[48]

Presbyterians in the Northeast and mid-Atlantic regions, unable to travel to North Carolina, were attracted to conference centers closer to home. Places such as the Rumney Conference Grounds in New Hampshire, Winona Lake in Indiana, America's Keswick in New Jersey, Mount Hermon in California, and Maranatha Bible and Missionary Conference in Michigan seemed to fill a similar role.[49]

The National Association of Evangelicals (1943)

That spirit of cooperation could also be clearly seen in other developments in which Presbyterian evangelicals played significant roles. A first was the founding of the National Association of Evangelicals (NAE). Although the organization was officially founded in 1943, its narrative properly begins much earlier.[50] Thanks to the work of the Evangelistic Association of New England (founded in

47. Peggy B. Murdock, *Bonclarken: A Story of Faith, Hope, and Tenacity* (Greenville, SC: Women's Synodical Union, Associate Reformed Presbyterian Church, 1975).

48. Robert Campbell Anderson, *The Story of Montreat from Its Beginning, 1897–1947* (Montreat, NC, 1949); Mary McPhail Standaert and Joseph Standaert, *Montreat*, Postcard History Series (Charleston, SC: Arcadia Publishing, 2009).

49. Elizabeth Evans, *The Wright Vision: The Story of the New England Fellowship* (Lanham, MD: University Press of America, 1991); Mary Ruth Macomber, "I Remember Growing Up with Rumney" (unpublished paper, Rumney Bible Conference, 1993); Vincent H. Gaddis and Jasper A. Huffman, *The Story of Winona Lake* (Butler, IN: Higley Huffman, 1960); Leona Hertel, *Sixty-One Years of Blessing: A Cameo History of Maranatha Bible and Missionary Conference* (Muskegon, MI: Maranatha Bible and Missionary Conference, 1971); and Elizabeth Evans, "The New England Fellowship" (unpublished paper, Rumney Bible Conference, 1995).

50. Arthur H. Matthews, *Standing Up, Standing Together: The Emergence of the National Association of Evangelicals* (Carol Stream, IL: NAE, 1992), and *Evangelical Action! A Report*

1889) and the New England Fellowship (founded in 1929), a strong ecumenical spirit was already alive, well, and clearly thriving in the rocky soil of New England by the 1930s. Quietly and without fanfare, J. Elwin Wright and his parents had been working tirelessly throughout the early decades of the century to build a network of evangelical Christians throughout the six New England states—facilitating scores of joint ventures in conferences, camps, evangelistic services, youth gatherings, radio outreach, publications, and vacation Bible schools.[51]

With their headquarters at the Rumney Conference Grounds, New England Fellowship's founder and president, J. Elwin Wright, became, as historian Randall Balmer phrased it, "a tireless advocate for evangelical cooperation."[52] A graduate of Nyack College, the unassuming and indefatigable Wright became the perfect institutional partner for the young Presbyterian pastor Harold J. Ockenga, who assumed the pulpit at Boston's historic Park Street Church in 1936. The process began, in fact, at a Rumney pastors conference in 1939, when the leadership of the New England Fellowship was asked to gauge interest across the country in establishing "a national association based on the principles of the Fellowship."[53] At the 1941 conference, Wright reported that such interest not only was apparent but also seemed to be growing. As a result, the participants at the 1941 pastors conference adopted the following resolution: "[we] feel a deep concern that the evangelical and evangelistic denominations, missions, associations, churches, and other religious organizations of America find some workable basis of co-operation and co-ordination which will enable them to present a united front against the inroads of modernism, infidelity and atheism." Consequently, "[we] resolve that it is the unanimous conviction of this Conference that immediate steps be taken by responsible leaders of these evangelical groups to bring into existence a central and representative organization operating under an appropriate name designating its purpose, through which evangelical Christians may become vocal."[54] By the following October, Wright had persuaded Will Houghton, president of Moody Bible Institute in Chicago, to call together and host a gathering of evangelical leaders to discuss the possibility of establishing a national organization on essentially the same principles as those that undergirded the New England Fellowship.[55]

of the Organization of the National Association of Evangelicals for United Action, Compiled and Edited by the Executive Committee (Boston: United Action Press, 1942).

51. Evans, *The Wright Vision.*

52. Randall Balmer, "J. Elwin Wright (1890–1973)," in *Encyclopedia of Evangelicalism,* rev. and expanded ed. (Waco, TX: Baylor University Press, 2004), 769.

53. Evans, *The Wright Vision,* 115.

54. Evans, *The Wright Vision,* 115–16.

55. The gathering at Moody Bible Institute was held on October 27–28, 1941. J. Elwin

As a result of those discussions, a National Conference for United Action among Evangelicals was convened on April 7, 1942, at the Hotel Coronado in St. Louis, Missouri. The conference opened on the morning of April 7 when Wright addressed the approximately 150 delegates. "For a number of years," he remarked, "many of us have been asking, 'Why does not someone start a movement to create some sort of central committee or office which will provide a clearing house for evangelicals in relation to matters of common concern?'" Then briefly reviewing the events that had led to the St. Louis gathering, he called on the delegates to answer that question by declaring their "essential solidarity as evangelicals," resolving "to go forward together unitedly for the truth," cultivating "a spirit of love and consideration toward those with whom we differ on less essential matters," and pledging "to God and each other" to henceforth "avoid carping and unkind criticism of our brethren of like precious faith."[56]

Wright's remarks were followed by an electrifying address by Harold John Ockenga. "Gentlemen," Ockenga began, "we are gathered here today to consider momentous questions and possibly to arrive at decisions which will affect the whole future course of evangelical Christianity in America." "Evangelical Christianity has suffered nothing but a series of defeats for decades," he reminded the delegates. "The programs of few major denominations today are controlled by evangelicals. Evangelical testimony has sometimes been reduced to the witness of individual churches." Evangelicals "are on the defensive or even the decline." Indeed, the time has come, he concluded, for the establishment of a "united front for evangelical action." "God help us to humble ourselves; God help us to be sane; God help us to do His will. God bless you, my brethren in the Lord. We stand together, under the shadow of the cross and cleansed by the blood of the Lamb. There let us unite for His glory."[57]

By the end of the address, it was clear that Ockenga's words had become for many delegates far more than just another conference speech. His concerns had become their concerns, and his call for united evangelical action had become theirs as well. Throughout the following year, in fact, a movement to establish such an organization continued to grow as Ockenga and others crisscrossed America spreading the word. By the time the International Constitutional Convention for United Evangelical Action convened at the La Salle Hotel in Chicago

---

Wright chaired the meeting. For a fuller account, see Rosell, *The Surprising Work of God*, 89–106.

56. Rosell, *The Surprising Work of God*, 96.

57. Harold John Ockenga, "The Unvoiced Multitudes," in *Evangelical Action!*, 19–39. The quotations are taken from this address.

the following year, nearly a thousand delegates had gathered to officially establish what came to be known as the National Association of Evangelicals.[58]

Not only did this fledgling organization take root, but by 1951 Wright and Ockenga, who had exercised such a catalytic effect in moving matters forward from New England to Chicago, also collaborated in the spread of this postwar enthusiasm for evangelical collaboration beyond the USA. They were among representatives from 21 nations meeting in summer 1951 in Woudschouten, the Netherlands, to reconstitute a faltering organization (the Evangelical Alliance, founded 1846) as the World Evangelical Alliance. This renewed organization, now representing the interests and concerns of evangelical Christians in 129 nations, is, in effect, the global matrix enabling coordination for the National Association of Evangelicals, with fraternal networks in other nations and continents.[59]

The Schaeffers and L'Abri

It was in this same postwar period of new evangelical initiatives that a young American couple, Francis and Edith Schaeffer, took their young family to Europe. Francis (1912–1984), a pastor in the Bible Presbyterian Church, had already served churches for a decade.[60] The self-consciously fundamentalist Bible Presbyterian Church was very concerned with separation from doctrinal error; in consequence, it was extremely wary of the surge in ecumenical activity that followed World War II.[61] Thus the Schaeffers went to Europe as missionaries of the Independent Board for Presbyterian Missions (the mission agency preferred by Bible Presbyterians) to advance the cause of a conservative evangelical ecumenical initiative meant to counter the emergence of the World Council of Churches and to continue the evangelizing of children, through a program known as Children for Christ.[62]

58. The International Constitutional Convention for United Evangelical Action met May 3–7, 1943. See Matthews, *Standing Up, Standing Together*. The Presbyterian Church in America, Evangelical Presbyterian Church, and Covenant Order of Evangelical Presbyterians are members of the NAE.

59. See the World Evangelical Alliance website, https://worldea.org/en/who-we-are/.

60. The circumstances surrounding the 1937 founding of the Bible Presbyterian Church, an offshoot of the just-founded Orthodox Presbyterian Church, are provided below on p. 305. This account is indebted to Colin Duriez, *Francis Schaeffer: An Authentic Life* (Wheaton, IL: Crossway, 2008).

61. The World Council of Churches held its inaugural meeting at Amsterdam in 1948.

62. Duriez, *Francis Schaeffer*, 61, explains that the Schaeffers had previously involved themselves with the evangelical organization Child Evangelism Fellowship (CEF). How-

Soon established in the Swiss canton of Valais, Francis and Edith pursued their educational evangelism among schoolchildren. But this canton, Roman Catholic by heritage, objected to their presence after the controversial conversion of an adult. Confronted with the demand that they promptly exit Switzerland, they reached an agreement that allowed them to remain in the country if they relocated to another canton, Vaud (Protestant by heritage), and purchase property there. Increasingly uneasy with the stridency of their mission board, the Schaeffers resigned and remained in Canton Vaud as missionaries directly supported by concerned individuals at home. Through school and eventually university relationships developed by their own daughters, a steady stream of inquisitive teens and university students beat a path to the door of what was soon called L'Abri. The emphasis on young schoolchildren gave way to work with young adults.

Before long, there were satellite extensions of L'Abri in Italy, England, Massachusetts, and Minnesota, each drawing streams of students with their questions.[63] And the lectures and talks from which Schaeffer prompted student discussions in L'Abri and in various university settings became the basis for the books for which he became so well known, first in the United Kingdom and subsequently in North America.[64] Schaeffer had gradually become a pioneer in evangelical cultural apologetics.

Though originally committed to a very angular doctrinal stance, the mature Francis Schaeffer became an "apostle" for theological orthodoxy wedded to the practice of Christian love. He was called on to advise various American Presbyterians as they wrestled with how to maintain evangelical orthodoxy in their wayward denominations and how to reunite after lengthy division.[65] Christians in and beyond the USA benefited by his film documentaries *How Shall We Then Live?* and *Whatever Happened to the Human Race?*[66] By the time of his passing in 1984, Francis Schaeffer had become a unifying and defining figure in global evangelicalism.[67]

---

ever, their excessive zeal for separation from doctrinal error inhibited their usefulness in introducing the CEF program into churches that, though interested, did not share their separatist zeal.

63. Duriez, *Francis Schaeffer*, 148, 196.

64. Among the most notable of his twenty books were *Escape from Reason* (1968), *The God Who Is There* (1968), and *The Church at the End of the Twentieth Century* (1970).

65. See a reference to Schaeffer's providing this counsel to concerned Southern Presbyterians below in chap. 18, p. 300.

66. The second of these involved collaboration with the renowned pediatric surgeon Everett Koop. The two film series were coproduced by Frankie Schaeffer, son to Francis. Duriez, *Francis Schaeffer*, 184, 190. The release of each film series was accompanied by the publication of a book of the same name.

67. It is significant to note that he influenced the wording of the Lausanne Covenant of

THE UNEASY CONSCIENCE

Four years after the founding of the NAE, evangelicals in America received a "wake-up call" from theologian Carl F. H. Henry (1913–2003) in the form of a short book entitled *The Uneasy Conscience of Modern Fundamentalism* (1947).[68] It was both a critique of the recent past and a call for renewal on the issue of the Christian responsibility to address contemporary societal needs and failures. This challenge was the brainchild of Henry and his close friend, Harold J. Ockenga. The two Christian leaders shared a vision for what they re-ferred to as "neo-evangelicalism." The terms "fundamentalist" and "evangelical" were not synonymous in 1947. George Marsden defined fundamentalism in the first sentence of his book *Understanding Fundamentalism and Evangelicalism*: "A fundamentalist is an evangelical who is angry about something."[69]

Evangelicalism has had a long and very successful history. Marsden argues that evangelicals reigned in American life from 1865 to 1890, the post–Civil War period. Following this evangelical heyday, the Progressive Era in United States history (c. 1890–1920s) was marked by the rise of the Social Gospel movement that was viewed by evangelicals as dangerous due to its liberal theology and its tendency to question the accuracy of the Bible. Marsden suggests that evangelicalism essentially split into two camps: theological lib-erals, "who in order to maintain better credibility in the modern age, were willing to modify some crucial evangelical doctrines, such as the reliability of the Bible or the necessity of salvation only through the atoning sacrifice of Christ,"[70] and "theologically conservative" evangelicals. In the mid-1920s, a more militant wing of the conservative evangelical Christians took the name "fundamentalists" and assumed the posture of crusaders against liberal the-ology. They were very wary of pacifism, ecumenism, and especially certain aspects of the Social Gospel.

Henry's *Uneasy Conscience* was addressed primarily to evangelicals in the separatist element in the fundamentalist camp. The word "separation" here includes separation from unorthodox doctrine as well the necessity of leading a life of holiness and a repudiation of all evil in one's personal life. Separatist fundamentalists insisted on a complete "separation" from "worldly

---

1974, by giving a major address on evangelism in that congress. See Barry Hankins, *Francis Schaeffer and the Shaping of Evangelical America* (Grand Rapids: Eerdmans, 2008), 146, 147.

68. Carl F. Henry, *The Uneasy Conscience of Modern Fundamentalism* (1947; reprint, Grand Rapids: Eerdmans, 2003).

69. George M. Marsden, *Understanding Fundamentalism and Evangelicalism* (Grand Rapids: Eerdmans, 1991).

70. Marsden, *Understanding Fundamentalism*, 3.

amusements including: dancing, smoking, drinking, playing cards, and going to a theater."[71] Ecclesiastical separation was a central issue—congregations and denominations must separate and not cooperate with any "liberals" or nonseparating groups. Distinguishing themselves from separatist fundamentalists, Henry argued, "If historic Christianity is again to compete as a vital world ideology, evangelicalism must project a solution for the most pressing world problems. It must offer a formula for a new world, a mind with spiritual ends, involving evangelical affirmations in political, economic, sociological, and educational realms, local and international. The redemptive message has implications for all of life; a truncated life results from a truncated message."[72] Neo-evangelicalism needed new expertise in relating doctrine to the problems encountered in the modern world.

Youth for Christ Congress on World Evangelization (1948)

The Congress on World Evangelization held in Beatenberg, Switzerland, in 1948 not only attracted five hundred delegates, representing forty-six nations and dozens of denominational groups, but its roster of participants reads like a Who's Who of future evangelical leadership, including a good many Presbyterians, throughout the second half of the twentieth century.[73]

"The burden of this conference," as the conference organizers phrased it, "is the final and complete evangelization of the entire world in our generation." We "are not here for a vacation," and "we are not here to trifle with time and opportunity." Rather, "the Holy Spirit has brought us together for prayer, for Bible study, for heart-searching, for waiting upon God. May it please [God] to give us a new and greater insight into the task of world evangelization and the means by which it can be accomplished NOW!" "May we go from the alpine heights of Beatenberg into the world," to do a new thing in our day.

The gathering in Beatenberg was only the beginning. Others soon followed. The first International Conference of Itinerant Evangelists was held in Amsterdam during the summer of 1983. Like the gathering in Beatenberg thirty-five years earlier, the participants—nearly five thousand from more than one hundred countries, meeting for ten days at the RAI Conference Center—gathered because of their shared interest in spreading the Christian gospel throughout

---

71. Marsden, *Understanding Fundamentalism*, 196.

72. Henry, *Uneasy Conscience*, 59–60.

73. For a report on the congress, see Harold John Ockenga, "Beatenberg," sermon 1442, Ockenga Papers, Gordon-Conwell Theological Seminary, South Hamilton, MA.

the world. The participants were carefully selected from lists of men and women who were "involved in evangelism at a grass roots level" in Asia (836 participants), Africa (750), Latin America and the Caribbean (452), Europe (753), Oceania (106), North America (857), and the Middle East (87).[74]

Amsterdam was an early indication in microcosm of much larger changes taking place within global Christianity. In his best-selling book *The Next Christendom*, Philip Jenkins called these changes nothing short of a "revolution." "We are currently living through one of the [most] transforming moments in the history of religion worldwide," wrote Jenkins in 2002, as "the center of gravity in the Christian world" shifts "inexorably southward, to Africa, Asia, and Latin America." The "era of Western Christianity has passed within our lifetimes," Jenkins argued, "and the day of Southern Christianity is dawning. The fact of change itself is undeniable, it has happened, and will continue to happen."[75]

A careful observer should not have been surprised by these shifts. The massive migrations of the nineteenth and early twentieth centuries had flooded our burgeoning cities with people from around the globe, and a world at war in the twentieth century had sent America's own sons and daughters to places they could scarcely have imagined while growing up in the small towns that dotted the American landscape. Equally important, one could argue, was the cumulative impact of the thousands of faithful missionaries who showed their slides at countless church suppers, who wrote letters home from the field, and who told fascinating stories around dinner tables when they were on furlough. How else can one explain the remarkable world vision that was embedded in the youth movements of the 1940s and the worldwide urban crusades of the 1950s?

Gatherings similar to Beatenberg and Amsterdam were held subsequently in places such as Montreux (1960), Berlin (1966), Lausanne (1974), Manila (1989), and Cape Town (2010). Not only did the focus of all these gatherings remain squarely on worldwide evangelization but also the documents they produced—including the Lausanne Covenant (1974), the Manila Manifesto (1989), and the Cape Town Commitment (2010)—clearly echoed

---

74. Figures are from the "Records of the 1983 International Conference for Itinerant Evangelists (Amsterdam 83)," Wheaton College, the Billy Graham Center Archives, Collection 253. Amsterdam's RAI Exhibition and Convention Centre, located near the RAI railway station, is one of the largest convention sites in the Netherlands.

75. Philip Jenkins, *The Next Christendom: The Coming of Global Christianity* (New York: Oxford University Press, 2002), 2-3.

that theme. Billy Graham's own ministry has been conducted literally around the globe—from Seoul, Korea, to Rio de Janeiro, Brazil.[76]

THE PRIORITY OF EVANGELISM

What held all these movements together seems to have been the priority of evangelism. "As America was coming to grips with the postwar world," historian Bradley Longfield helpfully reminds us, the Federal Council of Churches declared that "the time is at hand for evangelical Christianity to launch a movement to win America for Jesus Christ." Indeed, during "the years after World War II," he continues (quoting historian William McLoughlin), a "fourth great awakening" helped to bring "a new interest in the Christian ethos which underlies American civilization."[77]

With a global focus and a task far beyond the limited resources of a single denomination, Christians increasingly recognized the necessity of joining hands in the spread of the gospel to women and men, boys and girls from every tribe, tongue, and nation around the globe. Like those who had come before them, many also realized that the church would surely encounter enormous new challenges and obstacles as it seeks to spread the good news in an increasingly hostile world.

76. For a listing of the places where Graham preached, see *Just as I Am*, 736–39.
77. Bradley Longfield, *Presbyterians and American Culture: A History* (Louisville: Westminster John Knox, 2013), 177.

CHAPTER 18

Women, Civil Rights, and a New Confession

The post–World War II years in America were a time of remarkable change for society and the church. The beginnings of the Cold War and nuclear arms race, the Korean War, the space program, the sexual revolution, civil rights, the Vietnam War, abortion rights, gay rights, and the feminist movement all raised new theological and ethical questions. Presbyterian seminaries increasingly advocated adjustments to Christian faith in order to address these new challenges. Evangelicals in mainline churches, on the other hand, remained firm in their attachment to traditional Christian ethics and looked to find comrades in the larger evangelical movement.

As they were committed to encouraging and transmitting historic orthodox theology, they were prepared to make common cause with those who shared their concern. Thus, many supported the Evangelical Theological Society (ETS) from its founding in 1949. The ETS had been founded to provide "a medium for the oral exchange and written expression of thought and research in the general field of the theological disciplines as centered in the Scriptures."[1] Mainline evangelical leaders also hoped that Fuller Seminary in Pasadena would be "a new Princeton," offering an alternative to the theologically progressive curricula becoming standardized in the historically mainline seminaries across the United States.[2] Ockenga was the first president of the interdenominational school, and Billy Graham joined the board of trustees in 1958.[3] A distinguished faculty was assembled; five of the earliest professors

---

1. ETS Constitution, article 2, accessible at https://www.etsjets.org/about/constitution.

2. See Bradley J. Longfield and George M. Marsden, "Presbyterian Colleges in Twentieth-Century America," in *The Pluralistic Vision: Presbyterians and Mainstream Protestant Education and Leadership*, ed. Milton J. Coalter, John M. Mulder, and Louis B. Weeks (Louisville: Westminster John Knox, 1992), 99–125.

3. Ockenga commuted by air, weekly, between Boston and Pasadena during his presidency: 1947–1954 and 1960–1963.

were of Presbyterian affiliation: Everett F. Harrison, Paul K. Jewett, William Sanford LaSor, Wilbur M. Smith, and Charles Woodbridge.[4] Of the five, three were Princeton graduates and one a graduate of Westminster Seminary. Initially, the Presbytery of Los Angeles viewed Fuller as divisive and gave no welcome to Presbyterian students and professors at the seminary; but by the 1960s, the UPCUSA was accepting Fuller students as ministerial candidates. By the early 1980s, there were over five hundred Presbyterian students attending the Southern California seminary.[5]

In 1969, another evangelical seminary with substantial Presbyterian connections was established in the Boston area—Gordon-Conwell Theological Seminary. The new seminary was the merger of Conwell School of Theology (originally a part of Temple University) and Gordon Divinity School. Presbyterian businessman J. Howard Pew provided financial backing; Ockenga served as president and Graham as chairman of the board of trustees. A number of professors were Presbyterians,[6] and hundreds of evangelical students from both the UPCUSA[7] and the PCUS would be trained at Gordon-Conwell in the following decades. The young evangelicals attending Fuller and Gordon-Conwell were committed to staying the course and pursuing renewal in their denominations.[8]

WOMEN IN CHURCH OFFICE

Since the early decades of the nineteenth century, Presbyterian women had been involved in the church's ministry through interdenominational societies addressing social problems, Bible and tract societies, Sunday schools, and financial support for seminary students. They also took a prominent role in home and foreign missions, providing financial support and serving as missionaries. Sarah Foster Hanna had addressed the 1875 United Presbyterian Church of North America (UPCNA) Assembly, which endorsed her efforts to

4. Charles Woodbridge, a PCUS minister and Fuller professor of church history, became the fourth president of the Evangelical Theological Society in 1952.

5. George M. Marsden, *Reforming Fundamentalism: Fuller Seminary and the New Evangelicalism* (Grand Rapids: Eerdmans, 1987), 102–7.

6. Richard Lovelace, Deane Kemper, Meredith Kline, Gwen Walters, John Jefferson Davis, Garth Rosell, Rick Lints, Bill and Aida Spencer.

7. Formed by the 1958 union of United Presbyterian and Presbyterian Church in the USA bodies.

8. Garth M. Rosell, *A Charge to Keep: Gordon-Conwell Theological Seminary and the Renewal of Evangelicalism* (Eugene, OR: Wipf & Stock, 2020).

organize the Women's General Missionary Society, the first national Presbyterian women's organization. Eliza Clokey of the UPCNA had originated the Thank Offering for women, which was a one-dollar gift above the usual contribution to the Women's General Missionary Society. In the 1870s, women's groups were organized regionally by the PCUSA to support missions, and the Cumberland Presbyterians founded a Woman's Board of Missions in 1880.[9]

When women began to speak and pray in public gatherings in the nineteenth century, the 1832 General Assembly censured it: "To teach and exhort, or to lead in prayer, in public promiscuous assemblies, is clearly forbidden to women in the Holy Oracles." The Assembly clarified in 1874 that women speaking and praying in the weekly church prayer meeting was at the discretion of the pastors and elders. In 1872 the Reverend Theodore L. Cuyler was rebuked by the Brooklyn Presbytery for allowing a Quaker preacher, Sarah Smiley, to speak at the Sunday evening service. Reverend Isaac See allowed two women to speak from the pulpit in 1878, and charges against him were sustained by the Assembly. In both cases, the General Assembly referred to its 1832 statement as its definitive judgment on the matter.[10] Cumberlands would be the first Presbyterians to have a female minister, Louisa Woosley, who was ordained by Nolin Presbytery in Kentucky in 1889. There was a prolonged controversy over the legality of her ordination, but eventually she was recognized as a legitimate Cumberland Presbyterian minister. Woosley's case was unique; women deacons, elders, and ministers would not become acceptable in the PCUSA and PCUS until decades later in the twentieth century.[11]

The UPCNA had discussed women deacons in the 1870s but did not officially approve them until 1906. Cumberland Presbyterians approved the ordination of women deacons in 1921, and the PCUSA followed suit over the following two years. The PCUS did not allow the ordination of women as deacons until 1964. Cumberlands were first to allow the ordination of women elders in 1892, but there was ongoing controversy over the next few years. A proposal in the PCUSA to allow women elders was defeated in 1920, but by 1929 women elders were permitted while the prohibition of women clergy remained in place. The UPCNA refused to endorse women's ordination as elders or ministers in both 1920 and 1944. In 1946, the PCUSA Assembly passed an overture allowing ordination of women ministers, but the measure was defeated in presbytery

9. See R. Pierce Beaver, *American Protestant Women in World Missions: History of the First Feminist Movement in North America* (Grand Rapids: Eerdmans, 1980).

10. Lois A. Boyd and R. Douglas Brackenridge, *Presbyterian Women in America: Two Centuries of a Quest for Status*, 2nd ed. (Westport, CT: Greenwood, 1996), 95–100.

11. Woosley explained her position on women clergy in *Shall Woman Preach?*, published in 1891.

voting, 128 to 108. In 1953, the Assembly formed a committee to study the issue, which ultimately recommended women's ordination as ministers, stating, "the Bible neither provides specific direction for nor prohibits the ordination of women to the Gospel ministry."[12] In 1956, a majority of presbyteries voted in favor of the change, and Christian educator Margaret Towner became the first ordained female minister in the PCUSA. When the UPCNA and PCUSA entered union discussions in the 1950s, the diverse denominational practices on women elders and ministers surfaced. The UPCNA was promised that her congregations would not be forced to accept women elders or ministers.[13]

In parts of the South, the journey to women's ordination proceeded more slowly. In 1955, a PCUS Assembly study committee recommended that women be ordained as deacons and elders. The committee report stated, "We believe the Holy Spirit is leading us today into a new understanding of the place of women in the Church." The General Assembly voted to proceed with this plan, but the overture was defeated in the presbyteries, 44 to 39. The southern presbyteries took another vote on women's ordination in 1963, this time including women ministers along with deacons and elders. The vote was 53 presbyteries in favor and 27 presbyteries opposed, indicating significant numbers still held traditional views. Reaction in the PCUS ranged from welcoming the constitutional change as faithful to the gospel to deploring the move as undermining biblical authority. In 1965, the PCUS ordained its first clergywoman, Dr. Rachel Henderlite, a professor at the Presbyterian School of Christian Education in Richmond.[14] Traditional Presbyterians strongly disagreed with this innovation. William Childs Robinson, Columbia Seminary professor, had argued in 1956 that while the Bible mentions deaconesses, women prophesying, and women missionaries, the apostle Paul has given the church instructions "against women participating in authority to preach or administer the sacraments."[15]

The Associate Reformed Presbyterians endured an intense battle on women's ordination. The ordination of women deacons was approved by Synod in 1971 with very little opposition, but ordaining women elders or ministers produced impassioned sentiments on both sides. In the 1970s, church periodicals as well as presbytery and Synod minutes were filled with editorials,

12. *Minutes of the General Assembly of the Presbyterian Church in the United States of America*, part 1 (Philadelphia: Office of the General Assembly, 1955), 97.

13. Boyd and Brackenridge, *Presbyterian Women in America*, 129.

14. E. T. Thompson, *Presbyterians in the South*, vol. 3, *1890–1972* (Richmond, VA: John Knox), 478, 479.

15. William Childs Robinson wrote three 1956 articles opposing women's ordination for the *Southern Presbyterian Journal* (April 25, 1956; August 15, 1956; October 17, 1956).

essays, and overtures arguing from Scripture texts either for or against women's ordination. In 1981, a memorial from First Presbytery to Synod, asking for the approval of women's ordination, was turned down. A compromise proposal calling for a study committee to examine the biblical basis of female ordination was defeated, 136 to 101; opponents of the motion argued that the biblical question had already been debated, and ongoing discussion would be divisive.[16]

In the 1960s and '70s, the UPCUSA General Assemblies pressed forward with inclusion of women at every level of church life. The 1967 Assembly approved a report observing that while women may now serve as elders and pastors, "our Church is still bound by many old attitudes and traditions." A 1969 report from the Special Committee on the Status of Women in Society and in the Church pointed to parallels in discrimination against minorities in society and discrimination against women in the church, noting that "a profound bias against women continues to exist." The 1970 Assembly initiated directives on equality for women that would continue throughout the decade. Pulpit committees were directed to consider women, and congregations were instructed to elect women deacons and elders in numbers that reflected the female constituency of the congregation. Fair representation of sex and race in all agencies, boards, and committees of the church was required, as well as discontinuing generic use of masculine language in church documents. Congregational, presbytery, and synod compliance with these directives was monitored. In 1974, a Joint Task Force on Racism and Sexism was established, and the following year the Assembly approved Four Directives for Mission—one of which was "Justice for Women and Racial and Ethnic Minorities." By 1979, the UPCUSA's affirmative action for women became mandatory for all when "Overture L" ordered that women *shall* be elected to the office of deacon and ruling elder. The vote in the presbyteries was 79 to 70, and opponents decried this prejudicial action against those who still held traditional views. The 1980 Assembly responded to the conservative protest by allowing presbyteries to grant temporary waivers to congregations with no women officers as long as they were moving toward compliance.[17]

While the northern church still contained many older ministers opposed to women's ordination, there had been increasing opposition to ordaining new clergy who held traditional views. In 1974, Pittsburgh Seminary graduate

16. Lowery Ward and James W. Gettys, *The Second Century: A History of the Associate Reformed Presbyterians, 1882-1982* (Greenville, SC, 1982), 322-28.

17. Douglas Brackenridge and Lois A. Boyd, "United Presbyterian Policy on Women and the Church—an Historical Overview," *Journal of Presbyterian History* 59, no. 3 (Fall 1981): 400-406.

Walter Wynn Kenyon was denied ordination by the UPCUSA because he did not believe in the ordination of women. Kenyon was a son of the church; his father and grandfather had been UPCNA pastors. Kenyon had stated before the Pittsburgh Presbytery that on conscience grounds he could not participate in the ordination of a female based on his understanding of the Bible. However, he was willing to work with women clergy in the denomination and would not stop a congregation he served from ordaining a woman elder. Pittsburgh Presbytery approved Kenyon by a vote of 147 to 133, but the action to approve was appealed. The UPCUSA Permanent Judicial Commission (PJC) overturned the presbytery's action, and Kenyon was barred from ordained ministry.[18] Rejecting Kenyon for Presbyterian ordination, the PJC stated, "It is the responsibility of our Church to deny ordination to one who has refused to ordain women." Older pastors, who had not changed their views since ordination, felt ostracized because they did not conform to the new dogma.[19]

The Civil Rights Era

Beginning in the late 1930s, the PCUS began calling attention to the plight of blacks, who suffered from economic, social, and political disadvantages in American society. Addressing Christian responsibility in race relations, the 1939 Committee on Moral and Social Welfare noted that loving one's neighbor as oneself meant challenging discrimination in the South. In the '40s and '50s, there was a growing sense that social concerns were part of the church's responsibility, despite its historic affirmation of the "spirituality of the church" perspective on social/political issues.[20] A 1949 Committee on Christian Relations study paper, "States Rights and Human Rights," acknowledged that as two-thirds of the country's blacks live in the South, southerners had unique responsibility to lead in civil rights for all. The paper debunked the "permanent-child theory," which characterized blacks as inferior, arguing that backwardness among blacks stemmed from lack of opportunity and pointing out that in Christ there is "neither male nor female, bond or free, but all are one."

In 1954, the PCUS General Assembly adopted a paper, "The Church and Segregation" (by 236 to 169), which stated that "every person is of infinite

---

18. Kenyon went on to have a valuable teaching career at Belhaven College (University) in Jackson, Mississippi, a school with historic Presbyterian connections.

19. Brackenridge and Boyd, *United Presbyterian Policy on Women*, 404; see *Minutes of the General Assembly*, part 1 (Philadelphia: Office of the General Assembly, 1975), 220, 254–59.

20. Thompson, *Presbyterians in the South*, 3:504–29.

value, and therefore of equal value in the sight of God. In his sight there is no superior race"; thus Christians must pursue the "welfare and happiness of all people." A second document that year, "A Statement to Southern Christians," was written after the Supreme Court decision (*Brown v. Board of Education*, 1954) calling for desegregation of public education with all "deliberate speed." The PCUS paper argued that southern concern about widespread miscegenation as a result of desegregation was fictional. It also asserted that the church was lagging behind the state in moral leadership by not combating the evils of forced segregation. The 1954 Assembly approved a resolution commending the Supreme Court ruling. There was resistance to this call for desegregation by a few individuals, congregations, and presbyteries, but the PCUS became the first major southern denomination pressing her congregations to end segregation. By 1974, the PCUS had its first black moderator, the Reverend Lawrence Bottoms.[21]

The Associate Reformed Presbyterian Church (ARP) also had a prolonged struggle with desegregation. Ministers in the ARP had strongly decried injustices and lynching of blacks in the South in the 1930s. When World War II began, ARP writers compared southern white supremacist attitudes to the racial theories of Nazi Germany. Southerners should remember they are immigrants, the writers held, but blacks were forced here against their will. Writing for a September 1948 issue of the denomination's paper, one ARP author accused the Democratic Party in South Carolina of manipulating voters by spreading fear and prejudice against blacks and trying to prevent Negro progress. In the 1950s, many Associate Reformed Presbyterians supported a "separate but equal" arrangement, but others opposed it. The denomination had been hesitant to issue a public statement on integration, in order to preserve peace.

Tensions became more open in the 1960s during the ARP General Synod debates. A committee of nine, tasked with studying race relations, offered majority and minority reports to the 1964 meeting of Synod. The majority report called for church membership and participation in all Synod activities to be open to all regardless of race. The minority report (adopted 121 to 75) observed that there were differences among races and stated that no actions of Synod should "encourage or tend to promote a situation whereby intermarriage of the races would naturally follow." Therefore, it was unwise to endorse integration

---

21. James H. Smylie, "The Bible, Race and the Changing South," *Journal of Presbyterian History* 59 (Summer 1981): 201-7; Dwyn M. Mounger, "Racial Attitudes in the Presbyterian Church in the United States," *Journal of Presbyterian History* 48 (Spring 1970): 61-68. See also Andrew E. Murray, *Presbyterians and the Negro—a History* (Philadelphia: Presbyterian Historical Society, 1966).

of the races in ARP churches or institutions. An intense debate over integrating its own Erskine College ensued as a result of the 1964 Civil Rights Act. Colleges could sign the Assurance of Compliance Form stating that admissions policies would not discriminate by race. The 1965 Synod gave permission (102 to 80) to Erskine trustees to sign the document, and the board approved compliance (24 to 10). Immediately there was an avalanche of both support for the decision and opposition to compliance. Opponents argued that with compliance the federal government would interfere with the independence of the college, thus it was a church-and-state issue. The board issued a statement the following year, reaffirming its policy of nondiscrimination based upon race, color, or national origin. In 1968, the Synod adopted a paper affirming that segregation in the church is opposed to the will of God.[22]

North Carolina–born and ARP-raised Billy Graham had taken a stand against segregation in his 1953 book *Peace with God*; Graham dedicated the book to his father-in-law, Presbyterian medical missionary L. Nelson Bell. Graham charged that the church had failed in its responsibility to deal with the race issue. Christians should voluntarily be doing what courts are making happen by law. Graham wrote, "But in the final analysis the only real solution will be found at the foot of the cross where we come together in brotherly love. The closer people of all races get to Christ and His cross, the closer they will get to one another."[23] In 1957 Graham invited Martin Luther King Jr. to share the platform with him at a New York crusade in Madison Square Garden. In the South, Graham's crusades did not allow for separate seating for blacks. His 1964 crusade in Birmingham was the most integrated meeting in the city's history. Dr. Bell supported his son-in-law's position, stating in 1956 that "there is no biblical or legal justification for segregation."[24]

In 1946, the PCUSA had adopted the Federal Council of Churches' call for a "non-segregated church in a non-segregated society." Segregated synods were dissolved in the 1950s, but congregations remained mostly segregated. Northern Presbyterians were supportive of King and his peaceful protests for racial equality in the South. Stated Clerk Eugene Carson Blake was arrested for attempts to desegregate an amusement park in Maryland in 1963, and the following year the Reverend Elder Hawkins became the first black moderator in the UPCUSA. The UPCUSA established the Commission on Religion and

22. Ward and Gettys, *The Second Century*, 349–65.

23. Billy Graham, *Peace with God* (Garden City, NY: Doubleday, 1953), 195.

24. David L. Chappel, *Stone of Hope: Prophetic Religion and the Death of Jim Crow* (Chapel Hill: University of North Carolina Press, 2004), 117. On the other hand, Bell opposed mixed marriage, forced integration, and the civil disobedience of the 1960s.

Race in 1963, appointing black minister and Pittsburgh Seminary professor Gayraud S. Wilmore as the executive director. Wilmore was cofounder of the National Conference of Black Churchmen in 1966, an organization for pro-black power ministers advocating for black consciousness. Through Wilmore's lobbying efforts, atheist Black Panther James Forman addressed the 1969 General Assembly. Forman called for reparations from white religious institutions for complicity in slavery according to the "Black Manifesto."

The UPCUSA took initiatives to help working-class blacks, establishing the Presbyterian Economic Development Corporation in 1969, which distributed millions in low-interest loans to minority business owners. The UPCUSA provided a grant of $10,000 toward the defense of Angela Davis in 1971, a black communist who had been arrested in California for kidnapping and murder. Outrage throughout the church was so overwhelming that twenty black Presbyterians repaid the grant out of their own pockets to show their commitment to justice for a black woman. Wilmore returned to the classroom after the Davis affair, writing a number of books on black theology; he also coedited, with James Cone, the two-volume *Black Theology: A Documentary History, 1966–1979*.[25]

ECUMENISM AND A NEW CONFESSION

There was an ecumenical spirit in the air in the years following World War II. The PCUSA and PCUS were members of both the National Council of Churches (NCC) (est. 1950) and the World Council of Churches (WCC) (est. 1948). The northern and southern churches, separated since the Civil War, had approached the subject of reunion as early as the 1930s, but not until the 1950s was there an official vote on a plan of union. By 1951 the UPCNA had entered discussions about a three-way union. Many in the PCUS were opposed to union, raising objections to numerous faults in the PCUSA, including questions about theological liberalism, centralized polity, political action, and property ownership. The union plan was approved 283 to 169 by the PCUS Assembly in 1954 but failed to attain the required three-fourths vote of the presbyteries (42 in favor, 43 opposed).[26] Though southern partic-

25. Douglas H. Brown, "A Presbyterian Prophet of Black Power: The Witness of Gayraud S. Wilmore," *Presbyterian Outlook*, December 17, 2018; see Gayraud S. Wilmore, *Black Religion and Black Radicalism: An Interpretation of the Religious History of African Americans*, 3rd ed. (Maryknoll, NY: Orbis, 1998).

26. Thompson, *Presbyterians in the South*, 3:559–74; Sean Michael Lucas, *For a Con-*

ipation in the union was dead, a merger took place between the PCUSA and the UPCNA to form the United Presbyterian Church in the United States of America (UPCUSA) in 1958. The united body was the largest Presbyterian church in America, with over three million members.

By 1961 ecumenical discussions had begun on a larger scale between the UPCUSA, the PCUS, the Protestant Episcopal Church, the United Method- ist Church, the United Church of Christ, and others. The discussions were known as the Consultation on Church Union (COCU). Evangelicals were concerned about these deliberations, which were dominated by liberal church- men preoccupied with social policy, oftentimes to the exclusion of evangelism and missions.

A major influence on American theology by midcentury was Karl Barth (1886–1968) of the Reformed Church of Switzerland. After World War I, a new theological movement emerged that became known as neoorthodoxy, identified with the work of Barth, Emil Brunner, Dietrich Bonhoeffer, and American Reinhold Niebuhr of New York's Union Seminary. Barth wrote a commentary on Romans in 1919 charging German liberalism with having sub- verted the gospel in its embrace of essential human goodness. In the 1930s, he became part of the anti-Nazi Confessing Church, helping to write the Barmen Declaration, a protest against the Nazi German church. Barth emphasized human sinfulness and God's grace in Jesus Christ, but his understanding of election implied universalism—Christ is the only elect one, and all will be saved in him. Barth accepted the results of higher criticism and accentuated God's subjective revelation to individuals through Scripture rather than an objective revelation in Scripture itself as the written Word of God. His scathing attack on liberalism was welcomed, but many evangelicals were unconvinced, perceiving Barth's theology as a new version of liberalism. In 1962, Barth, at age seventy-five, lectured in the United States for seven weeks to high praise, appearing on the cover of *Time* magazine. Neoorthodoxy's revision of old lib- eralism was taught in mainline seminaries, and it influenced new statements of the Reformed faith.[27]

The UPCUSA produced a new confession and revised ordination vows in 1967. The Confession of 1967 (C-67) was neoorthodox in orientation, empha- sizing "God's work of reconciliation" in the world, and was noteworthy, not so much for what it said but for what it left unsaid—it neglected to address

---

tinuing Church: The Roots of the Presbyterian Church in America (Phillipsburg, NJ: P&R, 2015), 135–61.

27. Stanley J. Grenz and Roger E. Olsen, *Twentieth-Century Theology: God and the World in a Transitional Age* (Downers Grove, IL: InterVarsity Press, 1992), 63–77.

many historic Reformed doctrines.[28] Modern theological trends were followed by C-67, which spoke of Christ as the "Word of God" rather than Holy Scripture, which was the emphasis of the Westminster Confession, chapter 1. The new confession highlighted the importance of the church's social witness in the midst of American racism, nationalism, poverty, and "anarchy in sexual relationships." All this was a significant shift away from the old Calvinism of Westminster and was a sign of things to come.[29]

Alongside the new confessional statement, the UPCUSA adopted a *Book of Confessions* that contained numerous historic Reformed confessions, and ordination vows were modified to address this expanded confessional basis of the church. Presbyterian ministers now promised to be "under the continuing guidance of the confessions of this Church," but evangelicals wondered if this vague oath had any meaning at all. A new ministerial vow concerning Scripture was unmistakably Barthian: "Do you accept the Scriptures of the Old and New Testaments to be the unique and authoritative witness to Jesus Christ in the Church catholic and by the Holy Spirit God's Word to you?" The new vow appeared to undermine the objective authority of Scripture as divine revelation, and the *Book of Confessions*, it was feared, would dilute clergy accountability to historic Reformed faith.[30]

ETHICAL CONCERNS

In the 1970s, UPCUSA evangelicals relentlessly contested progressive ideas on abortion and homosexuality. Several evangelical organizations within the UPCUSA attempted to combat these liberalizing trends in the northern church.

28. John R. Fry argues that C-67's focus on "reconciliation" transformed the UPCUSA. The new confession became the basis for accepting theological diversity, understanding "mission" as any churchly activity, and providing marching orders for reorganizing the UPCUSA; see *The Trivialization of the United Presbyterian Church* (New York: Harper & Row, 1975), 1–37. Gayraud Wilmore was the only black member of the committee that drafted the Confession of 1967.

29. Milton Coalter, John M. Mulder, and Louis B. Weeks, *The Re-forming Tradition: Presbyterians and Mainstream Protestantism* (Louisville: Westminster John Knox, 1992), 131–33.

30. See James Moorhead, "Redefining Confessionalism: American Presbyterians in the Twentieth Century," in *The Confession Mosaic: Presbyterians and Twentieth-Century Theology*, ed. Milton Coalter, John M. Mulder, and Louis B. Weeks (Louisville: Westminster John Knox, 1990), 59–83; the *Book of Confessions* included the Nicene Creed, Apostles' Creed, Scot's Confession, Heidelberg Catechism, Second Helvetic Confession, Westminster Confession of Faith and Catechisms, Theological Declaration of Barmen, Confession of 1967, and a Brief Statement of Faith.

The Presbyterian Lay Committee (PLC) and Presbyterians United for a Biblical Confession (PUBC) were both established in 1965 to serve as collective voices for evangelicals to address problems in the UPCUSA.[31] The PLC had been started by a group of businessmen concerned about an impending new confession (C-67). Beginning in 1968, the *Presbyterian Layman* was launched as a conservative periodical committed to addressing issues facing the UPCUSA. In 1970 the church came out in favor of legalizing abortion, declaring that "termination of a pregnancy is a matter of the careful ethical decision of the patient." Evangelicals in the mainline founded Presbyterians Pro Life in the coming years, standing firmly in opposition to the pro-choice position of their denomination.[32]

The conservative PUBC and PLC did find success fighting liberalizing trends on human sexuality. The New York Presbytery asked the General Assembly for advice about a homosexual candidate, and a task force was appointed in 1976 with four evangelicals assigned to it. The majority report recommended letting presbyteries use their discretion, but the 1978 Assembly rejected this, instead adopting a minority report. The minority report (reflecting evangelical concerns) included a set of guidelines; these acknowledged that some Presbyterians "are persuaded that there are forms of homosexual behavior that are not sinful and that persons who practice these forms can legitimately be ordained." Encouraging congregations to welcome homosexuals, the Assembly statement admitted that "data in psychology and the social sciences have appeared to challenge the church's traditional posture on this matter"; it also noted that frequently "the results of scientific inquiry are tentative and inconclusive." The General Assembly statement reflecting this minority report, while leaving the door open for further study, clearly affirmed the position of historic Christianity: "We conclude that homosexuality is not God's wish for humanity . . . it is neither a gift from God nor a state nor condition like race; it is a result of our living in a fallen world. . . . We anchor our understanding of homosexuality in the revelation in Scripture of God's intention for human sexuality. . . . Nature confirms revelation in the functional compatibility of male and female genitalia and the natural process of procreation and family continuity." While this statement was a traditionalist victory, it was clear to evangelicals that the push for gay ordination was not going away.[33]

31. After the ratification of the Confession of 1967, the PUBC became "Presbyterians United for Biblical Concerns."

32. The Presbyterian Church (USA) in 1992 adopted its most comprehensive pro-choice statement supportive of *Roe v. Wade*: "The considered decision of a woman to terminate a pregnancy can be a morally acceptable decision, though certainly not the only or required decision." See "Report of the Special Committee on Problem Pregnancy" published by the Office of the General Assembly Presbyterian Church (USA), 1992, 11.

33. "Statement of the Ordination of Homosexuals: Policy Statement and Recommenda-

THREE EMERGING LEADERS

It was in this context of evangelical Presbyterian conservatives toiling to restrain liberalizing tendencies in UPCUSA theology that we can acknowledge the role played by three leaders in particular. The senior figure was John Gerstner (1914–1996), from 1950 a professor of church history at Pittsburgh-Xenia Seminary and (subsequent to a denominational reunion in 1958) the merged Pittsburgh Theological Seminary. In thirty years of classroom teaching and very extensive writing, he became one of the most outspoken advocates of evangelical and Reformed orthodoxy in America. While his own theological convictions were well to the right of center in his home institution, over a long teaching career he was able to mentor a large group of future pastors, many of whom themselves became pronounced defenders of Reformed orthodoxy.[34]

One of the most influential of these Gerstner students was R. C. Sproul (1939–2017). Converted in college, Sproul graduated from Pittsburgh Theological Seminary and went on to study at Amsterdam's Free University. Ordained by the UPCUSA in 1965, he labored as an evangelical in that communion until 1975, when he was received as a minister of the Presbyterian Church in America (PCA). A gifted communicator with a passion for teaching Reformed theology to laypersons, Sproul launched the Ligonier Valley Study Center in 1971, following a pattern similar to that utilized by Francis Schaeffer's L'Abri ministry in Switzerland; the center was eventually renamed Ligonier Ministries and moved from the Pittsburgh area to Orlando, Florida, in 1984.[35] Sproul's teaching ministry gained wide attention through videotapes; conferences; books; a monthly magazine, *Table Talk*; and his radio program, *Renewing Your Mind*. During his years of Christian ministry, Sproul was not only a popular writer and speaker but also served as a local church pastor, as well as teaching at several colleges and seminaries.[36]

Both Gerstner and Sproul came to be associated with a third northern

---

tions," in *Minutes of the General Assembly of the United Presbyterian Church in the United States of America* (NY: Office of the General Assembly, 1978), 261–67. The PCUS adopted the same statement in 1979.

34. Gerstner's career and wider influence have been most helpfully explored in the recent intellectual biography by Jeffrey S. McDonald, *John Gerstner and the Renewal of Presbyterian and Reformed Evangelicalism in Modern America* (Eugene, OR: Wipf & Stock, 2017). Gerstner's role, during his post-1980 retirement years, in urging others to leave his theologically comprehensive denomination is explored below at p. 308 n. 9.

35. Reference has been made to Schaeffer's launching of the L'Abri ministry above at pp. 277–78.

36. See Justin Taylor, "R. C. Sproul (1939–2017)," *Gospel Coalition*, December 14, 2017, www.thegospelcoalition.org/blogs/justin-taylor/r-c-sproul-1939-2017/. Sproul's most pop-

Presbyterian evangelical leader, James Montgomery Boice (1938–2000), pastor of Tenth Presbyterian Church, Philadelphia, from 1968 until his untimely death. A native of Pittsburgh, Pennsylvania, and a Harvard graduate, Boice also gained degrees at Princeton Seminary and the University of Basel. After his studies, Boice initially served as an assistant editor for *Christianity Today* magazine. His long ministry at Tenth continued the Barnhouse expository tradition and yielded a host of expositional commentaries, as well as a range of works on doctrinal themes.[37] Beginning in 1974, under Boice's pastoral leadership, Tenth Presbyterian began to host an important annual conference, the Philadelphia Conference on Reformed Theology; it was originally an attempt to reassert conservative Reformed theology within the Presbyterian mainline and within American evangelicalism.[38] Gerstner and Sproul, who, like Boice, were advocating this same stance within the UPCUSA, were often featured speakers in those annual meetings, which in time spread to the West Coast and the American Midwest. In light of that denomination's 1979 insistence that all congregations elect female elders, the congregation reaffiliated first to the Reformed Presbyterian Church, Evangelical Synod (RPCES) and then to the PCA, when the RPCES was received into the PCA in 1982.[39]

Southern Evangelicals Organize

Evangelicals in the PCUS, responding to encroaching liberal theology, started a new periodical in 1942, the *Southern Presbyterian Journal*, as a voice of conservative concern. Under the leadership of L. Nelson Bell, the *Presbyterian Journal*, as it was later renamed, became a rallying point for addressing concerns in the PCUS. Conservative southern Presbyterians were especially supportive of Billy Graham's ministry, which was followed closely in the pages of the *Southern Presbyterian Journal*. In 1952 Bell wrote, "The *Journal* has rejoiced in the results of the Billy Graham campaigns across America. . . . We rejoice in the results of this ministry because it is the message of historic Christianity based

---

ular books were *The Holiness of God* (1985) and *Chosen by God* (1986). For a biography, see Stephen Nichols, *R. C. Sproul: A Life* (Wheaton, IL: Crossway, 2021).

37. "Obituary: Boice, 61, Dies of Liver Cancer," *Christianity Today*, August 7, 2000, https://www.christianitytoday.com/ct/2000/august7/8.19.html?ctlredirect=true.

38. Boice described the initial success of these conferences in a March 1975 *Christianity Today* article, "Is the Reformed Faith Being Rediscovered?" The article is viewable at https://www.christianitytoday.com/ct/1975/march-28/is-reformed-faith-being-rediscovered.html.

39. D. G. Hart and John Muether, *Seeking a Better Country* (Phillipsburg, NJ: P&R, 2007), 239–40.

solely on faith in the authority and the complete reliability of the Scriptures."[40] Dr. Bell, who had been a missionary in China prior to World War II, became a prominent American evangelical spokesman in the postwar decades because of his famous son-in-law, Billy Graham, and his part in founding *Christianity Today* (1956). Bell wrote columns for *Christianity Today* over many years.[41]

Evangelical angst over creeping universalism, which undermined the priority of the Great Commission, motivated the organization of Presbyterian Evangelistic Fellowship (PEF), founded by Bill Hill in 1964, to support both home and foreign missions. PEF leadership would become instrumental in conservatives pushing to leave the PCUS. Southern conservatives were concerned enough about the theological direction of the Presbyterian seminaries that they discussed starting a new school for ministerial preparation. These discussions were accelerated by brief essays in the *Presbyterian Outlook* by four PCUS seminary professors who argued that the church did not need an infallible Bible.[42] A handful of laymen and ministers prayerfully began plans for a new seminary, which opened in 1966 as Reformed Theological Seminary in Jackson, Mississippi. Sam Patterson, the first president, along with two professors and seventeen students, made for a meager beginning that in time would expand to nine campuses, becoming one of the largest seminaries in the United States. A number of Reformed Seminary graduates would participate in a movement to establish a new southern Presbyterian denomination.[43]

An evangelical organization committed to remaining in the PCUS and pursuing denominational renewal was the Covenant Fellowship of Presbyterians (CFP). The roots of the CFP can be traced back to a meeting of moderate Presbyterian leaders in 1967. Dr. William M. Elliott Jr., senior pastor of Highland Park Presbyterian Church in Dallas, called these leaders together to discuss

40. *Southern Presbyterian Journal*, August 15, 1952.

41. L. Nelson Bell, *While Men Slept: A Concerned Layman's View of the Church Today* (Garden City, NY: Doubleday, 1970). This book is a collection of Bell's essays in *Christianity Today*. Bell's commitment to Christian social ministry was self-evident in his medical missionary labors in China (1916–1941); John Pollock, *A Foreign Devil in China: The Story of Dr. L. Nelson Bell* (Minneapolis: World Wide Publications, 1971).

42. "Do We Need an Infallible Bible?," *Presbyterian Outlook*, December 24, 1962, 5, 6. Dr. James H. Gailey Jr., OT Professor at Columbia Theological Seminary, argued that God is infallible, not the Bible. Using unmistakable Barthian language, he stated, "The Bible is the authoritative and inspired witness and instrument of God's redemptive work."

43. John Muether, *A Mind for Truth, a Heart for God: The First Fifty Years of Reformed Theological Seminary* (Montgomery, AL: Walker360, 2016). Muether notes that as Fuller Seminary shaped the direction of American evangelicalism, so Reformed Theological Seminary has "played a significant role in shaping Reformed evangelicalism in America over the past fifty years" (13).

tensions between liberals and conservatives in the PCUS. The group issued an "Open Letter" to the PCUS, addressing the conflict between extreme groups in the denomination; each was represented by a church periodical: the liberal *Presbyterian Outlook* and the conservative *Southern Presbyterian Journal.* The "Open Letter" declared that "the overwhelming majority of our people stand somewhere between these two positions but they are largely without a voice, and are earnestly longing for leadership which represents their convictions." The letter argued for recognizing the principles of both liberals and conservatives (personal salvation, social action) and calling for better communication between the groups in order to resolve differences.[44] The battle between liberals and conservatives in the PCUS had been going on for decades, but the General Assembly of 1969 appeared to be a turning point for liberal hegemony. In 1969 the southern Assembly set in motion the mechanisms for accomplishing the liberal agenda—union presbyteries, restructuring synods and presbyteries, restructuring boards and agencies, a new confession. All these actions were directed toward union with the UPCUSA, which conservatives had resisted. By this time the northern church had adopted C-67, a new *Book of Confessions,* and new ordination vows; it appeared that the southern church was moving in the same direction.[45]

When the "moderate middle" CFP was publicly launched in 1970, it staked out its position by affirming its evangelical principles, including the priority of proclaiming the good news to sinners and recognizing a call to action in areas that affect the whole life of humankind. CFP leadership declared: "We, therefore, call all the members of the Presbyterian church in the United States to join with us to rededicate ourselves to the Lord Jesus Christ as our only Savior and living example and to one another in humility, forbearance, and love on the basis of the historical Christian faith as taught in the Scriptures."[46] CFP's ministry over two decades would include advocacy of evangelical views in church courts, organizing annual evangelistic youth conferences, encouraging pastors, supporting evangelical seminary students, and sponsoring Lay Renewal Weekends in local congregations.[47] The PCUS in the mid-1970s was moving

44. Harry S. Hassall, *On Jordan's Stormy Banks I Stand: A Historical Commentary on the Life and Times of the Covenant Fellowship of Presbyterians* (unpublished manuscript, 1989), 6–9.

45. See *Minutes of the General Assembly,* PCUS, 1969; Thompson, *Presbyterians in the South,* 3:576–82; Bradley J. Longfield, *Presbyterians and American Culture: A History* (Louisville: Westminster John Knox, 2013), 195, 196.

46. Hassall, *On Jordan's Stormy Banks I Stand,* 19.

47. A key leader of CFP was Clayton Bell, pastor of First Presbyterian in Rome, Georgia. Bell was the son of L. Nelson Bell and the brother of Ruth Bell Graham, wife of Billy

forward to adopt a new confessional document, A Declaration of Faith, and a *Book of Confessions*, mirroring the UPCUSA's new confessional basis. Due in large part to the efforts of CFP, both were defeated in 1977; nevertheless, the persistent move toward union with the northern church continued unabated. The leadership of CFP believed it could support a PCUSA/PCUS union under the right circumstances, and proceeded to exert their influence within reunion discussions, hoping for favorable conditions for evangelicals.[48]

PRESBYTERIAN CHURCH IN AMERICA

Many southern Presbyterians were becoming convinced that separation from the PCUS was inevitable given the trajectory of theological drift in their denomination. Chief among conservative concerns was the persistent push for ecumenism within the PCUS—increasing support for NCC policies, participation in COCU, and the quest for reunion with the UPCUSA. Underlying this ecumenism, conservatives perceived erosion of biblical authority, a universalist theology, and a diminished commitment to historic Reformed theology. There were practical implications from this ecumenism for evangelism and missions, as these ecumenical relationships accented social justice as the primary mission of the church versus the evangelization of a world spiritually lost without Christ. For L. Nelson Bell, the bottom line in all these matters was mainline progressives' changing perspectives on the Bible; that is, they no longer affirmed its full authority, which meant that commitment to a biblical gospel, morality, and evangelism had so dissipated that the result was "a religion which is not Christianity."[49]

Conservatives who had connected with one another in like-minded organizations for decades began to contemplate leaving the PCUS and establishing a new denomination. One of these groups was Concerned Presbyterians (CP), established in 1964 for conservative laymen within the PCUS. Nelson Bell had been one of the original founders of CP, but over time he became uncomfortable with the group's direction when separation from the PCUS was contemplated. In 1968, CP met together with a group of ministers in Atlanta to discuss ways of reforming their denomination. Out of this meeting came

---

Graham. In 1973, he succeeded Dr. William Elliott as pastor of Highland Park Presbyterian in Dallas, which by the early 1980s was the largest Presbyterian church in the United States, with 7,500 members. Clayton Bell also served as chairman of the board for *Christianity Today*.

48. Hassall, *On Jordan's Stormy Banks I Stand*, 54–63.

49. L. Nelson Bell, "Not 'New'—but Very Different," *Presbyterian Journal*, May 26, 1965, 7, 8.

a "Declaration of Commitment," declaring commitment to Presbyterian ordination vows and the Westminster Confession, opposition to any new creed
and to COCU, and affirmation of biblical infallibility and the necessity of faith
in Christ for salvation. Another gathering was held the next year in Atlanta
with over 1,500 in attendance as momentum was building in the Continuing
Church Movement—that is, the old Southern Presbyterian Church and its
principles would be "continued" in a new denomination. D. James Kennedy,
pastor of the large Coral Ridge Presbyterian Church, addressed this group, declaring the importance of faithfulness to Scripture and evangelism, and noting
that the movement was not about preserving segregation.[50]

After the 1971 General Assembly, twenty-nine men met in July and adopted
"A Plan for the Continuation of a Presbyterian Church Loyal to Scripture and
the Reformed Faith," which set in motion the impending departure of congregations from the PCUS. At a September meeting in Atlanta, conservative
leaders issued "A Declaration of Intent," stating their desire for a church "Presbyterian in government, Reformed in doctrine, fervent in evangelism and concerned for human welfare." At a meeting of the steering committee tasked with
directing plans toward a withdrawal, Presbyterian cultural apologist Francis
Schaeffer addressed the group: "When it is no longer possible to practice discipline in church courts, then you must practice discipline in reverse and leave,
but your leaving must be with tears, not with flags flying and bands playing."

In May of 1973, a convocation of sessions met in Atlanta, to set in motion
plans for a new Presbyterian denomination comprised of churches departing
the PCUS. In December of that year, the first Assembly of the National Presbyterian Church convened at Briarwood Presbyterian Church in Birmingham
(pastor, Frank Barker) with representatives from 212 churches. The next year
the name of the new denomination was changed to the Presbyterian Church
in America (PCA).[51] The 1973 Assembly issued a statement setting out its
justification for separation from the mother church, citing these issues: "a
diluted theology, a gospel tending towards humanism, an unbiblical view of
marriage and divorce, the ordination of women, financing of abortion . . . , and
numerous other non-Biblical positions . . . all traceable to a different view of
Scripture from that which we hold and that which was held by the Southern
Presbyterian forefathers."[52]

---

50. Kennedy Smartt, *I Am Reminded: An Autographical, Anecdotal History of the Presbyterian Church in America* (Chestnut Mountain, GA: n.p., 1998), 46–54.

51. The National Presbyterian Church in Washington, DC, objected to the use of its
name; thus a new name was chosen at the second General Assembly in 1974.

52. Lucas, *For a Continuing Church*, 281–314; see also Morton H. Smith, *How Is the
Gold Become Dim: The Decline of the Presbyterian Church, U.S., as Reflected in Its Assembly*

The founders of the PCA were intentional about returning to a former era of Presbyterian faithfulness. In their zeal to establish a "continuing church," they adopted the earlier version of the Westminster Confession and Catechisms endorsed by the nineteenth-century Southern Presbyterian church. The PCA's polity also revisited historic Presbyterian practice by limiting church office (ministers, elders, and deacons) to men. From the beginning, the PCA wanted to be a grassroots movement that avoided the clergy-run centralized bureaucracy they had experienced in the PCUS. Therefore, parity of teaching and ruling elders was required by church polity, and denominational structure would be organized by committees answerable to the General Assembly rather than independent boards. The first moderator of the PCA was layman W. Jack Williamson, and the stated clerk was Dr. Morton Smith, who had been a theology professor at Reformed Seminary, Jackson, Mississippi.

The group of ministers that shaped the PCA was roughly divided into two groups: those who had a vision of the PCA as a historically confessional Presbyterian body and a larger group who found their primary identity in being evangelical Presbyterians driven by the concerns of evangelism and world missions.[53] These diverse emphases were not mutually exclusive but were the cause of ongoing tension in the young denomination as it defined its place among the Presbyterian family of churches. When division finally arrived in 1973, in many ways it was simply formalizing a reality that had already existed. Many conservatives felt that the ever-changing PCUS had left them, while their convictions had never wavered. They desired a continuing southern Presbyterian church committed to evangelism and the historic Reformed tradition—something that, from their perspective, had ceased to exist in the mainline church. Westminster Theological Seminary, Philadelphia, which was highly respected by southern Presbyterian evangelicals, trained many new pastors for the PCA. A number of Westminster faculty members (including the president at that time, Edmund Clowney) and trustees would be members of the PCA.

Actions, 2nd ed. (Jackson, MI: Premier Printing Company, 1973), published by the Steering Committee for a Continuing Presbyterian Church, Faithful to the Scriptures and the Reformed Faith. The document was published under the name *A Message to All Churches of Jesus Christ throughout the World from the National Presbyterian Church*. It is viewable at https://pcahistory.org/documents/message.pdf.

53. Kennedy Smartt, one of the PCA founders, commented on the 1986 General Assembly's affirmative vote to join the NAE (352 in favor, 274 opposed): "Those who were in favor felt it was important for our testimony before the watching world (Schaeffer) and also for the ministry and testimony of Mission to the World [PCA's world missions committee]." Smartt, *I Am Reminded*, 174.

With its southern roots, the PCA has been sensitive to racial issues in the South, both in the past and in the present. In 2004, the PCA General Assembly adopted a pastoral letter on "the gospel and race." The paper acknowledged the sin of unbiblical forms of slavery and encouraged soul-searching and repentance from ongoing sins of racism in congregations. Again in 2016, the PCA addressed the race issue with the overture "Pursuing Racial Reconciliation and the Advance of the Gospel." In 2018, a final paper entitled "Racial and Ethnic Reconciliation," building upon the 2016 overture, was approved.[54]

All the American Presbyterian denominations have historically been involved in both foreign and home missions. Many have mission boards or committees that strategize, oversee funding, recruit missionaries, and support them on the field. The contemporary Presbyterian exemplar of fervent evangelism and world missions over the last half century has been the PCA, the second-largest Presbyterian denomination in the United States. In the almost five decades since its founding in 1973, the PCA has grown from just over 200 congregations to almost 1,600, a product of its aggressive church-planting efforts coordinated by Mission to North America, its home missions agency.

A leading voice for aggressive church planting in the PCA since the 1990s has been Tim Keller, founding pastor of Redeemer Presbyterian Church in Manhattan. After serving as a professor at Westminster Theological Seminary, Keller founded Redeemer Church in 1989. Within two and a half decades, the church had grown to over five thousand attending worship on Sundays in three locations throughout the city; most of the church attendees are young urban professionals. Keller has had a burden not only for reaching urban America but also for planting new congregations in global cities. In 2001, he founded Redeemer City to City as a church-planting network for training and resourcing leaders to plant urban churches in the United States and around the globe. By 2020, City to City had helped with over 750 new church plants in 150 global cities throughout Africa, Asia, Australia, North America, the Middle East, and Europe. These churches have organized themselves into sixty city networks that are continuing to plant churches in their urban centers.[55]

---

54. *Minutes of the General Assembly of the Presbyterian Church in America*, 2004, appendix H, 427–57. See also *The Pursuit of Gospel Liberty: The PCA Position Papers on Racism and Racial Reconciliation* (Atlanta: PCA Committee on Discipleship Ministries, 2019).

55. See www.timkeller.com, www.redeemercitytocity.com; Timothy Keller, *Center Church: Doing Balanced, Gospel-Centered Ministry in Your City* (Grand Rapids: Zondervan, 2012). Keller's sermons and writings have been extremely popular and respected among American evangelicals. His best-selling books include *Reason for God: Belief in an Age of Skepticism* (New York: Penguin Random House, 2008) and *The Prodigal God: Recovering the Heart of the Christian Faith* (New York: Penguin Random House, 2008).

Redeemer's mercy ministries and efforts by groups such as Desire Street Ministries in New Orleans reflect the PCA's ministry to the urban poor. Though the PCA was primarily a white southern church from its founding, it has proactively reached out to minorities and currently has about fifty black pastors and over forty Hispanic congregations.

Reformed University Fellowship (RUF) is the PCA's ministry on university campuses across the country. By 2019, RUF was in forty states and on 169 campuses (including 16 international campuses). RUF has been intentional about outreach to minorities as well as international students. Campus ministers are ordained PCA ministers and are joined by additional campus staff and annual interns, many of whom end up going to seminary and entering full-time ministry. The PCA's foreign mission endeavors are implemented through Mission to the World, which supports about six hundred missionaries in sixty countries around the globe.[56]

56. These statistics come from 2019 PCA reports and from information supplied by ministry leaders within the PCA.

CHAPTER 19

Evangelical Marginalization and Resurgence

The 1980s coursed with optimism in domestic and foreign affairs: economic prosperity in the United States, the introduction of personal computers, the completion of the first successful Space Shuttle mission, a War on Drugs, a military buildup challenging the Soviet Union, conclusion of the Cold War and toppling of the Berlin Wall. There were international challenges: famine in Ethiopia, the Chernobyl disaster, and wars—Iran/Iraq, Soviet Union/Afghanistan, and the First Intifada in the Gaza Strip and West Bank. In the 1990s, there was genocide in Rwanda and Bosnia and the first Gulf War, which became a precursor to ongoing US military involvement in the Arab world combating Islamic terrorism. On the home front, domestic terrorism hit the United States with bombings at the New York World Trade Center and in Oklahoma City. An international War on Terror began to drain American military and economic resources.

Racial issues in the 1990s were ever present in the media frenzy over the Supreme Court confirmation hearings of Justice Clarence Thomas (1991) and the O. J. Simpson trial (1995). Homosexuality was becoming more acceptable in society, and a sitting US president took sexual advantage of a young White House intern. In 2005 Hurricane Katrina hit New Orleans and the Gulf Coast, causing billions in damage, and a 2007–2008 collapse of the housing market led to failed banks, bailouts of the auto industry, and a significant rise in unemployment. Congregations and denominations felt this economic downturn in reduced giving and expressed a new urgency to care for unemployed church members. By 2005, the United States had its first black female secretary of state, Presbyterian Condoleezza Rice, and in 2008 elected its first black president.[1] These three decades were full of massive cultural changes, bringing with

---

1. Dr. Condoleezza Rice, professor of foreign policy and director of the Hoover Institute at Stanford University, served as national security advisor and then as secretary of

them increased political polarization over economics, education, the environment, gay marriage, abortion, transgender rights, and racism.

Presbyterianism in the United States became progressively a divided house, sometimes mirroring the divisions in the nation. Most of the theological differences boiled down to competing understandings of biblical authority in a pluralistic society. Was Christianity just one of several legitimate religious options, or was Christ the only way of salvation for a lost humanity? Does Holy Scripture have the final word on human sexuality? Presbyterians gave sundry answers to these questions, and ultimately it produced more schism.

CHURCH UNIONS AND REUNIONS

At the end of the first decade of the Presbyterian Church in America (PCA) in 1982, it united with the Reformed Presbyterian Church, Evangelical Synod (RPCES). The RPCES had been formed by the 1965 union of the Evangelical Presbyterian Church (EPC) and the Reformed Presbyterian Church in North America, General Synod (RPCNA, GS). The origin of the EPC is traceable to a schism within the Orthodox Presbyterian Church (OPC); J. Oliver Buswell and Carl McIntire led a group of ministers out of the OPC in 1937, taking with them the Independent Board for Presbyterian Foreign Missions. The Buswell/McIntire group took the name Bible Presbyterian Church (BPC) and were distinguished by their commitment to premillennialism, their abstinence from alcohol, and their separatist attitudes toward both those considered doctrinal apostates and those who fellowshiped with them. By 1956 McIntire had separated again by leading a group out of the BPC; those remaining in the BPC changed their name to the Evangelical Presbyterian Church in 1961.

The RPCNA, GS, with whom the Evangelical Presbyterians merged, had roots going back to the Scottish Covenanters who immigrated to America. Union with the Evangelical Presbyterians in 1965 seemed the best way of ensuring their own continuation. The merged church was henceforth known as the RPCES.[2] In 1982, the OPC (founded 1936) was included in union discussions with the PCA and RPCES but ultimately did not join in a three-way

state during the George W. Bush administration (2001–2009). She spent her childhood in Birmingham, Alabama, where her father, John Wesley Rice Jr., was a Presbyterian minister and then dean of students at Stillman College in Tuscaloosa, a historically black college started by Presbyterians. See Sheryl Henderson Blunt, "The Unflappable Condi Rice: Why the World's Most Powerful Woman Asks God for Help," *Christianity Today*, September 3, 2003, 42–46.

2. George P. Hutchinson, *The History behind the Reformed Presbyterian Church, Evangelical Synod* (Cherry Hill, NJ: Mack, 1974), 224–407.

union. Only the RPCES joined the PCA, bringing with her two RPCES institutions, Covenant College in Lookout Mountain, Georgia, and Covenant
Seminary in St. Louis.[3]

The year after the PCA/RPCES "joining and receiving," the reunion of
the Northern and Southern Presbyterian churches finally became a reality.
Despite the failure of reunion negotiations in the early decades of the twentieth century, those who favored north-south union kept the issue before the
church in the years after World War II. Even after another failed attempt at
merger in the 1950s, the ecumenists in the United Presbyterian Church in
the United States of America (UPCUSA) and the Presbyterian Church in the
United States (PCUS) would not be deterred. In 1969, the two Presbyterian
bodies adopted a plan for "union presbyteries" that allowed presbyteries in
the PCUS and UPCUSA to be members of both denominations. The two
denominations also decided to hold their General Assemblies in the same
city in alternate years in another attempt to foster fraternal relations. Those
opposed to reunion viewed union presbyteries as reunion through the back
door and resented it.

In the late 1970s, reunion discussions between the PCUS and UPCUSA
were on a fast track, and conservatives were torn about what a reunion might
bring. Some evangelicals believed reunion to be a good thing; combining the
conservative influence in both churches could potentially produce a stronger voice for biblical faithfulness. Other evangelicals viewed the reunion as
another minimalist attempt to advance Christian union at any cost. In an
adroit ecclesiastical move, Southern Presbyterian evangelicals secured a special provision in the Plan for Reunion; PCUS churches would have the option
of withdrawing from the reunited church. This provision, known as "Article
Thirteen," gave Southern churches up to eight years after reunion to leave
for another Reformed body, along with their church property. The Plan for
Reunion stipulated: "If two thirds of those present and voting vote to request
dismissal, this particular church will be dismissed under the special provisions of Article Thirteen of the Articles of Agreement, and will retain all of its
property, subject to any existing liens and encumbrances, but will surrender
its membership in the Presbyterian Church (U.S.A.)."[4]

---

3. See Frank J. Smith, *The History of the Presbyterian Church in America*, silver anniversary
edition (Lawrenceville, GA: Presbyterian Scholars Press, 1999), 372, 373. The RPCES had several larger churches with women deacons that were "grandfathered" when entering the PCA.

4. *The Plan of Reunion of the Presbyterian Church in the United States and the United
Presbyterian Church in the United States of America*, 13.3.e, prepared by the Joint Committee
on Presbyterian Reunion, final edition, 2nd printing (Stated Clerk of the General Assembly
of the Presbyterian Church in the United States, 1981), 29.

ARTICLE THIRTEEN PROVISIONS: CONSEQUENCES

The church property component of Article Thirteen was a key provision; state courts had given markedly different interpretations of the PCUS constitution's understanding of property ownership during the 1970s when the PCA was in formation. Under this exclusive arrangement to appease southern conservatives, the evangelical PCUS churches would be more likely to vote in favor of reunion, knowing that they would have unencumbered freedom to withdraw if the reunion proved unsatisfactory. Because a Supreme Court decision in 1979 had favored local churches,[5] both the PCUS and the UPCUSA strengthened constitutional provisions making explicit the denominational ownership of property. While the Plan for Reunion granted the right of property ownership to southern congregations choosing not to remain in the reunited church, it also strengthened denominational ownership of all church properties for the rest of the churches.

Another major issue for conservatives in the PCUS was the ordination of women and "the right to hold conscientious differences." Conservatives considering the proposed union had objections in principle to the controversial "Overture L" of the UPCUSA; this mandated the election of women and minorities of all ages to church sessions. The final version of the Plan for Reunion stipulated that women must be elected as church officers, but it provided for exceptions if "effort is being made to move toward compliance."[6]

In 1983 the Plan for Reunion was approved by the UPCUSA presbyteries (152–3) and the PCUS presbyteries (53–8); five of the negative PCUS presbytery votes were from South Carolina. The reunited church took the name Presbyterian Church (USA), redrew presbytery lines, united all organizations within the two previous bodies, and moved denominational headquarters from Atlanta (PCUS) and New York (UPCUSA) to a new joint office in Louisville, Kentucky.[7] The mainline church had finally mended the breach that had divided it north and south since 1861. The reunited PC(USA) now contained 3.2 million members; however, major decline in membership had already been taking place for several decades and continued after the reunion.[8]

---

5. SCOTUS upheld the decision of the Georgia Supreme Court (*Jones v. Wolf*) that the property of Vineville Presbyterian Church, a member of Augusta-Macon Presbytery, was not held in trust for the PCUS.

6. *The Plan of Reunion*, 129, 131.

7. From this point onward, this work utilizes the term PC(USA) to refer exclusively to the post-1983 merged denomination.

8. Bradley J. Longfield, *Presbyterians and American Culture: A History* (Louisville: Westminster John Knox, 2013), 197–99.

Evangelical Presbyterian Church

A group of evangelical ministers and churches (within both the PCUS and the UPCUSA), during the latter years of reunion negotiations, began considering the formation of yet another Presbyterian body. One catalyst for considering departure from the mainline was the 1979 Mansfield Kaseman controversy in the UPCUSA. Kaseman, a United Church of Christ (UCC) pastor, was called to be copastor of a UCC congregation in Maryland, a union congregation with joint membership in the UCC and the UPCUSA. During his examination before National Capital Union Presbytery of the UPCUSA, Kaseman was asked to affirm that "Jesus is God," to which he replied, "No, God is God." Despite this denial of Christ's deity, his pastoral call was approved by the presbytery. A number of evangelicals in the presbytery filed a complaint. The Permanent Judicial Commission (PJC) of the UPCUSA heard the complaint and referred the matter back to the presbytery for further examination. Kaseman was approved again by the presbytery, 165 to 58, and the decision was upheld by the PJC. After widespread complaints, the 1981 UPCUSA General Assembly did make a pronouncement affirming the deity of Christ, but the PJC's handling of the Kaseman case was a breaking point for some, who decided an exodus was required since the UPCUSA had accepted apostasy in one of its ministers.[9]

Two ministers were uniquely instrumental in leading the new exodus out of mainline Presbyterianism, Bartlett Hess and Andy Jumper. Hess was pastor of Ward Presbyterian Church in Detroit (UPCUSA) and had served on the Joint Committee of Union (JCOU); Jumper, pastor of Central Presbyterian Church in St. Louis (PCUS), had likewise served on the JCOU. Both men had front-row seats to reunion negotiations and had lobbied JCOU regarding evangelical concerns on women's ordination and church property. Jumper had been a chief architect of Article Thirteen in the Plan for Reunion. At the conclusion of the 1980 UPCUSA General Assembly, which Hess had attended, he met with the Ward Session to discuss three problematic actions of the 1980 General Assembly—the refusal to denounce Kaseman; the reaffirmation of Overture L, making women's ordination mandatory; and the approval of a constitutional amendment giving ownership of local church property to the denomination. The Ward Session created a "reasons for withdrawing" document, adding

9. For an overview of the Kaseman debacle and Pittsburgh professor John Gerstner's charge of "apostasy" against the UPCUSA, see Jeffrey S. McDonald, *John Gerstner and the Renewal of Presbyterian and Reformed Evangelicalism in Modern America* (Eugene, OR: Wipf & Stock, 2017), 146–52. In 1981, when the UPCUSA Assembly reaffirmed its belief in the deity of Christ, Gerstner walked back his charge of apostasy. Gerstner would join the PCA in 1990.

to these three issues its concerns about UPCUSA neglect of missions and evangelism, support for liberation theology, advocacy of abortion, and official recognition of a gay caucus. Later that year, Hess and Jumper convened a meeting in St. Louis to set in motion plans to establish the Evangelical Presbyterian Church (EPC). The EPC (1981) adopted this name since the earlier EPC (1961) had surrendered the name in its merger with the RPCNA, GS, to form the RPCES in 1965. A steering committee was directed to edit provisional constitutional documents and report to the first General Assembly (1981), which convened at Ward Presbyterian Church. The first EPC Assembly, with representatives from fifteen churches, adopted a *Book of Government*, ordained six ministers, received a new congregation, and elected Dr. Ed Davis as stated clerk, a position he held until 2000. After 1983, additional congregations were added from the reunited PC(USA), including some former PCUS congregations that withdrew under provisions of Article Thirteen. A few independent churches and new church plants also joined the EPC.[10]

The EPC constitution included a modern-English version of the Westminster Confession and Catechisms with the additional 1903 chapters, "The Holy Spirit" and "The Gospel of the Love of God and Missions." An "Essentials of the Faith" document was written by the EPC, but the statement would cause dissension in future years due to early confusion about its purpose. A few EPC ministers considered the "Essentials" the minimal standard of belief for ordination rather than the Westminster Standards. One of the problems with this idea was that the "Essentials," though adopted by the first General Assembly, had never officially been part of the EPC constitution. In 2002, the EPC officially inserted a reference to the "Essentials" into an ordination vow but then added "An Explanatory Statement to 'Essentials of Our Faith'" in the Book of Order that explained, "The Westminster Confession of Faith is our standard of doctrine. . . . 'Essentials of Our Faith' is an irenic statement of historic evangelicalism. . . . It is not to be construed as a substitute for the Westminster Confession of Faith." These amendments strengthened the EPC's Reformed identity.[11]

Another test of the EPC's Reformed commitments was its handling of the controversial charismatic movement that had stirred American evangelicalism in the 1960s and 1970s. Within the mainline Presbyterian churches, the

10. S. Donald Fortson III, *Liberty in Non-Essentials: The Story of the Evangelical Presbyterian Church* (Livonia, MI: Evangelical Presbyterian Church, 2016), 27–80. The original document, "Essentials of the Faith," was later retitled as "Essentials of Our Faith" during the controversy over the function of the "Essentials" in the EPC.

11. Fortson, *Liberty in Non-Essentials*, 137–66.

charismatic movement had touched a number of ministers, as well as stagnant church members, who were either genuinely converted or revitalized by this effusion of the Spirit. While tongues and "prophetic gifts" were associated with the movement, it was distinct from Pentecostalism and the emphasis was on genuine conversion, committed discipleship, and evangelism. The EPC founders wished to affirm not only legitimate parts of the charismatic renewal but also the priority of Scripture.

In the early years, the EPC Assembly adopted a "Position Paper on the Holy Spirit" and in 1992 added further interpretive statements that expressed a balanced Reformed understanding of the Spirit's work by carefully defining "the baptism in the Spirit" as regeneration and not a second work of grace. On the other hand, the EPC declared, "As a Reformed denomination, we adhere strongly to our belief in the sovereignty of God, a belief that does not allow us either to require a certain gift or to restrict the Spirit in how He will work." This nuanced perspective reflected EPC membership, which included both charismatic and noncharismatic congregations and ministers.[12]

One factor that distinguished the EPC was its unique neutrality on women officers. Women's ordination to all church offices had been a "given" in the mainline church for decades. Many evangelicals had come to terms with this situation, believing it constituted no grounds for separation, and some were convinced that Scripture allowed for women to serve in ordained office. Numerous conservative Presbyterian churches (north and south) had women officers and wanted to preserve this practice in the EPC. There were others who held traditional views on women's ordination and had been marginalized for it in the mainline. The denomination staked out new territory by neither requiring nor forbidding women officers, believing women's ordination was a "nonessential" about which faithful believers reach different biblical interpretations. The EPC General Assembly adopted a "Position Paper on Women's Ordination" in 1986, acknowledging that "people of good faith who equally love the Lord and hold to the infallibility of Scripture differ on the issue."[13] The 2011 General Assembly modified the *Book of Government* to allow a congregation to transfer to a bordering presbytery if a female candidate/minister is prohibited from admission in a presbytery predominantly opposed to women clergy. The compromise retained the EPC's position on women's ordination by providing constitutional safeguards that affirmed both a local church's liberty to call a minister of its choosing and a presbytery's authority to determine its own membership.[14]

12. Fortson, *Liberty in Non-Essentials*, 99–101, 122–25.
13. *Minutes of the General Assembly*, EPC, 1986, 39–41.
14. Fortson, *Liberty in Non-Essentials*, 61–62, 95–99, 208–20. This policy has worked

A new wave of PC(USA) churches began inquiring about membership in the EPC during the first decade of the new century. Concerned about being overwhelmed by a large influx of new congregations, the EPC adopted a new structure in 2007 called a "transitional presbytery." Under this policy, churches might be received into a transitional nongeographic presbytery; the provision would only exist for five years. Churches and pastors received into a transitional presbytery would apply to be received by a permanent geographic presbytery. After the five years, a church that had not been received into an existing EPC presbytery would be dismissed to independency. The five-year structure provided an extended time of deliberation for congregations considering the EPC so that both sides could insure a good fit. A number of congregations belonging to a support network of conservative PC(USA) churches called New Wineskins voted to be dismissed from the PC(USA) and into the EPC transitional presbytery. During the years 2007–2011, the EPC received 120 congregations from the PC(USA), and by 2019 had grown to over 600 congregations and 145,000 members.[15]

Human Sexuality and Scripture

The beginning of the gay rights movement in America is associated with the 1969 Stonewall riots in New York City. Gay demonstrators were arrested, eliciting sympathy; thereafter, the gay community commenced organized efforts to achieve legal and social rights. In 1973, the American Psychiatric Association (APA) removed homosexuality from its officially approved list of psychiatric illnesses, bolstering gay activists' efforts to aggressively pursue public approval of homosexuality.[16] To achieve this goal, gay advocates began talking about gayness through every available venue of the mainstream media. The strategy was to make gays look acceptable and to vilify opponents in the public eye. The goal was to attain social tolerance and eventually the celebration of homo-

---

reasonably well since 2011; according to Jeff Jeremiah, stated clerk of the EPC, by 2020 no more than eight congregations have transferred to a bordering presbytery, with at least two "coming back" to their geographic presbytery after the woman pastor retired or took a call to another church.

15. Fortson, *Liberty in Non-Essentials*, 186–96.

16. See Robert R. Reilly's *Making Gay Okay: How Rationalizing Homosexual Behavior Is Changing Everything* (San Francisco: Ignatius, 2014), which includes a thorough overview of gay activism within psychology influencing the APA 1975 statement that "being gay is just as healthy as being straight." Reilly asserts that there is "no credible science to substantiate this assertion" (127).

sexuality.[17] There was pushback from the public, and in 1996 the US Congress passed the Defense of Marriage Act (DOMA), which defined marriage as the union of one man and one woman. However, in *Lawrence v. Texas* (2003), the US Supreme Court declared homosexual activity between consenting adults legal. This decision, striking down a Texas law that criminalized sodomy, invalidated similar laws in thirteen other states. The states continued to be divided on same-sex marriage as a result of contradictory court rulings and voter initiatives that had mixed results. Alongside gay political activism, a gay Christian movement emerged with the similar goal of gaining approval in American churches. All the mainline denominations would experience prolonged battles over homosexuality from the 1970s forward, most of them eventually approving full inclusion of the LGBTQ community within the church.

In 1972, the United Church of Christ (UCC) became the first denomination to ordain an openly gay minister, and five years later it ordained the first lesbian minister. It would be another forty years before the PC(USA) would approve gay ordination.[18]

The 1978 UPCUSA "Statement on the Ordination of Homosexuals: Policy Statement and Recommendations" had welcomed gays and lesbians into church membership, but "self-affirming, practicing homosexuals" were not eligible for ordination to church office. There were ongoing ecclesiastical battles over human sexuality in the '80s, and by 1993 the General Assembly of the PC(USA) decided to call a three-year voting moratorium on issues related to the ordination of gay and lesbian members to church office. In 1997, evangelicals were able to gather enough votes to push through an amendment to their constitution that required candidates for ordination "to live either in fidelity within the covenant of marriage between a man and woman, or chastity in singleness." A substitute amendment in 1998, requiring "fidelity and integrity in marriage or singleness" (and deleting references to celibacy or defining marriage as a union of a man and woman), failed. Again, the next year there was a move to delete the "fidelity and chastity" clause, but it was defeated. In 2001, there was another attempt to remove the "fidelity and chastity" provision, but once more the vote fell short. It appeared traditional views were holding their ground, though each time the votes got closer, as prohomosexual views gained traction. In 2009 Presbyterians once more declined to modify the constitu-

---

17. See Marshall Kirk and Hunter Madsen's *After the Ball: How America Will Conquer Its Fear and Hatred of Gays in the 90s* (New York: Doubleday, 1989).

18. S. Donald Fortson III and Rollin G. Grams, *Unchanging Witness: The Consistent Christian Teaching on Homosexuality in Scripture and Tradition* (Nashville: B&H Academic, 2016), 9–26, 143–63.

tional "fidelity and chastity" requirement for ordination. Finally, the "fidelity and chastity" constitutional language was jettisoned in July 2011 by a majority vote of the regional presbyteries. This paved the way for ordaining openly gay persons to the Presbyterian ministry, which began with the October 2011 ordination of Scott Anderson to serve a congregation in Wisconsin.[19]

In June 2014, the Assembly approved a policy allowing pastors to perform same-sex ceremonies in states where the practice was legal. The vote was 371 in favor and 238 opposed, a 61 percent margin of victory for progay Presbyterians. An additional vote to change the definition of marriage to "two people" rather than "a woman and a man" passed by 71 percent. The following year, in the *Obergefell v. Hodges* (2015) case, the US Supreme Court ruled that same-sex couples have a constitutional right to legal marriage.[20] The changes in PC(USA) policy on gay marriage had kept pace with the changing attitudes of American society. Those who affirmed gay marriage appealed to biblical justice, arguing that the church was following the Holy Spirit. The Spirit had led the church to modify its interpretations of Scripture on slavery and women's ordination, and was now "challenging us to give up culturally conditioned prejudices against people of homosexual orientation."[21] By contrast, the majority of evangelicals in the PC(USA) affirmed historic Christian teaching forbidding homosexual practice, basing their perspective upon what they believed was transparently taught in the Bible—that men and women were created by God for each other. A prominent spokesman for the traditional view was Pittsburgh Seminary New Testament professor Robert Gagnon, author of *The Bible and Homosexual Practice: Texts and Hermeneutics* (2002). Gagnon argued that interpreting the Bible in its ancient Near Eastern and Greco-Roman context convincingly showed that the Old Testament and New Testament consistently condemn all forms of homosexual practice.[22]

While the PC(USA) positions on gay ordination and gay marriage were changing along with evolving Western culture, the PCA and EPC were taking countercultural stands resisting gay ordination and defending traditional

---

19. Fortson and Grams, *Unchanging Witness*, 156–57.

20. Fortson and Grams, *Unchanging Witness*, 157–58.

21. Jack Rogers, *Jesus, the Bible, and Homosexuality: Explode the Myths, Heal the Church*, 2nd ed. (Louisville: Westminster John Knox, 2009), 58.

22. Robert A. J. Gagnon, *The Bible and Homosexual Practice: Texts and Hermeneutics* (Nashville: Abingdon, 2002). On the other side, some PC(USA) "evangelicals" claimed to have changed their minds on gay marriage; see Mark Achtemeier, *The Bible's Yes to Same-Sex Marriage: An Evangelical's Change of Heart* (Louisville: Westminster John Knox, 2014). Gagnon was terminated by Pittsburgh Theological Seminary in 2017 and currently is a professor at Houston Baptist University.

marriage between one man and one woman. The burning question for the
evangelical Presbyterian denominations was, What does Scripture teach? As
early as 1977, the PCA had declared, "The act of homosexuality is a sin according to God's Word. . . . In light of the biblical view of its sinfulness, a
practicing homosexual continuing in this sin would not be a fit candidate
for ordination or membership in the Presbyterian Church in America."[23] In
1986, the EPC produced a position paper on homosexuality, stating its views
as follows: "The witness of God's Word in both the Old and New Testaments
is clear, declaring that the practice of homosexual behavior, including lust, is
a grievous sin. . . . Unrepentant homosexual behavior is incompatible with the
confession of Jesus as Lord, which is required of members of the EPC. Unrepentant homosexual behavior is incompatible with the ordination vows for
the offices of Deacon, Ruling and Teaching Elder."[24] The PCA and EPC were
supportive of the DOMA and state referendums across the United States that
prohibited gay marriage. On the issue of human sexuality, one could discern
a clear difference between PC(USA) perspectives on Scripture and those of
the evangelical Presbyterians who still affirmed the finality of biblical authority. The historic doctrine of Scripture had long since been relinquished by
PC(USA) scholars.[25]

ECO: A Covenant Order of Evangelical Presbyterians

As the EPC was receiving a fresh wave of former PC(USA) congregations, another Presbyterian group began to consider organizing themselves as a distinct
ecclesiastical body. A considerable number of evangelical congregations had
chosen to remain in the PC(USA), hoping for reform. There was dismay over
the perpetual numerical decline of the church and what this indicated about
the absence of mission. It was becoming more difficult to be evangelical in

23. See PCA statements under "homosexuality," at http://pcahistory.org/pca/studies
/index/html; see also the May 2020 paper by Ad Interim Committee on Human Sexuality,
which will be presented to the 2021 General Assembly, available at https://pcaga.org/wp
-content/uploads/2020/05/AIC-Report-to-48th-GA-5-28-20-1.pdf.

24. "Position Paper on Homosexuality," in *Minutes of the General Assembly, Evangelical
Presbyterian Church*, 1986, 35–39. The EPC adopted a more comprehensive position paper on
"Human Sexuality" in 2017; see http://epcoga.wpengine.com/?s=Human+Sexuality+paper.

25. Modern evidence of how mainline Presbyterians came to adopt weaker stances on
biblical accuracy and authority was furnished by the publication of Jack B. Rogers and
Donald K. McKim's *The Authority and Interpretation of the Bible* (San Francisco: Harper
& Row, 1979).

the PC(USA), and there was a concern to protect their ability to do effective ministry. Seven Presbyterian pastors began fresh discussions about something new. What would it look like to be part of a movement committed to ministry and mission rather than to relentless distracting theological debates in a bureaucratic denomination? The seven pastors invited other leaders in the PC(USA) to join them in the conversation and to explore together something potentially new. By late summer 2011, about two thousand gathered to pray and consider a way forward. Out of this gathering emerged the Fellowship of Presbyterians, which was an association of like-minded folk seeking to equip and encourage one another for ministry. Within this new association, a number of churches, pastors, and seminary students began to sense God's call to leave the PC(USA). In January 2012, the Fellowship of Presbyterians sponsored a covenanting conference that was attended by representatives from over five hundred congregations. Responding to battles over gay ordination and years of frustration with the direction of the denomination, a new Presbyterian body was launched—ECO: A Covenant Order of Evangelical Presbyterians. The name ECO is not an acronym but points to a denominational ethos committed to "strengthening the ecosystems of local churches."

The new denomination was committed to biblical authority and a "missional centrality" focused on growing and planting churches. The ECO churches describe themselves: "We believe that the Church is a living organism that needs life-giving resources to help it grow, thrive, and multiply. ECO is committed to cultivating a healthy, diverse, resource-rich ecosystem where pastors and congregations can flourish." The name ECO points to three priorities: "to make disciples of Jesus Christ (Evangelical), connect leaders through accountable biblical relationships founded in God's grace (Covenant), and commit to a shared way of life together (Order)."[26]

In 2012 the ECO churches adopted the PC(USA) *Book of Confessions*. This would be a unique feature of the ECO, distinguishing it from the other new Presbyterian bodies of the twentieth century (OPC, PCA, EPC), who had all adopted the old Presbyterian creed, the Westminster Confession and Catechisms. The ECO also adopted an "Essential Tenets" document as a witness to the confession's common core. Intending to refine its confessional identity as the ECO matured, the church began a denomination-wide study within a few years. A theological task force was created to guide this process and resource presbyteries and sessions in their examination of the *Book of Confessions* and the "Essential Tenets." The plan was to have presbyteries present motions to the January 2018 Synod (national gathering) on potential options: keep the

---

26. See the ECO website http://eco-pres.org.

Book of Confessions, modify it, or write a new confession. The Synod decided on a collection of confessional documents, with the "Essential Tenets" as the theological center. The revised list of confessions included the Apostles' Creed, the Nicene Creed, the Heidelberg Catechism, the Westminster Confession and Catechisms, and the Barmen Declaration.[27]

Another feature setting the ECO apart from the other evangelical Presbyterian denominations was its dedication to an "egalitarian ministry," one of its eight "core values." Church polity has avoided rigid bureaucracy in favor of allowing flexibility in practice as deemed necessary, especially recognizing the challenges faced by large congregations. The denomination's constitution includes the "Essential Tenets," polity, and rules of discipline.[28] An ECO presbytery is defined as a "covenant community" that exists for the "nurture and benefit of its congregations," which must meet at least twice per year. Presbyteries are purposefully small, consisting of not more than 20 churches, according to ECO polity. The ECO's leadership has focused its energies upon the movement's church-planting efforts and leadership development. By 2019 the denomination had over 400 congregations with about 150,000 members.[29]

The Korean American Phenomenon

Presbyterians have historically had a close relationship with Koreans, which is rooted in nineteenth-century Presbyterian missionary work in Korea; this had produced about ten million Presbyterians in South Korea by the early twenty-first century. The earliest immigrants from Korea came to work on sugar plantations in Hawaii immediately after the turn of the twentieth century. Additional immigrants came to the United States after the Japanese annexed Korea in 1910, and more followed after 1945, when Japanese occupation of Korea ended after World War II. When strict immigration quotas were abandoned in 1965, the numbers dramatically increased. By 2017 there were about one million Korean immigrants in the country, with the vast majority being new immigrants since 1970.

About half of Korean immigrants to the USA have previous connections to Christian churches in Korea, and they seek out their ethnic community in America through affiliation with Korean American churches here. While in

27. "ECO Confessional Standards," 2018, accessible at http://eco-pres.org.
28. "ECO Constitution: Essential Tenets, Polity and Rules of Discipline," 2018, accessible at http://eco-pres.org.
29. Statistical information is from ECO executive director Dana Allin.

Korea about 70 percent of the Protestants are Presbyterians of some stripe, in America the percentage of Korean American Christians who are Presbyterian is much smaller. Many Korean Presbyterians are members of congregations who have affiliated with established American Presbyterian denominations.[30] Currently, there are over 400 Korean congregations in the PC(USA) and over 250 in the PCA.[31] Both denominations have several Korean-language non-geographic presbyteries. In the late 1970s, two distinct Korean American denominations came into being. In 1976 the Korean Presbyterian Church in America was founded; currently comprising 300 congregations, it changed its name in 2012 to the Korean Presbyterian Church Abroad.[32] The year 1978 witnessed the creation of the larger Korean-American Presbyterian Church; it now comprises 600 congregations.[33]

PRESBYTERIAN CONNECTIONS

The story of interchurch relations among the American Presbyterian family of churches offers a complex picture of ecclesiastical connections. The PC(USA) has maintained its ecumenical connections in the National Council of Churches, World Council of Churches, and the World Communion of Reformed Churches (WCRC, 2012), formerly the World Alliance of Reformed Churches. The Cumberland Presbyterian Church, the Cumberland Presbyterian Church of America, the EPC, the ECO, and the Korean Presbyterian Church Abroad are also members of WCRC. The EPC, ECO, and PCA are members of the National Association of Evangelicals (NAE), while the RPCNA, ARP, and OPC are not in the NAE. The RPCNA, ARP, OPC, PCA, as well the Korean-American Presbyterian Church are members of the North American Presbyterian and Reformed Council (NAPARC, 1975). A new global Reformed organization, the World Reformed Fellowship, came into existence in 2000, as the result of the merger of two previous organizations; the ARP,

---

30. Sang Hyun Lee, "Korean Presbyterians: A Need for Ethnic Particularity and the Challenge of Christian Pilgrimage," in *The Diversity of Discipleship: Presbyterians and Twentieth-Century Christian Witness*, ed. Milton J. Coalter, John M. Mulder, and Louis B. Weeks (Louisville: Westminster John Knox, 1991), 312–30.

31. As this is written, two Korean American PCA leaders have assumed the presidencies of prominent national evangelical organizations. Dr. Walter Kim assumed the presidency of the NAE in January 2020, while Dr. Julius Kim assumed the presidency of the Gospel Coalition in February 2020.

32. See www.kpca.org.

33. See www.kapc.org.

ECO, EPC, and PCA are member churches. Fraternal relations between individual evangelical Presbyterian denominations has been quite diverse and
sometimes involves official fraternal relations with the exchange of delegates
at assemblies/synods and collaborative ventures (church planter assessment,
conferences, shared curriculums, etc.). While each denomination has been
primarily focused on its own ecclesiastical affairs, and supporting its own
domestic church planting and foreign missionaries, these ecumenical connections speak to Presbyterian commitment to catholicity.

CONCLUSION

Presbyterians as Evangelicals

Presbyterians have been an important part of American life and culture for a very long time. With roots planted deep in the English and Scottish Reformations, growing numbers of Presbyterian families began to settle throughout the American colonies during the seventeenth and eighteenth centuries, bringing with them a deep respect for the Bible, a yearning for spiritual renewal and spread of the gospel, a theological seriousness, and a desire for a society transformed by Christian principles.

It is true that American Presbyterians have sometimes been as well known for their theological divisions as for their unifying proclivities.[1] These deep divisions are, of course, an essential and important part of the Presbyterian story. They are not, however, the whole story. While there is more than sufficient evidence to demonstrate that Presbyterians have often struggled to find a workable balance between unity and purity, there have also been periods, to borrow the language of the Eighty-Fifth Psalm, when love and faithfulness have met together and when righteousness and peace have kissed.[2]

The authors of this volume, as diligent readers will surely have noticed, have not been hesitant to identify the frequent divisions and debates within American Presbyterianism. Neither have they been reluctant from time to time to highlight the unique history, theology, and contribution of particular

1. American Presbyterianism is represented institutionally by approximately thirty denominational identities, including the four that are represented by the authors of this study: namely, the PCA, the EPC, the ECO, and the PC(USA). See Bradley J. Longfield, *The Presbyterian Controversy: Fundamentalists, Modernists, and Moderates* (New York: Oxford University Press, 1991), and George M. Marsden, *Reforming Fundamentalism: Fuller Seminary and the New Evangelicalism* (Grand Rapids: Eerdmans, 1987).

2. Ps. 85:10 ESV.

Presbyterian denominations or series of events. While this is certainly a worthy task, it has not been our primary focus.

Rather, the writers of this volume have sought to identify those continuities, shared passions, and underlying similarities that have tied the Presbyterian communities together and to explore how the Presbyterian presence in America has influenced the surrounding culture and how, in turn, it has been influenced by that culture. More particularly, and perhaps of even greater significance, the writers have sought to highlight the symbiotic relationship that has frequently existed between American Presbyterianism and American evangelicalism. It is a simple matter of fact that myriads of evangelical Christians have called themselves Presbyterians, and as many Presbyterians have called themselves evangelicals!

Whether or not one appreciates the linkage, there can be little doubt that a close relationship has existed between the two movements from the moment those early Presbyterian settlers landed on the shores of the New World to the present day. Evangelicals have attended Presbyterian seminaries in great numbers, and they have served as pastors in hundreds of Presbyterian churches. Presbyterian students, similarly, have attended evangelical seminaries in great numbers and have served as pastors in hundreds of Presbyterian churches. What has enabled this remarkable relationship to continue for so many years has been a shared allegiance by Presbyterians and evangelicals alike to the list of commitments with which this chapter began: namely, a deep respect for the Bible, a yearning for spiritual renewal and spread of the gospel, a theological seriousness, and a desire for a society transformed by Christian principles.

Biblical Authority

In the 1640s, English Puritans and Scottish Presbyterians declared their allegiance to the primacy of Scripture in chapter 1 of the Westminster Confession of Faith: "Holy Scripture is absolutely essential . . . the written word of God includes all the books of the Old and New Testaments. All of these books are inspired by God and are the rule of faith and life. . . . The Bible speaks authoritatively and so deserves to be believed and obeyed. The Old Testament in Hebrew . . . and the New Testament in Greek . . . were directly inspired by God. . . . They are therefore authentic and are to be the church's ultimate source of appeal in every religious controversy."[3] This high view of Scripture

---

3. *The Westminster Confession of Faith and Catechisms in Modern English* (Signal Mountain, TN: Summertown Company, 2004).

was brought to the New World by colonial Presbyterians. When American Presbyterians officially adopted a Form of Government in the late 1780s, the first ordination vow for ministers was a pledge to honor the final authority of Scripture: "Do you believe the Scriptures of the Old and New Testament, to be the word of God, the only infallible rule of Faith and Practice?"[4]

Historic Presbyterian commitment to biblical authority has been a shared value with American evangelicalism. Historians have always identified submission to biblical teaching as a key mark of the evangelical movement.[5] In the United States, the National Association of Evangelicals affirms in the first article of its statement of faith: "We believe the Bible to be the inspired, the only infallible, authoritative Word of God."[6] Likewise, the Lausanne Covenant, in article 2: "We affirm the divine inspiration, truthfulness and authority of both Old and New Testament Scriptures in their entirety as the only written word of God, without error in all that it affirms, and the only infallible rule of faith and practice."[7] One can hardly miss the Presbyterian overtones in these statements about Scripture from the larger evangelical movement in America and global Christianity. This fidelity to biblical authority has continued unabated among Presbyterian evangelicals; they have consistently pressed the standard of biblical authority ever since the Reformation.

Support for Spiritual Renewal

The early stirrings of America's Great Awakening emerged during the 1720s in New Jersey's Raritan Valley.[8] Led originally by Jacobus Frelinghuysen, a Dutch Reformed pastor in that region, the revivals soon spread to the growing numbers of Presbyterians then settling throughout the middle colonies. Gilbert Tennent, pastor of the Presbyterian church in New Brunswick and son of the founder of the Log College at Neshaminy, Pennsylvania, caught the revival spirit and began

4. *Draught of the Form of Government and Discipline of the Presbyterian Church in the United States of America* (New York: S. and J. Loudon, 1787), 19.

5. See George Marsden, ed., *Evangelicalism and Modern America* (Grand Rapids: Eerdmans, 1984); David W. Bebbington, *Evangelicalism in Modern Britain: A History from the 1730s to the 1980s* (London: Unwin Hyman, 1989); Alister McGrath, *Evangelicalism and the Future of Christianity* (Downers Grove, IL: InterVarsity Press, 1995); Mark A. Noll, David W. Bebbington, and George M. Marsden, eds., *Evangelicals: Who They Have Been, Are Now, and Could Be* (Grand Rapids: Eerdmans, 2019).

6. See https://www.nae.net/statement-of-faith/.

7. See https://www.lausanne.org/content/covenant/lausanne-covenant#cov.

8. Lefferts A. Loetscher, *A Brief History of the Presbyterians*, 4th ed. (Philadelphia: Westminster, 1983), 67–72.

to emphasize the necessity of conversion, as did Jonathan Dickinson, pastor of the Presbyterian church in nearby Elizabethtown, New Jersey. Soon other Presbyterian pastors, along with growing numbers of ministers in other denominations, began to preach the necessity of "new birth" and transformation of life.

The revivals proved to be a godsend throughout virtually every one of the colonies from Maine to Georgia—flooding congregations from Northampton, Massachusetts, to Dinwiddie County in Virginia with thousands of new members.[9] Although an Anglican evangelist, George Whitefield, emerged as the most famous of the Great Awakening preachers, Presbyterian luminaries such as Samuel Davies, Gilbert Tennent, and Dickinson also played significant roles in the awakening.[10] As difficult as it has been for Presbyterians to arrive at a consensus concerning revivals, it appears even more difficult to make sense of American Presbyterianism without including the stories of its regular, widespread, and enthusiastic participation in religious revivals. Indeed, from its earliest years in the New World to the present day, Presbyterians in great numbers have yearned for, prayed for, and participated in literally hundreds of efforts designed to help believers experience a fresh touch of God's Spirit in their lives and congregations. However some Presbyterians might feel about such gatherings, it is simply impossible to tell the Presbyterian story without including these spiritual awakenings.

The Missionary Impulse

Although the 1837 General Assembly of the Presbyterian Church in the USA is mainly remembered for the "Old School" and "New School" schism that primarily occupied its delegates, the Assembly might just as appropriately be remembered as the official beginning of the first national Presbyterian missionary board. With the approval of an overture from the Synod of Pittsburgh, the General Assembly voted to take over the work of the Western Foreign Missionary Society, the synod's missionary sending organization, thereby establishing what eventually came to be known as the Presbyterian World Mission.[11]

9. James H. Smylie, *A Brief History of the Presbyterians* (Louisville: Geneva, 1996), 48–49.

10. Thomas S. Kidd, *George Whitefield: America's Spiritual Founding Father* (New Haven: Yale University Press, 2016); Joseph Tracy, *The Great Awakening* (Edinburgh: Banner of Truth Press, 2019); and William Yoo, ed., *The Presbyterian Experience in America: A Sourcebook* (Louisville: Westminster John Knox, 2017), 15–24.

11. See Michael Parker, "History of World Mission: 175 Years of Presbyterian World Mission," Presbyterian Historical Society, 2012, https://www.history.pcusa.org/history-online/topics-note/history-world-mission.

Presbyterianism's growing commitment to missionary outreach, however, had been evident from its earliest years of settlement in America. While this interest was primarily focused on what might be called "home missions" during the colonial period, it shifted dramatically toward "overseas missions" early in the nineteenth century. While some within the church have raised concerns about the means, the motivations, and the cultural impact of the modern missionary movement—and some have even questioned its legitimacy—the spread of the Christian gospel around the globe has continued to play a central role in the agenda of worldwide Christianity. Evangelical Presbyterians and Presbyterian evangelicals, with rare exception, have helped to fan this missionary flame—convinced, as they are, that Christ's "great commission" remains the obligation and sacred privilege of every believer to share the good news by word and deed with an increasingly needy world.

THEOLOGICAL SERIOUSNESS

Our survey of American religious history demonstrates that one of the greatest contributions made by Presbyterians to national life has been in thinking and speaking clearly about God, his Son Jesus Christ, the Holy Scriptures, and the Christian gospel.

Such a claim does not require that Presbyterians were the first to do this. Because of their chronological precedence in arriving on American shores, representatives of the Congregationalists and the Church of England were surely active in speaking for God and teaching the Word before Presbyterians came to be well represented.[12] This claim does not require either that Presbyterians were the pioneers in advanced theological study; that honor falls to the Congregationalist initiative Andover Seminary, founded in 1805.[13]

But with these caveats, the claim can still be made that Presbyterians both early and regularly have made a weighty contribution by their serious study of and proclamation of the Scriptures. The founding of the first American Presbyterian seminary (at Princeton in 1812) brought into being an institution that, in its first century, provided an expression and conception of the Christian faith

12. Polly Ha, *The English Presbyterians: 1590-1640* (Palo Alto, CA: Stanford University Press, 2011), demonstrated that English Puritans of Presbyterian sympathy were present in the early Massachusetts settlements seeking the same relief of conscience as other immigrants. We have also seen that there were New England commissioners at the Westminster Assembly of Divines.

13. To this point, instruction in theology had been provided in the various colleges (e.g., Harvard, Yale, King's College [now Columbia University]) established earlier.

that was congruent with the dominant current understanding of Christianity in America.[14] Because of this orientation, it was early on turned to by persons of various denominations for sound instruction in the faith. Before long, a future chaplain of the US Senate and Episcopal bishop of Ohio (Charles P. McIlvaine), a future Lutheran seminary president (Samuel Schmucker), and a future Baptist seminary president (James Pettigru Boyce) would all pass through its classrooms.[15]

Though the claim to have published the first journal of theology in America is contested, it appears that the launch of the *Biblical Repertory and Princeton Review* in 1825 secures this honor.[16] Consistent with that leadership, Presbyterian thinkers and biblical scholars at Princeton and beyond earned the trust of Christians in America and elsewhere.[17] Well into the twentieth century, the theologies of Charles Hodge, Robert L. Dabney, W. G. T. Shedd, Benjamin Warfield, and William Adams Brown were the staples in ministers' libraries across North America.[18] This role of Presbyterians serving as systematic theologians for the evangelical church at large has continued into our time with theologies recently produced by Robert Reymond, John Frame, and Douglas F. Kelly.[19]

CULTURAL TRANSFORMATION

In his influential book *Discovering an Evangelical Heritage*, historian Donald W. Dayton details the central role that evangelical Christians have played as fervent and often outspoken prophetic advocates for social justice and reform. As Day-

14. James H. Moorhead, *Princeton Seminary in American Religion and Culture* (Grand Rapids: Eerdmans, 2012). The rise of theological seminaries gave them an existence distinct from liberal arts and colleges.

15. See entries in Timothy Larsen, ed., *Biographical Dictionary of American Evangelicals* (Downers Grove, IL: InterVarsity Press, 2003).

16. The claim of precedence made on behalf of the journal *Bibliotheca Sacra*, begun in New York in 1843 and soon thereafter continued in Andover, Massachusetts, seems to reflect the fact that Princeton's journal went through a series of name changes.

17. Paul Gutjahr has shown that Charles Hodge's Romans commentary was available in French translation by the 1840s. *Charles Hodge: Guardian of American Orthodoxy* (New York: Oxford University Press, 2011), 124.

18. With the exception of work of the latter, W. A. Brown, all these nineteenth-century systematic theologies remain in print.

19. Robert L. Reymond, *A New Systematic Theology of the Christian Faith*, 2nd ed. (Nashville: Nelson, 2010; original 1998); Douglas F. Kelly, *Systematic Theology*, 2 vols. (Fearn, UK: Christian Focus, 2008, 2014); John Frame, *Systematic Theology: An Introduction to Christian Belief* (Phillipsburg, NJ: Presbyterian and Reformed, 2013).

ton suggests, many of the most important reform movements of the nineteenth century—including abolitionism, women's rights, prison reform, and social welfare—emerged "directly from the ranks of evangelical Christianity."[20]

Indeed, many of the most prominent leaders of those movements have been evangelical Presbyterians.[21] In the aftermath of the fundamentalist-modernist controversies of the early twentieth century, such a conclusion seems suspect at best and downright misleading at worst. It is true, of course, that some evangelical Presbyterians, following the bitter battles of the 1920s, embraced personal piety at the expense of social engagement. Indeed, some were so averse to modernism that they turned inward and virtually abandoned their long-standing commitment to social justice.

Many other evangelical Presbyterians, however, were unwilling to turn their backs on their long heritage of social engagement. The "Justice and Peace Evangelicals," as theologian Gabriel Fackre has called them, sought to express their faith in more radical political and ecclesial idiom. Whether from an Anabaptist or high Calvinist perspective, they called into question what they understood to be an "accommodation" by church and culture alike "to affluence, militarism, and unjust social and economic structures." Many of them, Fackre argued, personally sought "to embody their faith in an alternative style of life through intentional Christian communities."[22]

While most would not have called themselves "Justice and Peace Evangelicals," many evangelical Presbyterians nonetheless resisted any bifurcation of the personal and the social by continuing their long-standing efforts to feed the hungry, to care for the sick, and to do battle with systemic evil. Convinced that the Bible required them to love their neighbor and to treat others as they wished to be treated, they prayed and worked for what H. Richard Niebuhr famously called the transformation of culture.[23] Nowhere is this commitment more clearly seen, it can be argued, than on the mission field. While many Presbyterian missionaries would have blanched at being labeled "social gospel

20. Donald W. Dayton, *Discovering an Evangelical Heritage* (New York: Harper & Row, 1976); the quotation below is taken from the book's cover. See also Timothy L. Smith, *Revivalism and Social Reform* (Baltimore: Johns Hopkins University Press, 1980), and Norris Magnuson, *Salvation in the Slums: Evangelical Social Work, 1865–1920* (Metuchen, NJ: Scarecrow, 1977).

21. Examples include Charles Grandison Finney, who was ordained by the Oneida Presbytery, and Charles Blanchard, who, upon graduation from Andover Theological Seminary, served for a time as pastor of Cincinnati's Sixth Presbyterian Church.

22. Gabriel Fackre, *The Religious Right and the Christian Faith* (Grand Rapids: Eerdmans, 1982), 6, 7.

23. H. Richard Niebuhr, *Christ and Culture* (New York: Harper & Row, 1951).

advocates," they nonetheless continued to serve as doctors and nurses in clinics around the globe, to make sure that people had clean water to drink and healthy food to eat, and to provide relief when natural disasters struck.[24]

In their best moments, it would seem, evangelical Presbyterians and Presbyterian evangelicals have characteristically opted for a robust and winsome application of biblical truth to every arena of life. After all, as pastor Timothy Keller has expressed so eloquently, "all problems, personal or social, come from a failure to apply the gospel in a radical way." However, Keller concluded, if "the gospel is expounded and applied in its fullness in any church, that church will begin to look very unique," for in it, by God's grace, a needy world will discover the refreshing and life-giving combination of "flexibility," "moral conviction," and genuine "compassion."[25]

THE PRESBYTERIAN EVANGELICAL CHALLENGE

Five features of Presbyterian evangelicalism have been named; it can fairly be said that they have characterized the experience of Presbyterian believers and churches in past centuries. A question deserving to be asked, however, is what the current and future prospects of these important distinctive pillars are.

As to respect for biblical authority, there is good reason to affirm that evangelical Presbyterians have continued to robustly affirm and show regard for the supreme authority of Scripture. The regroupings of conservative Presbyterians—certainly since the 1930s—have been attempts at recovering and reasserting biblical authority when it was perceived to be in eclipse. Evangelicals in that era were prescient in discerning that the Hocking Report, in combination with the expressed doubts of Pearl S. Buck, was the harbinger of change in how world mission would be conceived of and pursued.[26] In our own day, contemporary shifts away from upholding the sanctity of the life of the unborn and the truth that marriage, as ordained by God, is intended to be the permanent union of a man and a woman have been similarly judged to be departures from what is revealed.[27] But at the same time, Presbyterian

24. See the story of Bob Pierce and the founding of World Vision and Samaritan's Purse in Marilee Pierce Dunker, *Man of Vision, Woman of Faith* (Nashville: Nelson, 2005).

25. Timothy Keller, "The Centrality of the Gospel," in *The Presbyterian Experience in the United States: A Sourcebook*, ed. William Yoo (Louisville: Westminster John Knox, 2017), 141–53. Tim Keller is the founding pastor of Redeemer Presbyterian Church, New York City. See an extended reference to him in chap. 18.

26. See chap. 16 above.

27. See chap. 19 above.

children and adults show too many signs that they participate in the prevailing culture-wide decline of biblical literacy. The profession of the supreme authority of the Bible is undermined when professed believers lose a close familiarity with the Bible's actual teachings.

As regards evangelization and the need for national religious awakening, Presbyterian evangelicals can acknowledge with gratitude to God the fact that great spiritual harvests in American life have occurred at intervals since the days of Cotton Mather and Solomon Stoddard. This volume has drawn attention to the ministry of the Tennents and Samuel Davies, to Wilbur Chapman and Billy Sunday. But it is worth acknowledging that almost a half century has passed since a Presbyterian evangelist of national reputation has emerged; evangelist Leighton Ford (b. 1931) was the last to "do the work of the evangelist" (2 Tim. 4:5) on this earlier scale. Admittedly, the population is more wary of large evangelistic gatherings today than it was prior to 1970; this is a reality faced by all who want public evangelizing to continue. But it would appear that Presbyterians do not show leadership in this area as they once so clearly did.

It has also been noted that the substantial congregational growth experienced by evangelical Presbyterian congregations, while noteworthy in a period when many denominations are in numerical decline, is largely attributable to the transfer or reaffiliation of existing believers. Church growth by direct evangelism is at best modest.[28]

The chapters in this volume have highlighted a long-standing, high level of evangelical Presbyterian support for the sending of intercultural missionaries.[29] International ecumenical relationships nurtured by this intercultural mission are ongoing. But candid observers note that sacrificial giving by Presbyterians (as by other Christians) to all Christian causes (including missions) is slipping. Consequently, it is taking missionary candidates much longer than formerly to raise the support needed before departure.[30] It is also of special concern that the actual teaching of missionary subjects by seminary faculty members who are designated "professors of mission" has declined markedly

28. L. Roy Taylor, outgoing stated clerk of the PCA General Assembly, writing in denominational periodical *By Faith*, in May 2020 pointed to a modest 2 percent annual growth in PCA membership. He noted, "We are not reaching noncollege graduate, working-class people effectively. We are not experiencing a lot of growth by professions of faith." L. Roy Taylor, "The PCA, Facing the Future," *By Faith*, May 18, 2020, https://byfaithonline.com/pca-facing-the-future/.

29. See chap. 17 above.

30. Recently, the figure of two years was mentioned as a customary period for support raising.

over a generation. This lack does not itself constrict missionary recruitment, but it may be said to handicap that recruitment by leaving the training of missionaries to the sending agencies themselves.

Theological reflection and writing has not lost its place among evangelical Presbyterians. In addition to drawing on writers from within their own constituencies,[31] evangelical Presbyterian leaders have been ready to draw on writers from the wider Reformed theological tradition and beyond. Our General Assemblies are regularly provided with study reports that reflect very well on the acumen of the ministers and ruling elders who constitute the study committees. But at the same time, there are some developments that furrow the brow. Two are paradoxically the obverse of the other.

On the one hand, theological instruction tends to be highly reiterative, as if the mere repetition and maintenance of the theological opinions of another age constitute our theological task in the here and now. This can border on nostalgia, when what is called for is the creative restatement of our faith in changed times.[32] At the same time—with all due acknowledgment of the need for contemporary theological restatement—it needs to be admitted that the confessional and catechetical heritage of our churches is being sorely neglected. The catechizing of children is increasingly looked on as passé, while the confessional standards of our churches seem to function only in the examining of ministerial candidates by presbyteries and in officer training at the congregational level. The question needs to be asked as to how this relative neglect of our own particular theological heritage can bode well for our continued faithfulness. We should be able to recognize that this same neglect has already led to sad consequences in the mainline churches.

As for commitment to the transformation of culture, we can draw particular encouragement from the fact that a century ago, our forebears were acutely aware of the needs of immigrants to both coasts.[33] Presbyterian evangelicals continue to support efforts of this kind today through the settlement programs coordinated by the World Relief Commission of the National Association of Evangelicals.[34] Domestically, evangelical Presbyterian initiatives such as Desire Street Ministries and the Chalmers Center[35] are pointing the way forward for evangelicals by demonstrating how social, economic, and spiri-

---

31. Past and present examples have been named above at p. 324 and in chap. 18.

32. Taylor, "The PCA, Facing the Future," has cautioned against a nostalgia that "seeks to live in the past or to recreate the past. Nostalgia is crippling."

33. See chap. 14 above.

34. See https://worldrelief.org/refugees-immigrants-and-displaced-people/.

35. See the websites of these organizations: https://desirestreet.org/ and https://chalmers .org/.

tual advance can be pursued holistically within our decaying urban areas. We draw encouragement from the fact that our denominations now contain many congregations of Southeast Asian, African American, African, and Latino orientation, while acknowledging that our denominations remain predominately Anglo-Saxon.

All in all, Presbyterian evangelicals have a host of reasons to be grateful for the past while acknowledging that we still have a "charge to keep" in days to come.

American Presbyterian Denominations
Ranked by Membership

Presbyterian Church in the United States of America	1,245,354[1]
Presbyterian Church in America	384,793[2]
Evangelical Presbyterian Church	145,000[3]
ECO: Covenant Order of Evangelical Presbyterians	127,500[4]
Korean American Presbyterian Church	80,000[5]
Cumberland Presbyterian Church	70,810[6]
Korean Presbyterian Church Abroad	55,000[7]
Orthodox Presbyterian Church	31,112[8]
Associate Reformed Presbyterian Church	29,317[9]
Cumberland Presbyterian Church in America	15,142[10]
Reformed Presbyterian Church of North America	7,076[11]

1. https://www.pcusa.org/news/2021/4/21/pcusa-2020-statistics-show-no-change-de cline-rate/; accessed Oct. 5, 2021.

2. https://www.pcaac.org/resources/pca-statistics-five-year-summary/; accessed Oct. 5, 2021.

3. https://eco-pres.org/faqs/; accessed Oct. 5, 2021.

4. https://epc.org/about/faq/; accessed Oct. 5, 2021.

5. https://kapc-org.translate.goog/%ec%b4%9d%ed%9a%8c-%ec%97%ad%ec%82%ac%ec %99%80-%ec%86%8c%ea%b0%9c/?_x_tr_sl=ko&_x_tr_tl=en&_x_tr_hl=en&_x_tr_pto =nui,sc; accessed Oct. 5, 2021.

6. Roger E. Olson, ed., *Handbook of American Denominations* (Nashville: Abingdon, 2018), 102.

7. https://www.thearda.com/Denoms/D_930.asp; accessed Oct. 8, 2021.

8. Olson, *Handbook*, 108.

9. Olson, *Handbook*, 99.

10. Olson, *Handbook*, 103.

11. Olson, *Handbook*, 114.

Genealogical Table of American Presbyterians

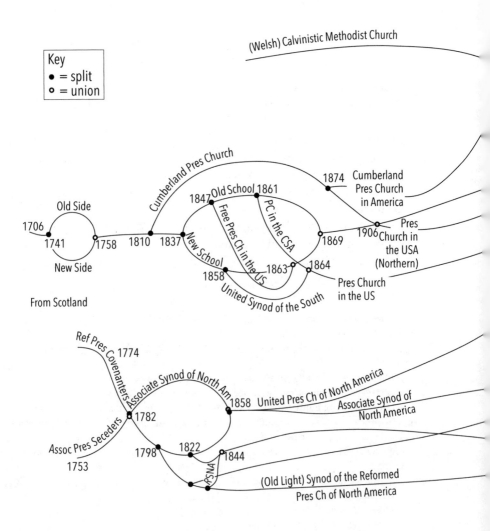

Key
- • = split
- ○ = union

(Welsh) Calvinistic Methodist Church

Cumberland Pres Church

Old Side

1706

1741   1758   1810   1837

New Side

From Scotland

1847 Old School 1861

Free Pres Ch in the US

New School

1858

United Synod of the South

PC in the CSA

1869   1906

1863   1864

1874   Cumberland
       Pres Church
       in America

Pres
Church in
the USA
(Northern)

Pres Church
in the US

Ref Pres Covenanters 1774

Associate Synod of North Am 1858 United Pres Ch of North America

Assoc Pres Seceders

1753

1782

1798   1822   1844

PSNA

Associate Synod of
North America

(Old Light) Synod of the Reformed
Pres Ch of North America

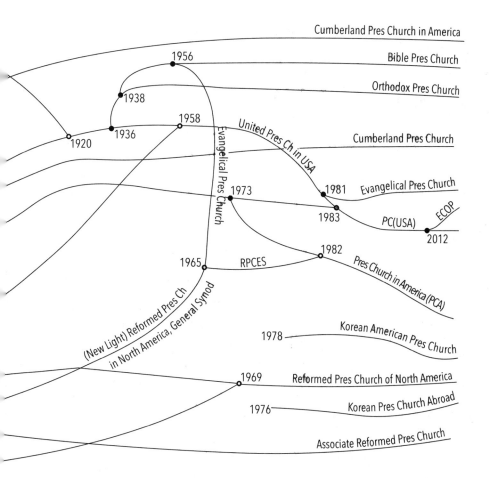

Presbytery, 1706
The first Presbytery was organized in Philadelphia in 1706.

Old Side / New Side, 1741–1758
During the first Great Awakening, Presbyterians split over the issue of revivals. Gilbert Tennent's 1740 pro-revival sermon "The Danger of an Unconverted Ministry" decried anti-revivalists as Pharisees and blind men. The minister John Hancock responded with 1743's "The Danger of an Unqualified Ministry." Unable to contain the dispute, the church split into the revivalist New Side and the anti-revivalist Old Side. Seeking what Tennent called "the Peace of Jerusalem," the factions reunited to form the Synod of New York and Philadelphia in 1758.

Synod of New York and Philadelphia, 1758–1788; Presbyterian Church in the U.S.A., 1789–1837
The Old and New Sides reunited in 1758 to form the Synod of New York and Philadelphia. In 1788, the body reorganized itself into four synods and resolved to meet in 1789 as the Presbyterian Church in the U.S.A.

Cumberland Presbyterian Church, 1810–1906
In 1810, objecting to the denomination's requirement that ordained ministers be formally educated, and disputing the necessity to assent to the Westminster Confession, a group of Kentucky ministers withdrew from the PCUSA to form the independent Cumberland Presbytery. The presbytery grew into the Cumberland Synod by 1813, and the Cumberland Presbyterian Church by 1829. In 1906, roughly two-thirds of the denomination reunited with the PCUSA.

Old School / New School, 1837–1869
In response to the Second Great Awakening, Presbyterians split once again over revivals and the primacy of the Westminster Standards. At the General Assembly of 1837 in Philadelphia, the Synods of Western Reserve, Utica, Geneva, and Genesee were refused entry. They left to hold a separate assembly nearby, constituting the New School. Ecclesiastical and theological differences were ultimately trumped by the national division over slavery, and the Old School and New School reunited in 1869.

Free Presbyterian Church in the U.S., 1847–1863
Staunch Presbyterian abolitionists organized the Free Presbyterian Church in one synod, the Free Synod of Cincinnati. Free Presbyterians seceded from both the Old School and New School in protest of both denominations refusing to exclude slaveholders from church membership. Reunited with Presbyterian Church in the U.S.A. (New School) in 1863.

United Synod of the South, 1858–1864
Separated from New School, 1858. Merged into the Presbyterian Church in the Confederate States of America, 1864.

Presbyterian Church in the Confederate States of America, 1861–1865; Presbyterian Church in the U.S., 1865–1983
Believing slavery to be divinely ordained, ministers separated from both New School and Old School to form the Presbyterian Church in the Confederate States of America in 1861. At the conclusion of the Civil War, the denomination became the Presbyterian Church in the U.S. The longest-running of American Presbyterianism's schisms ended with the reunion of Northern and Southern streams in 1983.

Presbyterian Church in the U.S.A., 1869–1958
Old School and New School Presbyterians reunited in 1869.

Cumberland Presbyterian Church in America, 1874–
A separate denomination for African

Americans was organized by the Cumberland Presbyterian Church as the Colored Cumberland Presbyterian Church in 1874. It was later renamed the Second Cumberland Presbyterian Church. The denomination continues as the Cumberland Presbyterian Church in America.

Cumberland Presbyterian Church, 1906–

At reunion in 1906, about one-third of the Cumberland Presbyterian Church refused to join the PCUSA.

Orthodox Presbyterian Church, 1936–

The fundamentalist Princeton Theological Seminary professor J. Gresham Machen, along with a group of likeminded professors, founded Westminster Theological Seminary in 1929. Objecting to what he saw as modernist dilution of the Reformed tradition, Machen founded the Independent Board for Presbyterian Foreign Missions. In 1934, the PCUSA General Assembly condemned this action and removed Machen and his cohorts from the ministry. In 1936, the group organized a new denomination, known as the Presbyterian Church in America; it changed its name to the Orthodox Presbyterian Church in 1939.

Bible Presbyterian Church, 1937–

The Bible Presbyterian Church broke from the Orthodox Presbyterian Church in 1937, advocating total abstinence from alcohol, and disputing whether the 1000-year reign would come before or after the return of Christ. The denomination persists today with fewer than thirty congregations.

Evangelical Presbyterian Church, 1956–1965

In 1956 the Bible Presbyterian Church split into two Synods, headquartered in Collingswood, N.J., and Columbus, Ohio. In 1961 the Bible Presbyterian Church, Columbus, Synod changed its name to the Evangelical Presbyterian Church. The denomination merged with the General Synod of the Reformed Presbyterian Church in North America in 1965 to form the Reformed Presbyterian Church, Evangelical Synod.

Reformed Presbyterian Church, Evangelical Synod, 1965–1982

The Evangelical Presbyterian Church merged with the General Synod of the Reformed Presbyterian Church in North America in 1965 to form the Reformed Presbyterian Church, Evangelical Synod. The denomination merged into the Presbyterian Church in America in 1982.

Reformed Presbytery, "Covenanters," 1774–1782

Upon the formation of the Church of Scotland, Presbyterians objecting to the establishment of an official state church refused to join. Known as "Covenanters," their descendants came to America, organizing the Reformed Presbytery in 1774.

Associate Presbytery, "Seceders," 1753–1782

At several times in the mid-eighteenth century, Presbyterians objecting to patronage, or the power of landowners to nominate ministers, often over the opposition of a congregation, broke with the Church of Scotland. Known as "Seceders," they came to America, organizing the Associate Presbytery in 1753.

Associate Synod of North America, 1782–1858

In 1782 a portion of the Associate Presbyterians did not join the Associate Reformed Presbyterian Church, continuing as the Associate Synod of North America until 1858.

Associate Reformed Synod, 1782–1801; Associate Reformed Presbyterian Church, 1803–1858

In 1782 a portion of the Associate Presbyterians joined the Reformed Presbytery to organize the Associate Reformed Synod, later known as the Associate Reformed Presbyterian Church.

Reformed Presbytery, 1798–1808;
Reformed Presbyterian Church, 1809–1833
The Reformed Presbytery was reorganized as a single presbytery in 1798 from the few churches that had refused to merge with the Associate Presbytery; a synod was organized in 1809 and given the name of church; the Synod divided into subordinate synods in 1831; in 1833 it separated into Old Light and New Light factions.

(New Light) Reformed Presbyterian
Church in North America,
General Synod, 1833–1965
Throughout the eighteenth century, Reformed Presbyterianism held that any state governed by a document that did not declare the supremacy of Jesus Christ was illegitimate. Reformed Presbyterians therefore abstained from voting, jury service, and political activity. In 1833 the Reformed Presbyterian Church in North America separated into Old Light and New Light factions over this stance. New Lights found civic activity permissible. They merged with the Evangelical Presbyterian Church to form the Reformed Presbyterian Church, Evangelical Synod, in 1965.

(Old Light) Synod of the Reformed Presbyterian Church of North America, 1833–
In 1833 the Reformed Presbyterian Church in North America separated into Old Light and New Light factions over whether to permit civic activity. Old Lights maintained that civic activity was impermissible. The names of the two bodies fluctuated throughout the 1830s; Old Lights eventually settled on the Synod of the Reformed Presbyterian Church of North America. In the 1960s, the church's stance on political activity softened; by 1969, church members were allowed to vote and to run for political office. The denomination continues as the Reformed Presbyterian Church of North America.

Associate Synod of North America,
1858–1969
Associate Presbyterians opposed to the merger that created the United Presbyterian Church of North America in 1858 continued as the Associate Synod of North America, merging with the Reformed Presbyterian Church of North America (Old Lights) in 1969.

Associate Reformed Synod of the
South, 1822–1934; Associate Reformed
Presbyterian Church, 1935–
Associate Reformed Synod of the South; originally the Synod of the Carolinas and Georgia in the Associate Reformed Presbyterian Church, it withdrew as an independent coordinating body in 1821; it received the Associate Presbytery of the Carolinas in 1844; name changed to General Synod of the Associate Reformed Presbyterian Church in 1935.

Reformed Synod of North America,
1840–1844
Followers of the Brush Creek, Ohio, minister, David Steele, unable to tighten the Reformed Presbytery of North America's restrictions on voluntary associations, withdrew in 1840 to found the Reformed Synod of North America. In 1844, most of the denomination united with the Associate Reformed Synod of the South. Other Steelite bodies persist, generally with one charismatic leader, including the Reformed Presbyterian Church (Covenanted), the Covenanted Reformed Presbyterian Church, and the Reformed Presbytery in North America (General Meeting).

United Presbyterian Church
of North America, 1858–1958
The Associate Reformed Presbyterian Church and the Associate Synod of North America united on May 26, 1858, at Seventh and Springfield Streets in Pittsburgh,

forming the United Presbyterian Church of North America. The UPCNA merged with the Presbyterian Church in the U.S.A. in 1958, also in Pittsburgh.

Welsh Calvinistic Methodist Church, 1828–1869; Calvinistic Methodist Church in the U.S.A., 1869–1920
Welsh immigrants to upstate New York in the 1790s brought the Welsh Calvinistic Methodist Church with them. On May 10, 1828, four churches of Oneida County met in gymnava or assembly at Penycaeran. The growing denomination renamed itself the Calvinistic Methodist Church in the U.S.A. in 1869, and merged into the Presbyterian Church in the U.S.A. in 1920.

United Presbyterian Church in the U.S.A., 1958–1983
The United Presbyterian Church of North America and the Presbyterian Church in the U.S.A. met jointly in General Assembly at Pittsburgh in 1958, forming the United Presbyterian Church in the U.S.A.

Presbyterian Church in America, 1973–
The Presbyterian Church in America left the PCUS in 1973 in protest of the denomination's liberalism.

Evangelical Presbyterian Church, 1981–
The Evangelical Presbyterian Church left the UPCUSA in 1981, rejecting the liberalism of the Northern stream.

Presbyterian Church (U.S.A.), 1983–
The General Assemblies of the United Presbyterian Church in the U.S.A. and the Presbyterian Church in the U.S. met in Atlanta in 1983 to reunite, forming the Presbyterian Church (U.S.A.). The PC(USA) remains among the largest American mainline Protestant denominations.

ECO: A Covenant Order of Evangelical Presbyterians, 2012–
Objecting to the ratification of Amendment 10-A to the PC(USA) Book of Order, conservative Presbyterians met in Orlando, Florida, in January 2012 to form ECO: A Covenant Order of Evangelical Presbyterians.

Korean Presbyterian Church in America, 1976–2012; Korean Presbyterian Church Abroad, 2012–
Korean Presbyterian Church in America, now the Korean Presbyterian Church Abroad (name changed in 2012) is an independent Presbyterian denomination in the United States. It was founded in 1976 as a union of three Korean-language Presbyteries. The mother church was the Presbyterian Church in Korea (TongHap).

Korean American Presbyterian Church, 1978–
The KAPC is a conservative denomination formed in 1978 by Korean immigrants on the campus of Westminster Seminary in Philadelphia.

CREDITS

Sources
This timeline is most heavily dependent on the Presbyterian Historical Society, especially the work of David Staniunas. Other sources consulted were *For a Continuing Church* by Sean Michael Lucas, *History of Presbyterianism in America* by Don Post and Chuck Frost, and *Historical Roots of the Presbyterian Church in America* by Don Clements.

Index

Abbott, George, 26–28

Account of the Life of the Late Reverend David Brainerd, An (Edwards), 75

Act against Covenants and Conventicles (1662), 62

Act against Puritans (1593), 15

Act of Indulgence (1672), 59

Act of Parliament (1649), 73–74

Act of Supremacy (1559), 14

Act of Uniformity (1559), 12, 14

Act of Uniformity (1662), 56–59, 79

Act Rescissory (1661), 61

Adger, John B., 180–81

Adopting Act (1729), 97–98, 112, 160–61

"Advertisements" of 1566, 14

African Free School (New York City), 171

Agassiz, Louis, 202, 206

Ahlstrom, Sydney, 140, 197

Aid for Colleges Committee (Synod of California), 229

Aikin, Samuel Clark, 138, 140, 142–43

Alarm to the Unconverted, An (Alleine), 67

Alesius, Alexander, 4

Alexander, Abraham, 122

Alexander, Archibald, 102n9, 154, 204–5, 242–43

Alexander, James W., 185

Alexander, Samuel, 195

Alison, Francis, 113, 163

Alleine, Joseph, 67, 79

Allen, Jonathan, 133

American and Foreign Anti-Slavery Society, 171

American Anti-Slavery Society, 170, 171, 173

American Bible Society, 153, 170

American Board of Commissioners for Foreign Missions (ABCFM), 130–33, 135, 159

American Civil Liberties Union (ACLU), 259–60

American Colonization Society, 168, 171

American Home Missionary Society, 131

American Psychiatric Association (APA), 311

American Revolution, x, 74, 84, 114–23; British taxes and trade laws, 118–19; first Continental Congress, 119–20, 123; preludes to, 114–15; Presbyterian clergy not backing the patriot cause, 122–23; Presbyterian support for, 120–21; and Scots-Irish settlers in the Carolinas, 121–23; Synod of New York and Philadelphia's "pastoral letter" to the colonies (May 1775), 119–20; Witherspoon and, 120

American Temperance Society, 184

American Tract Society, 215–16

America's Keswick Christian Retreat & Conference Center (New Jersey), 274

Amsterdam's Free University, 295

Anabaptists, 6, 109

Anderson, Scott, 313

Belfast Society, 94
Belhaven College (University) in Jackson, Mississippi, 288n18
Bell, Clayton, 270, 298–99n47
Bell, L. Nelson, 290, 296–97, 299
Bellamy, Joseph, 145
Beman, Nathan S. S., 138, 142–43
Bethany Sunday School (Philadelphia), 191
Beza, Theodore, 21
Bible and Homosexual Practice, The: Texts and Hermeneutics (Gagnon), 313
Bible and Medical Missionary Fellowship (now Interserve), 270
Bible Presbyterian Church (BPC), 277, 305
Bible School Movement, 259
biblical authority: Briggs controversy, 243–45, 255–56; contemporary views and future of, 326–27; and evangelical "the Bible alone" outlooks, xi; and fundamentalist-modernist controversies, 208, 254–56, 258; and historical-critical method, 236–38, 243–45, 252, 254–56; historic Presbyterian commitment to, 320–21; Hodge-Warfield 1881 essay in the *Presbyterian Review* ("Inspiration"), 254–55; inerrancy of Scripture and biblical inspiration, 208, 254–56, 258; mid-nineteenth-century American universities and changes in ministerial education, 241–45; Portland Affirmation (1893) on biblical inerrancy, 256; and Princeton theology, 204, 205, 242–43, 254–56; and Second Great Awakening, 241; social sciences and comparative religions approach, 246–47; and theological liberalism, 243. *See also* fundamentalist-modernist controversies of the early twentieth century
biblical literacy, decline of, 327
Biblical Repertory and Princeton Review, 148, 324
Bibliotheca Sacra, 324n16
Biddle Institute, 195
Bishops' Wars against Scotland, 31
Black Acts, 22–23
black Presbyterians: Civil Rights era and desegregation, 288–91; first black presbyteries in the South, 195–96; and Gra-

ham's crusades, 290; ministers in early nineteenth century, 170–71; PCUSA's post–Civil War schools, 195; post–Civil War Northern missions to freedmen in the South, 194–95; post–Civil War segregated presbyteries, 195–96; Princeton Seminary's first black graduate, 171; and UPCUSA, 290–91. *See also* slavery debate
Black Theology: A Documentary History, 1966–1979 (Cone and Wilmore), 291
Blair, Samuel, 102, 104, 106, 138
Blair, W. C., 187
Blake, Eugene Carson, 290
Blanchard, Charles, 325n21
Boice, James Montgomery, 296
Bolam, C. G., 57n30
Bonaparte, Napoleon, 234, 235
Bonclarken Conference Center (North Carolina), 274
Bonhoeffer, Dietrich, 292
Book and Slavery Irreconcilable, The (Bourne), 167
Book of Common Order, 15n46, 16, 30, 70–71n41
Book of Common Prayer, 7, 9, 10, 11, 41, 54, 56, 182
Book of Confessions (UPCUSA), 293, 315–16
Book of Government (EPC), 309, 310
Book of Reformation, 14. See also *First Book of Discipline*
Boston, Thomas, 67
Boston Massacre (1770), 119
Boston Tea Party, 119
Boswell, fourth Earl of (James Hepburn), 18
Bottoms, Lawrence, 289
Boudinot, Elias, 131, 135
Bourne, George, 167–68
Boyce, James Pettigru, 324
Bradford, William, 81
Brainerd, David, 75, 107–8
Brakel, Wilhelmus à, 100
Bray, Gerald, 42n35
Brazil, 186
Breckinridge, John J., 177

325; accommodationist responses to theological modernism, 248–51, 257–59, 325; biblical inspiration and the inerrancy of Scripture, 208, 254–56, 258; and Darwinian evolution, 247, 249, 250, 259–62; militant fundamentalist opposition to modernism, 248–49, 251–53, 325; Princeton Seminary and struggle against accommodation to modernism, 252–53, 258; and Princeton theology, 254–56; rise of theological modernism, 248–53; Scopes trial of 1925, 259–62; and uniformitarian understanding of geology, 247
Fundamentals, The (1910–1917), 223, 259

Gagnon, Robert, 313
Gailey, James H., Jr., 297n42
Galapagos Islands, 199
Gale, George, 139, 142–43
Galileo Galilei, 230
Garrison, William Lloyd, 162, 171, 173n29
gay ordination, 294, 311–14
Gellatly, Alexander, 128
General Associate Synod, 128
General Conference of the Evangelical Alliance (1873), 194
General Union for Promoting the Observance of the Christian Sabbath, 183–84
Geneva Bible, 12, 66
George I, 59, 60
German universities: Harnack and modern university curricula, 235–36; the PhD and doctoral dissertation, 236, 243; the University of Berlin, 235–36. *See also* liberal Protestantism, nineteenth-century
Germany and World War II, 266, 292
Gerstner, John, 295–96, 308n9
Gill, John, 109n32
Gillespie, George, 37n15
Gillett, Eliza, 134
Gillett, Moses, 140, 142–43
Girardeau, John L., 176–77
Gladden, Washington, 214–15, 250
Glamis, Lord, 21
Good Earth, The (Buck), 269
Goodman, Christopher, 11, 12, 16
Gordon Divinity School, 284

Gordon-Conwell Theological Seminary, 262, 284
Gospel Coalition, 317n31
Gospel Light Publications, 273
Gospel Literature International, 273n45
Graf, Karl, 240
Graf-Wellhausen Hypothesis. *See* Documentary Hypothesis (Graf-Wellhausen Hypothesis)
Graham, Billy, 270–71, 282, 283–84, 296–97; and Civil Rights movement, 290; and Henrietta Mears, 273
Graham, Ruth Bell, 299n47
Graham, William, 154
Grand Remonstrance, 32–33, 34, 35
Gray, Asa, 201–2
Great Awakening (1730s and 1740s), 99–113, 146, 321–22; evangelical preaching and revival in the colonies, 102–5, 232–33, 321–22; and Frelinghuysen, 100–103, 321; Gilbert Tennent, 102–3, 105–6, 321–22; interdenominational rivalries, 108–11; Jonathan Edwards, 104–5, 233; reunion of New Side ("New Lights") and Old Side ("Old Lights"), 111–13; roots in Continental Pietism, 99, 101; roots in English Puritanism, 99–101; roots in Reformed tradition, 100–102; schism of New Side ("New Lights") and Old Side ("Old Lights") Presbyterians (1741), 105–7; and Scots-Irish outdoor communion festivals ("holy fairs"), 71n28, 101, 136–37; the Synod of New York, 107–13; Tennent's Log College and ministerial training, 101–2, 105, 106; Whitefield, 105–6, 233, 322. *See also* Second Great Awakening
"Great Awakening" in Wales (1735), 69–70
Great Ejection of 1662, 57–60, 66
Great Migration of 1717, 29, 92–93
Great Philadelphia Wagon Road, 110
Green, Ashbel, 131, 242
Green, Jacob, 165–66
Greene, William B., Jr., 223, 224
Green Lake Conference Center (Wisconsin), 273
Greifswald University (Germany), 239, 240
Griffin, Edward Dorr, 131–33
Grimke, Francis James, 196

Whitefield, George, 101, 105–6, 116, 127, 232, 233, 322

White Horse Inn (Cambridge), 4

Whittingham, William, 12

Whitworth College (Spokane, Washington), 273

Who Wrote the Bible? (Gladden), 250

Wilberforce, Samuel, 200

William III of England, 59, 64, 74n43, 92–93, 116

Williams, Daniel, 75, 80

Williams College (Massachusetts), 130, 131

Williamson, W. Jack, 301

Willock, John, 7, 9, 11–13, 16n49

Wilmore, Gayraud S., 291, 293n28

Wilson, John, 86, 87

Wilson, John Ruggles, 263

Wilson, Joseph, 189

Wilson, Joshua, 177

Wilson, Woodrow, 189, 202, 263–65

Winona Lake Bible Conference (Indiana), 273, 274

Winram, John, 16n49

Winter, Ralph, 270

Wishart, George, 10

Witherspoon, Elizabeth, 117

Witherspoon, John, 117–18, 120, 163, 170, 241–42

Wittenberg, 1, 4–6

women in church office (women's ordination), 283–88, 307; ARP and battle over, 286–87; EPC and neutrality on, 310; PCUS and UPCUSA reunion discussions and "Article Thirteen" provisions, 307

Women's General Missionary Society, 285

Women's Occidental Board of Foreign Missions of the Presbyterian Church, 227–28

women's suffrage, 212, 250

Women's Union Missionary Society, 133–34

Woodbridge, Charles, 284

Woodrow, James, 202–4

Woosley, Louisa, 285

Worcester, Samuel, 132, 133, 135

Worcester House Declaration (1660), 52n8

Word of Life Fellowship (New York), 273

Working People and Their Employers (Gladden), 215

World Alliance of Reformed Churches, 317

World Christian Fundamentals Association, 260

World Communion of Reformed Churches (WCRC), 317

World Council of Churches (WCC), 277, 291, 317

World Evangelical Alliance, 277

World Reformed Fellowship, 317–18

World Relief Commission of the National Association of Evangelicals, 328

World War I, 212, 263–66

World War II, 266–67, 289

Wright, Benjamin, 139

Wright, J. Elwin, 275–77

Wright, Theodore Sedgwick, 171

Wycliffe, John, 2

Wycliffe Bible Translators, 270

Yale College, 115–16, 137–38

Yale University, 232, 243

Young Life Campaign, 271, 272

Young Men's Christian Association (YMCA), 185–86, 265

Youth for Christ, 271, 280–82

Youth for Christ Congress on World Evangelization in Beatenberg, Switzerland (1948), 280–82

Zinzendorf, Nikolaus Ludwig Graf von, 110

Zion Presbyterian Church (Charleston), 176–77

Zubly, John Joachim, 122–23

Zwingli, Ulrich, 3, 5–6